The Tale of the Living Vampyre

"[O]ften as she told him the tale of the living vampyre, who had passed years amidst his friends, and dearest ties, forced every year, by feeding upon the life of a lovely female to prolong his existence for the ensuing months, his blood would run cold, whilst he attempted to laugh her out of such idle and horrible fantasies; but Ianthe cited to him the names of old men, who had at last detected one living among themselves, after several of their near relatives and children had been found marked with the stamp of the fiend's appetite; and when she found him so incredulous, she begged of him to believe her, for it had been remarked, that those who had dared to question their existence, always had some proof given, which obliged them, with grief and heartbreaking, to confess it was true."

(John Polidori, "The Vampyre," *New Monthly Magazine* 11, 1, April 1819, 199)

The Tale of the Living Vampyre
New Directions in Vampire Studies

Kevin Dodd

Universitas Press
Montreal

Universitas Press
Montreal

www.universitaspress.com

First published in July 2021

Library and Archives Canada Cataloguing in Publication

Title: "The tale of the living vampyre" : new directions in Dracula and vampire studies / Kevin Dodd.
Names: Dodd, Kevin, author.
Identifiers: Canadiana 20210272120 | ISBN 9781988963327 (softcover)
Subjects: LCSH: Vampires. | LCSH: Vampires—History—19th century. | LCSH: Vampires in literature. |
   LCSH: Vampires in popular culture. | LCSH: Vampires—Folklore. | LCSH: Dracula, Count (Fictitious character)
Classification: LCC BF1556 .D63 2021 | DDC 398.2109—dc23

This book is dedicated to

Deborah Lorraine Dodd
& Natalie Elise Dodd

Contents

ix
Foreword by John Edgar Browning
xi
Introduction
xvi
Acknowledgements

Beginnings of the Nineteenth-Century Vampires

1
"Long After His Body Had Been Buried, It Vexed Many:"
The European/English Revenant and the Beginnings of the Vampire

33
"Materializing Shadows:"
The Norse "Again-walker" as a Remote Template for the Vampire

69
"An Evil Kind of Animal:"
300 Years of the Monstrous Vampire Bat up to the Nineteenth Century

The Vampire Bat and Monster

86
"Blood Suckers Most Cruel:"
The Vampire and the Bat in and before Dracula

106
"That Demonical Face with Staring Fixed Saucer Eyes:"
The Other Nineteenth Century "Blood-Sucking Vampire"

Gender and Sexuality

140
"With Whom Do You Think You Have Been Dealing?"
Making Love to Evil: Woman, the Devil, and the Nineteenth-Century Vampire

155
"A Person of My Sex:"
The Transgendered Vampire of the Nineteenth Century

170
"A Yearning Drove Me Here to You:"
The Male Homosexual Vampire of the Nineteenth Century

188
"Now I Know What Love Is!:"
The Lesbian Vampire of the Nineteenth Century

The Sympathetic and Merciful Vampire

211
"My Greatest Torture is Life Itself:"
The Tragic or Sympathetic Vampire in the Nineteenth Century

230
"I Am Not as These: I Have Mercy:"
The Benign or Benevolent Vampire of the Nineteenth Century

Foreword

by John Edgar Browning

For peoples spanning every continent save Antarctica, vampires have been and remain still today a universal language, their nightmarish history an admixture of humankind's need to cope with death, decomposition, and dread; death came, quite literally, from the dead, or so believed cultures for millennia. By the nineteenth-century, however, the vampire's promise of death, as Kevin Dodd demonstrates exceedingly well in the present volume, evolved into a prelude to desire.

In Britain as well as America, periodicals throughout the nineteenth-century used stories of past and present vampire hysteriæ to improve their selling power and expand their readership. Folklorist Michael E. Bell would unearth such stories in his seminal work on the topic, *Food for the Dead: On the Trail of New England's Vampires* (Carroll & Graf, 2001), which chronicles America's own history with vampire exhumations that lasted well through the 1890s. More often than not, however, the vampire or "vampyre" (the more ornate rendering that was eventually phased out by the mid-1800s) appeared in nineteenth-century newspapers as a pejorative to describe corporations, certain businessmen, as well as banks, landlords, and, as today, politicians. Manufacturers would also embrace the vampire in print advertisements to describe certain illnesses like scrofula (a form of tuberculosis) to help raise awareness about their new medicinal treatments. Even scientists invoked the vampire to classify and name certain species of bat and squid, a stroke of fortune for newspapers who found themselves only too willing to publicize these and similar scientific breakthroughs in the wake of the vampire's growing popularity with the publication of John William Polidori's "The Vampyre: A Tale" (1819), which he published after his dismissal from Lord Byron's employ as a traveling physician. Indeed, it was the confluence of the vampire's seemingly omnipresence in the American and British press, together with humanity's fear of death and the need reconcile that fear with forbidden desires, that arguably fueled the vampire's rise in literary and creative expression in the nineteenth-century.

Today, the vampire has transcended literature to become an icon of stage and film, television and video games, comic books and pornography, in popularized iterations that thematically appropriate 'un-death' ironically to celebrate life. But for a few cultures across the world, these days the vampire is safely bound by art. However, its extraordinary journey there is one we owe to the nineteenth-century, and to one of its disgruntled doctors.

While the vampire and its kin alike have enjoyed many names, their shared essence has almost always remained the same: they evoke fear, sustain themselves on the blood or vital energy of others, and don't easily die. The vampires we know today in popular entertainment function much in the same way, only now they serve more or less as socio-political billboards that the cultural moment can tear down and re-paper depending on our needs. Among other things, vampires tell us metaphorically whom to go and not go to bed with, who a society's advantaged and disadvantaged people are, and who should and should not have power. The present volume recaptures the modern vampire's genesis in the nineteenth-century through years of painstaking researches, adding new light in areas left previously dark or little trodden.

Vampires are the archaeologist's digging site, the geologist's multi-layered rock face, and the crime scene investigator's murder weapon; through them, we learn more about ourselves. Vampires are pure culture, and culture needs 'diggers' like Kevin Dodd.

John Edgar Browning
Georgia Tech University
2020

Introduction

Nina Auerbach, in her classic 1995 *Our Vampires, Ourselves*, wrote that "there are many Draculas—and still more vampires who refuse to be Dracula or to play him" (1); that "There is no such creature as 'The Vampire;' there are only vampires" (5); that "vampires are easy to stereotype, but it is their variety that makes them survivors" (1); and that "every age embraces the vampire it needs" (145). It is the variety, the refusal, and the adaptability that interest me, yet these are much richer than Auerbach may have imagined. And whereas Auerbach was focused on background issues—her book "is a history of Anglo-American culture through its mutating vampires" (1)—I want to draw attention to types, to characteristics of specifically the nineteenth-century vampire itself, including those that appear in French and German literature, regardless of when or in what context they appeared.

I am concerned with *Dracula* only indirectly. Bram Stoker, the author of *Dracula*, had to have been familiar with the application of the word "vampire" to assassins,[1] animals, politicians, etc., as well as with some of the ways the bat was said to be vampire, even though the identity of the actual sources he knew appears to have died with him. It must have been of interest to him almost as much as instances of the literary vampire, because it was in the cultural air he breathed. Most scholars have treated the nineteenth century as leading up to *Dracula*, as if it were the apex of a century's work; hence a picture is painted in broad, but also biased strokes. Most of my chapters, on the other hand, are on the era per se, apart from Stoker, so they provide a more nuanced historical view.

Not a lot of creative research has transpired on the nineteenth-century vampire since the 1980s and 90s when Carol A. Senf wrote her *The Vampire in Nineteenth-Century English Literature* (1988), Christopher Frayling his *Vampyres: Lord Byron to Count Dracula* (1991), Roxanna Stuart her *Stage Blood: Vampires of the 19th-Century Stage* (1994), and Sabine Jarrot her *Le Vampire dans la Littérature du XIXe au XXe Siècle* (1999). Jarrot actually added nothing by way of source material. Yet a lot has happened since then for researchers with the maturation of the internet. Analysis of books and other materials that were generally inaccessible is now possible with a few "clicks." And translations have continued apace. Yet few have taken advantage of either to develop a new outlook on the period. Instead pretty much the same sources delineated in the texts above are continuously recycled and displayed along with different concerns—philosophical, theological, psychological, political, social, sexual, etc. Scholars and avid amateurs treat the *topoi* as largely settled.

I am an unlikely person to write a book like this. I was, of course, influenced by the monsters that appeared on television shows such as *Chiller*, *Jeepers Creepers*

---

[1] Stoker, in his preface to the Icelandic version, may have used Jack the Ripper in developing his Dracula. See Stoker and Ásmundsson, *Powers of Darkness: The Lost Version of* Dracula.

Theater, and *Million Dollar Movie* in my youth, but I outgrew them and seldom looked back. I did read *Dracula* when I was eleven years old but that was as a punishment from my fourth-grade teacher for pretending I had read *War and Peace*, one of the few books we had in our house, for a book report.

I received a Ph.D. from Vanderbilt University in the history of Christianity, when I was forty, but like many men in my class, I was unable to find a full-time teaching position, so I turned to adjunct positions at several colleges and universities. The longest stint I had was at Watkins College of Art, Design, and Film in Nashville teaching philosophy, religion, and mythology; it lasted seventeen years, until I quit to take care of my mother-in-law, one of the most wonderful people on earth.

It was while at Watkins that I watched and then read *Let the Right One In* and saw immediately the potential this myth had for a class. In 2012 I began my studies on the subject of vampires, and then narrowed it to the nineteenth-century ones. I never taught the course, yet I continued my research while caregiving for my mother-in-law. I would say at the time, when asked why, that it was simply inertia. I did not consider myself a fan, although I very much enjoyed my work.

I begin this book with background issues concerning the nineteenth-century vampire. The first concerns the Continental and British revenant (or "returner"), for this is the stream from which the vampire emerged. If there had not been such a creature in its folklore, early representatives of the culture would have dismissed the reports coming in from Greece and Slavic regions, treated them with derision, found them eccentric, or considered them humorous as many later did. What makes the initial reports of vampires different from reports of previous revenants was that they were vouched for by respected, skeptical Western sources. Western societies were becoming "enlightened" and were depending more on empirical data for its judgments. So I call the revenant a proto- or urvampire—"ur" just being German, the first language the word appears, for "proto." I put them into four categories. In addition to the vampiric revenant, there are communal ones, those who have unfinished business, and those connected with religion.

From there I turn to the Norse revenant. The *aptrgangr* ("again-walker"), or *draugr* (a [corporeal] ghost or phantom) as it is normally called, has been treated as a vampire uncritically for well over two hundred years as the nineteenth century began. It is in actuality a remote influence on the developing idea of the vampire on the Continent but it is also much different—for example, its tendency to hoard the wealth with which it was buried and to wrestle with those who have entered its burial mound to pilfer it. I develop a typology of the creature to aid in a more critical dialogue between Norse and vampire scholars. I propose fifteen categories: the violent, the contagious or pestilential, the conjugally assertive, the pestering, the tempting, the retributive, the evoked or conjured, the evoking or recruiting, the helpful, the comforting, the revelatory or didactic, the providential, the unprepared, the indifferent, and the communal *aptrgangr*.

The final background issue is the huge blood-sucking bat. This bat had been around ever since the European explorers and conquerors entered the New World in the late fifteenth century and was named "vampire" in the mid-eighteenth century, when it was mainly designated as "vampire" rather than vampire bat. It was actually the standard vampire bat at least until the second decade of the nineteenth century, whereas today the true one is known to be a microbat. Along the way of charting the development of descriptions of this bat, I conjecture on some of the reasons Europeans may have identified the vampire with a large bat. For one thing, the "monstrous" bat, as it was called, is plentiful in Central and South America and the real vampire often stalks alone, is stealthy and can escape quickly if one awakens, for they "attack" while one is asleep. But this is not sufficient, for within a century of its discovery, its range was extended to the Old World, where no sanguivorous bat had ever been reported. To account for this I think it is primarily due to Christian demonology, with support from bestiaries, classical mythology, indigenous tales, and the natural tendency to exaggerate dangers.

I now turn to the first paper I wrote on the topic under the rubric of the vampire bat and the monster. In 2016, it occurred to me that a number of texts that had been interpreted in terms of the monster were actually about the bat. The nineteenth century used the word "vampire" to denote both the monster and the bat, causing confusion among contemporary scholars. I therefore look into works of art, literature, and scholarship that have been said to pave the way to Stoker's use of the bat to see how many were actually about the bat. In this chapter I also support the thesis that the metamorphosis of the monster into the bat and *vice versa* predated *Dracula*, although the transformation was tepid compared to Stoker's development of it. This contains some substantial additions to the published version that appeared in *Athens Journal of Humanities and Arts* (2019).

We then look at the nineteenth-century giant vampire bat from several different sources: Naturalists, Soldiers, Travelers, and Popularizers; Journalists and Newspaper Reporters; Poets; Authors; Illustrators. Reports can be accurate, exaggerated, fantasized, or metaphorical; poetry might treat the bat imaginatively or literally; literature is able to deal with it in passing, metaphorically, or substantively; illustrations may be divided into bat attacks, exaggerated bat-faced vampires, human-faced vampires, both general and specific, and the humorous.

The next category deals with the subject of the nineteenth-century vampire with reference to gender and sexuality. In my explorations into various background issues, I became aware of a particular French lineage of demon women or succubi tempting men to have sexual intercourse with them, who turn into vampires in the nineteenth century, so I devote my attention to that first. The chapter delineates two main trajectories—one with a negative view of women demonstrating the fear of an independent woman as the source of male temptation and the other with a male fantasy of a powerful woman falling hopelessly and eternally in love with him. This was all played out in stories of devils, then of vampires. The tales are sometimes nearly identical.

Alternatives to binary relationships have been a topic for years now with the vampire, but not much has been done with the nineteenth-century vampire. One not analyzed at all is transsexuality or transgenderism in the nineteenth century, so I break this ground in "'A Person of My Sex:' The Transgendered Vampire of the Nineteenth Century." I find one text that goes beyond about anything in today's literature, but the rest are either cross-dressing or cross-sexing, by which I mean a temporary switching, even if it lasts for years, rather like Tiresias in Greek mythology.

In my study of the transgender vampire the matter of romantic friendship was touched upon. It plays a much larger role in the investigation of male homosexuality and lesbianism—deep, tender, and physically intimate platonic associations. I count them as homoerotic, although I recognize that they would not have been so at the time. In my third essay on the subject of vampire gender identities (concerning gay homosexuality), I find that romantic friendships actually comprise about half of the texts including such standard-bearers as *The Picture of Dorian Gray* and "The Sad Story of a Vampire." I treat them as homoerotic, as I noted above, because that is the current category that makes the most sense of the phenomenon. Of the actual homosexual texts, one is antierotic, two are nonerotic, one erotic but humiliating, and only one fully and poignantly erotic. In fact the last one, "Manor," I consider to be the most moving vampire story of the entire nineteenth century.

With lesbianism, I was surprised and a little dismayed to find that all but two cases universally acknowledged by vampirologists to be lesbian seemed simply to be about pseudo-romantic friendships, even the celebrated examples *Christabel* and *Carmilla*. Of the two remaining, one concerns simply the intimacy between a stepmother and stepdaughter. The one legitimate one, in my estimation, is made up of a single, short scene in a rather lengthy book. It appears then that lesbianism was not the option for nineteenth-century vampires that it has been made out to be.

In the final category, I look at the sympathetic and merciful vampires of the nineteenth century. With regard to the sympathetic vampire, vampire scholars have given us seven examples to work with, three of which must be eliminated right from the beginning. Instead of being restricted to the remaining four, I arrange around fifty examples and place them in eleven categories: tragic pre-vampires, tragic due to religion or philosophy, to inevitability or necessity, to longevity, to an assignment, to unintentionality, to the loss of companionship, to separation by death, to misidentification, to the need to be loved, and to no desire to victimize.

This leads me to a related, but much more narrow topic as my final chapter: "'I am not as these: I have mercy:' The Benign or Benevolent Vampire of the Nineteenth Century." Because many experts are so certain that the nineteenth-century vampire is absolutely evil, there has been no attempt, so far as I know, to locate such vampires. I, therefore, single out sixteen examples and organize them under three categories: vampires that act beneficently, those that are benign; those that are benevolent.

These articles were composed to stand alone and therefore there are certain duplications of material across the chapters. It is my hope that each overlap will look at the story from a different angle and therefore remove the tedium to the reader of going over the same material again.

I should add that I am uninterested in building some theoretical edifice here, some philosophical, psychological, economic, or social complex erected on Marx, Freud, or Nietzsche or their numerous descendants, like Adorno, Lacan, or Heidegger. I am unwilling to focus on the vampire as some figurative embodiment or suspension of boundary resistance. I do not desire to concentrate on every reference to blood as anti-Semitism or to biting as sexual perversion or on its character as indicative of a changing aristocracy or bourgeoisie. I simply want to investigate applicable texts and see what they have to say about certain topics.

It should be obvious by now that I see the nineteenth-century vampire as far richer territory than has been previously acknowledged. But this book is not meant to be the final word on the subject, rather it is to be a preliminary one. More study is called for. I have not combed through all that is available in English on the internet, especially newspaper articles, and my French and German are too elementary for a close examination of sources in those languages. So I throw down the gauntlet and hope that there are those who will pick it up. Every conclusion I draw may be overturned with time, but that is one of the pleasures of academic research: to see a field progress beyond oneself.

Works Cited

Auerbach, Nina. *Our Vampires, Ourselves*. Chicago: University of Chicago Press, 1995.

Stoker, Bram; Ásmundsson, Valdimar. *Powers of Darkness: The Lost Version of Dracula*. Trans. Hans Corneel de Roos. New York: Overlook Duckworth, Peter Mayer Publishers, Inc., 2016.

Acknowledgements

> [H]e who is unable to live in society,
> or who has no need because he is sufficient
> for himself, must be either a beast or a god ...
> A social instinct is implanted in all men by nature.
> Aristotle, *Politics* 1.1253a

I am neither a god nor a beast. I have, all my life, depended on kindness from others. The writing of these essays has relied first and foremost on the encouragement of family and friends. My wife and daughter have supported me most; the book is dedicated to them. Although my parents have now passed away, I wish to honor them here: Barbara Timmermann, Benno Timmermann, Robert Dodd, and Felecia Dodd. Norma Sparrow, my late mother-in-law, receives a special word of thanks.

Friends and additional family include Charly Fallon, Ted Olsen, the Marsh family—Harry, Trudi, Clayton, Seth, and Julian—Richard Spann, Ashley Beasley, John Rawls, Lisa Tackett, Ashley Shelton, Hugo Martinez, Michael Walker, Michael Bielaczyc, Julia Buzzell, Patrick Thomas, Murutamanga and Françoise Kabahita, my nephew Jonathan Stiles, my cousin Sharon Treadgold, and my brother Brien. I must add here John Edgar Browning who has particularly been helpful in fulfilling this dream, as well as Douglas A. Anderson and Mike Ashley who read the lengthy first draft of my first paper. Emily Smith at Region's Bank has kept up with this project and has heard just about everything about its progress.

As I have been writing I have enjoyed the status of Visiting Scholar at Vanderbilt University. I was provided this by Dr. William Hook, who had been nice enough to renew it each year. The position gave me access to Vanderbilt Interlibrary Loan (ILL) and to the wonderful staff that works there, especially James Toplon and Rachel Adams. They have gone well beyond any sense of duty to provide me with the books and articles I requested. My privileges were coming to an end in the school of religion, but I have Dana D. Nelson to thank for picking it up in the English Department.

My thanks also go out to all the workers at ILLs around the country. And then my gratitude extends to the many, paid and unpaid, who have posted books, magazines, journals, newspapers, librettos, and plays on the internet. They have made most of my research possible.

Anderson Gaither translated almost all the Latin texts; I would find the passages and he would render them into English. Without him I would have been lost. Marcia Epelbaum corrected my Spanish. Breanna King-Butterworth and Anne Cornet checked my French in the cases when I had difficulty with seventeenth- and eighteenth-century manuscripts. Dr. Wayne Barnette translated two Icelandic texts for me: versions of "Af Petro þrœl." I owe a significant debt to each one. All mistakes remain my own, of course, for I did not have help in most cases and I adapted Prof. Gaither's translations to my own peculiar English.

I have sent each article as I have finished to three readers. Anthony Hogg is first. He contacted me shortly after my first essay was rejected and I had decided to give up. His interest in my project has been key to the arrival at this moment. He introduced me to Andrew Boylan who has always been supportive. And then there is Dr. Michael Rose, a composer and instructor by profession, a neighbor and an expert on horror by fortune, who has always counselled me to pursue my passion even though I receive no recognition for it.

Then there is my peer reviewer. They went completely out of their way to correct the text and make specific suggestions for change. I was amazed at the thoroughness of their reading of the text. And my editor at Universitas Press, Dr. Cristina Artenie has been helpful beyond description providing help, advice, and direction. The main one to thank for this publication is Dr. J. Gordon Melton. I had sent off my first paper to a number of experts and no interest was expressed. And it was rejected by several journals. With no expectations, I sent off the paper to Dr. Melton and received a response within a few hours. He liked my effort, so I sent him more. He came up with the idea to put the articles together as a book, he found a publisher, he sought out John Edgar Browning and Joseph Laycock to write the preface and afterword. He has, with good humor, dealt with all my revisions even well after I submitted the essays to him. And he found the individuals to provide "blurbs" for the text. The kindness from this stranger, whom I now count as a friend, will long be remembered, at least until my dotage.

I.

Beginnings of the Nineteenth-Century Vampire

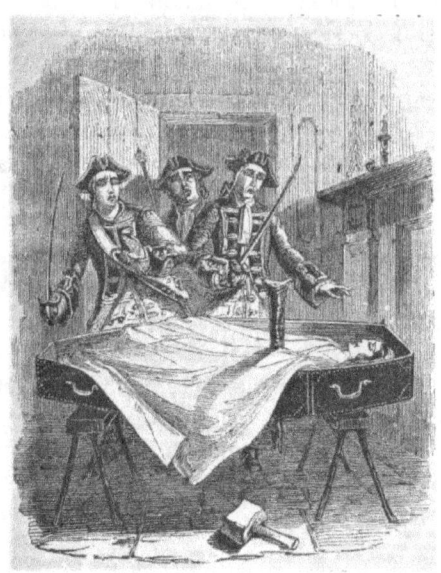

James Malcolm Rymer, *Varney the Vampire: Or, The Feast of Blood* 1845 chapter 51.

Wolf Neubauer, "Pfählen einer Frau" *Neubauersche Chronik* 1616.
In *Justiz in Alter Zeit (Band VI Der Schriftenreihe des Mittelalterlichen Kriminalmuseums Rothenberg ob der Tauber)* 1984, 306/68.

1.
"Long After His Body Had Been Buried, It Vexed Many:" The European/English Revenant and the Beginnings of the Vampire

Introduction

There has been a lot of investigation into the medieval and early modern revenant. Among these studies, keeping to sources just in English, are: *The Return of the Dead* (1996), *Phantom Armies of the Night: The Wild Hunt and Ghostly Processions of the Undead* (1999) and *The Secret History of Vampires* (2010) by Claude Lecouteux; "Wraiths, Revenants and Ritual in Medieval Culture" (1996), "Revenants, Resurrection, and Burnt Sacrifice" (2014) and *Afterlives: The Return of the Dead in the Middle Ages* (2016) by Nancy Caciola; *Ghosts in the Middle Ages: The Living and the Dead in Medieval Society* (1998) by Jean-Claude Schmitt; *Medieval Ghost Stories: An Anthology of Miracles, Marvels, and Prodigies* (2001) by Andrew Joynes; "Repentant Soul or Walking Corpse? Debatable Apparitions in Medieval England" (2003) by Jacqueline Simpson; "'Dead Man Walking': The Historical Context of Vampire Beliefs" (2006) and *The Trial of the Pig, the Walking Dead, and Other Matters of Fact from the Medieval and Renaissance Worlds* (2007) by Darren Oldridge; "Was the Vampire of the Eighteenth Century a Unique Type of Undead-Corpse?" (2006) and *Troublesome Corpses: Vampires and Revenants from Antiquity to the Present* (2007) by G. David Keyworth; "The Demise of the Walking Dead: The Rise of Purgatory and the End of Revenancy" (2007), Elif Boyacioğlu's Master's Thesis for Bilkent University; *History and the Supernatural in Medieval England* (2007) by C. S. Watkins; *The Penguin Book of the Undead* (2016) by Scott G. Bruce; and "Animated Corpses and Bodies with Power in the Scholastic Age" (2017) by Winston Black.

There has been, in spite of all this work, little on the precise relationship between the revenant and the early modern vampire, which I can only deal with in the introduction and conclusion, because this chapter is primarily about the revenant.[2] I tend to elide the two, focus on medical or archeological explanations, and/or concentrate just on the essential differences between them. The revenant or Wiedergänger (Again-Walker) I call the proto- or urvampire. "Ur" simply means "proto" in German. Since "vampyr" was first used in German, I prefer "ur" to "proto."

---

[2] "Revenant" simply means "returner" or "one who returns." One of the first published appearances of the word was in the anonymous *Les Esprits, ou Le Mary fourbé*, published in Liège in 1686 (93). It was popular enough to reach dictionary status in the 1690 *Dictionnaire universel de Furetière*: "Those who return (*Les revenants*) from great journeys owe God great thanks. We hold that there are returning spirits (*des esprits revenants*) in this house." Under *revenir* or "to return" we read, in addition to returning to a normal mental state, like "that man returned to his senses," that one may say, "Spirits return to a house, when those who live there believe they see specters and apparitions, as servants or clever people make a noise there at night to frighten the master, conduct their business, or give themselves entertainment."

The early modern vampire is a construct of the European imagination in the seventeenth and eighteenth centuries working with certain Slavic and Greek superstitions. Greece was under Ottoman rule at the time, so was outside the orbit of Europe. This means, however, that the vampire did not arise in a vacuum. The Slavic and Greek sources would have been dismissed as something wholly eccentric, meaningless, humorous, or worthy of derision had there not been something already in the culture that corresponded to the vampire.[3]

As James Twitchell in his *The Living Dead* (1981) writes, because of the "vampire epidemics" in the Balkans during the early eighteenth century, the vampire became a serious subject of study in Europe: "Treatise after treatise was written, not necessarily affirming the vampire's existence (that was already generally accepted), but rather explaining the vampire as a personification of demonic energies on earth" (33).

The difference between the urvampire and the vampire is not, as David Keyworth ("Was the Vampire" 241-60; *Troublesome Corpses* 191) holds, that one living-impaired creature sucks blood and the other does not, for a number of seventeenth-century vampires and several eighteenth-century ones did not exsanguinate their victims, and a few urvampires did. The vampire first became associated with drinking blood with Paul Ricaut's *The Present State of the Greek and Armenian Churches* (1679), and it became more common after that. It really became tied to it with the famous case of Arnont Paole in 1732.

Nor is it, in addition to bloodletting, human corporeality that sets them apart, for urvampires likewise had human bodies.[4] And it is misguided to cut the eighteenth century off from the seventeenth as the era of vampires, presumably due to the fact that it was when the word first appeared, because the creature was in continuity with the preceding century's monster. Almost everyone includes Joseph Pitton de Tournefort in their timeline of vampires. His work dates back to 1700-1701 (published in 1717) and includes the classic Greek vampire of the 1600s. Finally it is not the lack of putrification as Keyworth purports that sets them apart, for many of the revenants are found rotting as well.

What really sets the early modern vampire apart from the revenant is the emphasis on reports of the undead from unbiased, respected, and skeptical Westerners.[5] Spectral evidence, trials by ordeal, confessions under torture, and hearsay, such as were used in witch trials, were giving way to more uniform, formal rules of juridical law and to modern scientific procedures to ascertain facts. This is the time leading up to the Enlightenment after all. Accounts were mediated through a Western or Western-trained individual and committed to writing within only a few months or years of the episode. If they did not actually witness the vampires, they vouched for the reputations of those who said they did.

---

[3] Bruce A. McClelland in his masterful treatment of the rise of the vampire in Eastern Europe and Russia *Slayers and Their Vampires: A Cultural History of Killing the Dead* 2006 seems completely unaware of this aspect of the Western development of the concept of the vampire and so treats the West as virgin territory awaiting Eastern ideas on the subject.
[4] In fairness Keyworth wants to add "human corporeality" because not all vampires suck blood and not all revenants take on *human* corporeality. So he is covering his bases.
[5] This is the reason that I agree with J. Gordon Melton's timeline in his 2011 *The Vampire Book* (xxi), including his assertion that the first "modern" vampire text was by Leo Allatios: *Beliefs of Modern Greece* (1645). I disagree, however, with his addition of revenant texts from the twelfth century. This is what I meant by eliding the two. I also would not call it the first modern treatment but the first treatment, period.

Some intellectuals recognized this as pivotal. In his 1722 *Huetiana, ou Pensées diverses*, Pierre-Daniel Huet wrote, "I shall not examine here whether the events that are reported are true or are instead common error, but it is certain that those who have reported them are such competent and credible authors and such direct witnesses that one must not take sides without paying serious attention to them" (83). Put negatively, Jean-Jacques Rousseau in *Letter to Beaumont* (1763): "If there is a well-attested history in the world, it is that of the Vampires. Nothing is missing from it: interrogations, certifications by Notables, Surgeons, Parish Priests, Magistrates. The judicial proof is one of the most complete. And with all that, who believes in Vampires?" (68).

So the way people heard the reports from Slavic and Greek regions was filtered through familiarity with European revenant stories. This is the reason why vampire studies must spend time with the European/English revenants and not simply quote a few well-known cases. One thing we must note about the European vampire is that Europe was in constant geographical flux. So we will notice several of the revenant tales are already from relatively obscure provinces under Western domination.

There are the most famous cases of the era: the peasant man from Blow and the woman of Levin, introduced by Neplach of Opatovice (1322-1371) in his "Chronicon" (*Fontes rerum Bohemicarum* III, 480-481) and regularly repeated afterward; the skull from Breslau (Joseph Klapper, "Die Quellen" 1911 [c. 1350], 202-31); Stephen Hubener (Andreas Hondorff, "Vorrede," *Promptuarium exemplorum* 1584, ii.); the Shoemaker of Breslau (Carolus Weinrichius, "Proaemium" 1612, 1-13); his Maid (Henry More, *An Antidote Against Atheism*, 1653, 213-14); Johann Cuntz (Martinus Weinrichius, *De ortu monstrorum*, 1595, 13-22); the Pharmacist of Crossen (George Sinclair, *Satan's Invisible World*, 1685, 132-34), the dead man who would leave his shroud at his grave (Martin Zeiller, *Theatrum Tragicum*, 1624, 25-26)—all are stories that derive from Bohemia, Silesia, or Moravia, which are all Western Slavic territories. Numerous kings of Bohemia were elected to be Holy Roman Emperors; Silesia became a possession of the Crown of Bohemia under the Holy Roman Empire in the fourteenth century; Moravia became an imperial state of the Holy Roman Empire in the eleventh century. So Slavic influence was already in the Western revenant, which is all the more reason why Westerners did not ignore or dismiss the vampire as pure superstition.

I therefore agree, to a degree, with Michael Pickering that "eighteenth-century German-speaking academics largely constructed the vampire as it came to be known in Europe and beyond. The genesis of this construction was in fact the military reports sent to Vienna from the southern and eastern reaches of the Habsburg Monarchy" ("Attitudes" 120).[6] My main argument with him is that he sets the timeline forward a century—the eighteenth rather than the seventeenth.

Another significant perspective comes from Thomas Bohn in his 2016 *Der Vampir*, regarding the vampire's ties to previous revenants. He states the roots of the vampire are "in England of the twelfth century and in Bohemia of the

---

[6] In a later paper, he phrases it as "the representatives of the Habsburg State—military officers and surgeons—[who] facilitated inadvertently the construction of the vampire in the 1720s and 1730s.... They drew upon a tradition of writing about wandering corpses in Western, Central, and Northern Europe.... Discussing vampires in relation to wandering corpses provided a framework in which learned writers could couch their responses to utterly foreign beliefs coming from the South" ("'Sie Mußten ins Feuer,'" 12-13).

fourteen century" (31). He adds that a prototype lacking blood sucking is found in the Icelandic sagas of the thirteenth century. It is, then, "a European myth" as he subtitles his book. As I will try to demonstrate, it is much more complex than this.

Nick Groom's perspective in *The Vampire* (2018) is of equal importance: "[V]ampires are ... creatures of the Enlightenment: their history is rooted in the empirical approaches of the developing investigative sciences of the eighteenth century, in European politics and in the latest thinking. . . . Vampires came into being when Enlightenment rationality encountered East European folklore" (4-5). But, as Bohn reminds us, their actual roots lie in England as well. The Enlightenment (and proto-Enlightenment) encountered the East European (and Greek) revenant folklore through the mediation of the European revenant.

It is important to evaluate all the revenants, not just the ones that influenced the Western response to the vampire. So, in addition to the vampiric revenants, we have revenants that are communal, others that have unfinished business, and ones that are linked to Christianity in a particular fashion, e.g., the devil invading or manufacturing a body. I will stress the locations to show how widespread they are. I will also rather capriciously cut off the revenant stories with the beginning of the eighteenth century, so that famous sources like the *Magia Posthuma* and Marquis d'Argens' *Lettres Juives* are excluded. I am not interested in setting these observations and stories in their historical contexts. That would mean dealing with only a fraction of them because of the length of explanation.

Communal Revenants

From Western Slavic regions come three tales from the eleventh century, reported by Thietmar of Merseburg in his 1013 *Chronicon*. Night guards saw in a cemetery candles burning and heard two dead men singing the invitatory and all of the morning praises in order (76).

A priest accustomed to singing matins saw a multitude of dead people bringing offerings to a priest who was standing before the doors of the church. He pushed his way through, but soon thereafter died, as one of the dead prophesied he would (75).

A priest saw a group of the dead making offerings in the cemetery and church and heard them singing. When he related this to his bishop he was told to sleep in the chapel. The dead threw him and his bed out. After he shared this with the bishop, he was ordered to sleep there again and was blessed with sacred relics and holy water to protect him. This time the dead picked him up and, before the altar, burned him to fine ash. These dead keep to themselves and should be left alone (76-77). The bringing of offerings demonstrates that the dead live a parallel existence to the living (see Caciola, "Revenants" 318, 329-330).

Two sixteenth-century European works—Olaus Magnus' *A Description of the Northern Peoples* (1555) and Jakob Ziegler's *Quae Intus Continentur Syria* (1532)—tell of five drowned Icelanders who appeared to their acquaintances before they knew of their deaths and greeted them (see Magnus 95 who quotes Ziegler 93 almost verbatim).

In Geoffrey of Burton's *Life and Miracles of St. Modwenna* (c. 1150), two English peasants fled from their monastic estate to the protection of the secular ruler, Count Roger. He was so affected by their account of the monks that he moved militarily against the monastery but was miraculously repelled. Then the two peasants were suddenly struck dead and were spotted carrying their coffins and heard shouting at the inhabitants in their homes. They unleashed such disease that the village was almost decimated, and the Count traveled to the monastery to beg for pardon (92-99).

An English gentleman was on a pilgrimage and was on night watch for his companions. He sees a host of the dead passing by and in the midst was an infant boy rolling in a shoe. When questioned the baby revealed that he was the man's premature son buried unbaptized and nameless in a shoe by his mother in his father's absence. The father christened and named him; thereafter he stood on his feet and walked proudly in the procession. There are a number of other sightings of marches, regular and armed, and of hunting parties.[7] I will cover three of the most colorful here. One is apparently of a hunting party, another a general march, and the last an army.

King Herla, of the ancient Britons, according to Walter Map, a late-twelfth-century English courtier, writing in *De Nugis Curialium* c. 1182, was approached by a dwarf who offered his hand in friendship. He foretold him that the King of France would soon offer him his son to marry and that he would attend the wedding and then one year later Herla would attend his. The dwarfs were present at Herla's daughter's marriage and were celebrated for their lavish gifts and sumptuous food. One year later the king went to the dwarf's nuptials in his mountain palace. After three days he left with gifts for hunting and a dog who, until it jumped down from the horse, signaled that the party must not dismount. When they reached the sunlight, the king met an old shepherd and asked about his queen. The shepherd was bewildered and said that a queen by that name had died some two hundred years before. Some of his entourage then descended from their steeds and instantly turned to dust. So his party marched endlessly and were seen by many until the coronation of King Henry, at which time, they disappeared (Map 15-18). Apparently the dog finally jumped.

In the second book of *The Ecclesiastical History of England and Normandy* (1141), Oedericus Vitalis (1075-c.1142) tells the story of a priest, Walkelin, who was out late the night of the new year in France when he witnessed hordes of people suffering a purgatorial march. The first legion was comprised of robbers carrying all the things they stole on their heads. Following them, dwarfs with barrel heads were being carried. In their midst was a priest-murderer being tortured by a demon. Next was a crowd of women on horseback sitting on burning nails, confessing their sins, and then a host of clergy, monks, rulers, and judges, many considered pious in life, all pleading with him to remember them in prayer. Thereafter was an army of warriors howling in pain. Recognizing then this to be Harlequin's people he tried to find a memento so people would believe him when he returned; thus he tried to take an unmanned horse but the first bolted and the second had stirrups that severely burned and a saddle that was unbearably frozen.

---

[7] For such tales see Claude Lecouteux, *Phantom Armies*; Schmitt, *Ghosts in the Middle Ages* 92-121; Nancy Caciola, *Afterlives* 157-205.

Four knights became angry with him for trying to take what was theirs; three tried to grab him but one stopped them saying he wanted him to grant a favor—to convey a message to his wife. He refused, which set the man in a rage and he attacked him. Walkelin cried out to Mary for help and was immediately saved by his dead brother, who rode up with sword drawn. He told him secrets from their past but Walkelin denied everything, afraid of what might happen given the circumstances, until reminded of all his brother had done for him—then he confessed the truth in tears. His brother explained his torment and related to him that trying to steal the horse was an offence that should require him to join the crowd, but the mass he had sung that morning saved him. He asked him to continue praying for him; their father had just been released to paradise and he was hoping to leave punishment within a year. With this he rode away and Walkelin lived sixteen more years bearing witness to his experience and carrying the scar on his face from the attack (511-520).

A story arising out of France in the thirteenth or the fourteenth century, known as "An Army White as Snow," tells of two dukes at war with each other: the duke of Sardinia, Eusebius, and that of Sicily, Ostorgius. They could not have been more different. Although Ostorgius was much richer and had many more soldiers, he was not devout whereas Eusebius had his treasure laid up in heaven, praying and doing all he could for the dead. While Eusebius was gone, Ostorgius moved against his city and captured it. Eusebius made the decision that he would retake the city, or more likely, die trying. He would be doing it for the glory of God. As he was waiting to ambush Ostorgius' forces an all-white army came and camped in front of them. Eusebius sent messengers to them to determine their intent and learned that they were comprised of God's emissaries to fight against his enemy. God's army approached Ostorgius and demanded that he restore twice of all he had seized from Eusebius and place himself under his authority. Terrified, Ostorgius agreed. When Eusebius queried as to who they really were they replied, "We are those souls of the departed that the Lord's generous indulgence has released for your acts of kindness and your alms" ("An Army White as Snow" 154-160).

Another story is told by William of Malmesbury, in his *Chronicle of the Kings of England* (c. 1140). A young Englishman after his marriage put his wedding ring on a statue of Venus to play sports. When he returned it was gone. That night when ready for intimacy with his wife, Venus interposed herself between them claiming him for herself. To aid him in getting back the ring he contacted a necromancer who told him to be at a crossroad at a certain hour of the night and a parade of hell-bound revenants would pass by. He was to pass a letter the necromancer had prepared to the master of the march, who could then retrieve the ring from Venus for she would also be in the group. She reluctantly yielded it and he was able to consummate his marriage (232-234).

In his *The General History of Ireland* (1631), an Irish Catholic priest, Geoffrey (or Jeoffrey) Keating, related the story of the Tuatha de Danans in Ireland, a tribe with magical powers. On their way ultimately to Ireland to invade it, they were in Athens when the Assyrians attacked. As adepts of necromancy they would revive the Athenian dead after each battle to fight again the following day. The Sumerians were ready to give up when a Druid enlightened them as to how they may stop it. They needed to stake the fallen. They did this and when the Tuatha de Danans saw that they had been foiled, they fled (Keating 40-41).

There are Festive Revenants. Walter Map, an English author of Welsh origin quoted above, revealed that a "certain knight buried his wife, who was dead beyond a doubt, and got her again by snatching her from a band of dancers; and he was afterwards presented by her with children and grandchildren. Their posterity survives until this day" (97). The dancers are elsewhere identified as "a great throng of women" (218), no doubt revenants like her.

In his encyclopaedic *Otia Imperialia* (c. 1215), Gervase of Tilbury, an English author who spent time in Italy, France, and Germany, wrote "In Catalonia there is a crag which levels out to form a fair-sized plateau. On its summit at about midday knights are seen wearing armour and charging each other with spears as knights do. But if anyone goes near the place, nothing at all of this kind of thing is visible" (668-669). Elsewhere, there is mention of an English hunting party "of infinite wandering, or maddest meandering, of insensate silence, in which appeared alive many who were known to be dead." They wandered abroad "with chariots and beasts of burden, with pack-saddles and bread-baskets, with birds and dogs, with men and women running side by side" (Map 233-234).

In a story, "The Hand of Reyneke" (c. 1360), told by Heinrich von Herford, the German revenant Reyneke, a confessed Christian, manifested himself as a hand which was touched by many and answered questions. This parallels the one above about the group of dead persons making offerings. He explained that he and his clan lived inside a mountain. "We eat, drink, marry, have children, arrange the weddings of our daughters and the marriages of our sons. We sow and we reap and we carry on our lives just like you." They were well-established and noble. Those in a neighboring mountain were "bandits who cause great disturbances and invade their neighbours' land" (Herford 116-117).

Some are tricksters. In an account (*Anecdotes historiques, légendes et apologues*, 1261) related by Étienne de Bourbon, a French peasant bringing home a bundle of wood at night saw countless hunting dogs and a multitude of people following. He asked one of them who they were and was told they were the retinue of Arthur whose court was nearby. He was invited to join them, and he entered a palace where knights and ladies danced, feasted, and drank. After this, in which he evidently joined, he went to bed in a richly ornamented bed where a beautiful woman was lying. He woke in the morning "draped over his firewood as the butt of a joke" (qtd. in Caciola, *Afterlives* 197-198). Another peasant witnessed a similar company. One of the horsemen spun his head around backward and asked, "Is my hood on straight?" (198). This was repeated endlessly, and a group of women dancing seemed to be doing the same.

Religion and Revenants

Map relates a story (1182) in his *De Nugis Curialium* of an Englishman who died in unbelief who was wandering about in an orchard. All the townsfolk surrounded him, so he walked to his grave, but fled when he saw a cross on it. The cross was removed and he returned, fell into the grave, covered himself with soil. When the cross was replaced, he stopped his visitations (126). A Flemish priest by the name of Thomas of Cantimpré, in *Bonum universale de apibus* (1260), wrote that a nun, worthy of God, kept her regular hours of prayer. One morning a dead body was in the chapel. The devil seeing an opportunity to stop her moved the body in the coffin. "The virgin therefore crossed herself and bravely shouted to the Devil, 'Lie down! Lie down, you wretch, for you have no power against me!' Suddenly the Devil rose up with the corpse and said, 'Truly, now I will have power against you, and I will revenge myself for the frequent injuries I have suffered at your hands!' When she saw this, she was thoroughly terrified in her heart, so with both hands she seized a staff topped with a cross, and bringing it down on the head of the dead man, she knocked him to the ground. Through such faithful daring she put the demon to flight" (see Caciola, "Wraiths, Revenants and Ritual" 11).

A similar story from Belgium is told of in the anonymous *Ida the Eager of Louvain* (1425): "One night she spied a kind of bier in front of her. She was quite shocked and puzzled. The Demon's cunning made a corpse appear on it, ready for burial, and then—inventor that he is of all malice and skilled at the switching of skins—he leapt into that body and stood it upon its feet. Thus identified with it, he stepped forward to wrestle with Ida, grabbing her arms and then twisting them violently for a long time. But soon she implored help from on High and the Demon had to vanish, routed in confusion. While the fright of this fantastic vision had indeed upset the holy woman's heart, and had done so disproportionately, nevertheless it was still she who triumphed and she who carried off the palm of victory from the combat. It was still she who reduced the enemy's roaring savagery to nothing. In fact, that was a time when her heart was *experiencing great hope and trust in God* (cf. Dan 13.35),[8] especially inasmuch as that very day she had been refurbished with the victorious and life-giving Sacrament of the Lord's body" (*Ida the Eager* 8). It was the sacrament that gave her the presence of mind to overcome the revenant.

A great doctor of divinity died, according to Richard Baxter in his 1654 *The Saints' Everlasting Rest*, sat up in his bier and said *Justo DEI judicio accusatus sum*, "I am accused at the just Judgement of GOD."[9] "At which voice, the people ran all out afrighted. On the morrow when they came again to perform the Obsequies, to the like words as before, the Corps rose again, and cried with a hideous voice, *Justo DEI judicio judicatus sum*; I am Judged at the Righteous Judgement of GOD. Whereupon the People ran away amazed. The third day almost all the City came together, and when they came to the same words as before, the Corpse rose again, and cried with a more doleful noise than before, *Justo DEI judicio condemnatus sum*, I am condemned at the just Judgement of GOD" (123). Since someone of this caliber was subject to such severe judgment, some of the witnesses went and established a stricter monastic order.

The Hungarian king, St. Ladislas, was portrayed by an unknown illustrator in the *Anjou Legendarium* (1330s) as praying when he was attacked by a devil animating a dead body. It threw a catafalque at the saint and Ladislas displayed the cross and it had to flee. A German knight led a life of crime. Caesarius of Heisterbach in the second volume of his *The Dialogue on Miracles* (1220-35) penned

---

[8] This reference from the Book of Daniel pertains to the story of Susanna and the Elders.
[9] The story goes back at least to 1515 and Francisco Puteo's "Vito Altera;" it putatively occurred in 1082 (see Puteo 493-94).

"At midnight the devil by raising his body upright on the bier terrified all who were present. His friends fearing outrage by the devils, bound the body before the mass and buried it" (see Caesarius of Heisterbach II, 300). Again Caesarius testified about a German knight who lived a horrible life and came back. "He could not be driven away by the sign of the cross, or by a sword, not be driven

St. Ladislas driving out the devil.[10] From fragments of a collection of legends prepared on the occasion of the trip to Italy by Charles Robert and the child Prince Andrew.

away by the sign of the cross, or by a sword. He was often struck with a sword but could not be wounded, giving off the sound of a soft bed being struck. His friends consulted John the lord bishop of Trèves and he advised them to pour water on a nail of crucifixion and to sprinkle the house and his daughter and the man himself, if he was present. That being done he never appeared again" (II, 303).

The archbishop of Genoa, Italy, de Voragine wrote in his 1260 *Legenda aurea sanctorum* of the hermit Peter. "The devil appeared to him often in the likeness of a naked woman, and joined herself to him naked, and the more he defended himself, the more the devil approached, tempting him shamelessly. After she had troubled him like this, he took the stole off a priest's neck and wrapped hers with it, and straightaway the devil departed and left lying there a stinking and rotten corpse. So great a stench issued from it that there was none that saw it but said that it was the body of some dead woman which the devil had taken" (251).

Revenants with Unfinished Business

We will start with revenants who serve as life-examples. Revenants were very rare until the eleventh century with only two authors covering them before that, as far as I know. One of them is Gregory the Great (the other is St. Germanus

---

[10] It is on a page displaying four moments in the life of St. Ladislas. See https://www.hung-art.hu/frames.html?/magyar/zmisc/miniatur/14_sz/anjou/anjou_1.html. This is all we have of the story. Béla Zsolt Szakács, in his 2006 "Between Chronicle and Legend" relates that "A detailed textual source for this event is not known; the legend mentions only that the king frequently prayed at night in church" (151).

of Auxerre who will be covered later). Gregory I was pope from 590 to 604. His *Dialogues*, an extremely influential work through the medieval period, appeared in the third year of his papacy. He has four examples that concern us, all set in Italy. A pious deacon, Paschasius, died with only one sin still held against him. A bishop, visiting the public baths, saw Paschasius there ready to wait on him, knowing that he had died. He asked him why he was there and he replied by referring to his one unconfessed sin. He asked the bishop to pray for him and he was absent when the deacon came back. He should not have been without some punishment, we are told (Gregory the Great 236-37). There is another similar story but it is the Eucharist that is offered. The sacrament is of great profit, we learn, seeing spirits that are dead desire it (248-52)

A chaste but prattling nun died and the keeper of the church saw her divided in two, one-half burned at the altar, and the other untouched. The following day he saw marks of a fire on the altar. The lesson is that being buried in holy ground gives no benefit if one is unworthy (Gregory the Great 245-46, 248). A dyer was buried and the sexton heard from his grave at night the words "I burn, I burn." The following day his coffin was dug up and his garments were untouched, but his body was nowhere to be found. The same lesson is taught (248).

Buried in the second volume of the Benedictine Abbey of Marmoutier's *Acta sanctorum ordinis S. Benedicti* is "De Rebus Gestis" (c. 1175). A storehouse manager in a French monastery had a habit of stealing grain due to be offered to the dead. Two dead monks appeared and upbraided him. He hardened himself so they returned threatening punishment. When he still did not mend his ways they beat him so mercilessly that he lay in bed for half a year as one dead and never recovered completely. We learn to consider what the future holds for those who cheat the dead from what is owed them ("De Rebus Gestis" 400).

Caesarius of Heisterbach has two more tales in his second volume apart from the one that appeared under "Religion and Revenants." In Germany two families were locked in a mortal feud and the two heads of the family died the same day. They were buried in the same grave and the ruckus that arose from the grave was enough for the inhabitants to disinter them and place one far away from the other. This taught the villagers to live together in peace. (Caesarius of Heisterbach II, 286). Both this story and the one above from "De Rebus Gestis" could also be categorized as communal. In the work of the prior of Heisterbach Abeey there is also a story of a dead father who came to his son to offer him some of the fish he lived on. Because he was not admitted to the house he hung them on the door. In the morning the son went out and found a bundle of snakes and toads which is, according to the story, the food cooked in hell over the sulfurous flames (see Caesarius of Heisterbach II, 305).

Another example is what Joseph Klapper calls "the oldest version of the tale of the dead guest" written in the mid-fourteenth century, an oft-repeated story from Germany.[11] A drunk came across a skull in a graveyard and invited it home with him to which the skull answered he would follow in a little while. Once home, he refused the skull entrance until it threatened him. The skull was attached to a decomposing skeleton, disgusting everyone present. It ate nothing but then invited the host to its mausoleum home the following week. Because

---

[11] See Klapper, "Die Schlesischen Geschichten von den Schädingenden Toten." There are several other versions present in the text as well.

one cannot say "no" to the dead, he went and a sumptuous meal was served him while the dead man sat in the shadows with black bread served on a dirty table, for that is all he was worthy of, considering he himself had been a drunk when alive. He advised the man to go home and change his behavior. The man returned terribly disfigured but he lived out the rest of his life in piety (see Caesarius of Heisterbach II, 202-31).

Thomas Hariot in his 1588 *A Briefe and True Report* wrote of two men from the Algonquian people on Roanoke Island. One was dead and buried and on his way to Popogusso, where one burns continually. A god stopped him and sent him back to teach his companions what to do in order to avoid this place of torment. The other likewise was dead and buried and had entered paradise where there "grewe most delicate and pleasaunt trees, bearing more rare and excellent fruites then euer hee had seene before or was able to expresse." He met his father who charged him to return to explain what was needed to go to that place (37-38). There are quite a few stories of people coming back from the dead to share what they had seen. This will represent them all, because it is an unusual instance, being outside Christianity, although it is unclear whether and how much Hariot changed the stories to fit his readers' expectations.

Most of those that commence in the following selections have to do with penitential or repentant revenants. There are a lot of them, so the choice is almost arbitrary. In the eleventh century the Benedictine Abbey of Marmoutier in France compiled sixteen miraculous tales in the 1084 *Acta sanctorum ordinis S. Benedicti*, of which four concern us. Paragraph 2 concerns two dead monks appearing to the abbot so he will upbraid those not saying prayers for the dead; paragraph 4, a dead monk complained to his confessor that he was being punished for sins not adequately confessed—his confessor took responsibility and the monk was freed; paragraph 8, afraid that the monks would stop praying for a dead priest who gave all his possessions, including debts owed to him, to the monastery, because one of his debtors refused to pay, the priest appeared to a chaplain asking him to intervene on his behalf and tell the man to pay. Paragraph 10 has to do with the two dead brothers who beat the storehouse manager above ("De Rebus Gestis" 395-400).

St. Germanus of Auxerre, the other pre-eleventh century author besides Gregory, as told by Constantius of Lyon's "The Life of Saint Germanus" (c. 480), was camping for the night among some deserted ruins when "[s]uddenly there appeared . . . a dreadful spectre, which rose up little by little as he gazed on it, while the walls were pelted with a shower of stones." Germanus queried in the name of Christ who he was and what he was doing. The revenant replied that after committing many crimes, he was executed, and his shackled body was left unburied there and so he could find no rest. That is why he was bothering the living. Germanus asked him to show him where his body was. The following morning, he gathered together some neighbors and they cleared away the rubble and found his body. He had the irons removed, a grave dug, his body covered with dirt, and he himself said prayers of the dead over him. "There was repose for the dead and quiet for the living. From that day onwards the house lost all its terrors and was restored and regularly occupied" (Constantius of Lyon 84-85).

There are a number of German stories as related by Caesarius of Heisterbach in the second volume *The Dialogue on Miracles*, written in 1220: a young nun, impregnated by a priest and having died in childbirth, confessed to the Abbot and the effects of her sin were lessened by the Abbot's and her family's intervention (II, 315-16); a dead teacher told the Abbot that he was suffering torments for his sins but because his intentions were good the Lord had been merciful (II, 318-19); a dead man explained to his wife that his almsgiving had helped him not at all in the afterlife, for he had done it for vain glory and not charity (II, 305-306); a nine-year-old girl used to whisper to her friend in church before she died; she now must return four times to the church in which she sinned during evening prayers to bow every time "Our Lady" was mentioned (II, 323-25).

There is a particularly interesting one in Caesarius' first volume. An older and younger monk had sex together once and then confessed it to each other rather than to the Abbot. The older, when deathly ill, finally confessed it but refused to reveal his partner. He later appeared after death to the younger monk and told him to confess, for it would help them both, and otherwise the young man would suffer eternal punishment. Finally, after much procrastination, he did (Caesarius of Heisterbach I, 157-59).

Joseph Klapper's selected moral anecdotes, in his 1911 *Exempla aus Handschriften des Mittelalters* from collections of sermons found in the Royal and University libraries in Breslau that span from the end of the twelfth through the fifteenth centuries. The selection of 115 included a number of ones that were related to penitential revenants and were set in graveyards. A priest sprinkled holy water in a cemetery and the dead reached up to receive it (Klapper, *Exempla* 17); a bishop was upbraided by the dead as he passed through a cemetery because he suspended a priest who frequently performed masses for the dead (36); a priest's foot was seized in a cemetery and was released only when he promised to pray for the dead, which was not his habit before that time (37); a man was chased by his enemies into a cemetery where he was protected by the dead, since he habitually prayed for them (43). The last is a little like the story of Ostorgius and Eusebius.

Another one, from the fifteenth century, gathered from Breslau, was of a usurer who was buried unlawfully in a monastery. He rose from the dead each night and would howl and beat the monks with a stick, who then, the next morning, would find themselves in front of the city in a field. After repeatedly burying him, a holy man finally asked him why he haunted them. He replied that he could find no rest because he hounded the poor day and night for their money. They could find rest from him, however, by burying him outside the monastery. This was done and he molested them no longer and there are no reports he molested anyone else (Klapper, "Die schlesischen Geschichten" 68). This is a particularly peculiar story because the dead man asks for and receives no remedy for himself. It appears he only wanted to be buried in unconsecrated ground.

A French abbot by the name of Peter the Venerable in *De Miraculis libri duo* (1142) told of a monk confronted by his abbot who died a few days previously. He confessed to the monk that he was in terrible torment but with his assistance he could pass through this more quickly. "Therefore, I pray to you that moved by my plea you might beseech the lord abbot and all of the brethren to pour forth prayers before almighty God for my freedom and to do everything that they can to release me from such great evils." He did go to them and they did pray (Peter the Venerable 103-104). Also by Peter is a story of a powerful nobleman, who had done many evil deeds, converted and went on a pilgrimage to Rome to repent. He died on the way home. A few years later he appeared to a man, telling him of his agony and his narrow escape from eternal punishment by his visit to Rome, and requested him to appeal to the abbot to pray and perform masses for him. "It is worthwhile to believe that through these works [he] would be freed from his hardships and find the rest of the faithful," the author writes (105-107).

Walter Map again relates a story about an English soldier's dead father who visited him and asked for a priest. He had been excommunicated because he withheld his tithes. But the general prayers of the church and the aims of the people had availed him so much that he could now ask for absolution. He was absolved and a whole procession followed him to his grave, into which he fell with the ground of its own accord covering him up (Map 127-28). Another of Klapper's *exempla* from the fifteenth century tells of the corpse of a woman in Italy who was unburied after seventy years and was found to be utterly intact. The corpse was leaned against a wall and the townsfolk gathered around to see it. That night, however, when the sexton went into the church to light the matin lamps, the body followed him and told him that it could not decompose because she had been excommunicated. She asked that the papal legate be called to absolve her. He did, sprinkled the body with holy water, and it immediately turned to dust.

A tale concerning a Swiss man who bequeathed his property to a local monastery with the consent of his brother is told by Baltherus Seckinganus (*Hie endet sich Sant Fridolinus*) in the thirteenth century).[12] But upon his death his brother reneged on the deal so the abbot Fridolin took him to court. The judges demanded that the dead man appear so Fridolin traveled to his grave and asked him to accompany him back. Fridolin took him by the hand and led him to court where he upbraided his brother. The brother relented and bequeathed his own property as well (Seckinganus eIII-eV). Another tale from Caesarius of Heisterbach relates about a citizen of Strasbourg who died but his soul returned and he told his wife unless they relinquished all their ill-gotten property they could not be saved. He was with her for three days as they got everything in order and then he died again (269).

This variation of the three kings is from a fifteenth-century English manuscript. It is taken from John John Audelay's *The Three Dead Kings*. Three French kings, all of them dismissive of or cruel to their servants and subjects, were riding away from a successful boar hunt. They became lost in a fog and their retainers fled, when they saw three dead men approach them. "[O]ut of the grove, three men come in view:/ Shadowy phantoms, fated to show,/ With legs long and lean, and limbs all askew,/ Their livers and lights all foetid." They contemplated running away, but feared the consequences. They called them ghouls and devils, but they turned out not to be. "Fiends? Demons? Nay! You're

---

[12] A very similar story is told of St. Stanislaus and Piotr. See Antoine Augustin Calmet, *Traité sur les apparitions des esprits* 9-12; also Calmet, *The Phantom World* 12-15.

mistaken!/ We're your fathers—salt of the earth—soon forgotten." They were complaining that masses were not said for them, but their actual purpose was to call out their sons for their brutality, for their love of pomp and pride. Rather they must think of their deaths. "When the finest man dies/ His worst works are decried!" says one of the dead. Another confesses his heartlessness and concludes "Time, remorseless and cruel/ Leads me on to the Doom." The three living kings repented and transformed themselves accordingly (see Audelay 4-14).

Abbot Fridolin and the Dead Man. In *Hie endet sich Sant Fridolinus leben mit der vorrede vund gezugnuss vnd grossen wunderwerck die er gewurket hat vnd die got durch in gewurket hat nach synem tode* 1408, 105.

Master of the Munich Boccaccio: "The Three Living and the Three Dead" c. 1470. Christine Kralik, "Dialogue and Violence" 2011, 145.

George Sinclair in his 1685 *Satan's Invisible World* instructs the reader about a Scottish woman who was a servant to a minister but was turned out by the back door. After a time she came back haunting the place and even throwing a stone at the back door. She died and soon was seen at the minister's home throwing rocks. The pastor came home one night and right after he shut the back door a heavy stone hit it, leaving a dent. A veteran servant was smartly hit with a rock in her back. The dead woman grabbed the heel of a stable boy frightening him and even threw a long-lost horse comb at his bed, but no one was hurt. She threw a number of stones at the gardener and one hit him sharply. Also, the "house was sometimes troubled within with some small Noise and Din" (144-147). Obviously she was getting even for being fired.

Two more English narratives occupy a place here. They are taken from The Byland Abbey Manuscript (c. 1400). A dead man "used to leave his grave at night and disturb and frighten the townsfolk." A courageous youth captured him and a priest came and demanded, in the name of Jesus Christ, that he answer a question. Asked, the corpse confessed his sins and the priest absolved him. He haunted the village no more (see Byland 42). A man wrestled a revenant, got the upper hand, and forced him to speak. The dead man was a canon in the church but was excommunicated because of stealing spoons. He told the man where to find them and for him to take them to the prior to seek absolution. The prior granted it and the man rested in peace (43-44).

The anonymously written *Sad and Wonderful Newes* (1661) asserted that an Englishman died and for five months he caused a hideous noise in the house. He appeared as a black cat and a goat before taking his human form, in which he identified himself to the maid as her master. His eyes were "half sunk in his Head, his face extraordinarily black, and in the same Cloathes he used to wear when he was alive" (3-4). He struck one individual on the leg and he was lame thereafter. Whenever confronted with a religious utterance he would disappear. Finally a minister asked him in the name of God the Father, Son, and Holy Ghost why he was not at rest and he said that he had unjustly dealt with his granddaughter. "And then immediately after some Sighings, and Groans, it seemed to vanish" (5). This is another unusual story with no remedy asked for or given unless he just needed to confess his wrongdoing.

In the same document there was a shorter story told. It was of a dead man who after seven years walked again. He appeared to his daughter at noon one day and took her by the hand and asked how she was, frightening her terribly. Finally she answered "Well I praise God. I wish the like to you. Father, what is your business, would you speak with my Mother?" (8) He replied in a most hideous voice, "No." He would utter such horrible groans that the neighbors had to take lodging further away. He sometimes appeared with a plaster on his face as if he were murdered. One night four doctors were present as he issued sad groans and heavy sighs and they tried to see him and discover the cause of his walking, but he was invisible to them so it was difficult to ascertain whether his blood had been shed violently, "for true it is, that Muther will certainly cry aloud for Vengeance, till satisfied by Justice."

In 1694 the English pamphlet, *An Account of a Most Horrid and Barbarous Murther*, appeared excoriating the evils of murder. Captain Brown was a man of upstanding character and well-liked by all that knew him. He was set upon while traveling by his servant in the company of seven country laborers, slain, and robbed. They cut off his head and buried it together with his body in a field. Soon afterwards, he appeared to some gentlewomen of his acquaintance as they lay in bed. With a smile he pulled the curtain and opened the window casements. He then disappeared. He then visited an elderly friend who was sick and sat down with his son. While the son chatted with him, the captain smiled but said nothing. He then got up and again vanished. The servant who had returned alone from the journey was arrested on suspicion of murder after an extensive search was conducted and turned up no body. Later the seven workers were arrested after being overheard speaking of the deed and put in jail "in order to receive their just Punishment for so horrid and barbarous a Murther."

George Sinclair weighed in on the topic with three tales. A young man encountered his dead father-in-law at night who told him to say to his wife not to worry about him: "God has showed me mercy contrary to my deserts." He also directed him to pay a debt he owed and to explain to his son that he must get rid of the sword he inherited at a particular place. The debt was paid and when the son arrived at the designated place his father took the sword and placed where he had buried a man he had murdered with that sword. Then he disappeared (Sinclair 102-108).

Not long after her death, a mistress knocked at her maid's door and told her to follow her. She took her to a field and said that her father acquired this land wrongfully so it must go to the poor. Since this must be worked out with the mistress' brother-in-law, she told her maid a secret known only to the two of them. The brother-in-law initially laughed at the request, but upon hearing the secret he relinquished the land and it has been used by the poor to this day (Sinclair 128-31).

Then there are four particularly intriguing ones. Sinclair's third story tells of a servant to an Apothecary from Silesia, then under Austrian rule, who had recently died. He came back to the shop and, although appearing ghastly, he did everything he did before except he was belligerent to his master. He eventually left the shop and wandered abroad visiting the homes of his old friends but saying nothing. He did, however, speak to a maid, telling her where a treasure was buried. It ended up the valuables were nothing but an old decayed pot with a bloodstone in it. She therefore had him exhumed and stripped of all the items he was buried with; he was seen no more (Sinclair 132-34).

Hervé Martin in his "À la recherche de la culture populaire bretonne" tells of a baker who passed away (c. 1475), but as his family were kneading the bread suddenly the dead man appeared in their midst and "commenced to roll his shirt sleeves up to his elbows and join them in kneading the dough and spur them on, often in a loud voice, telling them to work skillfully and vigorously." This frightened them so their neighbors cast him out. He thereafter stood obnoxiously outside their homes and cast stones at passers-by. Because he avoided paths when ambling about he was covered to his knees in dirt. Due to this mischief, the people went out and disinterred him, finding him with mud to his knees and flour to his elbows. They filled the grave back up but he continued to vex the townspeople, so they unburied him again and broke both his legs (Martin 32-33).

In a letter from 1070, Peter Damian informs the reader of a young woman from Rome on the feast of the Assumption of Mary at a basilica dedicated to the virgin who caught sight of her godmother who had died about a year before. She asked her how she was getting along. "Until today a heavy punishment oppressed me because I had disgraced myself in my youth by succumbing to the enticement of wanton lust with girls my own age." She had died with the sin unconfessed. That day, however, Mary had forgiven her and many others as well so they were all there to pay homage to her (Damian 239-40).

Dante, in Italy, related in his 1314 *Inferno* how an individual who was alive when he embarked on his journey to hell was there being punished. Dante learned that this acquaintance had actually been there for a while, but since his body had been allotted a certain number of years, until his time had run out a demon inhabited his corpse. This is especially interesting, because it means that souls can be removed from their bodies after a wicked deed is performed with no time for contrition, repentance, and forgiveness. And a demon in a body is not noticeable (see Dante 159-61).

If there is anything consistent here it is its inconsistency. Some very minor infractions are dealt with harshly, even outwardly pious individuals are damned, whereas some who have committed particularly heinous deeds experience leniency.

Proto- or Urvampires

We have already read about the two runaway peasants with the pestilence they unleashed, the revenant put down by water poured over a nail from the crucifixion, and the dead woman who wrestled the monk. A dead Englishman crawled into bed with his wife and nearly crushed her according to William of Newburgh in his "History" (c. 1198). After a couple of nights of this, she prevailed upon her neighbors to keep watch. They did and scared him away. He then successively attacked his brothers, his friends, and his neighbors until all of them were watching over each other. He then began to appear in the daylight, exposing himself to just a few at a time. The people pleaded with their bishop to do something and, instead of dismembering him, he prepared a letter of absolution. He was exhumed, the letter placed on his chest, and reburied, thus ending his terror (see William of Newburgh 656-57).

In 1575 Stephan Gerlach averred that a Greek man was disinterred two years after he had died and was not found decomposed That is why whoever saw him at night immediately died, fifteen in all. The Greeks accused him and the Turks burned him (see Gerlach 94). All of mainland Greece and most of the Aegean islands were in the hands of the Ottoman Turks at the time.

Walter Map again (c. 1182) writes about an English soldier in Wales who sought the help of a bishop because a malefactor who died in his lodging was visiting the house nightly and summoning one of the inhabitants, who never failed to fall ill and die. The bishop advised him "to dig up the corpse, cut the neck, and besprinkle the body and the grave with holy water, and then rebury it. Although this was done, nonetheless the survivors continued to be assailed by the restless spirit." Finally the dead man called out the soldier himself, but he had had enough and charged the specter with sword drawn. The dead man fled to his grave. The soldier dug him out and beheaded him thereby terminating his hauntings (Map 125-26).

There are four more tales pertaining to England. The first three are by William of Newburgh (c. 1198). A great rogue, having been buried, sallied forth, was pursued by a pack of barking dogs, and was frightening people. A group of young men was conscripted to deal with him. They dug him up, severed all his limbs, and committed his body to the flames. Peace seemed restored, but then a pestilence broke out, carrying away the majority of the citizens (see William Of Newburgh 657-58). No happy ending here. An immoral priest died and, unable to haunt the holy monastery, went instead to his confessee, a frequent donor to the convent, terrorizing her. She confided this to a friar and he kept watch over the cemetery until late into the night when the body rose and rushed at him with a great noise; he buried a hatchet into his chest. With help he exhumed the body, saw the gaping hole in its breast, and reduced it to ash (658-59).

The third is unique in that it actually calls the revenant a *sanguisuga* or bloodsucker "filled with the blood of many persons." A scoundrel spied on and caught his wife in infidelity but mortally injured himself in the process. After his burial, he wandered through the town causing the inhabitants to lock their doors lest he beat them black and blue, but his foul carcass emitted a "pestiferous breath" killing most of the townsfolk anyway. Finally, some young people took matters into their own hands, dug up the body, pulled out the "hell-hound's" heart, tore it to pieces, and then burned the carcass. Actually it was rumored the body would not burn until the heart was removed and ripped up so that is what they did. The air being purified, the illness ceased (William Of Newburgh 660-61).

The fourth is found in The Byland Abbey Manuscript (c. 1400) and tells of a rector who was buried but "used to go out by darkness and one night he put out the eye of his concubine." The abbot had his body removed from its grave complete with its coffin and ordered that it be taken to the river. While his coffin was being thrown into the river the oxen almost sank into the water with fear. This is the only one that has the urvampire clearly sucking human blood (see Byland 42-43).

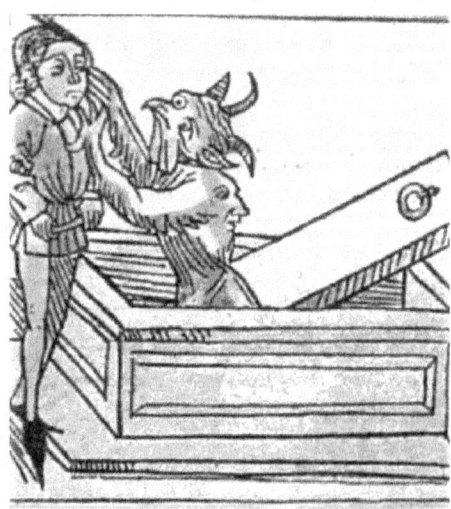

Vampire attacking a Christian[13]

---

[13] "Vampiro attacando cristão." This is a misidentification. It is not a vampire but a revenant. It is a German engraving from the fifteenth century, published in *Mito y Realidad de los No-muertos* (2003) by Miguel G. Aracil, 38. 1

Richard Baxter in *The Certainty of the World of Spirits Fully Evinced* (1691), described a pious, English woman, whose husband was visiting Ireland, who was in bed for the night. She endured a strong wind outside during which time her husband appeared and asked if he could join her. As she was praying she told him "no" and averred that he was not her husband, to which he took umbrage. She and some other godly women prayed through the night but the apparition constantly interrupted them. Two nights later he revealed himself again but this time with "an insufferable stench, like that of a putrefied carcass," emitting smoke, and again interrupted their prayer by uttering incomprehensible words and by "striking them so that the next morning their faces were black with the smoak, and their bodies swollen with bruises." She left the house lest she tempt the Lord by staying in such danger (Baxter 24-26).

A French nobleman on his deathbed made his wife promise she would not marry his avowed adversary otherwise he would kill her with a salt mortar according to Gervase of Tilbury writing in his *Otia Imperialia* circa 1215. She, being in such grief, felt coerced to agree to it. After his death, her friends began to push her to marry the man and they utterly discounted her concerns. Under their pressure she married him; and her dead husband picked up a mortar and shattered her skull (Gervase of Tilbury 752-55). In Germany Caesarius of Heisterbach (*The Dialogue on Miracles*, 1220-35) related the story of a nurse who took the children out to relieve themselves when she saw a woman dressed in white with a pallid complexion looking at them over the fence and then moving over to stare at the neighbor's home. The two children, their mother and the nurse all passed away, along with the neighbor and his son (118-19). She apparently is still at large.

Circa 1297, *The Chronicle of Lanercost* told of an excommunicated monk in Scotland who died and "[l]ong after his body had been buried, it vexed many," riding roofs at night and by day terrifying and molesting the household of a knight. "And when men either shot at him with arrows or thrust him through with forks, straightway whatever was driven into that damned substance was burnt to ashes in less time than it takes to tell it. Also he so savagely felled and battered those who attempted to struggle with him as well-nigh to shatter all their joints" (118-19). The eldest son of the knight challenged him and died. He could still be lurking about. Also from the same source: in Scotland a couple was riding home from market when the wife asked to dismount the horse and walk the rest of the way on foot. Her husband went on ahead. She encountered a girl scarcely seven years old and of pallid complexion who attacked her, leaving her for dead with a huge gash on her back, the skin torn from her arms, and bruises all over her body. Two days later she passed away (104-105). That young girl may also be on the loose

We come now to two of the most popular revenant stories of the medieval and early modern eras, which were then usurped at the beginning of vampire literature. The accounts that are most detailed come from Wenceslaus Hagecius von Libotschan in his *Böhmische Chronik* (1541) so I will use them for my synopses, although they were preceded by some 170 years by Neplach of Opatovice, also Bohemian, writing in much more summary fashion (*Summula chronicae tam Romanae quam Bohemicae*) and followed by at least Martin Zeiller's *Theatrum Tragicum* (1624, 25-26) and Heinrich Roch's *Neue Lausitz'sche Böhm* (1687, 4-5). They were first referenced in vampire literature by Johann Weichard von Valvasor *Die Ehre deß*

Hertzogthums in 1689 (335-36) and most famously by Antoine Augustin Calmet in *Traité sur les apparitions des esprits* (1751, 9); see also *The Phantom World* (1759, 31).

The first features a shepherd from Blow, now in the Czech Republic, buried near the church. "The same arose every night, circulated among the villages, frightened the people, spoke with them in no other way than when he was alive, even strangled some of them; and before whatever dwelling he would stop, if he called out someone's name, the same had to die before eight days had passed." The townsfolk staked him, but he chided them saying that they have only given him a stick to ward off the dogs. "He went forth that same night and killed more people than before." They loaded him on a cart and bound him where he bellowed like an ox and when placed on the pyre he brayed like an ass. Since he was burned the troubles were brought to an end (Libotschan 552).

The second has to do with a witch from Levin also presently in the Czech Republic. She practiced her craft openly until admonished by some priests after which she practiced secretly. She died mysteriously and was buried at a crossroads. She revived and often changed her form into an animal and chased the flocks causing the herders extensive trouble. She also walked about in her human form. She regularly went to town and the surrounding villages, entering "people's homes, appearing in different ways, talking with folks, but terrifying a part of them and bringing about their death." They disinterred her and saw she had "devoured half of the veil that was wrapped about her head; it was pulled from her throat covered in blood." They staked her and returned her to her grave. "After a short time, she let herself be seen publicly much more than she did before, frightening and killing people, and those who died, she jumped on with her feet. Therefore, they had her exhumed again . . . and they found that she had pulled out the stake that had impaled her and that she held it in her hands. Because of this, she was taken out and burned together with the stake, and then the ashes, mixed in with earth, were poured in the grave and it was covered over again" (Libotschan 552).

Illustration by Albert Decaris in Jean Mistler's 1944 *Le Vampire*.

Heinrich Roch in his *Neue Lausitz'sche Böhm* (1687) gives three examples. The people of Künern in Poland "were sorely plagued by a ghost on June 8 [1612], and because the coarse shepherd came to their minds, his body was exhumed and found to be fresh as if barely a day had passed since he had been laid to rest. The corpse was committed to the flames and the troubles stopped" (236). The inhabitants of Görsdorff in Poland had been plagued for a long time by a revenant and finally a man who had died three years previously and his wife, eight weeks prior, were mentioned. "The two were disinterred and found to appear fully composed and to bleed freely. On the 22nd of May [1614], they were burned to ash and soon thereafter the calamity ceased" (242). "In August [1651], the people around Freudenthal [in the current Czech Republic] were harassed by spirits of the night, so that even their livestock were sucked on [*ausgesogen*] and killed, before they would return to their graves; therefore the people forsook their markets and land, and went to live in other, more secure places" (307-308). The last implies bloodsucking; it seems unlikely that drinking milk could kill livestock.

A wealthy man named Steffan Hubener died in Bohemia according to Andreas Hondorff's "Vorede" to his 1584 *Promptuarium exemplorum* (see ii). This is duplicated nearly exactly by Johann Wolf (*Lectionum memorabilium et reconditarum* 1600): "It came to pass . . . that soon after his death and burial, his corpse and body (or, as I believe, the devil in his diabolical power, directed and walked about visibly in his body) pressed so hard upon so many people that many of them died. Some, however, recovered and they unanimously confessed that they had been pressed upon, according to all external appearances, by none other than the rich man after his death, but as they knew and saw him beforehand" (848). Hubener was exhumed and although dead twenty weeks, he was found corpulent and intact. His head was cut off, his body sliced up, and his heart removed; all his blood flowed out as if from a living man under torture, and he was completely incinerated.

Carolus Weinrichius wrote the "Proaemium." to the 1612 edition of Giovanni Francesco Pico's *trix* and told of a Polish shoemaker who slit his throat.[14] Because suicide was a disgrace, the family went to great lengths to conceal the fact, but rumors nonetheless circulated. Then came the visitations day and night. The revenant "scared many people through its very form, awakened others with noises, oppressed others, and others it vexed in other ways, so that early in the morning one heard talk everywhere about the ghost." The family complained to the authorities about the accusations, because they besmirched his character, but things only got worse. "For the ghost was there right after sundown, and since no one was free of it, everyone looked around constantly for it. The ones most bothered were those who wanted to rest after heavy work; often it came to their bed, often it actually lay down in it and was like to smother

---

[14] Paul Barber (1988, 10-14) in his seminal work, *Vampires, Burial, and Death*, translated this story. He used as his source J. Grässe *Sagenbuch des preussischen Staats* 1868, 176-180. Grässe's anthology was itself carefully documented, and he attributed it to his source: Christian Stief, *Schlesisches Historisches Labyrinth* (1737), 351-362. Stieff, in his introduction, referred back to the original by Carolus Weinrichius (Karl Weinrich in German), affixed to the 1612 edition of Giovanni Francesco Pico della Mirandola's work (first published in 1523), 1-13. I am using Barber's translation with additions from Henry More's 1655 *An Antidote Against Atheism*, 209-213.

the people. Indeed, it squeezed them so hard that—not without astonishment—people could see the marks left by its fingers" (1-13).

The body was dug up and though buried eight months previously was like it was when just put under except bloated. It was put on display and guarded but the ghost continued to rage terribly, "thereby causing great inconvenience to many citizens as well as his good friends." Finally the widow confessed and now the corpse could be dealt with properly. It was beheaded, dismembered, its heart cut out, burned, and the ashes strewn in flowing water. Although he was dealt with, his maid became a revenant as well.[15] She lay on a fellow servant so that her eyes bulged, caught another by the throat so that it swelled, mishandled an infant so that had not the nurse entered it would have died. She pulled another number of other tricks for a month until her body was dug up and burned.

Johann Cuntz, also a Pole, died from an accident according to Martinus Weinrichius (13-47) and More's 1655 *An Antidote Against Atheism*. Scarcely a day had passed after his burial before the hauntings began. At night people witnessed things being thrown around the house. He galloped up and down like a wanton horse; he bruised a child to death "making his very bones so soft, that you might wrap the corps on heaps like a glove;" he terrified a friend "vomiting out fire against him . . ., and biting of him so cruelly by the foot, that he made him lame;" he pressed one's lips together so hard he had a hard time pulling them apart; he beat a woman in the form of a dwarf; he emitted a horrible stench from his mouth almost driving a family out of their house; he flung dung into milk bowls (see More 215-226).

A further list was provided which included "[h]is defiling the Water in the Font, and fouling the Cloth on the Altar on that side that did hang towards his grave with dirty bloody spots: His catching up Dogs in the streets, and knocking their brains against the ground: His sucking dry the Cows: . . . His looking out of the Window of a low Tower, and then suddenly changing himself into the form of a long staff" (More 223). He tried to have sex with women including an aged one who told him "Mr. Cuntius, thou seest how old, wrinkled, and deformed I am, and how unfit for those kind of sports" (224), whereupon he laughed and vanished. He was finally exhumed but he was "unwilling" to move from the church, to be carried to the place of his execution, and to be burned. Until the body was torn to pieces the people and the executioner had a terrible time with each task. The executioner cut the body up, burned it, and cast the ashes into the river.

The following is an unusual example from seventeenth-century Silesia in Prussia found in Julius Wilhelm Otto's 1877 *Deutscher Sagenschatz*. A bagpipe player asked that his instrument be buried with him when he died. He passed away and at midnight he rose from his grave and began playing dance songs. The other tombs opened, and the dead stepped out and began to dance. The watchman in the turret witnessed it and the next day he spread the word about what happened. That night many curious spectators gathered together to view the spectacle, but the dead went after them and many fainted from fright and several died. The clergy tried to stop the piper but in vain. Several university scholars advised them that the dead be disinterred, decapitated, a stake thrust through their hearts, and any that bled burned. This done, the dance of the dead ended (see Otto 139-140).

---

[15] This is not in the original account but appears to have been added by Henry More (213-214).

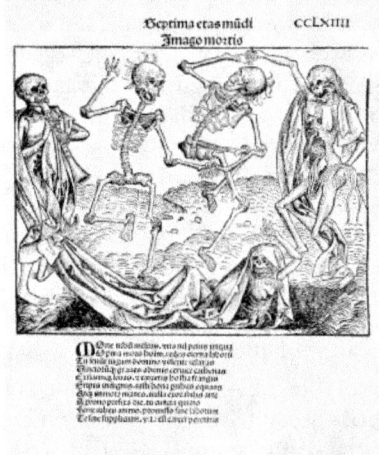

"The Dance of Death" illustrated by Michael Wolgemut. In *Liber chronicarum*, 1, by Hartmann Schedel (1493), CCLXIIII.

François de Rosset's 1614 "D'un demon qui apparoist in forme de Damoiselle," presents a French city guard, La Jaquière, renowned for visiting prostitutes, feeling particularly randy one night, telling his friends that "if at this moment I met the devil, he would never escape my grasp until first I had had my way with him." Suddenly an attractive woman appeared on the street. He and two friends approached her and offered to see her home safely. Upon reaching her home, having learned that she was married but that her husband was away, they entered the house and he seduced her into sexual intercourse. When over he said although she had his oath of secrecy, she did not have such from his two friends, so after some serious cajoling, she went to bed with them as well. Afterward they were all praising her appearance when she surprisingly said "If you knew who I am, you would never say such things." She immediately turned into a stinking rotten corpse and the house was reduced to ruins with the three thrown on to heaps of garbage and manure. One died right away, La Jaquière just had time enough to confess, and the last one lived long enough to recount the adventure. We learn the lesson that "lechery leads to adultery, adultery incest, incest the sin contrary to nature, and after that, God allows that one couple with the devil" (Rosset 329-344).[16]

A young man, in a story related by François du Carroy, *Histoire prodigieuse d'un gentilhomme* (1613), returned home to find a finely dressed Parisienne with refined manners waiting in the rain on his porch for her coach. He invited her in and eventually wore down her reluctance to do so.[17] They supped and then, because the coach had not come, he yielded his bed to her and would sleep on the front room himself. Because he had found her responsive to his flirting, he later entered the chamber to ask how she was doing and from there wooed her.

---

[16] The short story was translated into German by Martin Zeiller by 1628 (*Theatrum Tragicum*). The tale would enter vampire literature first as reworked by Jan Potocki in his *Le Manuscrit trouvé à Saragosse* (1805, 101-109; 1810, 125-34); he says he is translating it from E. G. Happelii *Grössester Denkwürdigkeiten der Welt*, 537-39. If so, its ultimate source was with Zeiller not Rosset. Charles Nodier will tell the same version, but in condensed form, as "Les Aventures de Thibaud de la Jacquière" and published it in his *Infernaliana* (1822), 95-111.
[17] The narrative was developed by Nicolas Lenglet Dufresnoy, "Histoire prodigieuse" (1751) and was vampirized by Collin de Plancy, *Histoire des Vampires* (1820).

She finally admitted him into bed with her and he experienced "pleasures he believed to be perfect" (Plancy 129). The next morning he vacated the room, so that both would appear chaste, and sent his servant to wake her. She asked to be given more time since she had not slept well. The young man circulated about town for a while and returned only to find her dead. He called some justices and physicians to examine her and pass judgment on her death but they all recognized her as one who was hanged a while back. Suddenly a cloud of smoke arose from the bed, the body disappeared, and a foul odor was all that was left.

The Nachzehrer, those who devoured their burial clothes often spreading plague at the same time, were also treated as ur- or protovampires. We have already noted the witch from Levin. In 1517, we are told in Nikolaus Pol's 1630 *Jahrbücher der Stadt Breslau* that 2000 people died from illness in Breslau (1). He continued that a shepherd had been buried and in his grave had "smacked like a sow." He was exhumed and his clothes were found bloody in his mouth. He was beheaded and his head placed at the front of the churchyard (1-2). Martin Luther, the German monk who sparked the Reformation, in entry 6823 of his *Tischreden* (published posthumously in 1566) was informed "how a woman in a certain village had died and now, since her burial, she [was] eating herself in her grave, causing every person in that village to die." Luther responded that it was a matter of faith; because they believed it was for real, they were dying off whereas if they confronted Satan, who is perpetrating it, with faith and set him to flight, no one would succumb. "[T]hey should all gather together in the church to ask God that their sins be forgiven for Christ's sake and to resist the devil" (Luther 214).

In German Lutheran pastor, Martin Böhm's 1601 *Drey Grossen Landtplagen*, some thirty-five years after Luther's "table talk," is stated that "[i]t has been heard to occur in times of pestilence, that the dead, especially women, who have died of the plague, make a smacking noise in their graves, like a sow when eating, and that with this smacking, the pestilence grows worse, and those likewise of the same lineage die one after another. . . . In 1553, as the plague was raging here in Lauben, the same thing happened—a woman had also made smacking noises in her grave. With the deaths at Sangerhausen in the year of our Lord 1565, Heinrich Rorhsey writes of something similar occurring to them. [So too in Merseberg in 1581 and in Schiselbein in 1584.] Here is the question that is posed: In such an event, what can be done? Actually the counsel given was that the grave of the one smacking should be opened and the body decapitated with a spade. Those who have so done say that the veil placed over the mouth and lips has been devoured and that when the head is chopped off, fresh blood may flow out" (Böhm 141). He says that because the body and soul were separated at death it had to be the devil animating the corpse. This is similar to Luther, but in distinction from him, he held that more than faith was required to stop it.

Circa 1650 in today's Czech Republic, as told by M. Philipp Rohr, *Dissertatio Historico-Philosophica de Masticatione Mortuorum* (1679), Part 1, Thesis 7, a corpse was found that had devoured not only his own burial clothes but also those of a nearby woman; in 1672 in the same region a body was dug up and found to have been eating itself.[18] Concerning the feeding on oneself, Christian Friedrich

---

[18] Summers (*The Vampire in Europe* 185-186) has translated all of Rohr's dissertation but as is so often the case it is misleading. The corpse, according to Rohr, is not eating the adjoining woman, as Summers asserts, but her shroud; the man is not eating his limbs but himself, however likely it is his limbs he is devouring.

Garmann (*De miraculis mortuorum*, 1670) adds that the devouring dead, which is primarily composed of the "weaker sex," "consume with their mouth as much as they can touch" (27).

Also in Czech territory, according to Martin Zeiller in his *Theatrum Tragicum* (1624), an honest man was buried in the churchyard, "but he continually at night would rise up and kill people. He would always leave his death shroud lying by his grave and when he was ready to lie back down therein, he would put it back on." One night the guards occupying the church tower saw him disrobe and rushed down and took his grave clothes in his absence. When he returned he called to the watchers that they must return his shroud or he would break all of their necks. In great fear, they did exactly what he demanded. "Later the executioner had to exhume his body and hack it into pieces. Thereafter there was no more trouble. The executioner drew from the corpse's mouth a large, long shroud he had devoured from his wife's head. He displayed it to those who were standing around saying, 'Behold! how greedy this scoundrel was!' After he was taken from the grave, the executioner continued, 'Things worked out well for you, because his wife also died and was laid beside him. Otherwise they both would have killed half the town.'"[19]

Conclusion

Before the eleventh century there was a general concern, embodied by St. Augustine, to eradicate any form of the "pagan" practice of worshiping the dead, and to work out the struggle between good and evil in the cosmic terms of God, angels, and saints vs. the Devil and its minions. I do not like the word "pagan." It was used by Christians to denote all religions but their own. The five stories of St. Gregory and St. Germanus were exceptions. So, under Augustine, the dead were shut off from the living, unaware of their goings-on, and preoccupied with their own concerns. This idea of a strict divide between the dead and living, however, began to weaken in the eleventh century.

In his collection of medieval stories *Ghosts in the Middle Ages* Jean-Claude Schmitt (see 4-5, 28, 33-34, 60-62) finds the reason to be in the development and consolidation of the masses said on behalf of the dead at the beginning of the tenth century and of the concept of purgatory. But he also notes that for some, there was probably an eschatological interest—that these portended the end of the world—for others, it may be due more to an idea of the uniqueness of their own time and thus, the desire to chronicle it.

As William of Newburgh in his "History" explained around 1198: "It would be strange if such things should have happened formerly, since we can find no evidence of them in the works of ancient authors, . . . for if they never neglected to register even events of moderate interest, how could they have suppressed a fact at once so amazing and horrible" (658). Schmitt also mentions the pressure to inflate narratives and to present more appealing representations.[20] Thomas

---

[19] I have translated this from Erasmus Francisci's 1690 *Der Höllische Proteus* (259-60).
[20] Rob Hebblethwaite, in "The Good, the Bad and the Rotten: How the Living Dealt With the Dead in England" (2017), conjectures that the Norse *aptrgangr* may have been influential on the development of the English revenant (see 31-36).

M. Bohn, in *The Vampire* (2019) adds that "A key precondition for the emergence of the belief in vampires [i.e. revenants] was the gradual replacement of the practice of cremation and the funeral pyre with that of entombment or burial in the earth" (xi).

Without these cultural changes there would have been no vampire, for, as we saw in the introduction, it grew out of the European and English revenant. So what have we learned of these urvampires? Not all of them are technically revenants, except in terms of their bodies, for they do not have their own souls. Because there is still a legacy of the division between the dead and the living, the explanation is that Satan is inhabiting the body. Yet this is true of several vampires as well. Penitential ones differ: some have clearly done evil from the standpoint of the church like the men who have sex with each other or the woman, who in her youth, succumbed to the enticement of wanton lust with girls her own age; some are guilty of minor offences like the canon taking and hiding silverware (for which he was excommunicated!); some seem, to our minds, wrongly accused like a nun who was no doubt raped.

With regard to the post-mortem state, some suddenly sit up while they are on display before their burial; two become animated in order to scare pious virgins in prayer; one experiences an earthly purgatory awaiting inebriated passers-by and then using fear and wisdom to turn that one from sin; some make a racket; some return to their vocations; some hit people; some try to have sex with women; some cause sensations of suffocation in their victims. A few are shape-shifters—as animals or as a dwarf; several never leave their coffin—they sometimes cause and intensify disease by chewing on the veil that covers their face in the grave or their own limbs. A sizable number actively kill: a seven-year-old girl attacks a young woman by a river and mortally wounds her; a pale woman exits the cemetery and kills the inhabitants of two homesteads simply by staring at them; one sucks human blood and two others implied to do the same with livestock; some murder but are impervious to weapons, including those of the church; one undresses himself, kills people naked, and then returns to his grave to redress. Many of these things are attributed to vampires as well, a number by attributing these stories directly to them.

There is no single way to deal with them. Something that stands out is nonviolent alternatives to bodily mutilation. Many are absolved—even one who is not seeking it, but nonetheless a certificate is placed on his chest and his body is quieted. The wandering revenant that is surrounded in an orchard, promptly buries himself when the cross is taken from his grave and then remains subdued when it is replaced. Feuding corpses are separated. Martin Luther's *Nachzehrer* is to be dealt with by faith alone. Other cases that do not include violence to the revenant are single cases where the urvampire is specifically targeting a person or persons and is not returning for more. The pale woman who kills with her gaze (or just indicates with it who is next to die) is never pursued; the dead knight who brings a meal from hell is not either; nor is the seven-year-old girl. Some communities of the dead should not be engaged but actively avoided or one can die. A good, dancing wife is welcomed back by her husband with open arms—no one would think of harming her. There are analogies here especially with the Greek vampires of the seventeenth and early eighteenth centuries.

Others do meet a violent end, however, and this places them closest to the Slavic vampires. A man is exhumed, inspected, and reburied. When that does not work his legs are broken. One unbeliever is disinterred, holy water thrown on the body, and his neck cut. When this proves insufficient the carcass is dug up again and beheaded. There are a number of instances where a simple beheading or staking or being cut into pieces is not enough and the body must be burned. Some cremations are from God as with the nun that has half her body burned and another reduced to ash in his grave after yelling "I burn, I burn!" The rest are done by humans. One is attacked with an ax, burned, and its ashes discarded. In fact a lot of ashes are scattered either to the wind or in water. The shepherd of Blow and the witch of Levin are impaled but this proves unsuccessful and both must be cremated. One has his head cut off, his body sliced up, and his heart removed, and then completely incinerated. The body of one, it was said, would not burn unless the heart was first removed and sliced up; another's was "unwilling" to burn until it was torn in pieces. Still another was beheaded, dismembered, its heart cut out, burned, and the ashes strewn in flowing water. Even cremation sometimes does not spell the end. Undead corpses are committed to the flames but this unleashes a lethal disease severely depopulating the town.

So the revenant or Wiedergänger is a proto- or urvampire. The vampire in the eighteenth century is largely an inert body, swollen with blood, and surprisingly uncorrupted over time, on which could be blamed pestilence, progressive emaciation, superstitions, or night terrors, i.e. feelings of suffocation, and other parasomnias. On this may be added wandering. In Europe and England the vampire came to be tied inextricably to exsanguination or bloodsucking in 1732 with the bestselling account of Arnont Paule. All of these are found among revenants. So was the remedy of violating the body, which was typical in the Nordic countries as well. But revenants came with much more developed stories, with extensive narratives of their deeds, and this helped set up the vampire for literature.

Works cited

An Account of a Most Horrid and Barbarous Murther and Robbery Committed on the Body of Captain Brown. Edinburgh: s.n., 1664.
"An Army White as Snow" [Thirteenth or fourteenth century]. *The Penguin Book of the Undead: Fifteen Hundred Years of Supernatural Encounters*. Trans. Scott G. Bruce. New York: Penguin Books, 2016. 154-160.
Audelay, John. *The Three Dead Kings* [Fifteenth century]. Trans. Giles Watson. Morrisville, NC: Lulu, 2011.
Barber, Paul. *Vampires, Burial, and Death: Folklore and Reality*. New Haven: Yale University Press, 1988.
Baxter, Richard. *The Certainty of the World of Spirits Fully Evinced*. London: T. Parkhurst, 1691.
Baxter, Richard. *The Saints' Everlasting Rest*. London: Thomas Underhill and Francis Tyton, 1654.
"De Rebus Gestis" [1084]. *Acta sanctorum ordinis S. Benedicti* 2. Benedictine Abbey of Marmoutier. Venice: Sebastianum Coleti & Josephum Bettinelli, 1733.

Black, Winston. "Animated Corpses and Bodies with Power in the Scholastic Age." In *Death in Medieval Europe: Death Scripted and Death Choreographed.* Ed. Joelle Rollo-Koster. London: Routledge, 2017. 71-93.

Böhm, Martin. *Drey Grossen Landtplagen—Krieg, Tewrung, Pestilentz—Welche Jetzundt vor der Welt Ende in Vollem Schwang Gehen.* Wittenberg: Christian Seelfisch, 1601.

Bohn, Thomas M. *The Vampire: Origins of a European Myth.* Trans. Francis Ipgrave. New York: Berghahn, 2019.

Bohn, Thomas M. *Der Vampir: Ein europäischer Mythos.* Cologne: Böhlau Verlag, 2016.

Boyacioğlu, Elif. "The Demise of the Walking Dead: The Rise of Purgatory and the End of Revenancy." Master's Thesis. Bilkent University, 2007.

Bruce, Scott G. *The Penguin Book of the Undead: Fifteen Hundred Years of Supernatural Encounters.* New York: Penguin Books, 2016.

Byland Abbey Manuscript. ("Twelve Medieval Ghost Stories") [c. 1400]. Trans. Pamela Chamberlaine. *M. R. James: Book of the Supernatural.* Ed. Peter Haining. Marlow: W. Foulsham & Co., 1979. 34-49.

Caciola, Nancy. *Afterlives: The Return of the Dead in the Middle Ages* Ithaca: Cornell University Press, 2016.

Caciola, Nancy. "Revenants, Resurrection, and Burnt Sacrifice." *Preternature: Critical and Historical Studies on the Preternatural* 3: 2 (2014), 311-338.

Caciola, Nancy. "Wraiths, Revenants and Ritual in Medieval Culture." *Past & Present* 152 (August 1996), 3-45.

Caesarius of Heisterbach. *The Dialogue on Miracles* [1220-1235]. Vol. 2. Trans. H. Von E. Scott and C. C. Swinton Bland. London: Routledge, 1929.

Calmet, Antoine Augustin. *The Phantom World* [1746/1751]. Vol. 2. Trans. Henry Christmas. London: Richard Bentley, 1850.

Calmet, Antoine Augustin. *Traité sur les apparitions des esprits et sur les vampires ou les revenans de Hongrie, de Moravie, &c.* New ed. Senones: J. Pariset, 1759.

The Chronicle of Lanercost: 1272-1346. Trans. Herbert Maxwell. Glasgow: James Maclehose, 1913.

Constantius of Lyon. "The Life of Saint Germanus of Auxerre" [c. 480]. Trans. F. R. Hoare. *Soldiers of Christ: Saints and Saints' Lives from Late Antiquity and the Early Middle Ages.* Eds. Thomas F. X. Noble and Thomas Head. University Park: Pennsylvania State University Press, 1995. 75-106.

Carroy, François du. *Histoire prodigieuse d'un gentilhomme auquel le diable s'est apparu et avec lequel il a conversé soubs le corps d'une femme morte, advenue à Paris le premier de janvier 1613.* Paris: François du Carroy, 1613.

Damian, Peter. *Letters of Peter Damian 151-180* [1067-1070]. Trans. Owen J. Blum and Irven M. Resnick. Washington, D. C.: Catholic University of America Press, 2005.

Dante. *The Inferno* [1314]. Trans. Henry Wadsworth Longfellow. *The Divine Comedy of Dante Alighieri.* Boston: Houghton, Mifflin, 1886.

Dufresnoy, Nicolas Lenglet. "Histoire prodigieuse, D'un Gentil-Homme auquel le Diable s'est apparu, & avec lequel il a conversé sous le corps d'une femme morte, advenue à Paris, le premier de Janvier 1613." *Recueil de dissertations anciennes et nouvelles* Tome 1, Partie II. Avignon, 1751. 71-81.

Les Esprits, ou Le Mary fourbé. Liège : Loüis Montfort, 1686.

Francisci, Erasmus. *Der Höllische Proteus, oder Tausendkünstige Versteller.* Nuremberg: Wolfgang Moritz Endters, 1690.

Furetière, Antoine. *Dictionnaire universel de Furetière.* Vol. 3. The Hague: Arnout & Reinier Leers, 1690.

Garmann, Christian Friedrich. *De miraculis mortuorum.* Leipzig: Joh. Gabr. Guttneri, 1670.

Geoffrey of Burton. *Life and Miracles of St. Modwenna* [c. 1150]. Trans. Robert Bartlett. Oxford: Clarendon Press, 2002.

Gerlach, Stephan. *Stephan Gerlachs deß Aeltern Tage-Buch*. Frankfurt: Johann David Zummers, 1674.

Gervase of Tilbury: *Otia Imperialia: Recreation for an Emperor* [c. 1215]. Trans. J. W. Binns and S. E. Banks. Oxford: Oxford University Press, 2002.

Glixelli, Stephan. *Les cinq poèmes des trois morts et des trois vifs*. Paris: Édouard Champion, 1914.

Grässe, J. G. Th. *Sagenbuch des preussischen Staats*. Vol. 2. Glogau: Carl Flemming, 1871.

Gregory the Great. *The Dialogues of Saint Gregory* [593]. Trans. P. W. London: Philip Lee Warner, 1911.

Groom, Nick. *The Vampire: A New History*. New Haven: Yale University Press, 2018.

Hariot, Thomas. *A Briefe and True Report of the New Found Land of Virginia*. London: for the author, 1588.

Happelii, E. G. *Größte Denkwürdigkeiten der Welt oder so genannte Relationes curiosae*. Vol. 3. Hamburg: Thomas von Wiering, 1687.

Haupt, Karl. *Sagenbuch der Lausik*. Vol. 1. Leipzig: Wilhelm Engelmann, 1862.

Hebblethwaite, Rob. "The Good, the Bad and the Rotten: How the Living Dealt With the Dead in England c.600-1200." Master's Thesis for the University of East Anglia, 2017.

Heinrich von Herford, "The Hand of Reyneke" In *Medieval Ghost Stories: Miracles, Marvels, and Prodigies*. Trans. Andrew Joynes. Woodbridge: Boydell Press, 2001. 116-117.

Henning Karl. *Das Hanoversche Wendland*. Lüchow: Selbstverlag des Vereins, 1862.

Hondorff, Andreas. *Promptuarium exemplorum dast ist, historien und Exempelbuch*. Frankfurt am Main, 1583.

Huet, Pierre Daniel. *Huetiana, ou, Pensées diverses de M. Huet, eveque d'Avranches*. Paris: Jacques Estienne, 1722.

Ida the Eager of Louvain [c. 1425]. Trans. Martinus Cawley. Santa Fe: Guadalupe Translations, 2000.

Joynes, Andrew. *Medieval Ghost Stories: An Anthology of Miracles, Marvels, and Prodigies*. Woodbridge: Boydell Press, 2001.

Keating, Geoffrey. *The General History of Ireland* [1631]. Trans. Dermo'd O'Connor. London: J. Bettenham, 1723.

Keyworth, G. David. *Troublesome Corpses: Vampires and Revenants from Antiquity to the Present*. Southend-On-Sea: Desert Island Books, 2007.

Keyworth, G. David. "Was the Vampire of the Eighteenth Century a Unique Type of Undead-Corpse?" *Folklore* 117: 3 (December 2006), 241-260.

Klapper, Joseph. *Exempla aus Handschriften des Mittelalters* [twelfth-fifteenth centuries]. Heidelberg: Carl Winter's Universitätsbuchhandlung, 1911.

Klapper, Joseph. "Die Quellen der Sage vom toten Gaste" [c. 1350]. *Festschrift zur Jahrhundertfeier der Universität zu Breslau*. Ed. Theodor Siebs. Breslau: M. & H. Marcus, 1911. 202-31.

Klapper, Joseph. "Die Schlesischen Geschichten von den Schädingenden Toten." *Mitteilungen der Schlesischen Gesellschaft für Volkskunde*. Band 11. Breslau: Selbstverlag der Gesselschaft, 1909. 58-93.

Kralik, Christine. "Dialogue and Violence in Medieval Illuminations of the Three Living and the Three Dead." In *Mixed Metaphors: The Danse Macabre in Medieval and Early Modern Europe*. Eds. Sophie Oosterwijk and Stefanie A. Knöll. Newcastle on Tyne: Cambridge Scholars Publishing, 2011. 133-54.

Lecouteux, Claude. *Phantom Armies of the Night: The Wild Hunt and Ghostly Processions of the Undead*. Trans. Jon E. Graham. Rochester: Inner Traditions, 1999.

Lecouteux, Claude. *The Return of the Dead: Ghosts, Ancestors, and the Transparent Veil of the Pagan Mind*. Trans. Jon E. Graham. Rochester: Inner Traditions, 1996.

Lecouteux, Claude. *The Secret History of Vampires: Their Multiple Forms and Hidden Purposes.* Trans. Jon E. Graham. Rochester: Inner Traditions, 2010.

Libotschan, Wenceslaus Hagecius von. *Böhmische Chronik* [1541]. Nuremberg: Baltdazar Joachim Endier, 1697.

Luther, Martin. *Tischreden* [1566]. *Weimarer Aufgabe: Luthers Werke: Tischreden aus verschiedenen Jahren.* 6. Weimar: Hermann Böhlaus Nachfolger, 1924.

Magnus, Olaus. *A Description of the Northern Peoples* [1555]. Vol. 1. Ed. Peter Foote. Trans. Peter Fisher and Humphrey Higgens. London: Hakluyt Society, 1998.

Map, Walter. *De Nugis Curialium (Courtiers' Trifles)* [c. 1182]. Trans. Frederick Tupper and Marbury Bladen Ogle. London: Chatto and Windus, 1924.

Martin, Hervé. "A la recherche de la culture populaire bretonne à travers les manuscrits du bas Moyen Age." *Annales de Bretagne et des Pays de l'Ouest* 87: 4 (December 1979), 631-33.

Melton, J. Gordon. *The Vampire Book: The Encyclopedia of the Dead.* Detroit: Visible Ink Press, 2011.

McClelland, Bruce A. *Slayers and Their Vampires: A Cultural History of Killing the Dead.* Ann Arbor: University of Michigan Press, 2006.

More, Henry. *An antidote against atheism; or, An appeal to the naturall faculties of the minde of man, whether there be not a God.* London: J. Flesher, 1655.

Neplach of Opatovice *Summula chronicae tam Romanae quam Bohemicae* [1371]. Vol. 3. Prague: Františka Palackého, 1882.

Neplach of Opatovice. *Summula chronicae tam Romanae quam Bohemicae* [1371]. Vol. 3. Trans. Niels K. Petersen. *Magia Posthuma.* 2007. Retrieved from http://magiaposthuma.blogspot.com/2007/08/.

Nodier, Charles. "Les Aventures de Thibaud de la Jacquière." *Infernaliana.* Paris: Sanson, 1822. 95-111.

Nodier, Charles. "The Adventures of Thibaud de la Jacquière" [1822]. *Infernaliana: Anecdotes, stories, and tales of ghosts, phantomes, demons, and vampires.* Trans. Sarah Archer. Kindle. Cozy Arcana: 2012.

Oldridge, Darren. "'Dead Man Walking': The Historical Context of Vampire Beliefs." *Vampires: Myths and Metaphors of Enduring Evil.* Ed. Peter Day. Amsterdam: Rodopi, 2006. 81-91.

Oldridge, Darren. *The Trial of the Pig, the Walking Dead, and Other Matters of Fact from the Medieval and Renaissance Worlds.* London: Routledge, 2007.

Peter the Venerable. "The Haunting of the Cloister." From *De Miraculis libri duo* [1142]. *The Penguin Book of the Undead: Fifteen Hundred Years of Supernatural Encounters.* Trans. Scott G. Bruce. New York: Penguin Books, 2016. 100-107.

Pico della Mirandola, Giovanni Francesco. *Strix, sive de ludificatione Dæmonum dialogi tres.* Strasbourg: Paul Ledertz, 1612.

Pickering, Michael. "Attitudes toward the Destruction of Vampire Bodies in the Habsburg Empire." *Inside and Outside the Law.* Eds. Shubhankar Dam and Jonathan Hall. Oxford: Inter-disciplinary Press, 2009. 119-132.

Pickering, Michael. "'Sie Mußten ins Feuer': Changing Policies within the Habsburg Monarchy on the Destruction of Vampire Bodies." *Evil and the State: Interdisciplinary Perspectives.* Eds. Kiran Sarma and Ben Livings. Oxford: Inter-disciplinary Press, 2013.

Plancy, Collin de. *Histoire des Vampires et des Spectres Malfaisans, Avec un Examen du Vampirisme.* Paris: Masson, 1820.

Pol, Nikolaus. *Jahrbücher der Stadt Breslau* [1630]. Vol. 3. Ed. Johann Gustav Büsching. Breslau: Johann Friedrich Korn, 1819.

Potocki, Jan. *Tales from the Saragossa Manuscript (Ten Days in the Life of Alphonse Van Worden).* Trans. Christine Donougher. Sawtry: Dedalus Limited, 1990.

Puteo, Francisco A. "Vito Altera" [1515]. *Patrologiae Cursus Completus: S. Bruno Carthusiensium Institor.* Vol. 152. Paris: J. P. Migne, 1853.

Richard, François. *Relation de ce qui s'est passé de plus remarquable à Saint-Erini isle.* Paris: Sabastien Cramoisy, 1657.

Richter, Julius Wilhelm Otto. *Deutscher Sagenschatz: Eine Auswahl der Schönsten Deutschen Sagen.* Vol. 3. Eisleben: Otto Mähnert, 1877.

Roch, Heinrich. *Neue Laussnitz- Bohm- und Schlesische Chronica.* Leipzig: Johann Herbodt Klossen, 1687.

Rohr, M. Philipp. *Dissertatio Historico-Philosophica de Masticatione Mortuorum.* Leipzig: Michael Voctii, 1679.

Rosset, François de. *Les Histoires memorables et tragiques de ce temps.* Paris: Pierre Chevalier, 1619 [1614].

Rousseau, Jean-Jacques. *Letter to Beaumont, Letters Written from the Mountain, and Related Writings* [1762-1765]. Trans. Judith Bush and Christopher Kelly. Hanover: Dartmouth College Press, 2001.

Sad and Wonderful Newes from the Faulcon at the Bank-Side. London: George Horton, 1661.

Schmitt, Jean-Claude. *Ghosts in the Middle Ages: The Living and the Dead in Medieval Society.* Trans. Teresa Lavender Fagan. Chicago: University of Chicago Press, 1998.

Seckinganus, Baltherus. *Hie endet sich Sant Fridolinus leben mit der vorrede vnd gezugnuß vnd [der] grossen wunderwerck die er gewurket hat vnd die got durch in gewurket hat nach synem tode.* Basel: Bernhard Richel, 1480.

Simpson, Jacqueline. "Repentant Soul or Walking Corpse? Debatable Apparitions in Medieval England" *Folklore* 114: 3 (December 2003), 389-402.

Sinclair, George. *Satan's Invisible World Discovered* [1685]. Edinburgh: Thomas George Stevenson, 1871.

Stieff, Christian. *Schlesisches Historisches Labyrinth.* Breslau: Michael Hubert, 1737.

Summers, Montague. *The Vampire in Europe.* New York: University Books, 1968 [1929].

Swieten, Gerhard van. *Vampyrismus.* In Mayer, Andreas Ulrich. *Abhandlung des Daseyns der Gespenster, nebst einem Anhange vom Vampyrismus.* Augsburg, 1768 [1755].

Szakács, Béla Zsolt. "Between Chronicle and Legend: Image Cycles of St. Ladislas in Fourteenth-Century Hungarian Manuscripts." *The Medieval Chronicle IV.* Ed. Erik Kooper. Amsterdam: Rodopi, 2006. 149-175.

Thietmar of Merseburg. *Ottonian Germany: The Chronicon of Thietmar of Merseburg* [1013]. Trans. David A. Warner. Manchester: Manchester University Press, 2001.

Twitchell, James. *The Living Dead: A Study of the Vampire in Romantic Literature.* Durham: Duke University Press, 1981.

Valvasor, Johann Weichard von. *Die Ehre deß Hertzogthums Crain.* Vol. 2. Laybach: Endter, 1689.

Vitalis, Oedericus. *The Ecclesiastical History of England and Normandy* [1141]. Vol. 2. Trans. Thomas Forester. London: Henry G. Bohn, 1854.

Voragine, Jacobus de. *Legenda aurea sanctorum, sive, Lombardica historia* [c. 1260]. Trans. Wyllyam Caxton. London: William Caxton, 1483; Ann Arbor: Text Creation Partnership, 2004-08.

Watkins, C. S. *History and the Supernatural in Medieval England.* Cambridge: Cambridge University Press, 2007.

Weinrichius, Carolus. "Proaemium." In Giovanni Francesco Pico. *Strix, sive de ludificatione Dæmonum dialogi tres.* Strasbourg: Paulum Ledertz, 1612.

Weinrichius, Martinus. *De orto monstrorum commentaries.* Leipzig: Sumptibus Heinrici Osthusii, 1595.

William of Malmesbury. *William of Malmesbury's Chronicle of the Kings of England* [1040]. Ed. J. A. Giles. London: Henry G. Bohn, 1847.

William of Newburgh. "The History of William of Newburgh" (c. 1198). *The Church Historians of England.* 4.2. Trans. Joseph Stevenson. London: Seeleys, 1856.

Wolf, Johann. *Lectionum memorabilium et reconditarum.* Lavinga [Lauingen]: Leonhardus Rheinmichel, 1600.

Zeiller, Martin. "Von einem Schaarwächter Leuten-Ampt zu Lyon in Franckreich wie ihme der Teuffel in einer Sdelichen Dame Gestalt erschienen." *Theatrum Tragicum, Das ist: Newe, warhafftige, trawrig, kläglich und wunderliche Geschichten.* Tübingen: Philibert Brum, 1628 [1624].

Ziegler, Jakob. *Quae Intus Continentur Syria, Palestina, Arabia, Aegyptus, Schondia, Holmiae, Regionum Superiorum.* Strasbourg: Petrum Opilionem, 1532.

2.
"Materializing Shadows:"
The Norse "Again-walker" as a Remote Template for the Vampire

The Connection Between the Aptrgangr and the Vampire

> ". . . [I]f I see, up in a tree
> a dangling corpse in a noose;
> I can so carve and colour the runes,
> that the man walks
> And talks with me."
> Odin, *Hávamál* in *The Poetic Edda*, 37, 1665

> All we have to go upon are traditions and superstitions. . . . [L]et me tell you, [the vampire] is known everywhere that men have been. In old Greece, in old Rome; he flourish in Germany all over, in France, in India . . . He have follow the wake of the berserker Icelander.
> Dr. Van Helsing, *Dracula* (1897 text), 222.

The *aptrgangr* ("again-walker;" pl. *aptrgangar*), or more often the *draugr* ("a [corporeal] ghost;" pl. *draugar*), has too quickly and easily been drafted as a kind of vampire. I prefer the use of *aptrgangr* over that of *draugr* for reasons outlined in the Conclusion. The confusion started in earnest in the nineteenth century from those on the vampire side as part of its drive to universalize the monster. Every known blood-sucker or walking dead sooner or later was cast as a vampire. Even a number of pests—insect, animal, and human—made it on the list. With regard to this context, Grendel was indirectly named in 1855;[21] others were done directly: Hrapp (1822); Thorgunna and the other *aptrgangar* in her story (1855);[22] Thorolf Halt-Foot (1855); Asvith (1859);[23] Hrapp (1859); Glámir (1863);[24] Thrain (1868)[25]; Raknar (1868); Kar (1868); Soti (1887).[26]

---

[21] The anonymous author of the article "Vampyres" published in *Household Words* (1855) writes "There is an old Anglo-Saxon poem on the subject of the Vampyre of the Fens" (43). Eugenio Olivares Merino, in "The Old English Poem" (2004), has traced this poem back to *Beowulf*.
[22]"Vampyres," 39-43.
[23] Nodier, "Le Vampire Harpe" 69-70; Mannhardt 276-277, 278-279.
[24] Baring-Gould, *Iceland* 115-131. This honour is usually reserved for Andrew Lang (in his 1897 book *The Book of Dreams and Ghosts*; see 245; 254-269). Ármann Jakobsson, in "The Fearless Vampire Killers," for example, has made much of this and he uses Lang to bolster his claim that vampire is a good word for Glámir (307-308). As a matter of interest, Glámir was called a vampire or höibo (used synonymously) in Vicary 230 (which also precedes Lang).
[25] Baring-Gould, *Curious Myths* 42-44.
[26] Vicary named Sote (231). He actually designated him a *höibo* or mound-dweller but he had just used vampire as a synonym for that on page 230. He is called vampire more directly in 1899 by Stephánsson and Collingwood in their 1899 *A Pilgrimage to the Saga-Steads of Iceland* (37).

In the twentieth century, scholars of old Norse literature began to do the same. Early on, it looks like this was mainly to make a connection with readers. For example, Hilda R. Ellis Davidson, in her classic *The Road to Hel*, compared the *draugr* to the vampire in several different ways: the burning of their bodies; their shared propensities and physicality; social familiarity with ideas of animated corpses; the unconsciousness of the *aptrgangr* and the greater awareness of the vampire (38, 92, 98, 148).[27] There are many quickly recognizable features of the vampire here, making *aptrgangar* less alien. Recently the use of "vampire" seems more tied to taking advantage of its popularity. It has been used, for instance, creatively and prominently in titles to articles by Ármann Jakobsson ("The Fearless Vampire Killers," 2009; "Vampires and Watchmen," 2011) and Matthias Teichert ("'Draugula,'" 2013).

From either side, these are mainly assertions based on the perceived similarities between two classes of the living-challenged. But there is something more substantial than bare claims: an actual historical connection that has yet to be explored. References in Latin to the Nordic living dead began making inroads into Continental Europe in the sixteenth century—in 1514, the first complete edition of Saxo Grammaticus' *Gesta Danorum*, which had stories of three revenants (the dead master, Asvith, and Mithothyn), was published; in 1555, Olaus Magnus (*Historia de gentibus septentrionalibus*) who largely expanded (62) on the ideas in Jakob Ziegler's 1532 *Quae Intus Continentur Syria* (93), quoting them almost verbatim, published his influential study on the "Northern peoples" with a chapter on Iceland entitled "The Materializing Shadows of the Drowned."[28]

De apparentibus vmbris fubmerforum.

"The Materializing Shadows of the Drowned"
Illustration in Olaus Magnus *Historia de gentibus septentrionalibus*, 62.

Toward the end of the sixteenth century, Adam of Bremen's tome, *Gesta Hammaburgensis ecclesiae pontificum*, was rediscovered and printed, containing the story of an excommunicated pirate who died in Norway and whose body was uncorrupted for seventy years until he received absolution (77). In his 1593

---

[27] She later reiterates this point (see Ellis Davidson, "The Restless Dead" 168).
[28] This is how my Latin translator, Professor Anderson Gaither, has translated "De apparentibus vmbris submersorum." I like it better than the official English translation (*Northern Peoples*): "On the Apparitions of Drowned Men" (Book II, chapter 3).

defense of Iceland, *Brevis commentarius de Islandia*, Arngrímur Jónsson relates an account told him of one who had died a year before, shortly after an attack by a "homicidal spirit," that wrestled and tried to strangle him. *The Poetic Edda* was published in 1665 with its tales on the seer in "Balder's Dreams" and on Helgi Hundingsbani in the second poem. The dialogue between Hervör and her long-dead father, Angantyr, a mound-dwelling *aptrgangr*, appears to be the first piece of Old Norse literature translated into a modern European language (English) in 1703, in George Hickes's *Linguarum Vett* (I:1, 193-95).[29]

Asvith, a heroic young man who became a horrifying, mindless revenant, seems to be the first to make it into early vampire literature. He appeared, for example, in Johann Weikhard von Valvasor's book, *Die Ehre deß Hertzogthums Crain* (1689) where the influential vampire story of Giure Grando, a contemporary "blood sucker," was told (338-339). In the twenty-eighth chapter, entitled "The Chewing Dead," of Erasmus Francisci's 1690 tome there was another lengthy mention of the tale (270-274); it was retold again in Michael Ranft's 1725 classic dissertation on the "masticating dead" (19) and Otto von Graben zum Stein's 1730 study on the "kingdom of ghosts" *Unterredungen von dem Reiche der Geister* (39-41).

The tale of Hrapp, a particularly violent *aptrgangr*, was related in the important book of 1689 by Thomas Bartholin on the "pagan Danes' disdain of death," *Antiqvitatum Danicarum de Causis Contemtae a Danis adhuc Gentilibus Mortis* (see 265-269) but was not referenced in vampire literature, so far as I am aware, until a short note appeared in the mid-eighteenth century. Yet that allusion was in the most prominent vampire book of the era: Dom Calmet's *The Phantom World* (24). The reference is in the 1751 revision of the 1746 original. The fact that Calmet picks it up only in his second edition, *Traité sur les apparitions des esprits* (26), is indicative that it was not widely cited before him.

So several Nordic stories that featured *aptrgangar* had already begun to enter into European consciousness at the very time the conception of the vampire was consolidating. One can say they provided a remote template for the construction of the vampire (along with Greek and Latin myths and legends). Jakobsson, therefore, understated the issue when he wrote "The literary vampire was . . . inspired by the Slavic vampire of folklore and not at all by its Western European counterparts, the *draugar*" ("The Fearless Vampire Killers" 307).

I cannot argue the case here, but I can give a brief overview. Continental or "Core" Europe and Britain had developed a rich literature on revenants since the eleventh century, some of which paralleled Nordic *aptrgangar*. The vampire reports that started filtering in from Greece and Slavic regions, including Russia, were placed largely in continuity with the revenant it already knew. From the 1720s on, the vampire was named and began to develop a singular set of common characteristics and this was picked up by literature mid-century. So, as it was developing, the Nordic *aptrgangr* was providing a very small, but discernable, part of the framework used. Therefore Jacobsson would do better to say "much more by the Slavic vampire of folklore than by its Western European counterparts, the *draugar*."

Also this means Ellis Davidson overstated the matter when she wrote, "The [Norse] creatures who leave their grave-mounds and cause damage wherever they go, who can usually only be overcome by physical force, and who are brought to an end when the body is destroyed, are the direct ancestors of the vampire rather

---

[29] The claim that this is the first translation into a modern European language is found in O'Donoghue ix. Hebblethwaite conjectures that the Norse *aptrgangr* may have been influential on the development of the English revenant (31-36).

than the ghost of later belief" (*The Road to Hel* 148). The line between them is not direct; that belongs again to the Continental and British revenants. Other than that, the comparison is apt. She says something similar to this later ("The Restless Dead" 173). There she equates the lineage of the vampire back equally to the British revenant and the Icelandic *draugr*.

The Approach of this Chapter

First, this will be a literary investigation, not a historical or geographic one. Stories from different regions and eras will be organized together for no other reason than that they share narrative themes and ideas.

In Jakobsson's "Vampires and Watchmen" he shows clearly the limitations of previous approaches to categorize *aptrgangar* and has chosen an avenue concentrating on differences of function as the most promising. Accordingly he distinguishes them into "vampires" and "watchmen." The latter are mound-dwellers who tend to guard and defend their grave treasure and are rarely aggressive outside it. The former, however, are aggressive, trying to craze human beings and "infect them with vampirism" (300). To deal with either of these revenants one may fight them oneself or depend on an outside expert. To dispatch one permanently several methods are used: relocating its grave further away (which often proves ineffective), beheading it, or incinerating it. Finally the main characteristic of both of them is selfishness—an unwillingness to give up their possessions and their bodies (300).

The twofold division between *haugbúar* or mound-dwellers and other *draugar* actually had already been pioneered by Chadwick, "Norse Ghosts (A Study in the *Draugr* and *Haugbúi*" in two parts (1946), followed over forty years later by Elizabeth J. Stern in her 1987 Ph.D. dissertation, "Legends of the Dead." Before Chadwick and even after Stern, "*haugbúi*" and "*draugr*" had and have been used to a large extent synonymously.[30] The duality, however, has become influential enough by now that Matthias Teichert in his 2013 study, "'Draugula," divided the unquiet dead the same way.

That the division is still in use is an indication that scholarship has yet to catch up to Fernando Guerrero. His 2003 Master's Thesis "Stranded in Miðgarðr" is the most extensive study to date. Cristina Spatacean used his typology in her dissertation "Women in the Viking Age" (2006) but that may be because her study was for the same institution: The University of Oslo. Be that as it may, Guerrero, by patient analysis, teases out four categories instead of two. He uses *draugr* as the inclusive term and then subdivides it into the *haugbúi* (a mound-dweller), the *aptrgangr* (a roving terrorizer), the *fyrirburðr* (a specter, usually acting as an omen), and the *uppsitjendr* (one who revives for a moment before becoming inert again).

---

[30] One can see this in one of the most important early works on the subject in English: Ellis Davidson's *The Road to Hel*. On Chadwick in particular see Guerrero 13-14. Although most of Gould's article, "They Who Await the Second Death," (1927) concerned howe-dwellers, the word *haugbúi* did not appear. On the other side of Stern, Aðalsteinsson's *A Piece of Horse Liver* (1998), used ghost, phantom, and mound-dweller synonymously. Sayers, in "The Alien and Alienated as Unquiet Dead" (1996), employed *aptrgangr, draugr*, and revenant to refer to the living challenged and treated the "grave-dweller" as a subset until page 256, where he clearly distinguishes the revenant from the *haugbúi*, albeit in a single sentence. It is not obvious, therefore, where to place him.

Rebecca Merkelbach, in "Hann lá eigi kyrr" (2012), has developed a distinctive threefold scheme of her own: Antagonistic Revenants; Groups of Revenants; Others. They are ranked according to the hypothesis that the more revenants interact with the living, the more antagonistic they are. So the first is the category of those directly hostile to human beings; they are essentially the *draugar* and *aptrgangar* in the above typologies. Like them, she draws parallels to vampires only here. The second is novel and contains those that form communities of their own. The last is made up of the ones whose hauntings are non-destructive and who interact little or not at all with people.

None of the first dual groupings nor Guerrero's fourfold one is useful in linking Norse *aptrgangar* with vampires, not least because one of the categories cannot really apply (the *haugbúi*) and two of Guerrero's are very rare (the *fyrirburðr* and the *uppsitjendr*). It is misleading to reduce all vampires to the single type. Merkelbach (11-28) is more helpful, because all three can apply at least to literary vampires. But even with her, the sheer diversity of Nordic revenants and of vampires makes her divisions too simple and the exceptions too many. Hence in attempting to present a new set of categories, I must be as comprehensive as Guerrero. The tendency to talk of the Norse undead by looking at a handful of examples blinds us to the variety of depictions. Merkelbach, for example, just looks at seven instances. One might consider my approach a systemization of what Gould did in his 1927 essay, "They Who Await the Second Death."

I propose fifteen categories: the violent *aptrgangr*, the contagious or pestilential, the conjugally assertive, the pestering, the tempting, the retributive, the evoked or conjured, the evoking or recruiting, the helpful, the comforting, the revelatory or didactic, the providential, the unprepared, the indifferent, and the communal.

The Variations: 1. The Violent

A. The Innately Violent *Aptrgangr*

Grendel and his mother in *Beowulf* (700-750 AD)[31] are what Claude Lecouteux has named "disguised revenants (*The Secret History* 194-197)." They are much like mound-dwellers, for they live in a dark cave underwater. Nevertheless they are not "watchers;" rather they are aggressively violent. They are bloodthirsty and seek out great men and warriors to devour. Beowulf hears of the trouble and offers his aid to the victims of this terror. He wrestles Grendel and mortally wounds him by tearing off his arm. He tracks Grendel's mother to her subaquatic cave and wrestles her as well. As he seems ready to lose, Beowulf is able to seize a sword that he finds in the cave and behead her. The maiming of their bodies is enough to end their rampages. They have been evil their whole lives; they are communal, but as mother and son. And these "revenants" are the only ones able to procreate, although they appear to have reached the end of their line. The incest taboo seems intact for revenants. Their victims do not become like them.

---

[31] Beowulf exists in a single manuscript which was written down circa 1000 AD.

Asvith or Aran—depending on which version one is reading—is a young hero devoted to his friend Asmund.[32] The two vow that if one should die, the other will accompany him into the burial mound. Asvith/Aran dies, so Asmund is shut in with him along with several animals. Asvith/Aran is reanimated and on two successive nights he consumes the animals; the third he attacks Asmund. Asmund has to cut off his friend's head; then he either impales or cremates him. Asvith/Aran is not a watcher, keeping his treasure to himself, but one who is innately driven to violence like a mindless zombie. Interestingly, as Aran, he speaks on the second night, inviting Asmund to dine with him on the raw flesh of his horse. Speech is rare among the aggressively violent; eating equally so. Finally he is acting in death contrary to everything he stood for in life. Chester Nathan Gould writes, "Not every person who died became a *draugr*, but every one who died might become one" (182). Whether good or bad while alive.

Hrapp in *Laxdæla Saga* (1230–1260), on the other hand, is largely antisocial in life. When he dies he is buried, according to his direction, standing up in the doorway so he can keep watch on his household. He begins to haunt the place and kill the servants. It is not long before the homestead is deserted. Hrapp is reburied further away and his visitations do taper off, but when his son and then his brother-in-law try to claim the estate, they quickly die under suspicious circumstances. The latter apparently dies from Hrapp shapeshifting into a seal. Finally the property is sold to an outsider, Olaf, and when Hrapp violently returns, Olaf pushes at him with his spear and Hrapp snaps it. When Olaf runs at him, Hrapp sinks into the ground with the spear head in hand. He has Hrapp's grave opened; Hrapp is found undecayed and the spear head with him. His body is burned and the ashes spread out in the sea. He has been consistently troublesome both in life and in death (see *Laxdæla Saga* 10, 11, 17, 18, 24).

In *Eyrbyggja Saga* (mid-late thirteenth century) Thorolf Halt-Foot is worse than Hrapp; he is actively sociopathic in life. When he dies his body becomes heavy and loathsome. He is buried in a distant mound. He kills a herdsman who is tending his cattle nearby, and animals that come close die or run off in a frenzy. He begins stalking further afield. In the winter he harasses his wife to death and kills many others. Each one who dies starts to accompany him, but no description is given of their involvement in his crimes. He is dug up and his disfigured and weighty body is hauled further away. The violence continues, however, so he is disinterred by Thorod, a victim of Thorolf's renewed fury, and found to be undecayed. He is committed to the flames. Yet a cow licks his ashes, becomes pregnant by an unknown bull, and gives birth to a strangely fast-growing bull which gores Thorod and then runs into a quagmire and sinks (see *Eyrbyggja Saga* 33, 34, 63). Thorolf is the first in our study who is contagious; those he kills haunt too. Vampires form packs rarely in the nineteenth century (and are contagious equally seldom; those things really await *Dracula* and the twentieth century.

Glámir is the high point for this kind of creature (*Grettis Saga*, c. 1320). Glámir becomes a shepherd for Thorhall, although he knows the homestead is haunted by an evil ghost. He is a good worker, but disliked by everyone. He is irreligious, shunning church and its rituals. He goes out on Christmas eve to tend the sheep in

---

[32] Asvith: Grammaticus, *Gesta Danoru* (late twelfth century), 5.334-38; *The History of the Danes*, 5.336-39. Aran: *Egils saga einhenda ok Ásmundar berserkjabana* (fourteenth century), 7.

a snowstorm and the following day he is found dead, black, and bloated; he appears to have wrestled the spirit and killed it. But apparently the *aptrgangr* was contagious. He cannot be buried at the church for he weighs too much to haul him there.

He proves to be restless in the grave they prepared for him and begins to haunt the people—driving them witless and initiating a horrible killing spree. He walks both day and night, but more in darkness than light, and in winter than in summer. Grettir hears of this and volunteers to fight him. When Glámir enters Thorhall's house he encounters Grettir; they wrestle furiously. Finally Grettir gets the better of him, yet before he can kill him, Glámir speaks and curses him; Grettir lives under that malediction the remainder of his life. Grettir then decapitates him, burns him, and buries his ashes far away from the homestead (see *Grettis Saga* 32-35). Glámir always acted by himself . . . and like Aran, he speaks.

Grettir later faces a troll woman, also called a "disguised revenant" by Claude Lecouteux (*The Secret History* 197-201). She has struck against Steinvor's household twice on successive Christmases, taking the lives of her husband and her farmhand. News reaches Grettir of this and he comes to spend Christmas with her. Like Glámir, the troll woman enters the building, sees him, and wrestles him. She is stronger than him, but he is craftier. They end up at the edge of a cliff with a waterfall cascading down, and there, in a quick move, he is able to free his hand, grab his short sword, and cut off her arm. She either falls into the gulf and is taken off by the river's current or is turned into a rock at the top where she died (*Grettis Saga* 64-67).

Grettir, elsewhere in the narrative, hears the story of Kar who after his death emerged from his barrow and "swept away" all the farmers who owned land there (*Grettis Saga* 18). He decides to pay him a visit in his mound, but more in another section. Raknar is also buried in a mound. After his death he murders his parents and many others. This will be developed later as well. Both are provoked to their fatal struggle; they do not initiate it on their own. But initially they are both aggressive.

In *Thorsteins Thattr Baejarmagns* (late thirteenth century), Earl Agdi has been a scoundrel all his life. At the end of it, he is fixated with killing Thorstein, who is abroad in Norway; he is homicidal because Thorstein first publicly humiliated him and then eloped with his daughter. Foiled by the power of Christianity from his revenge when he attacks him in Norway, he prepares a mound back home with his treasures placed therein, and enters. He dies and then emerges to destroy his old house. When Thorstein returns, builds a new home in its place, and moves in with his wife, Agdi tries again to strike, but is repelled by crosses on all the gates. Thorstein eventually enters the mound when Agdi is out, steals some valuables, hides, and when Agdi enters he runs out planting a cross in the doorway. The mound closes with Agdi trapped within. A Christian symbol is sufficient to stop him (see *Thorsteins* 12-13).

On a quest of love and vengeance, Halfdan arrives at the isolated house of Kol and his daughter Gullkula, who are notorious thieves, in *Hálfdanar Saga Eysteinsson* (mid-fourteenth century). Halfdan enters by force, fights Gullkula and ends up tearing her to pieces. When Kol comes home, Halfdan slits his throat. As he dozes off later, he is attacked by the two corpses; Halfdan's dog bites the groin of Gullkula and tears out her intestines; Halfdan breaks Kol's neck. He cremates their bodies and that is the end. They are communal as the living dead but only for a matter of minutes (see *Hálfdanar* 17). Perhaps what is most interesting here is the rapid reintegration of Gullkula's severed pieces.

In *Svarfdaela Saga* (late fourteenth century), Klaufi, who functions four different ways as a revenant, is said to have emerged from his burial mound after a long time of being quiet and his "violence became so horrendous that he did injury to both man and beast" (27). He is exhumed and burned, his ashes placed in a casket, and sunk in a hot spring. This is his final death. Kar, in *Grettis Saga*, is different. Just after he dies and is placed in his mound, he haunts the island on which he is buried and frightens away all the farmers. It appears he continues to haunt, but those who have found protection under his son can still live there and not be harmed. So one haunts after being freshly buried and the other only after a prolonged rest.

Another interesting perspective has to do with an unpopular man, Gardi, the overseer for Thorstein the farmer and his wife Sigrid in *Eiríks saga rauða* (thirteenth century). While Thorstein Eiriksson and his wife, Gudrid, are wintering at the farm, there is an outbreak of illness and the first to contract it and die is Gardi. Eventually Sigrid and Thorstein Eiriksson are dying in their beds. Shortly before her death Sigrid goes out to the privy and on the way back to the house she is stopped by a vision. And it is not just she who sees it, but Gudrid as well: all of the dead are lined up, including Sigrid and Eiriksson and Gardi seems to be trying to whip them. After Thorstein Eiriksson dies, he resuscitates briefly and voices his desire to have all the revenants buried at the church except Gardi, for he started the sickness from which they all died. He is to be burned (see *Eiríks* 6). There are folklore vampires like this; the first to die of a pestilence is the cause of all deaths that follow. We also have to do with *aptrgangr* on *aptrgangr* violence—and not for the last time.

A stronger story with multiple revenants is that of King Hrolf appearing in *Hrólfs Saga Kraka ok Kappa Hans* (circa fourteenth century). Among his vassals who must obey and pay tribute to him is King Hjorvard, who is married to Hrolf's half-sister, Skuld. Hrolf has surrounded himself with twelve berserkers, unrivaled in war, so he is considered invincible. But Skuld is elven on her mother's side and so has magical abilities. Angry at their subordination, she convinces her husband to attack Hrolf. In preparation, she gathers together a formidable army and, by spells, hides the build-up from her half-brother. When war breaks out, Hrolf and his companions begin easily overpowering Skuld's forces. But her warriors never diminish. Hrolf and the twelve realize that the dead are rising and fighting again, becoming even grimmer opponents than before. Given such a disadvantage, Hrolf and his men finally fall in battle (see *Hrólfs Saga* 7.47-52). The risen dead are called *draugar*, and this is translated by Peter Runstall as "zombies." That is exactly what they are.

There is the unique story of Peter of Grationopolis in Kygri-Björn Hjaltason's *Maríu Saga* (early thirteenth century).[33] He has his leg restored by the Virgin Mary and St. Hippolytus In gratitude he takes up residence in a small cell devoting

---

[33] Kygri-Björn Hjaltason, *Maríu Saga* 1.2.14; "Af Petro þræl" or "On Peter the Slave" was specially translated by Wayne Barnette for a reader I am preparing on the nineteenth-century vampire. This is most likely dated before 1238; the tale appears in Continental Europe in Voragine's *The Golden Legend* (circa 1260). They both may go back to a common source, but I have not located one yet. Guibert de Nogent (1053-1124) refers to the story in his *Liber de Laude Sanctae Mariae*, chapter 11, but it has only to do with the healing of Peter's leg. Or, because this tale follows the logic of the Nordic *aptrgangr*, albeit in reverse, this may be the original. In the normal setting a human trespasses from above the *aptrgangr*'s living space and wrestles the monster; here the *aptrgangr* enters from below a human's living space and wrestles the mortal.

himself to the service of God. The devil is unnerved by this, so he takes on a dead woman's naked body, and enters his cell through the cesspool. She caresses him and displays herself, but he is unmoved, so she tries to take him by force. Night after night they wrestle in his cramped room. Word spreads and many come to see whether the reports are true. During one of his nightly struggles, Peter calls to the onlookers to get him a consecrated stole and give it to him through the window. They do so and he places it around her neck, strangles her, and the devil is forced to flee the body; the corpse immediately returns to its state of decay. It is removed from his cell, burned, and the ashes scattered in water. The rags that the devil tore from the body are later found in the cesspool (see Hjaltason 1.2.14).

Finally, I would add the wooden man featured in the story of Thorleif Jarl's Skald (late fourteenth century) as another "disguised revenant." Hakon wants Thorleif dead so he fashions a wooden man. A human is sacrificed and through witchcraft, spells, troll power, and heathen charms, his heart is placed in it and it lives. It is named Thorgard and he is able to walk and talk among people without them noticing anything amiss. It sails to Denmark from Norway, finds Thorleif, and impales him. At the same time Thorleif swings his sword at Thorgard, but the wooden man suddenly falls into the ground.[34] He disappears like Hrapp. The most interesting feature here is Thorgard's ability to blend in with people. His aggressiveness is targeted on only one person and he is not bound by a lair so that he can make a long voyage across the sea (see *Thorleifs Thattr Jarlsskálds* 7). Some of these features make it approach rather closely to the literary vampire of the nineteenth century.

There is no single pattern here, except that all are aggressively violent. In life one can be good or evil; there can be no predictor. Asvith or Aran, at least, is a hero by the standards of the time and a faithful friend. The quiet mound-dweller after death does not apply to him. Grendel and his mother, Asvith or Aran, Thorolf, Kar, Raknar, and Klaufi are all exceptions. And expectations are reversed when a quiet human being in his cloistered cell is forced to fight an invading *aptrgangr* who wants to rob him of his treasure of piety. To wrestle seems universal but it is not. When Olaf runs at Hrapp to wrestle him, Hrapp disappears rather than confront him. The wooden man vanishes as well.

Muteness applies to most, but not all; Glámir has time before he is executed to give a rational speech cursing his executioner; Aran invites Asmund to dinner; the wooden man apparently talks with people like he is one of them.

Maiming is not the only way to deal with them after they are overcome. Christian symbols are sufficient for Earl Agdi and the demon-possessed body of the woman—although precautions are made in the latter case so that the corpse never be used again. Mutilation utterly fails with Kol, Skuld's army, and Gullkula. Even flames do not guarantee success. Thorod's ashes are licked and he, as the animal, is capable of killing one more time in an act of vengeance. They are not all loners. Some live in family units and in one case this is possible only by procreation, since mother and son have always been monsters; there must have been a father. Thorolf is contagious, so he turns his victims into revenants

---

[34] On the association of woodenness with the *aptrgangr* (and with humanity), see Chadwick 125-26 and Guerrero 20-33; 37.

and they accompany him.[35] The narrative, unfortunately, is not interested in developing this. Raknar is buried with 500 men who act as his front guard. In other words, all of the familiar tropes put forward by scholars fail.

B. The Provoked *Aptrgangr*

We have met Kar before—buried in a barrow, he walked abroad and drove the inhabitants from the island (*Grettis Saga* 18). Grettir enters Kar's malodorous mound at night and is gathering its treasures together at the rope to haul them up. Suddenly he is gripped strongly and a struggle ensues. They wrestle a long time, driving each other to his knees repeatedly until finally Kar falls backward and Grettir cuts off his head.

Grettir Feels Kar's Grip.
Illustration by Henry Justice Ford
in Andrew Lang's *Book of Romance*
1902, 362.

Much later in his story (*Grettis Saga* 66), Grettir takes on the companion of the troll woman, a giant, also designated by Lecouteux as a "disguised revenant" (*The Secret History* 197-201). Grettir descends the waterfall alongside of which he killed the troll woman, dives under it, and emerges on the other side near the opening of a cave where a fire is burning. He enters and the giant lunges at him with his weapon, but Grettir breaks it with his short sword. As the giant reaches back for his sword, Grettir thrusts him through and hews from his chest downward until his entrails spill out.

In *Hólmverja Saga* (late fifteenth century), Hord and his companions open up the barrow of Soti and two men die from the stench. Hord enters and finds Soti in the bow of his ship, horrible to behold. Soti asks Hord why he should invade his space—what has he ever done to him? Hord answers that he has come to rob treasure from an abominable man. Soti attacks him and easily is overpowering him. Hord calls to Geir, his companion, who is nearby and has a wax candle,

---

[35] Contagion is pretty rare, contra Merkelbach (10). So comparison to vampires is limited. Folklore vampires themselves were not considered to be contagious until the second or third decade of the 18th century.

telling him to approach them with it lit. Soti is immediately weakened. Hord tells Geir to approach closer and Soti plunges into the ground rather than endure the light (see *Hólmverja Saga* 15).

Thorgils, in *Flóamanna Saga* (1290-1330), is staying with Bjorn for the winter. They are regularly bothered by Bjorn's dead father thrashing about on the roof of the house. Thorgils, one night, goes outside and sees him standing before the door, "huge and hideous-looking." Thorgils chases him to his mound and then Bjorn's father turns on him and a grim match of wrestling begins. The *aptrgangr* falls on his back and Thorgils beheads him, thereby ending his hauntings. He was provoked by Thorgils (see *Flóamanna Saga* 13).

Thrain, in *Hrómundar Saga Gripssonar* (mid-thirteenth century) is the most developed of the *aptrgangar* in this section. Hromund descends into Thrain's mound to face this sorcerer king. He is black and huge. Thrain is particularly inert, however; he merely watches as Hromund gathers all his wealth together. When Hromund insults him, Thrain simply asks to be left alone. Hromund continues to chide and to shame him until he elicits a response. Thrain first prepares everything necessary to cook Hromund in order to eat him and then they begin their wrestling match. Hromund finally trips him and decapitates him. After that he cremates the monster (see *Hrómundar Saga* 3-4). Again we have the rare picture of a revenant eating or planning to eat. They never drink blood.

Again nothing can be taken for granted here. We do not know whether all were evil in life. It seems unlikely that Bjorn's father was. Not all mounds smell of death: the giant's, Bjorn's father's, and Thrain's are not mentioned as being such. Not all are indicated as hideous to look upon. Kar may be the exception, although his mound smells of death. There are various levels of provocation. All Grettir does is enter the giant's lair and he is immediately set upon. Kar waits until Grettir has gathered all his treasure and then attacks. Soti asks Hord why he has broken into his mound when he has done nothing to warrant it. After a particularly insulting answer he lashes out. Bjorn's father is outside his mound and playing the provocateur with his family. He fights only when cornered. Thrain makes no move as Hromond gathers his wealth and he does not want to wrestle him. Hromund relentlessly harasses him until he is pushed to respond.

Not all wrestle. The giant attacks with his weapon from the start. Only one uses a weapon found in the mound to dispatch the revenant: Hromund. They do not all speak. Bjorn's father and the giant do not. They are not all maimed. Soti is weakened by the light of a candle and dives into the ground to avoid it being brought any closer to him. This disappearing can be compared to the Wooden Man and Hrapp. They are not all alone. The giant is undoubtedly companion to the troll woman and probably related to her.

C. The Provocative *Aptrgangr*

We have already seen Bjorn's father as a provocateur. In *Hávarðar Saga Ísfirðings* (fifteenth century), seventeen-year-old Olaf goes to stay with a recently widowed woman, for her dead husband, Thormod, has been returning to his bed nightly. Olaf lies in his bed and when the deceased returns, he is angered by the intruder, for his bed is to be unoccupied, and they wrestle until Thormod trips backward and Olaf kills him "in a manner he found fitting." Not long afterward, Olaf runs across a shepherd who is out late in a winter storm. The sheep had left their shelter and all his attempts to drive them back are foiled by a man blocking their way. It is Thormod, standing quietly on a bank above them. Olaf runs at him while he waits, and only when he reaches him does Thormod react. It is as if he is taunting Olaf. After a long contest, they fall and roll downward one over the other, until they reach the bottom and, as fortune would have it, Olaf is on top. He breaks Thormod's back, swims out in the frigid sea with the body, and sinks it (see *Hávarðar Saga* 2-3).

In *Bárðar saga Snæfellsáss* (fourteenth century), Gest, although a so-called pagan, is spending the winter with the Christian king, Olaf, who wants him to convert. On Yule eve a tall, evil-looking, fully armed man enters the court. All the celebrants are stunned to silence; the man says that all he is wearing will go to the one who can take them from him. He then departs, leaving the stench of death behind him. He has dared them to confront him. Olaf sends Gest after him to get those treasures, for Gest believes that this is none other than the dead king Raknar. Gest travels a great distance, finds the mound, and enters with gifts Olaf has provided for him—for example a candle and a short sword. He encounters five hundred men in Raknar's buried ship; they want to attack but the candle light immobilizes them and Gest easily cuts off their heads with the exceptional blade of the short sword. He then finds Raknar deeper in the mound and asks for what was promised. Raknar surrenders everything with grace until Gest reaches for the sword. Then Raknar attacks him and quickly begins to overpower him, for the candle has gone out; also the five hundred now stand up. Gest calls on Olaf to help him and Olaf appears as an apparition, robbing Raknar's strength along with that of his men with his celestial light. Gest acts quickly and decapitates Raknar. Then he converts to Christianity (see *Bárðar saga* 18-21).

The stories are quite different from each other, but there is at least one thing that holds them together—the *aptrgangar* provoke non-violently but draw violence to themselves. Thormod has already entered his house to rest in his bed. When he meets his end with Olaf, he suffers what Olaf thinks is appropriate—probably he is beheaded. But this proves insufficient. He returns and what is unique in his provocation is Thormod's manner. With violent watchers in the howes, the invader most often arouses the dead and provokes an attack. With the innately aggressive, they simply attack on their own initiative. Here Thormod waits for the slayer to run uphill to him and hurl himself at him before he even moves. He is not maimed; his back is broken and he is sunk in the ocean.

Raknar travels a long distance to provoke King Olaf. Gest does not fight like the others after invading his mound. They rely on their own strength. He uses blest objects from the king to help him and depends on a divine miracle (a *deus ex machina*) to win the fight, thus stressing Christianity's power. Raknar is also not alone but is interred with five hundred other *aptrgangar*, who would be the first line of defense if not subdued by Olaf's candle and executed. When the candle sputters out, they resurrect although they were decapitated. Olaf stops the potential disaster with his heavenly light. Gest beheads Raknar and his entire entourage dies for a third time.

D. The Retaliatory *Aptrgangr*

Gunnar in *Brennu-Njáls Saga* (1270-90) is a warrior of renown yet he also has a tendency to shun counsel and make hasty judgments. For a particularly grievous infraction, he is banished as an outlaw; because he refuses to go into exile, he becomes a target for vengeance with impunity. He is assaulted and puts up a valiant fight but in the end he is slain and buried in a mound, sitting upright (see *Brennu-Njáls Saga* 78). One evening Gunnar's son and his friend are outside when they see the barrow standing open and Gunnar therein looking at the moon. They then hear him sing about how he stood his ground to the end. Thus he died proudly. The two hear this and know that he is singing to them to follow his example in life and retaliate. They prepare themselves and then exact revenge. Gunnar's son's friend, Skarphedin, may also speak a verse after death, but it is unclear whether he is alive or dead when he says it. And it seems mainly just to communicate his wife's grief when she learns of his death (130).

Klaufi in *Svarfdaela Saga* (late fourteenth century) is a celebrated instance of this category. We have already seen him as an aggressive mound-dweller. He will appear again as conjugally assertive and as a revelatory spirit. Klaufi is secretly murdered and beheaded at the behest of his wife. He mounts the roof of Karl's house, his kinsman, and calls for vengeance (see *Svarfdaela Saga* 18). Klaufi, then, carrying his head, takes his companions to the home where his brothers-in-law, who decapitated him, are hiding and swings his head against the door. Karl cuts their host in two. Reinforcements have been alerted and when they arrive wholesale war breaks out; therein Klaufi sings songs of revenge and of constancy, all the while he is engaged in the struggle, forcing the enemy to retreat before the head which he swings at them or because he is blocking their path.

Gunnar is widely admired and is considered to be a good man, even if rash; Klaufi is problematic. He starts slaying people at ten years old simply because they irritate him, costing his elders a small fortune in blood money. Neither, however, is evil even in death until the very end with Klaufi as an aggressive mound-dweller. Gunnar fights no one; he counsels revenge and then is heard from no more. No one needs to intervene to mutilate his body or drive him away. Klaufi is much more active, but he is not indiscriminate in his fights; he struggles alongside his kinsman for his posthumous honor. And he was mutilated. His head was removed and ritually placed between his legs, which was to guarantee he not return. Yet return he does and his decapitation simply provides him with a macabre weapon. Both act strictly as individuals, but they can interact with the living in a nonviolent manner while counseling violence.

E. The Recruiting and Vengeful *Aprgangr*

This is very similar to the category above, but while there the *aptrgangar* directed men to fight other men, here a revenant recruits a living person to fight against other revenants. There are several reversals of expectations in the following.

In *Thorsteins Tháttr Uxafóts* (1394), Thorstein, a very young man, is asleep on a mound when it opens and a man named Brynjar invites him in. Thorstein picks up his ax and follows him. Thorstein enters the barrow and sees eleven pleasant looking men on a bench on one side and twelve unpleasant looking on the other; they sit with the eleven. At the head of the opposite bench is Brynjar's evil brother, Odd, who is daily extorting the treasure from Brynjar's men so that soon everything will be his. Brynjar tells him that Odd is guarding gold that has the magical property of giving speech to the mute (see *Thorsteins Tháttr* 6). This is of particular interest to Thorstein since his mother cannot speak. Odd begins to call for donations but when Odd calls for Thorstein's contribution, all he can offer is his ax. Odd reaches out to receive it and Thorstein brings it down violently on his arm, severing it. Thus begins a terrible fight. Brynjar's men protect Thorstein as he chops away at his opponents. It turns out that he is the only one that can do damage to anyone, because when *aptrgangar* fight each other their wounds instantly heal. Thorstein prevails and Brynjar leads him out of the mound with a purse of the magical gold. He wakes up and the gold is with him, thus demonstrating the reality of his dream.

The mound is a place of contention between factions of the living dead, not a place of rest as it is elsewhere. Odd is maneuvering to have all the treasure for himself. The living man is brought in to restore order not to disrupt it, to defend justice, not to display greed or achieve glory. There is no wrestling; the conflict begins with weapons, as is the case with the giant. The triumphant revenant gives him some of the treasure—Thorstein does not steal it and Brynjar does not defend it against him.

To sum up this section on violent *aptrgangar*, we should recall what is said of Alberuni, the great Muslim scholar of the eleventh century, who once complained of Hinduism that there was nothing that one Hindu affirmed that was not denied by another (see Sharma 3). In like manner, there is nothing portrayed in one narrative that is not reversed in another. Violent revenants are not just drawn from bad people in life; they are from average and even good ones as well. Glámir was a sociopath; Asvith was considered a hero; Bjorn's father would be considered average. They do not represent only one socioeconomic class. Those buried in mounds are well-to-do, especially those buried with their ship and crew; Glámir is a hired shepherd.

The nature of their post-mortem violence varies. There are those that are innately violent or provoked or even provocative; others that are retaliative or retributive. Klaufi is both of the first and of the fourth. Some are indiscriminate in their violence, while others are selective. Some are set apart from the living as their enemies; others appeal to the living for help. Some are communal—either as relations (mother and son, father and daughter), or contagious, or buried with companions; most are strictly solo. In *Beowulf* a "disguised revenant" even procreates. Some are ugly, bloated, and heavy; others are said to look pleasant. One is disgusting but is made to appear beautiful for the sake of leading a monk astray. In the same way, some smell repulsive, but in one case the odor is masked even though the revenant is decayed and enters the cell through a cesspool. They prefer the night but can walk in the day as well. Some are mute, others speak, even aggressive ones. Mound-dwellers often hoard their treasures, but some are initially apathetic to robbery and one actually gives some away. Most remain fairly near to their graves, Roknar travels a great distance from his.

The methods of termination differ. Some are stopped forever by a simple maiming like the removal of an arm or a head. Others are undeterred by this. Gullkula is shredded but returns whole; Klaufi is decapitated and then uses his head as a weapon. Staking is very rare. It occurs only in the case of Asvith. Some are incinerated and their ashes scattered or buried, but their remnants may be licked by an animal allowing for a new manifestation. Many wrestle to the death, but a few start immediately with weapons. There may be no mutilation at all—Thormod's back is broken and his body sunk in water intact; some disappear into the ground; others are finished off by Christian symbols. Gunnar simply sings his song of retaliation and then never appears again.

Variations: 2. The Contagious or Pestilential *Aptrgangr*

Glámir has already been noted. What is significant there is how he becomes an *aptrgangr* in the first place (*Grettis Saga* 32). He knows when he is hired as shepherd that the homestead is haunted by an *aptrgangr*. On Christmas eve he is out tending the sheep; he is found the following day dead with the area around him torn up. He apparently wrestled the evil spirit and killed it, but died afterward. In a short while, he becomes far more dangerous and aggressive than the one he slayed. The insinuation is he became one of the undead after killing one; the first was contagious. We have already mentioned Thorolf Halt-Foot as well. After his death he becomes a violent *aptrgangr*, the bane of all the people of the region (*Eyrbyggja Saga* 34). "And all those people who died were then seen in Thorolf's company." The nature of "Thorolf and his company" is not developed unfortunately.

Thorgunna is at the center of a particularly unique and rather whimsical account (*Eyrbyggja Saga* 53-55). She dies after having given instructions that her bed things are to be burned; other than that almost everything is to go to the family with whom she is living to do with as they will. But the lady of the house, because of her strong acquisitiveness, refuses to abide by this and saves some of what Thorgunna designated to be burned. This sets up what follows.

When the entourage bearing her body to the church is treated inhospitably, Thorgunna rises from her casket, prepares dinner, and serves it to her bearers naked. After that, word spreads and everyone on the route treats them well. But burial is not the end of her: she then haunts the place as a seal.[36] She keeps to herself as such, but she also appears to orchestrate the development of two communities—possibly three—of *aptrgangar*. And because of the stress placed on her Christianity in this narrative, she must do so under divine direction.[37]

---

[36] On the seal or "seal-like creature" see Kanerva, "The Role of the Dead in Medieval Iceland" (2011), 28-32. Because Justin Noetzel (in "Outlaws and the Undead") does not hold the seal to be Thorgunna, he concludes that the "undead are not always evil in their intentions" (181). Thorgunna stands apart from the other undead, we are told, because of "her domestic impulse and action" (182). I agree that they are not always evil, but I do not hold that Thorgunna is the best example.

[37] If Thorgunna is the same as the one referred to in *Eiríks Saga*, who possesses "pagan" supernatural gifts, the datum is omitted here, and we must assume that omission is significant to the writer. Unless, of course, it is written after the *Eyrbyggja Saga*. Both documents are conjectured to be written in the thirteenth century. On the two Thorgunnas see Cavaleri 50-51.

Shortly after her burial, the shepherd of the household comes home distraught. After his death, sudden illnesses take seven lives one by one and they are buried at the church. An indication of the presence of a seal submerged in the stores of dried fish is followed by six men drowning. The seal then rises in the fireplace, looks at Thorgunna's bed gear, and is finally driven back down with a sledgehammer to the head. In the wake of that, the six who were drowned rise from their watery grave like the seal from the ashes and surprise everyone by coming into the house drenched, wringing out their clothes, and sitting by the fire; they do this night after night. Soon they are joined by those who were buried; interment at a church does not keep them down. They enter and shake the mud from their clothes on to the wet ones, in an apparent move to have better access to the fire. Meanwhile it is found that the seal has destroyed all the winter storage of fish, which is followed by another spate of six successive deaths and resurrections.

The story comes to an end when an appeal is made to the authorities. Delegates of the chief and a Christian minister join forces, carry out religious rituals in the home, burn the bed stuff, and summon the dead to court. The cases against them are presented, judgments are passed against the revenants, and they reluctantly leave. The hauntings and their end are nonviolent, with one exception, to which we shall refer in the summary.

In *Flóamanna Saga* (early fourteenth century), two families with their servants and companions are stranded for the winter in a deserted area after their ship breaks up off the coast of Greenland. They build a hut and partition it. Thorgils is Christian; his family observes Christmas with respect. Jostein and his family behave in an opposite manner. On Christmas Eve a shout is heard in the distance. The next day a knock is heard on Jostein's door. One of their party answers and quickly goes mad. He dies the following day. That night the same happens; the one who answers the door sees the man who died run at him. One after another Jostein's company dies and all become the living dead as in a spreading epidemic. They mainly haunt the side of the hut that was theirs in life and the main person they "attack" is Thorgils himself. No description of the attacks is offered. Thorgils has all the bodies cremated and there is no further problem. It is clear that the god Thor is at the bottom of this (see *Flóamanna Saga* 22).

Mithothyn represents another side of the pestilential *aptrgangr* in *Gesta Danorum* (circa 1215). He is described as an egocentric pretender of divinity. He eventually is murdered, but his evil does not end there. "[A]nyone nearing his tomb was quickly exterminated, and his corpse emitted . . . foul plagues." In other words, his body makes no out-of-grave appearances, nonetheless it spreads death to those who live nearby. The people, oppressed by this, dig up his body, behead it, and run a stake through its heart. This is the only instance in old Nordic stories of something similar to a particular revenant and early vampire in Continental literature: the *Nachzehrer* or "after-feeder," known in English sometimes as the "shroud eater" or "the smacking dead." The corpse devours its burial clothes in the grave and then turns to gnawing its own body or one adjacent to it. As long as it chews, it sends forth a plague on the land, so the body must be disinterred and meet a violent end (see *Gesta Danorum* 1.25).

So we have two types of contagion—the *aptrgangar* who "infect" their victims, making them revenants like themselves and the *aptrgangar* who spread disease without ever emerging from the grave. Almost all of the infectious ones spread their sickness nonviolently or at least it appears to be the case. We do not ordinarily think of illness as violent, although, admittedly, we use metaphors of war as it "invades" our bodies and we "fight" it off. There is one mention in the narrative of Thogunna of the first one that becomes a revenant, the shepherd, slamming the second, Thorolf Halt-Foot, against the door, but after that there is no indication of violence. We know nothing of the so-called "attacks" by Jostein's clan.

Some of the living challenged are communal, one is solo. With Thorgunna, there are two groups that form almost gangs. Jostein's family keeps the contagion among themselves and there's no sign of dissention in their ranks and no clear indication of whether one of them acts as a leader. Mithothyn acts alone. Finally there is no single way to end the hauntings. Jostein's family and Mithothyn are violently dealt with; in fact with the latter we have our second staking. The eighteen *aptrgangar* of Thorgunna's are charged with trespassing and legally banished; they disappear into the night with no harm to their bodies.

Variations: 3. The Conjugally Assertive *Aptrgangr*

Thormod has been introduced as a violent revenant and it is very hard to judge whether he belongs in this category as well. A recently widowed woman complains that he returns to her bed each night. Olaf, the would-be slayer, stations himself in bed and Thormod sees "that there was a man in bed where none was accustomed to lie." Is his bed shared with his wife? Is he surprised that a male is in his bed or that anybody is? There is no mention by the widow that he might be forcing her to have sexual intercourse, hence of assault and/or rape. He is asserting himself, but is not aggressive, so far as we know. He appears to be merely returning to sleep as he was accustomed to when he was alive. But it could be otherwise. Elizabeth Stern attributes it to Thormod being unaware that he is dead or due to experiencing discomfort in the mound (36).

There is no doubt that Klaufi (in the late-fourteenth-century *Svarfdaela Saga*), whom we have also covered, *is* conjugally assertive. His wife, Yngvild, arranges with her two brothers to murder him. She works him up into a fit of madness in which he can perform feats of preternatural strength, for he is a "berserkir." Then she calms him down, which renders him powerless, and begins sexually caressing him. While he is weak and distracted, the brothers slaughter him and drag him under a haystack. "Yngvild went to bed, and they prepared to leave. But in the moment that they left, Klaufi gets into bed with Yngvild," as if he were going to continue what they started. She sends word to her brothers; they return and behead him. He, of course, returns anyway, head in hand; this time for battle not for bed (see *Svarfdaela Saga* 17).

Another story like this, but with several key changes, is that of Sigrid, in the thirteenth-century *Eiriks saga rauða*. Thorstein Eiriksson and his wife, Gudrid, are spending the winter with another Thorstein and his wife, Sigrid. Early during their time there, Gardi, the unpopular overseer of the farm, becomes ill and dies; he is followed by a number of others. Sigrid and Thorstein Eiriksson then sicken. Sigrid has a vision that she is to die and in the morning she does. Her husband is out later in the day when he receives a message to return quickly, for Sigrid's corpse is trying to rise and get into bed with Eiriksson. He steps in just as she has reached the bed, so he takes his ax and buries it in her breast. The wound is enough to stop her from any further haunting (see *Eiríks saga rauða* 6). She does seem to be claiming Eiriksson as her husband in the afterworld.

Killer-Styr, as he is known, is a powerful chief and a reprehensible man (in the mid-thirteenth-century *Heiðarvíga saga*). After insulting a family he depends upon when traveling, he is murdered when on a visit. As his body is in transit back for burial, his retinue stops at the house of a farmer. When all have gone to bed, the eldest daughter feels she must look at the face of this infamous man about whom she had heard so much. She sneaks into the fire room and beholds his face. At that point he seems to sit up and recite a verse that dares her to kiss his lips and taste the mold on his beard (see *Heiðarvíga saga* 9). In a variation (mid- or late-thirteenth-century *Eyrbyggja Saga*) he holds her around the waist. She goes mad, cries and struggles throughout the night, and dies the next morning. He makes no further appearances although he has ample opportunity to do so, for he becomes so heavy he has to be left behind in a makeshift cairn until spring when he can be buried (see *Eyrbyggja Saga* 56). He is not maimed or burned, despite his wickedness in life and his behavior as a corpse. He also appears to be taking her to be his mate on the other side of death.

I know little about this phenomenon. What we have as two data are that the *aptrgangr* wants to get into bed, and sometimes does get into bed with a person of the opposite sex, or desires to find a mate. All sorts of assumptions can be made about this, but nothing is clear, so far as I know. The final two appear to be about claiming someone as their own in the afterlife and do not have sex as the object of their actions. The first may be simply about getting into one's bed— an indication that the corpse is not willing to give up some of its accustomed routines yet. The one that is almost certainly about sex is Klaufi, and all we can say is that he is returning to be caressed, not to force himself upon his wife. Intercourse may be his ultimate aim, but it appears to be dependent upon her initial willingness to participate. Most have a violent end, but not all. Related to this, Klaufi is mutilated but it is ineffectual.

Variations: 4. The Pestering *Aptrgangr*

We have already had the opportunity to present Bjorn's father. He hurts no one but bothers all. Directly following that story is another, also featuring Thorgils. Thorgils' friend, Audun, asks him for help, for his mother has died and "strange things had happened since her death. "All the men have run away, because no one dares remain," he says (*Flóamanna Saga* 13). We do not get an impression she is murdering or beating anyone; she is just frightening people. Thorgils makes a coffin for her and ties it with strong ropes. They begin to drag it away and plan on burying her. On the way, however, the ropes snap and

Audun's mother gets out and begins to walk off—she does not attack them. It takes all the strength of these two imposing men to bring her back. They end up cremating her.

Hallbjorn Slickstone-eye drowns, his body washes up on shore, and it is buried in a shallow grave. He haunts the area frequently. One of Thorkel the Bald's cows goes missing, so in the growing dusk he begins to search for it. After nightfall and in the light of the moon he believes he sees it on a rise, but as he approaches he notices it is Slickstone-eye instead. They begin to wrestle, but Hallbjorn quickly slips from his grasp and sinks into the ground (*Laxdæla Saga* 38). Hallbjorn does no more harm after this.

There does not seem to be any violence in these hauntings. They terrorize by annoyance and simply by being the undead. The termination of two is violent, but one disappears at the first sign of trouble. Is there actual cowardice among *aptrgangar*? We have seen this behavior before. Continental and British revenants as well as early vampires have their share of tricksters.

Variations: 5. The Tempting *Aptrgangr*

The story of the succubus starts with flirtations in order to fill Peter of Grationopolis with lust. But he is impervious to her advances. So the rest of the time she violently tries to overcome him. The *aptrgangar* who climb into bed with someone are never trying to tempt them, but, as we have seen, there is no proof of assault or rape either. On the other hand, there is evidence in some of the cases of early vampirism, for example Giure Grando.

But the following may be a case of temptation—albeit not of a sexual sort. Thorstein slips out from King Olaf's court and goes to the communal latrine alone, contrary to the will of the king, who commanded that the men go in pairs (*Thorsteins Tháttur Skelks* 1). He sits close to the door. Up through the seat farthest from him, from the cesspool beneath, comes a demon, identifying itself as Thorkel the Thin, a slain soldier from the war against King Harold War-tooth. He says he has come from hell. Thorstein asks who endures the torments best and who the worst. Thorkel answers to the first, Sigurd the Dragon Slayer; to the second, Starkead the Old.

Concerned that the devil would not leave his company unharmed, he knows he must alert the king. He has the demon howl like Starkead three times, each time louder. With each shriek, the demon moves closer to him. After the third, the next of which the demon would reach his seat, awakens the king and he rings the church bell causing the demon to fall and disappear. He is stopped by a Christian symbolic action and again there is a vanishing downward. Like Peter of Grationopolis we have a surrogate mound invaded by an *aptrgangr* from below. Humans, of course, violate mounds from above. Unlike the succubus story of Grationopolis, Thorstein does not live there nor does he wrestle the intruder.

John Lindow, in "Þorsteins Páttr *Skelks* and the Verisimilitude of Supernatural Experience in Saga Literature," cautions against seeing only the humor in Thorstein's narrative; it has serious undertones. It seems this is a temptation to renounce Christianity, forsake heaven, and demonstrate his courage in hell like Sigurd. In other words, the demon is there to steal a treasure of piety. Instead of succumbing to temptation, Thorstein demonstrates his boldness by facing the power of hell and outwitting it (264-280).

There is another case, and it is meant comically as well. In the story of Raknar, as told by John Christian Atkinson in *Lost or What Came of a Slip from 'Honour Bright,'* Gest travels a long distance with his companions, which includes a priest (146-56). Odin joins the party and preaches paganism to tempt them back from the Christian fold, but the priest hits him on the head with a crucifix and he falls into the ocean and disappears. This may not be a true example of an *aptrgangr*, but it is worth a mention. It appears to be the fifth case of such vanishing. In no case but one is there a mutilation of the body.

Variations: 6. The Retributive *Aptrgangr*

Gunnar and Klaufi have been covered under the rubric of "The Retaliatory *Aptrgangr*." Revenge was violent there; retribution is about attaining justice. Gunnar incites it through his recitation and then returns to the eternal beyond. Klaufi, however, leads the charge against those responsible. Brynjar invites Thorstein into his cairn so he will violently engage his adversaries and bring an end to the injustice of the dead. King Hreggvid, as we shall see, rejoices in retributive violence but does not instigate it. This is different from both it and the vengeful *aptrgangr* in that it is divinely instituted.

Thorgunna has been covered under "The Contagious or Pestilential *Aptrgangr*," but this aspect of the tale was only touched upon. Thorgunna is a Christian at port in Iceland (i.e. Fróðá) during the very time that Christianity becomes the national religion (see *Eyrbyggja Saga* 50-51). A local woman, Thurid, wants some of the goods Thorgunna is bearing with her and so invites her to her homestead, even though Thorgunna says nothing is for sale. One day while she is working, there is a cloudburst, yet it rains not water but blood. It quickly dries from everything except Thorgunna and what she has touched. She soon becomes sick and makes a few requests of her hosts—among them that her bedding be burned. She is certain that if this appeal be not followed, it will bode ill for the family, since the blood is clearly an omen.

She dies but Thurid takes some of the bedding for herself anyway. After this we know Thorgunna becomes a seal haunting the homestead and destroying their winter storages of food. In its one appearance to everyone, it carefully eyes the bed. At the end, her things are burned and that helps terminate the hauntings. All that happens, what is called the Fróðá Marvels, one can see, if one adheres only to the story itself, as divine retribution for disobedience with Thorgunna acting as God's agent.

It is a pretty nasty intervention of God, if Thurid has a conscience. She has to watch the death and haunting all around her and know it was due to her decision. God does not smite her down but the household. She loses her husband and most of her servants. There had been thirty, but at the end, eighteen are dead and five have fled. Thurid becomes ill herself and it appears that this plays a pivotal role in finally seeking help. Once the house is sanctified, the material destroyed, and the *aptrgangar* judged, she recovers to bear the memory of what she did. As William Sayers writes in "The Alien and Alienated as Unquiet Dead in the *Sagas of the Icelanders*," "Þúriðr's [Thurid's] acquisitiveness represents a dysfunctional relationship with the supernatural, and responsibility for the negative effects that are soon manifest ultimately lies with an individual [i.e. Thurid herself]" (249). The end announces that her son prospers but says nothing of her.

Variations: 7. The Evoked or Conjured *Aptrgangr*

First we consider the story of the vǫlva or seer in *Baldrs Draumar* (mid-tenth century). Odin, concerned with his son Baldr's dreams that seem to portend his death, rides to Hel. He stops at the grave of the vǫlva, a seer, and utters a "corpse reviving spell." She rises reluctantly and complains of the difficult road he has made her travel, for she has long been dead. Disguised, he asks her several questions and after the answer to each she wants nothing further to do with the interview. Finally he asks a question that reveals himself to her, seemingly purposely, and she sends him on his way, but he has learned all he wanted to know (see *Baldrs Draumar* 243-245).

In *Gesta Danorum* (circa 1215), Hadding and his lover, a giantess, stay at a home where the master has died and his body not yet buried. The giantess reanimates his tongue to tell the future of Hadding and he, furious at being called up from below and bound again to his body, viciously curses her (5: 135-36). The future bodes well for Hadding but she will soon be torn to pieces. This dead master is not a seer but a normal man. He knows the future simply by virtue of being dead.

In *Hervarar Saga ok Heiðreks* (circa 1250), Hervör, raised from youth more as a boy than a girl and being as strong as the boys, is on a quest to visit the burial mound of her father, Angantyr, and her paternal uncles. On a ship she has boarded under the guise of a man, the captain dies and she takes command herself. Upon landing, she walks the distance to the mound and addresses her father. She informs him that she has come for his renowned sword. Angantyr tries to dissuade her, including opening the grave-door to reveal the blazing fires engulfing the inside so that she cannot enter. When this and other warnings do not deter her and she threatens to curse him in turn, Angantyr relents and gives her the blade. She then thanks him and expresses her wishes that all in the barrow lie unharmed in the future (see *Hervarar Saga* 3). If one is looking for a proto-feminist in this literature it would be she.

Thorleif was a man of remarkable skills, according to *Thorleifs Þáttr Jarlsskálds* (circa 1300). Against an enemy one time, he used his power of recitation to make him itch intolerably in his groin and rectal areas, to bring a fog down on his court, and to call forth the weapons stored there to strike down the men. He was eventually killed by a wooden man, a substitute for a revenant, fashioned out of spite for that incident. In the same document, a shepherd, Hallbjorn, hoping to become a skald (poet) and trying unsuccessfully to create a praise poem about Thorleif, sleeps on his mound. He sees the mound open and Thorleif exit, feels him pull his tongue, and is given the first lines he seeks. He awakens and believes he catches sight of Thorleif's shoulders as he enters the mound. He memorizes the lines, makes the poem, and becomes a great skald (see *Thorleifs Tháttr Jarlsskálds* 4). His presence and desires, as well as Thorleif's wish to be remembered, evoke him up from the grave.

In mid-thirteenth century *Færeyinga Saga*, Sigmundur, along with his companions, Thorir and Einar, have jumped in the ocean to swim a mile to a nearby island. They are escaping from Thrond who is trying to kill them. Thorir and Einar drown; Sigmundur makes it to shore exhausted only to be decapitated by Thorim for his valuables. Years later, Thrond must prove he did not kill Sigmundur and find out who did. He suspects Thorim and so goes to his home, fetters him, lights fires, ritually prepares the house, and then waits. Eventually Einar and then Thorir enter in succession dripping wet and warm themselves by the fire. After they have left, Sigmundur steps in, bloody and carrying his head. He stands for a short while and then leaves, proving Thorim to be his murderer (see *Færeyinga Saga* 40).[38]

The way they conjure differs. Odin and the giantess use spells. Thrond ritually organizes the house. Hervör calls out to her father and he responds. The shepherd does not call Thorleif forth; the great poet responds on his own to Hallbjorn's ambition and to his own wish to be further celebrated. The vǫlva and Angantyr are reluctant: she because she would prefer being left where she is; he because he wants to protect his daughter. The dead master is livid and issues the prognostication of his conjurer as a curse. Sigmundur and company seem indifferent; they are simply on display. Thorleif comes forth willingly. None is harmed, except the giantess, and she not by the dead master; all return to their accustomed places after the one encounter.

Variations: 8. The Revelatory or Didactic *Aptrgangr*

We have already encountered most of these. After the battle where Klaufi swings his head about, he signals, as he rides across the sky, that Karl, his kinsman, is to die that day in battle (see *Svarfdaela Saga* 21). Thorolf Jarl's Skald walks out of his burial-mound in Thorleif's dream and gives him the first lines of a recitation that if he remembers upon awakening may make him a great poet. The vǫlva is conjured up reluctantly to reveal the meaning and purpose of Baldr's dreams. The dead master tells the future to Hadding and the giantess in a rage for being called back to his body. Sigmundur and his companions simply display themselves to indicate how they died. Gudrid has her fortune told by Thorstein Eiriksson and Thorir by Agnar. In a wholly different way, Thorgunna in her first appearance is teaching the people the importance of being hospitable to those engaged in funeral processions.

In *Laxdæla saga* (76), Gudrid is now married to her fourth and final husband, Thorkell. He has sailed to Norway to obtain a large load of lumber so he can build a church on his property. Later, as he is sailing home with the lumber, he and his crew drown in the midst of a storm. At the same time, Gudrid is on her way to church, for it is Maundy Thursday. When a stranger, an *aptrgangr* himself, tells her that he has news of great importance, she retorts that he keep it to himself. She thinks she sees Thorkell and his men, dripping wet, at the door of

---

[38] On the nature of these conjuring, necromantic rituals, see Foote 209-221.

the church, but she simply sidesteps them and enters, probably thinking they are returning home. After an extended time of prayer, she rises and seeks Thorkell but there is no trace of him or his crew. The following day she learns of his death.

Ogvald king of Rogaland was staying in Southern Norway (in early-fourteenth-century *Hálfs saga ok Hálfsrekka*). Haekling the Viking came with his raiders against him and he fell in battle. Years later a settler asks someone when the king had been laid in the barrow. A voice rings forth from within the howe that long ago Haekling and his men sailed the sea and he was "crowned king of this mound" (*Hálfs saga* 2).

Finally, there is the tale of the talking head in mid- to late-thirteenth-century *Eyrbyggja Saga*). Egil, a servant of Thorbrand, wants his freedom more than anything else. Thorbrand's sons promise it to him if he kills a member of a family against which they hold a grudge. He walks the distance to their home, but upon entering he is caught and then executed. There are many casualties in the battles that ensue. As Egil was on his ill-fated journey, a shepherd found a human head which sung out about the coming deaths (see *Eyrbyggja Saga* 43).

Some of these *aptrgangar* appear to be immaterial, others not. The talking head and the dead master are definitely not. There is little reason to believe that Klaufi is immaterial. He appears four times in the story and in each manifestation, he is a different type of revenant. Three of his "returnings" are physical, so it seems unlikely this one would be different. He appears to his kinsman, Karl, riding through the sky trailing behind him a sled with Karl's head therein. He tells him that he will join him this night in death. Thorolf pulls the shepherd's tongue, but in a dream; nonetheless when the shepherd awakens he believes he sees Thorolf's shoulder disappearing into the mound.

They all have their different motives. Klaufi is warning his kinsman to ready himself for a valiant death; the *vǫlva* and the dead master are forced to speak by spells; Thorkell is providing a sign that he has died; the talking head speaks arbitrarily; Thorolf is moved by the shepherd's desire and his love of renown. All are loners except for Thorkell; there is no maiming except for Klaufi, who is so twice, but not for this revelation.

Variations: 9. The Providential *Aptrgangr*

Under the rubric of the retributive revenant, we have dealt with this aspect of the Thorgunna narrative. She attributes the incident with the blood as a sign of coming death. It brings about her own death and signals danger to the family she is staying with, if it does not abide by her final directive. Because her Christianity is so stressed, when the hauntings begin due to disobedience to her requests, she appears to become an agent of divine providence to punish the family until it complies. Consonant with this being providential, the many revenants are never aggressive to the living, only inconvenient. The end of the hauntings comes about by submission to her wishes.

Thorstein Eiriksson has also been considered above, but not concerning this. Thorstein sits upright after he has died and calls for his wife, Gudrid. She answers his appeal lest his corpse "walk abroad, which I suspect will happen otherwise" (*Eiríks saga rauða* 5). It appears he has been crying, he whispers a few words in her ear, and he warns her openly that she not remarry a Greenlander but an Icelander; other than these he addresses Christian issues. He urges her to give their money to the church or to the poor. He declares that those who observe their faith properly are blessed but complains that not many do so. He wants a church burial, not only for himself but for all the revenants who have haunted the homestead over the winter, with the exception of the first to die, Gardi, who must be burned, for he is responsible for the illness that spread and took so many lives, including his own.

With such a long oration on Christian duty and piety, this resurrection must have been divinely commissioned. It also may have something to do with purgatory, which is well represented in Continental and British revenant stories. If so, perhaps this warrants a separate category: The Penitential *Aptrgangr*. Stern would recognize this category (34). But this does not read that way. He is not rectifying anything he has done or warning not to follow his example. To read repentance from tears in his eyes is tenuous at best.

In both these stories one can see concern about *aptrgangar*. To disobey the last wishes of a Christian can lead to divine judgment, which can include the appearance of revenants on the estate. To avoid the hauntings of the dead, bodies should be buried in a church yard. Interestingly, church burial is precisely what is ineffective in the first. Nonetheless, each is preventative, although the techniques vary.

Variations: 10. The Evoking or Recruiting *Aptrgangr*

We have already had the opportunity to introduce the Vengeful and Retaliatory *Aptrgangar*, but they are surrounded by violence. Hreggvid also belongs here but he shall be dealt with as a helpful revenant, for that is he category best suited for it. Helgi Hundingsbane has a place here as well, although he will be treated as a comforting *aptrgangr*. Nora Chadwick would place him here. She holds he is recruiting the help of Sigrun to play a part in a ritual substitution for the act of suttee (see Chadwick 57).

The tale of Olaf Geirstad-Alf further reverses expectations of a barrow-dweller in *Tháttr Ólafs Geirstaða Alfs* (1394).[39] A greatly admired king, but a non-Christian, he was warned of a coming plague, not in order to flee or to help his subjects, but to prepare for his death and that of his men. He and his men are overcome by disease and they are buried in a mound with a great treasure. Olaf becomes an *aptrgangr* to guard the treasure and wait. When the wife of his great-great-grand-nephew is ready to give birth, Olaf sends a dream to her husband's foster brother, Hrani, since her husband, Olaf's nephew, is deceased. He tells him to break into the mound, to decapitate him, and to plunder the mound, especially taking the symbols of his rule and power for the child. His belt is to be placed on the expectant mother (see *Tháttr Ólafs* 3-4). It appears this takes place so he may be reborn, this time as a Christian—in fact, as the great Saint Olaf.

---

[39] I have access to this in English only through secondary sources (Chadwick 58-59; Ellis 101, 138-139).

In *Laxdæla saga* (1230-1260), the elderly, widowed Gudrun spends hours in church at night praying. Her granddaughter receives a dream from a woman who complains of Gudrun praying over her body and weeping on her, for the tears burn. The floorboards are taken up and the bones of a sorceress are found. They are removed and placed a long way off in an isolated spot. According to the story, then, the sorceress' soul is still linked to what is left of her body and she is restless and miserable enduring Gudrun's crying, unable to move, but able to communicate and request help (see *Laxdæla saga* 76).

In *Landnámbók* (1275-1278), Asmund is buried in a ship with his slave beside him. Someone walks by his mound and hears Asmund singing that without a crew to crowd about him and with a slave who can offer but feeble support, he would prefer to be alone. The cairn is opened up and the slave removed (see 2.6).

In *Sörla þáttr* (early fourteenth century), Odin requires of his wife, Freyja, that she arrange for a perpetual conflict between two kings until a Christian should liberate them. She works this through the valkyrie, Göndul. Göndul first directs King Hethin of Serkland to Högni, king of Denmark and they become such close friends that they take mutual oaths of foster-brotherhood. Göndul then meets Hethin again, removes the vows from his memory, and convinces him that it would be a valiant deed to kill Hethin's wife and abduct his daughter. He does so. Shortly thereafter Göndul meets with him one last time and restores his memory. Hethin flees but Högni is in quick pursuit so they face off on the island of Hoy. Unable to reconcile, they and their armies clash. They are vicious in battle but when one falls, he is restored and re-enters the fray. This continues every night for 143 years until a Christian ship anchors there and Hethin asks for the aid of the guard. He wades into the fight finally killing all the warriors. Although all signs of the battle are gone in the morning, the blood on his sword testifies it was not a dream (see *Sörla þáttr* 49-57). We could create for this a new category: the cursed *aptrgangr*. Thorolf would also qualify (see *Eyrbyggja saga* 20), in the light of the curse placed on Arnkel by Katla that his father would be called evil.

So we have four very different scenarios where *aptrgangar* call for human help. King Olaf has guarded his treasure for generations, but then he conscripts the help of Hrani to do the opposite of what most mound-dwellers want. The pagan sorceress asks for help in getting away from the piety of Gudrun, for she can still feel pain in her body. Asmund needs the aid of the living in order to get rid of his servant. Hethin and Högni and their armies are locked in combat until Hethin conscripts the help of a living Christian. Helgi Hundingsbane should be placed here; a dead husband asks his wife for help in the afterlife. I have designated him, however, more as a comforting *aptrgangr*.

Variations: 11. The Unprepared *Aptrgangr*

There are more unprepared for the afterlife than those covered here, but they are the ones that remain with the living for reasons of vengeance, protecting their wealth (even if they intend later to give it away), or just being nasty and angry. But we must remember there are some unprepared to return as well, such as the vǫlva and dead master. I wish to look at others that are not so clear. The story of Grimhild has in the background an unresolved issue preventing her final death. She and Thorstein Eiriksson have been deathly ill. Grimhild is the first to die. When her husband, Thorstein the Black, steps out of the room, she raises herself up on her elbow and touches her feet to make sure she has her shoes on. When he re-enters, she collapses. Fernando Guerrero has argued that this gesture is probably linked to the "pagan" belief that one must walk to one's afterlife; they are called "hel-shoes" (see *Gísla saga Súrssonar* 16 and *Grænlendinga saga* 6).

In the second version, where Grimhild is named Sigrid (see *Eiríks saga* 6), when her husband is gone, she slowly makes her way to Thorstein Eiriksson's bed in order to climb in with him. When she has almost completed her task, her husband, who has been summoned, steps in and thrusts his ax into her chest. This may be due to another "pagan" idea, says Guerrero (123-124)—the dead looking for a partner for the afterworld. This concept underlies the practice of suttee, where a wife is buried alive with her dead husband.

We can see the same in the instance of Styr. He sits up and proposes that the young woman who is looking at him kiss him, causing her to die the next day (see *Grettis Saga* 33). Styr, although a vile man, never rises again, as if he had gotten what he desired and was content. This may also be behind the story of Glámir harassing Thorhall's daughter to such a degree that she dies as well as Thorolf pestering his wife until she passes away.

Returning to Thorstein Eiriksson, we will remember that he sits up and tells his wife, Gudrid, her fortune. In one rendition he tells her she shall marry an Icelander and in the other that she must not marry a Greenlander. Guerrero here conjectures that these may well have to do with jealousy (124-125). Thorstein the Black is now a widower and Gudrid a widow. There is a lot of pressure, Guerrero observes, to remarry quickly after a spouse dies in cultures such as this because farm life demands a couple to work together at it. Thorstein the Black, a Greenlander, had moved over to Gudrid, embraced her, and was consoling her when her husband sat up and disallowed her to marry an inhabitant of Greenland.

Variations: 12. The Helpful *Aptrgangr*[40]

Thorleif, who has been covered under the heading of the evoked *aptrgangr*, belongs here. On his own initiative he equips the shepherd with what he needs to succeed. There is a measure of this with Angantyr as well. He gives his daughter what she believes she needs, even though the sword is cursed. And we could place Brynjar, at least partly, here too. The gold he gives Thorstein will make his mother lose her muteness and it is offered without reservation.

In fourteenth-century *Göngu-Hrólfs Saga*, King Hreggvid dies in battle and is placed in an impregnable, bricked mound. Hreggvid himself, as a revenant, adds magic spells to protect it from outside access. The hero of the story, Hrolf,

---

[40] It is important to mention here that Stern writes that "The most fundamental difference in the nature of the *haugbui* is whether he is pictured as hostile or helpful to the hero" (29).

is able, by sheer force of strength, to penetrate the spells, but does not need to break in, for Hreggvid is outside to greet him. He tells Hrolf he would like him to marry his daughter, but he recognizes there is an immediate obstacle in Hrolf's way, so he provides him from his treasure the things he will require. These are to be kept secret; he gives other items as proof the barrow was broached, for he is sent on this impossible task by the king and by his false master, William. William then takes the credit for it before the king and in the story he tells, he follows the expected narrative: he himself broke through the spells, he had a terrible time opening the mound, he battled all night with "the great troll" within, and finally prevailed (see *Göngu-Hrólfs Saga*, 3,16, 32).

Hrolf visits him one more time, when he is battling the forces responsible for Hreggvid's death. Again, he is outside the mound expecting Hrolf. Hreggvid rejoices that vengeance will soon be his, although Hrolf is already involved in the war, without Hreggvid ever appealing to him for help. He has his own reasons for fighting the culprits. Hreggvid provides him once more with the wherewithal to be victorious and tells him not to worry even though things do not appear favorable at the moment. With Hreggvid's aid, Hrolf is victorious and marries Hreggvid's daughter.

In *Gull-Thóris Saga* (1300-1350), Thorir hears that there is a fortune to be made by raiding Agnar's mound, and thinks it worth it even if it is protected by spells and all attempts to break in have been failures with horrible consequences. Agnar, the son of Reginmod the Evil, was buried with great treasure and his entire crew. On the way, Thorir has a dream in which a man, imposing and splendid, appears to him, reveals that he, Agnar, is kin to Thorir, and offers him gifts and money if he will not invade his mound. He wants to keep the rest of his wealth for himself. Thorir agrees to it when Agnir offers to give him the location of another treasure—this time guarded by dragons. He wakes up from his dream and the items are before him. Furthermore, his companion has also seen Agnir and overheard the entire conversation in his sleep. Agnar returns the following night to tell Thorir many things that would come to pass and explain to him how to succeed in getting the treasure from the dragons (see *Gull-Thóris Saga* 1300-1350, 3; cf. *Hálfdanar saga Eysteinsson* 26).

In late-thirteenth-century *Reykdæla Saga og Víga-Skútu*, Hall's daughter is desired by a particularly evil man called Thorstein for his wife. Hall refuses and Thorstein challenges him to a duel. Hall cannot fight against him so he asks Thorkel to stand in for him and he agrees. Hall gives him a sword taken from the treasure in a burial-mound. Thorkel is victorious. Although this sword was from a grave and he is told he ought to keep it for himself, Thorkel refuses and has it returned. Skefil, the dead man whose sword it was, appears to Thorkel in a dream and says that because he showed himself courageous and upright, by returning it, he could keep the sword. He wakes up and the sword is with him (see *Reykdæla Saga* 19).

They are all mound-dwellers and they appear to have been good men in life, although there may be some doubt about Agnar. In other words, their afterlife seems to conform to their previous life. One might want to propose that they all have to do with violence, but arguably that is not the case. Four do provide weapons and one gives a gift to exalt the violence that others have performed in song, but this does not pertain to Thorstein and Brynjar, nor initially to Skefil. While there is considerable violence in the former episode, the gift itself is primarily to help Thorstein's mother speak. With reference to Skefil, he allows his sword to be taken from his mound without a fight, but would have resorted to lethal force, not against the one who took it, but he who used it, if it had not been returned, although no one in the story knows this. Finally, none of the living-challenged individuals is subject to a second death through violence.

Variations: 13. The Comforting *Aptrgangr*

We have already covered the story of the two revenants Thorstein Eiriksson and Sigrid, but there is a variation of it in early-thirteenth-century *Grænlendinga saga*, where Gudrid is the second *aptrgangr* instead of Sigrid. Thorstein dies. Later that night he sits up and calls for his wife. The host in whose house Thorstein has died, answers and Thorstein explains that he wants to tell Gudrid her fate "to make it easier for her to resign herself to my death." She will have a long life, he says, married to an Icelander (they are in Greenland), and will have numerous children and grandchildren. She will outlive her fourth and last husband (Thorstein was number three) and take holy orders during the waning years of her life (see *Grænlendinga saga* 5). In the other version, he mostly counsels her about correct Christian behavior and rituals (see *Eiríks saga rauða* 6). Gudrid, by the way, is the same one who was weeping above the sorceress' body, discomforting her.

The following may be better as a recruiting revenant, but I believe what he does is meant to comfort. Helgi Hundingsbane falls desperately in love with a Valkyrie, Sigrun (*Helgakviða Hundingsbana II*). She, however, is promised to another man, so Helgi slaughters everyone who could hinder their marriage, including most of her family. He saves one of her brothers who vows to serve him, but he ends up murdering Helgi for revenge. Sigrun curses her brother and mourns her husband. One night her maid sees Helgi return to his burial mound, accompanied by an army, and Sigrun is elated.

His wounds are bleeding so he has asked the maid to fetch his wife to staunch them. She arrives and wants first to kiss him; she notices how wet he is with dew and blood and how cold he is. But this does not deter her. She makes a bed for them and readies herself to sleep with him. He, however, tells her it is her tears that cover him like dew and blood, and asks that she mourn for him no longer, that she long no more to sleep in a dead man's arms. We may note a comparison here between Gudrin and the Sorceress. This is obviously how she can staunch his injuries and help him. They then do sleep together one last time. He leaves before dawn and never returns. Despite his counsel, she waits for him and then dies of grief.

This reverses the usual pattern of the man, unwelcomed, returning to the bed of his wife. Chadwick, in "Norse Ghosts," sees this as probably a substitute for a ritual burial with her husband; it makes their reincarnation possible and hence the continuation of their love story, for their love has preceded this event (57). If she is correct, his return guarantees they will meet again in another life. It is a sign of hope and comfort. Both stories have to do with dead husbands comforting their grieving wives.

Variations: 14. The Indifferent *Aptrgangr*

There are revenants who are going about their own business, oblivious to human beings and just happen to be observed. There should also be a place here for Thorgunna's revenants, for they do not interact with the living until the trial, as well as for Sigmundur and his companions, although both companies mean to be observed.

With his crew of nine slaughtered, Thorgeir (in *Fóstbrœdra Saga*, circa 1270-1300) fights valiantly, taking down thirteen before being killed himself. His enemies behead him and then the party of conquerors goes their separate ways. One segment carries his head with them and at each stop take it out and mock it. Eventually they bury it—a long distance from his body. A year later, two men are conversing outside and believe they see him and his nine crew members, covered in blood, walking along the fields until they disappear (see *Fóstbrœdra Saga* 19).

In *Brennu-Njáls saga* (1270-90), Svan and his crew are out fishing when they are overcome by a storm and drown. A number of fishermen see them walk into a mountain and hear them being greeted warmly (see *Brennu-Njáls saga* 14). Caciola notes that this is a very different vision of a burial mound than the one we usually encounter, for the mountain acts as one symbolically (*Afterlives* 347-363). The tale of Thorstein Codbiter in *Eyrbyggja Saga* (mid- to late thirteenth century) is similar. He too is out fishing and drowns, along with his crew. That evening a shepherd sees the north side of a mountain open with fires blazing and the sound of drinking-horns clacking within. He then hears Thorstein and his crew being welcomed and Thorstein being invited to sit in the high-seat alongside his father (see *Eyrbyggja Saga* 11).

These are represented in Continental European and British revenant literature as well, but context can make them quite different. These Nordic stories should be compared first to mound-dwellers before they are matched with ones in the south. Mounds are often dank, dark, and malodorous; they are almost always somber and quiet; they are never joyous; nor do they tend to open up in order to welcome newcomers. The mountain barrow provides a kind of parallel existence for the dead that mirrors earthly life at its best, much like the Christian heaven reflects life at its most religiously satisfying—however that be conceived. The first example above can be likened also to the medieval tales of ghostly hunters, armies, and processions.

Are they visions, immaterial apparitions in transit from the place of their death to their otherworld destiny, as Guerrero asserts (103-106)? Or are they physical with supernatural qualities as some (Ziegler 93 and Olaus Magnus 2.3) indicated in the sixteenth century?[41] I follow the latter, for I think the earlier writers should know. These creatures, living-challenged all, are like the other *aptrgangar*—i.e., material.

---

[41] "These spectres make themselves so apparent [manifest] to gatherings of their acquaintances that those who are ignorant of their death receive them as though they were alive and offer their right hands; nor is the mistake detected before the shades have vanished" (Olaus Magnus 2.3). Their presence is physical, but they can vanish, just as other *aptrgangar* do.

Variations: 15. The Communal *Aptrgangr*

As far as I can tell there are no noteworthy variations in being alone, so there will be no category for it. The *aptrgangr* is doing whatever it is doing by itself. But there are different ways of being communal. For example, there are those whose groups are those who are related; father and daughter (Kol and Gullkula) or mother and son (Grendel and his mother). Probably the giant and the troll woman belong here as well. There are larger groups like Jostein's and those associated with Thorgunna, which include servants.

Then there are those who were companions in life, die, and become revenants together. These can consist of those who are buried together in a mound, often as captain and crew or as king and select subjects. The dead entourage may play no further part in the story as, for example, the case of Olaf Geirstad-Alf and Agnar, who enter a barrow with all their men and turn into trolls alone, guarding the treasure. Those that do have a role are usually harmonious, but they can be in tension with each other. Asmund is discontent with his useless slave. Odd is exploiting Brynjar, and Brynjar is looking for a way to eliminate his tyrant brother. And there are *aptrgangr* soldiers who cannot die when fighting each other.

On the other hand, there are those like Svan and Thorstein Codbiter, who are welcomed into an already lively community. They are expected and they join in the revelry and feasting with enthusiasm. This mountain barrow is a place of reunion with lost loved ones. It is well lit, spacious, and warm, as opposed to the ones fashioned by human hands. Finally, however, like the cairn, it is a place of hierarchy.

There are communities formed by contagion. How the "disease" of revenantism is passed on is not explored, but it undeniably is. An *aptrgangr* that communicates it to others often takes on a leadership role. Thorolf Halt-Foot does to such a degree that his progeny disappear from the narrative apart from a mention of their existence. Sometimes the leader will even try to whip the others into shape, like Gardi. Jostein's household and friends, in contrast, seem to function with a kind of stable anarchism; there is no sense they follow the directives either of Jostein or the first one to die. And even with hierarchical order there can be rival gangs of *aptrgangar*. In the remarkable story of Thorgunna, Thorir Wooden-leg's group of the land-dead and Thorod's group of the drowned form mutually exclusive groups at the fire. It is even more pronounced between Odd's men and those of Brynjar.

Conclusion

At the risk of being impertinent, for I am writing as a vampire scholar, I would like to start by making two observations. I do not think that *draugr* is the best word to describe the Nordic undead. Besides "vampire," the most used word for the living dead today, there is the French word "revenant" (returner) which is virtually identical in meaning with the German "Wiedergänger" (again-walker). I think we ought to utilize the Old Norse word that is most closely related to "revenant" and that is *aptrgangr*. No matter how many times it was or was not used for the revenant in the classic Nordic literature, "ghost," even "corporeal ghost," is misleading to those who are not scholars in the field. *Aptrgangr* carries its physicality with it. As Guerrero (40) indicates, the choice of *haugbúi* is rather arbitrary since other words are used for the mound-dweller as well. And as Jakobsson ("Vampires and Watchmen" 284) and Merkelbach (11) point out, the word *draugr* is not used in some of the most celebrated cases of the Nordic revenant.

Second, there was a reason that *draugr* and *haugbúi* were originally used synonymously. Barrow-dwellers have, all too often, a nasty habit of having time outside the mound and can be quite violent. On the other hand, those who walk abroad are, with one clear exception (Earl Agdi), always to be found in their graves when at rest. I do not think it is that helpful a distinction. Aðalsteinsson, in his 1998 *A Piece of Horse Liver*, does not even single out *draugr* in his study. My approach may prove to be unsatisfactory but I think something like it will prove a better avenue to pursue—*aptrgangar* with different literary functions and characteristics, yet involving a fair amount of overlap. The search for exclusive categories here is bound to fail.

Let us take a look briefly at what this all means, focusing just on those who dwell in tumuli. They have an enormous range of variability, which "watcher" cannot capture. Soti is a watcher pure and simple and the giant appears to be one as well. Thrain has been a watcher, but initially, when being robbed, he is disinterested. Rocknar is a watcher who travels far abroad to dare Christians to come and take his treasure. During that time he is not being watchful. Kar at first leaves his mound for violence but now spends most his time indoors and watching. But he still goes out. Agnar barters with his relative not to rob him by offering him information and a few things from his treasury, so he can be free to watch over the remainder. Angantyr is a watcher but gives of his wealth to his daughter once persuaded of her intransigence.

But Thorleif helps a struggling poet from his storehouse of talent. Hreggvid helps make his mound impregnable except to the intrepid hero he has chosen for his daughter; he then freely offers him everything he will need from his interred wealth. Skefil allows his sword to be taken, but is ready to kill its user, not its thief, if it be not returned. When he does, it is given him. Olaf Geirstad-Alf guards his treasure for generations until he appears in a dream to Hrani and directs him to break into his mound, decapitate him, and plunder his wealth. Brynmar, an *aptrgangr*, is generous with his treasure to a living young man as a reward for killing the *aptrgangar* who were hoarding it. Peter of Grationopolis protects his treasure of piety against an invading *aptrgangr*. So too Thorstein against Thorkel the Thin but in a weaker way.

Then there are those who are not watchers at all, no matter how qualified. Grendel and his mother simply abide in their surrogate mound and wander abroad seeking violence. Earl Agdi actually leaves his mound utterly unattended as he walks about unsuccessfully looking for violence. Klaufi, after a long time of quiet, terrorizes those about his mound who are not bothering him. Bjorn's father departs from his sanctuary to bother his family. Helgi apparently has left his howe vacant for a considerable time and then returns to his wife's delight.

Gunnar stays within, with his cairn open, and sings out a song for vengeance, while Haekling shouts out an answer to a question with his cairn closed. They are indifferent to their riches. Asvith/Aran does not walk outside, but viciously attacks his friend who out of devotion is buried with him and has no designs on his buried wealth. Mithothyn spreads disease from his mound without ever stepping outside. Finally Svan and Thorstein Codbiter enter their mountain mound to join dead relatives in endless celebration where there is nothing to fear from outsiders.

The benefit of this approach, broadly if not in detail, for medievalists specializing in Old Norse literature, is greater precision in working with *aptrgangar*. For vampire historiographers, it moves discussion forward beyond generalities to the possibility of careful comparison. For example, now one can see how there might be useful parallels in some cases between the "again-walker" with its mound, and the vampire with its grave.

Works cited

Adam of Bremen. *Gesta Hammaburgensis ecclesiae pontificum. History of the Archbishops of Hamburg-Bremen*. Trans Francis Joseph Tschan. New York: Columbia University Press, 2002.

Aðalsteinsson, Jón Hnefill. *A Piece of Horse Liver: Myth, Ritual Folklore in Old Icelandic Sources*. Trans. Terry Gunnell & Joan Turville-Petre. Reykjavík: Háskólaútgáfan, 1998.

Atkinson, John Christopher. *Lost or What Came of a Slip from 'Honour Bright.'* London: Sampson Low, Son, and Marston, 1870.

Baldrs Draumar. "Baldr's Dreams." *Poetic Edda*. Trans. Carolyne Larrington. Oxford: Oxford University Press, 1996. 243-245.

Bárðar saga Snæfellsáss. "The Saga of Bard the Snowfell God." *Icelandic Histories and Romances*. Trans. Ralph O'Connor. Stroud: Tempus, 2002. 109-138.

Baring-Gould, Sabine. *Curious Myths of the Middle Ages*. London: Rivingtons, 1868.

Baring-Gould, Sabine. *Iceland: Its Scenes and Sagas*. London: Smith, Elder and Co. 1863.

Bartholin, Thomas. *Antiqvitatum Danicarum de Causis Contemtae a Danis adhuc Gentilibus Mortis*. Copenhagen: Joh. Phil. Bockenhoffer, 1689.

Beowulf. Trans. Seamus Heaney. New York: Farrar, Strauss, & Giroux, 1999.

Brennu-Njáls Saga. "Njal's Saga." Trans. Robert Cook. *The Complete Sagas of Icelanders* 3, ed. Viðar Hreinsson. Reykjavik: Leifur Eiríksson, 1997. 90-92.

Caciola, Nancy Mandeville. *Afterlives: The Return of the Dead in the Middle Ages*. Ithaca: Cornell University Press, 2016.

Calmet, Antoine Augustin. *The Phantom World*. 2. Trans. Henry Christmas. London: Richard Bentley, 1850.

Cavaleri, Claire. "The Vínland Sagas as Propaganda for the Christian Church: Freydís and Gudríd as Paradigms for Eve and the Virgin Mary." Master's Thesis. University of Oslo, 2008.

Chadwick, N. K. "Norse Ghosts (A Study in the Draugr and the Haugbúi)." *Folklore* 57: 2-3 (June-September 1946), 50-65; 106-127.

Collingwood, W. G.; Stephánsson, Jón. *A Pilgrimage to the Saga-Steads of Iceland.* Ulverston: W. Holms, 1899.
Egils saga einhenda ok Ásmundar berserkjabana. Egil One-Hand and Asmund Berserkers-Slayer. *Seven Viking Romances.* Eds. & trans. Hermann Pálsson and Paul Edwards. London: Penguin Books, 1985. 228-257.
Eiríks saga rauða. "Eirik's Saga." *The Vinland Sagas: The Norse Discovery of America.* Trans. Magnus Magnusson & Hermann Palsson. London: Penguin Books, 1965. 73-105.
Ellis [Davidson], Hilda R. *The Road to Hel: A Study of the Conception of the Dead in Old Norse Literature.* Cambridge: Cambridge University Press, 1943.
Ellis Davidson, Hilda R. "The Restless Dead: An Icelandic Ghost Story." *The Folklore of Ghosts.* Eds. Hilda R. Ellis Davidson and W. M. S. Russell. Cambridge, Mass.: Boydell & Brewer Ltd., 1981.
Eyrbyggja Saga. "The Saga of the People of Eyri." Trans. Judy Quinn. *The Complete Sagas of Icelanders* 5. Ed. Viðar Hreinsson. Reykjavik: Leifur Eiríksson, 1997. 131-218.
Færeyinga Saga. Faroe-Islander Saga: *A New English Translation.* Trans. Robert K. Painter. Jefferson: McFarland & Co., 2016.
Flóamanna Saga. "The Saga of the People of Floi." Trans. Paul Acker. *The Complete Sagas of Icelanders* 3, ed. Viðar Hreinsson. Leifur Eiríksson, 1997. 271-304.
Foote, Peter. "Færeyinga Saga: Chapter 40." In *Aurvandilstá: Norse Studies.* Viborg: Odense University Press, 1984.
Fóstbrædra Saga. "The Saga of the Sworn Brothers." Trans. Martin Regal. In *The Complete Sagas of Icelanders* 2. Ed. Viðar Hreinsson. Reykjavik: Leifur Eiríksson, 1997. 329-402.
Francisci, Erasmus. *Der Höllische Proteus, oder Tausendkünstige Verstelle.* Nürnberg: Wolfgang Moritz Endter, 1695.
Gísla saga Súrssonar. "Gisli Surrson's Saga." Trans. Martin S. Regal. *The Complete Sagas of Icelanders* 2. Ed. Viðar Hreinsson. Reykjavik: Leifur Eiríksson, 1997. 1-48.
Göngu-Hrólfs Saga. Trans. Hermann Pálsson and Paul Edwards. Toronto: University of Toronto Press, 1980.
Gould, Chester Nathan. "They Who Await the Second Death: A Study in The Icelandic Romantic Sagas." *Scandinavian Studies and Notes* 9: 6 (May 1927), 167-201.
Grænlendinga saga. "The Saga of the Greenlanders." Trans. Keneva Kunz. *The Complete Sagas of Icelanders* 1. ed. Viðar Hreinsson. Reykjavik: Leifur Eiríksson, 1997. 19-32.
Grammaticus, Saxo. *Saxo Grammaticus. Gesta Danorum: The History of the Danes.* 1. Ed. Karsten Friis-Jensen. Trans. Peter Fisher. Oxford: Clarendon Press, 2015.
Grettis Saga. "The Saga of Grettir the Strong." Trans. Bernard Scudder. In *The Complete Sagas of Icelanders* 2. Ed. Viðar Hreinsson. Reykjavik: Leifur Eiríksson, 1997. 49-191.
Guerrero, Fernando. "Stranded in Miðgarðr: Draugr Folklore and Old Norse Sources." M.Phil. thesis. University of Oslo, 2003.
Guibert de Nogent. *Liber de Laude Sanctae Mariae. Patrologiae cursus completus, serie latina.* Ed. Jacques Paul Migne. Vol. 156. Paris: Migne, 1853. 11, 301-312.
Gull-Thóris Saga. "Gold-Thorir's Saga." Trans. Anthony Maxwell. *The Complete Sagas of Icelanders* 3. Ed. Viðar Hreinsson. Reykjavik: Leifur Eiríksson, 1997. 335-59.
Gylfaginning. The Prose Edda. Snori Sturluson. Trans. Jesse Byock. London: Penguin Books, 2005.
Hálfdanar Saga Eysteinsson. "The Saga of Halfdan Eysteinsson." Trans. George L. Hardman. *Germanic Mythology: Texts, Translations, Scholarship.* http://www.germanicmythology.com/FORNALDARSAGAS/HalfdanEysteinssonHardman.html
Hálfs saga ok Hálfsrekka. "The Saga of Half and His Heroes." Trans. Peter Tunstall London: Northvegr, 2005.
Hávarðar Saga Ísfirðings. "The Saga of Havard of Isafjord." Trans. Fredrik J. Heinemann. *The Complete Sagas of Icelanders* 5. Ed. Viðar Hreinsson. Reykjavik: Leifur Eiríksson, 1997. 314-19.

Hebblethwaite, Rob. "The Good, the Bad and the Rotten: How the Living Dealt With the Dead in England c.600-1200." Master's Thesis. University of East Anglia, 2017.

Heiðarvíga saga. "The Saga of the Slayings on the Heath." Trans. Keneva Kunz. *The Complete Sagas of Icelanders* 4. Ed. Viðar Hreinsson. Reykjavik: Leifur Eiríksson, 1997. 79-81.

Helgakviða Hundingsbana II. "Second Poem of Helgi Hundingsbane." *The Poetic Edda*. Trans. Carolyne Larrington. Oxford: Oxford University Press, 1996. 132-141.

Hervarar Saga ok Heiðreks. *The Saga of Hervor & King Heidrek the Wise*. Trans. Christopher Tolkien. London: Thomas Nelson & Sons Ltd., 1960. 14-19.

Hickes, George. *Linguarum Vett. septentrionalium thesaurus grammatico-criticus et archeologicus* I: 1. Oxford: E Theatro Sheldoniano, 1703.

Hjaltason, Kygri-Björn. *Maríu saga: legender om Jomfru Maria og hendes jertegn: efter gamle haadsckrifter*. Ed. C. R. Unger. Christiania: Brögger & Christie, 1871.

Hólmverja Saga. "The Saga of Hord." Trans. Alan Boucher. *Three Icelandic Outlaw Sagas*. Viking Society for Northern Research, 2004. 267-327.

Hrólfs Saga Kraka ok Kappa Hans. "The Saga of Hrolf Kraki and His Companions." Trans. Peter Tunstall. London: Northvegr, 2003.

Hrómundar Saga Gripssonar. "The Saga of Hromund Greipsson." *Stories and Ballads of the Far Past*. Ed. & trans. Nora Kershaw. Cambridge: Cambridge University Press, 1921. 58-78.

Jakobsson, Ármann. "The Fearless Vampire Killers: A Note about the Icelandic Draugr and Demonic Contamination in Grettis Saga." *Folklore* 120 (December 2009), 307-316.

Jakobsson, Ármann. "Vampires and Watchmen: Categorizing the Mediaeval Icelandic Undead." *Journal of English and Germanic Philology* 110: 3 (June 2011), 281-300.

Jónsson, Arngrímur. *Brevis commentarius de Islandia*. 1593. *The Principall Navigations, Voiages, Traffiques, and Discoveries of the English Nation*. Richard Hakluyt. Vol. 1. Trans. Richard Hakluyt. Edinburg: E. & M. Goldsmid, 1880 [1598].

Kanerva, Kirsi. "The Role of the Dead in Medieval Iceland: A Case Study of *Eyrbyggja saga*." *Collegium Medievale* 24 (November 2011), 23-49.

Landnámbók. *The Book of Settlements*. Trans. Hermann Pálsson and Paul Edwards. Winnipeg: University of Manitoba Press, 2007.

Lang, Andrew. *Book of Dreams and Ghosts*. London: Longmans, Green, and Co., 1897.

Laxdæla Saga. "The Saga of the People of Laxardal." Trans. Keneva Kunz. *The Complete Sagas of Icelanders* 5. Ed. Viðar Hreinsson. Reykjavik: Leifur Eiríksson, 1997. 1-120.

Lecouteux, Claude. *The Return of the Dead: Ghosts, Ancestors, and the Transparent Veil of the Pagan Mind*. Trans. Jon E. Graham. Rochester & Toronto: Inner Traditions, 1996.

Lindow, John. "Þorsteins þáttr skelks and the verisimilitude of supernatural experience in saga literature." *Structure and Meaning in Old Norse Literature: New Approaches to Textual Analysis and Literary Criticism*. Eds. John Lindow, Lars Lönnroth and Gerd Wolfgang Weber. Odense: Odense University Press, 1986. 264-280.

Magnus, Olaus. *Historia de Gentibus Septentrionalibus*. Ed. Peter Foote. *Description of the Northern Peoples* 1. Trans. Peter Fisher & Humphey Higgens. London: Hakluyt Society, 1996.

Mannhardt, Wilhelm. "Über Vampyrismus." *Zeitschrift für deutsche Mythologie und Sittenkunde*. 4, 1859. 259-82.

Merino, Eugenio Olivares. "The Old English Poem: 'A Vampyre of the Fens': A Bibliographic Ghost." *Miscelánea: A Journal of English and American Studies*. 32 (2005), 87-102.

Merkelbach, Rebecca. "Hann lá eigi kyrr'—Revenants and a Haunted Past in the Sagas of Icelanders." MPhil Thesis. University of Cambridge, 2012.

Nodier, Charles. "Le Vampire Harppe." *Infernaliana*. Paris: Sanson, 1822. 69-70.

Noetzel, Justin T. "Outlaws and the Undead: Defining Sacred and Communal Space in Medieval Iceland." *Dealing with the Dead: Mortality and Community in Medieval and Early Modern Europe*. Ed. Thea Tomaini. Leiden: Brill, 2018. 175-200.

O'Donoghue, Heather. *Old Norse-Icelandic Literature: A Short Introduction* Malden: Blackwell Publishing Company, 2004.
Ranft, Michael. *De Masticatione Mortuorum In Tumulis.* Leipzig: Breitkopf, 1725.
Reykdæla Saga og Víga-Skútu. "The Saga of the People of Raykjadal and of Killer-Skuta." Trans. George Clark. *The Complete Sagas of Icelanders* 4. Ed. Viðar Hreinsson. Reykjavik: Leifur Eiríksson, 1997. 257-302.
Saxo Grammaticus. *Gesta Danorum.* Ed. Hilda Ellis Davidson. *The History of the Danes, Books I-IX.* Trans. Peter Fisher. Cambridge: D. S. Brewer, 1979.
Sayers, William. "The Alien and Alienated as Unquiet Dead in the Sagas of the Icelanders." *Monster Theory: Reading Culture.* Ed. Jeffrey Jerome Cohen. Minneapolis: University of Minnesota Press, 1996. 242-263.
Sharma, Arvind, Ed. *Our Religions.* San Francisco: HarperCollins, 1993.
Sörla þáttr. Trans. N. Kershaw. *Stories and Ballads of the Far Past.* Ed. Nora Kershaw/ Cambridge: Cambridge University Press, 1921.
Spatacean, Cristina. "Women in the Viking Age: Death, Life after Death and Burial Customs." M.Phil. University of Oslo, 2006.
Stein, Otto von Graben zum. *Unterredungen von dem Reiche der Geister.* 1. Leipzig: Samuel Benjamin Waltern, 1731.
Stern, Elizabeth J. "Legends of the Dead in Medieval and Modern Iceland." Ph.D. dissertation. UCLA, 1987.
Stoker, Bram. 1897. *Dracula.* New York: Grosset and Dunlap, 1897.
Stoker, Bram; Ásmundsson, Valdimar. *Powers of Darkness; The Lost Version of* Dracula. Trans. Hans Corneel de Roos. New York: Overlook Duckworth, 2016. Kindle.
Sturluson, Snorri. *Ynglinga Saga. Heimskringla* 1. Trans. Alison Finlay & Anthony Faulkes. London: University College, 2011.
Svarfdaela Saga. "The Saga of the People of Svarfadardal." Trans. Fredrik Heinemann. *The Complete Sagas of Icelanders* 4. Ed. Viðar Hreinsson. Reykjavik: Leifur Eiríksson, 1997. 149-192.
Teichart, Matthias. "'Draugula': The *Draugr* in Old Norse-Icelandic Saga Literature and His Relationahip to the Post-Medieval Vampire Myth." *Universal Vampire: Origins and Evolution of a Legend.* Eds. Barbara Brodman and James E. Doan. Madison: Fairleigh Dickinson, 2013.
Thorleifs Thattr Jarlsskálds. "The Tale of Thorleif, The Earl's Poet." Trans. Judith Jesch. In *The Complete Sagas of Icelanders* 1. Ed. Viðar Hreinsson. Reykjavik: Leifur Eiríksson, 1997. 360-69.
Thorsteins Thattr Baejarmagns. "Thorstein Mansion-Might." *Seven Viking Romances.* Trans. Hermann Pálsson & Paul Edwards. London: Penguin, 1985. 258-75.
Thorsteins Tháttur Skelks. "The Tale of Thorstein Shiver." Trans. Anthony Maxwell. *The Complete Sagas of Icelanders* 1. Ed. Viðar Hreinsson. Reykjavik: Leifur Eiríksson, 1997. 394-396.
Thorsteins Tháttur Uxafóts. "The Story of Thorstein Bull's-Leg." Trans. George Clark. *The Complete Sagas of Icelanders* 4. Ed. Viðar Hreinsson. Reykjavik: Leifur Eiríksson, 1997. 340-54.
Valvasor, Johann Weichard von. *Die Ehre deß Hertzogthums Crain.* 2. Nürnberg, 1689.
"Vampyres." *Household Words—a Weekly Journal.* 11: 255. 10 February 1855. 39-43.
Vicary, J. Fulford. *Saga Time.* London: Keagan Paul, Trench & Co. 1887.
Voragine, Jacobus De. *The Golden Legend: Readings on the Saints.* Trans. William Granger Ryan. Princeton: University Press, 1993.
Ziegler, Jakob. *Quae Intus Continentur Syria, Palestina, Arabia, Aegyptus, Schondia, Holmiae, Regionum Superiorum.* Petrum Opilionem, 1532.

In *Nouveau dictionnaire encyclopédique universal illustré* 5 (1885), 572.

In *Brehms Theirleben, allgemeine Kunde des Thierreichs* 1 1876:339
https://play.google.com/books/reader?id=bRfPAAAAMAAJ&hl=en&pg=GBS.PA339

3.
"An Evil Kind of Animal:"
300 Years of the Monstrous Vampire Bat up to the Nineteenth Century

Introduction: The Imperial Background

The European soldiers and settlers, as well as those who followed in their wake, did not invade the "New World" with a Lockean mental blank slate. Their encounters with a winged leech passed through a complex interpretive grid. Their worldviews were deeply shaped by Christian symbols and rituals, supplemented by Greek and Roman mythologies, and by Medieval and early Renaissance bestiaries, which predisposed them to link large bats, rather than small ones, with sanguivorous behavior.

Central to the first on the list is its centuries-old representations of the devil as having bat wings with a preoccupation with blood. The bat wings go back at least to Basil of Caesarea's fourth-century *Commentary on the Prophet Isaiah* (see Basil 110) and become embedded in Christian iconography with Giotto di Bondone in the late thirteenth century ("The Exorcism of the Demons" and "The Confession of the Woman of Benevento") and Duccio di Buoninsegna in the early fourteenth ("The Temptation of Christ on the Mountain" and "Descent to Hell"). Dante in his 1314 *Inferno* first wrote about it directly (385), spreading it out to a much larger audience (385).[42] Demons were depicted roughly as human size.

Christianity also is unique among the world religions for its celebration of an executed criminal as its founder as well as its devotional meditations on the manner of his death. His shed blood is one of the most prominent features of its theologies, its practices, and its mysticisms. Thus the bleeding of Christian bodies in the New World by bats, linked with the violence of conquest for the advancement of religion, would put them in mind of being martyrs. *Plures efficimur, quoties metimur a vobis; semen est sanguis christianorum* (roughly "The blood of the martyrs is the seed of the church") Tertullian declared in the late second century *Apologeticus* (139).[43] So it is not surprising that after Cortés' conquest at Tenochtitlan against the Aztecs and his gift of land to Juan Garrido, that Garrido built a chapel on it and named it "The Martyrs" in honor of fallen conquistadors. It was the Devil that was behind it all.

Greek and Roman mythologies have a number of large, deadly, bird-like creatures. Harpies, the Stymphalian birds, and the Furies are all mentioned in early reports of the blood-sucking bat of the Americas. Harpies were fearsome

---

[42] Dante is also important in establishing that the Devil's wings are that of a bat and not a dragon, as is held by Partha Mitter, in *Much Maligned Monsters* (9). Dante insisted that they were not feathered, "but were in form and texture like a bat's [vispistrello=pipistrello]."
[43] Translated here as "The oftener we are mown down by you, the more in number we grow; the blood of Christians is seed."

birdlike creatures, full of wrath and vengeance, with faces of women, who would torment the disobedient as they were delivering them to Tartarus. Stymphalian birds were monstrous beasts who had beaks of bronze with which they would devour their human prey. The furies were birdlike goddesses of retribution and revenge. They were known to deliver madness, disease, and famine to humans.

Also present in the myths were the hypnotic Sirens, the sleep-inducing Hypnos, and the batlike Strix (pl. Striges). The first, often pictured with wings, lured passing sailors by their hypnotic song off their ships, into the water, and to their deaths. The second was once summoned by Jason and on Hypnos' way to him "everything living and moving he persuaded to sleep under his golden wings" (see Pseudo-Orpheus, *The Orphic Argonautica*). Entrancement and sedation will become standard for the vampire bat in the eighteenth century. The last term became used for witches and then applied as an early name for vampire monsters. It was often depicted as an owl, but Samuel Grant Oliphant, in "The Story of the Strix" (1913) has made a strong case for it being based on the bat instead—and a carnivorous one at that.

Finally, bestiaries primed their imaginations to jump to exaggerated descriptions of the unfamiliar fauna. Add to these a subsequent exposure to native folklore and art, which would sometimes link bats with ritual human sacrifices (see Elizabeth P. Benson's 1991 "Bats in South American Folklore") as well as the human propensity to amplify and dramatize danger and we have an entrance to the complex context of those participating in the waves of conquest and national expansion. It is even more complex since leeches were considered benevolent in medicine.

The Monstrous Bat up to the Eighteenth Century

From the beginning size was an issue, so the vampire became identified with the largest bat in the Americas—what we know today as the *Vampyrum spectrum*. By 1511, Pietro Martire d'Anghiera in *De Orbe Novo* wrote that "in many places bats as large as pigeons flew about the Spaniards as soon as twilight fell, biting them so cruelly that men, rendered desperate, were obliged to give way before them as though they had been harpies" (1: 179). This statement was made available to English speakers in 1555 with a translation by Richard Eden, *The Decades of the Newe Worlde* (103). By 1516, Anghiera added that they could kill: "During the night the men were tortured by bats which bit them; and if one of these animals bit a man while he was asleep, he lost his blood, and was in danger of losing his life. It is even claimed that some people did die on account of these wounds" (1: 355).

Later in 1530 he observed that the bats "fasten upon any part of the human body which remains uncovered, biting quickly and sucking the blood (2: 376)." At this point, he told "an amusing story" of a dying man who needed to be bled immediately but the doctors could not open a vein, so he was given up as lost (2: 377). As the monks prepared for his burial outside the room, a bat descended on him, fed from his foot, and left with the toe still bleeding. The next morning, the monks, prepared to put him in his grave, found him out of danger and almost well.

Gonzalo Fernández de Oviedo y Valdés informed the readers of his 1526 *Sumario de historia natural* about these same dangerous bats, saying that when landing with Balboa, "some Christians at the time died, and others were in danger of dying, until it was learned from the Indians how to treat those who had been bitten by them. These bats are neither larger nor smaller than those here [in Spain] and at night are in the habit of biting, for the most part, the tip of the nose, or the tips of the fingers or toes, and extract so much blood from the wound, that one needs to see it in order to believe it" (50-51). This is the only source that said their size was nothing extraordinary.

In 1555 Álvar Núñez Cabeza de Vaca wrote a commentary of his experiences in Brazil. There he described a particular type of bat that he called "an evil kind of animal." "They are larger than our doves in Spain with teeth so sharp that their bite is not felt" (Cabeza de Vaca 199). They cut off the combs of the fowl so that they died. They frightened the horses terribly, fastening themselves to their ears, and they bit humans at the toe or the tip of the nose. One bit the toe of a man who woke up later with his leg cold from the loss of so much blood (199-200).

"They served us a bad trick on one occasion," he wrote. "When we were starting on our voyage of exploration, we had six pregnant sows, and hoped to rear a race of pigs. When the little pigs were born, and tried to suck their mother, they could not find her teats, because these had been bitten off by the bats; so the young pigs died, and we had to eat the sows, because they were unable to rear their young" (Cabeza de Vaca 200). Interestingly, in 1810, Robert Southey, the future poet laureate of England, paraphrased this passage in his *History of Brazil* (adding the term "vampire" to the account, by the way, so it was widely available to English-speakers in the nineteenth century). This is the only description that has them eating flesh or at least cutting off areas of an animal's body (see Southey 134-35).

In his 1565 *History of the New World*, Girolamo Benzoni related that on the eastern coast of Costa Rica, the numerous bats tormented his party more than anywhere else south of them. He is obviously referring to large bats by their number and their fluttering of wings in his face. In Panama, for example, they bit his toes while sleeping, so delicately, that he never felt it. "But in this place, they have never bitten me without my feeling it, and suffering pain for two or three hours after. Sometimes they fluttered their wings about my face; and if I kept my stockings on, they would bite my hands; wherefore, having no other remedy, I used always to keep bandages where I slept, and as soon as I felt myself pecked, I bound up the wound; and thus they healed in three or four days without any more ado" (Benzoni 142). He held, therefore, that they were not dangerous.

Ulisse Aldrovandi's 1599 *Ornithologiae* is an interesting development, for he passed on sensational stories while at the same time distancing himself from them. He thereby made the bats very perilous. In the hot regions of the world, like India, he wrote, bats are reported to be savage. They are the size of doves and "attack the faces of people, by striking and wounding in such a way that they sometimes mutilate noses or ears or other parts" (579). We are told that Martire d'Anghiera described that bats "equaling our doves, as if incited by furies, attack people early in the evening and with their dreadful and stinking bite drive them nearly to madness." The inhabitants have been forced to flee as if confronted by Harpies and the Stymphalides birds. Finally, he related that Pompilius Azalius tells of a huge bat in the East Indies which prowls for prey and "often knocks to the ground people who are crossing that area, having been beaten by its wings, and that it even kills many" (579). Something more nuanced is happening in this narrative other than the provocative stories it contains—the bats are now placed outside of South and Central America.

Jacobus Bontius also set them beyond America. After confusing the Sunda flying lemur with a bat, he returned in 1642 (in *Historiae Naturalis et Medicae*) to the tropes to which we have become accustomed, yet with less drama: in the groves of Java, he narrated, are bats the size of doves which sometimes will fly into open windows, bite bare feet, and suck out a great quantity of blood, but they generate more fear than danger (Bontius 68-70). In other words, again they are not really deadly. And the next source once more disagrees.

Pison in his 1658 *De Indiae utriusque re naturali et medica*, wrote poetically that the bat "is a bipedal . . . animal of certainly marvelous configuration, a quadruped, walking not with its feet, flying not with [feathered] wings, seeing without light, blind in the light, it uses light outside the light, in the light it goes without light, a bird with teeth, without a beak, with breasts, with milk, carrying its young even during flight. They seek out every type of animal, and they take away their blood. Moreover . . . there is a certain type of bats which in the night attacks the bare feet of people sleeping: and they wound them with their beak for the sake of sucking out the human blood; . . . such a large amount of blood flows from the poisonous bite that only with difficulty can it be stopped: and so clearly does it bring to those sleeping a danger to life" (Pison 68-70).

Following Pison in 1667 was another English language treatise that mentions the vampire bat. It was authored by George Warren and was about his experience in Surinam (*An Impartial Description*. He wrote, "The *Bats* are found to be not a little noxious both to Men and Beasts, in the night drawing away their Blood, and so easily, that the loss is not perceivable, 'till it be past prevention, which (if I was not misinform'd) has forc'd several people to forsake their Dwellings, to save that little blood they had, which would have been otherwise sucked out. Some seem as big as Pigeons in their flight" (Warren 21-22).

Thus in the sixteenth and seventeenth centuries, many commentators have emphasized that these bats are capable of taking a human life if their bites are not treated. But a few have dismissed them as little more than nuisances. Some have even seen them rather like pranksters, healing a dying man, or biting off roosters' combs and pigs' nipples. The bite is generally painless and unnoticed by a sleeper, until blood shed during the night alerts one upon awakening, if one wakes at all, what has happened.

Descriptions of the bat are not plentiful. From the beginning, it is as large as a medium-sized bird—a pigeon or dove. Some have likened the bats to large mythological monsters—Stymphalian Birds or Harpies, driven forth as if by Furies. A few have placed them in the East Indies, but most describe them only in terms of the "New World." Their wings, when mentioned, are frightening, flapping around in one's face, or used for aggressive purposes, beating people and probably even helping to disfigure a victim from time to time.

The Eighteenth Century: Europe

The century starts with another leap forward for the bat. In 1731, Joseph Gumilla published a report, *El Orinoco ilustrado*, in which he wrote, "And who would believe or dare to speak, if it were not so evident and bloody and dreadful, of the nocturnal plague of bats. There are two types: some are as large as those we see in Spain, the others are so large that they measure some 3 ½ feet from wing to wing; both hunt all night long, in order to drink blood" (406). He repeated the trope of nocturnal bites on those who are exposed sleeping, even one's forehead. He continued, "if by misfortune a vein is opened, which happens not infrequently, they slip from dream to death, so subtle is the penetration of their teeth, while their wings softly beat the air to cool and lull the sleeper, whose life, they intend to take" (406).[44] We have now a large hunter that intends to kill, using its expansive wings to lull its victim into utter helplessness. Plus there are two bloodsuckers.

It is not clear whence he is pulling the flapping of the wings, no longer as aggressively dangerous, but as sedating, even entrancing, the sleeping victim (is it classical in origin like the story of Hypnos or the seductive song of the Sirens, or is it due to the overwhelming need of fanning oneself in the tropics, or from native folklore?), but its influence on the nineteenth century should not be underestimated. And he is giving wing measurements, which enhances the bat's size, for the span of a European dove's wings is substantially less (about 18 to 22 inches).

Charles Marie de la Condamine made a quick allusion to the situation in 1745, in his *Relation abrégée d'un voyage*, but one that included a phrase which proved to be very popular with later writers: "Bats which suck the blood of horses, mules, and even humans when they do not protect themselves by sleeping in the shelter of a house are a plague common to most of the hot countries of America. They are of monstrous size [*monstrueuses pour la grosseur*]; at Borja and in several other places they have entirely destroyed the large cattle that missionaries have introduced and were just beginning to multiply" (171).

Jorge Juan y Santacilia and Antonio de Ulloa wrote in their 1748 *Relación histórica*, that the blood loss was so great from their bites, that although one was near death one could not respond unless one woke up in time, because one did not feel it and the bats "create with their wings a breeze, the refreshment from which brings an insensitivity to the evil that is happening" (81).

Then in 1758 a fateful move was made: Carl Linnaeus, known as the father of modern taxonomy, in his *Systema Naturae*, identified the large or Malayan flying fox by the name "Vampyrus" (31). Today it is known as the *Pteropus vampyrus*.

Modern eyewitness reports of animated corpses, related by credible Europeans and Britons, had been filtering into intellectual circles in the West since 1645. Interestingly, in 1693, Pierre des Noyers, in an untitled piece, said the name of these creatures in Latin was Striges, the cannibalistic birds probably

---

[44] Leslie Klinger, in *The New Annotated Dracula*, in a bizarre pseudo-scientific move, adapts this myth of the wings for his readers. "Scientists are quite interested in the bat's saliva, which numbs the victim's skin and lulls the victim to sleep while preventing the blood from clotting" (232).

styled on bats, that we noted before (62-69). In 1725, a report about one Peter Plogojowitz, in Austrian Serbia, was filed to the Austrian court, which first used the word vampire in a Western European text (see Barber 5-9). This undead body was going around the village, lying on top of people in their sleep, throttling them, drinking their blood, and leaving them for dead. Nine had indeed died before he was exhumed, staked, and his body committed to the flames. "Vampire" was not yet presented in a modern Western language, but introduced as the Serbian and, incidentally, Latin word instead: *vampiri*.

It was seven years later, in 1732, that the term appeared as the German word *Vampyr*. The report in which it appeared was widely translated, so the term entered deeply into popular culture. It concerned Arnont Paule also in Austrian Serbia.[45] Within a month of his demise, four deaths had been attributed to him and thus his body suffered the same fate as Plogojowitz. But he also was said to have sucked the blood of livestock, which were then eaten, so all the recent corpses had to be disinterred to see if they were vampires as well. A good number were found to be so, since their bodies were full of blood and not decomposed.

The phenomenon that followed this report in Europe and the Anglophone world, has been called "vampiromania."[46] Voltaire (in the article "Vampires" in *A Philosophical Dictionary*) would write later "Nothing was spoken of but vampires, from 1730 to 1735; they were laid in wait for, their hearts torn out and burned. They resembled the ancient martyrs—the more they were burned, the more they abounded" (371-372). Part of the fascination, alluded to indirectly by Voltaire, was that the vampire was becoming something of an inversion of Christ, which received its high point in the nineteenth century with *Dracula*: the latter, innocent of any sin, shed his blood, rose from the dead at dawn, and ascended into heaven so that his followers may live; the vampire, arisen from the grave at dusk, and descending back into it at dawn, shed and drank the blood of the innocent so it might live. It was becoming an "anti-Christ."[47]

So it was only twenty-six years after Paule, that this term, which had first been applied to a monster, was used for a bat. Sometimes it was called a "vampire bat;" more often it was known simply as a "vampire."

Georges-Louis Leclerc, Comte de Buffon in his 1763 *Histoire Naturelle* (volume 10) picked up where Linnaeus left off and created another part of the myth that would last, sporadically, into the nineteenth century: the tongue was the agent that drew the blood (Buffon 55-65; 70-72). He called Linnaeus' Malayan flying fox a "roussette" and compared it to what he named the New World "vampyre," which today is known as the *Vampyrum spectrum* or "Linnaeus' false vampire bat (55-65)."[48] Buffon transferred the name from Southeast Asia to the New World because the Western bat was the one reputed to suck the blood of humans and animals whereas the flying fox was not. Nonetheless they

---

[45] See Barber 15-20; Frayling 22-23.
[46] See Dimic, "Vampiromania in the Eighteenth Century." Nick Groom, in *The Vampire: A New History*, writes that debates about vampires "detonated" across Europe (36).
[47] Leatherdale (190) has a list as well although it stretches the comparisons and focuses only on Dracula.
[48] Linnaeus is often attributed with the name *Vampyrum spectrum*, hence the South and Central American bat being known today as Linnaeus' false vampire bat. In actual fact, Linnaeus (1758, 31) named it *Vespertilio spectrum*. It appears that the name *Vampyrum* was first affixed to this bat in Rafinesque's 1815 *Analyse de la nature* (54).

shared enough characteristics for him to consider treating them together and simply because there were no reports of the first sucking blood, this was no proof it did not.

So he asked himself, in the absence of a specimen, how a vampire could possibly drink the blood of a victim without waking one up—especially animals that sleep lighter than human beings do. A bite would awaken one, a scratch from a nail would too. But not a tongue. A careful drawing of the lengthy tongue of a roussette, might set things straight he thought. "[T]his tongue is pointed and bristled with hard, very fine and very sharp papillae which are directed backward; these points which are very thin are able to insinuate themselves into the pores of the skin, enlarge them, and penetrate enough in order that the blood acquiesces to the constant suction of the tongue" (Buffon 71). Yet Buffon was very careful to make sure his readers knew this to be pure conjecture.

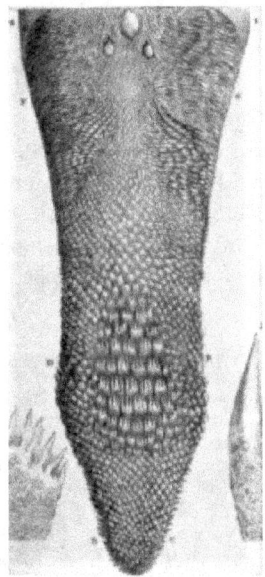

Illustration (Plate 15) of the tongue in Buffon's *Histoire Naturelle*.

He also added that the vampire's "aspect," compared to the other two "is as hideous as that of the ugliest bats; the head is unshapely, and the ears large, very open, and very straight; its nose is disfigured; its nostrils resemble a funnel, and have a membrane at the top, which rises up in the form of a sharp horn, or cock's comb, and greatly heightens the deformity of its face" (Buffon 57-58). So we have a hideously ugly bat that might be able to lay its tongue across the surface of the skin and pull blood from its pores. He describes the relative sizes this way: the vampire, when it flies, seems to be of the size of the pigeon; the roussette, the size of a large hen. Thus the vampire is large, but not the largest.

And then there was Phillippe Fermin who in the 1769 *Description Générale, historique, géographique et physique de la colonie de Surinam* followed the normal tropes. He described the bat as "monstrous" and "very dangerous, because of the damage it can do: for it sucks the blood of horses, and even that of men, if it finds them asleep" (Fermin 139-140).

Closing this European section of our study, we will provide two accounts, chosen rather arbitrarily, to show the state of things remained in a certain amount of flux at the century's end. E. A. W. Zimmermann, in *Geographische Geschichte des Menschen und der vierfüssigen Thiere* (1780), calls the Malayan flying fox the proper "bloodsucker," agreeing with Linnaeus, and conjectures that in the New World, there may be two species, following Gumilla. He calls the two, "undetermined animals." The first is likely the same as the flying fox and he calls it the large bloodsucker; the second is what he names the small bloodsucker (see Zimmermann 62-66; 408-409). There is, therefore, still a confusion in identifying the extent of the range the vampire inhabits and the number of species which belong under this heading.

Then there is Martin Dobrizhoffer in his 1784 *Historia de Abiponibus Equestri*. He limits his comments mainly to horses (1.268), but he does note the bats attack human bodies as well (3.378). He says they are large in number and size, and not only molest but injure the horses. "They sit upon the horse, and whilst they wound his back with their bills, create a gentle breeze by the continual motion of their wings, lulled by which the horse makes no resistance, and [allows] his blood to be sucked by the bat. The wound that remains, unless it be sprinkled with hot ashes, soon swells, and by degrees becomes ulcerated, which clearly proves that the bats are in some measure venomous" (1.268). So the exact nature of the seductive flapping of the wings was still open. When talking of human beings the consensus has been that the bat draws the sleeper into an ever deeper slumber; here with horses, however, it creates such a pleasant breeze that a conscious animal was willing to part with its blood in exchange for it. One is nonvolitional; the other involves consent.

The Eighteenth Century: England & Summation

Turning to England, the bat also commanded a lot of attention. In 1751 George Edwards's *A Natural History of Birds* quoted Condamine with a nice translation of its size: some were, he wrote, "of a monstrous Bigness" (4: 201). Twenty years later in his *Synopsis of Quadrupeds*, Thomas Pennant had almost all the lurid details for the bats at the time. "These monsters inhabit Guinea, Madagascar, and all the islands from thence, to the remotest in the Indian ocean. . . . Many are of an enormous size . . . [T]heir cry is dreadfull; their smell rank; their bite, resistance and fierceness great when taken. . . . Linnaeus gives this species the title of Vampyre, conjecturing it to be the kind which draws blood from people in their sleep. M. de Buffon denies it, ascribing that faculty to a species only found in S. America: but there is reason to imagine, that this thirst after blood is not confined to the bats of one continent, nor to one species . . . The Bat is so dexterous a bleeder as to insinuate its aculeated tongue into a vein, without being perceived, and then suck the blood till it is satiated; all the while fanning with its wings, and agitating the air, in that hot climate, in so pleasing a manner, as to fling the sufferer into a still sounder sleep" (361-362). Now the tongue enters a vein and does not lie simply upon the surface of the skin; it is no longer conjecture, but fact. Pennant was widely quoted in English naturalist studies and encyclopedia articles into the 1840s especially his phrases "so dexterous a bleeder" and "its aculeated tongue," but often without attribution.

Most influential on the nineteenth century, in the Anglophone world, was the personal account of John Gabriel Stedman (*Narrative, of a Five Years' Expedition*) published in 1795. This was excerpted or fully quoted into the twentieth century.[49] He described how he woke from a sound sleep with blood and gore all over, and ran to the military surgeon, who estimated a blood loss of "at least twelve or fourteen ounces." It was caused by "the vampire or spectre of Guiana," which was a bat "of a monstrous size" (142). He goes on to give his readers some background.

"Knowing by instinct that the person they intend to attack is in a sound slumber, they generally alight near the feet, where, while the creature continues fanning with his enormous wings, which keeps one cool, he bites a piece out of the tip of the great toe, so very small indeed that the head of a pin could scarcely be received into the wound, which is consequently not painful; yet through this orifice he continues to suck the blood, until he is obliged to disgorge. He then begins again, and thus continues sucking and disgorging till he is scarcely able to fly, and the sufferer has often been known to sleep from time into eternity" (Stedman 142-143). In a rather grotesque note later, he says: "Mr. Reynsdorp . . . took me in his sail barge for change of air to . . . one of his own coffee estates; where I saw a white man who had lately lost both his eyes in one night by the bats, or vampires, as they are called" (205).

Illustration from Steadman's book: "The Vampire or Spectre of Guiana"

So the bat in the eighteenth century, to compile the more colorful descriptions, is no longer just deadly, it is become sinister. It is not indigenous simply to Latin America but spreads out into the so-called East Indies. It is enormous. It has an insatiable thirst for blood, so much so it can fell a cow or horse weighing over half a ton. Not only is its bite indiscernible, but it now fans its victim with its gigantic wings to sedate one into an ever deeper sleep or to obtain consent for drawing blood. No longer does it kill as a consequence of its need for blood, but it actually seems to intend to bring about one's death.

---

[49] See Macmillan 137.

Its sucking may be due to the normal procedure of suction from the mouth, or due to the manipulation of the tongue. Stedman at last explains how it can drain victims much larger than itself of their blood: they drink until satiated, vomit it up, only to start again—like the legendary "pagan" orgies of Rome.

Indigenous Gods as Demons with Bat Wings: An Afterword

From the beginning, the effects these soldiers, naturalists, adventurers, missionaries, and physicians in South and Central America were describing, was due to the microbat *Desmodus rotundus*. It really does bite, honing in on "hot spots" where the blood flows close to the surface of the skin; its bite is rarely felt, unless the bat is young; it feeds on blood; blood does flow from the wound after the bat has moved on. Why was this not identified from the very beginning?

One reason is that this small bat is hard to detect in action and it is fast and agile in escape if its victim wakes. Another is that the largest bat in the region, the spectral vampire, is visibly numerous, it sometimes gets caught in enclosed spaces with humans or their animals therein where it flies around excitedly searching for a way out; it can brush against people, flutter about in their faces, and bite if put on the defensive, simulating an attack. So it is not outlandish to place the blame on them.

Yet more is going on. From America the misidentification fans out to the so-called Old World and its bats, where no sanguivorous activity has ever been witnessed. Why? It seems we have to return to where we started. Partly it is European mythology, as we have seen; partly it is the bestiary tradition that exaggerates the weird, based on a long history of describing exotica outside Western civilizations. More responsibility, however, will have to go to the tendency to imagine what is foreign and alien as demonic.

The early mainstream church wasted little time transforming the gods of the Hebrews' enemies—the so-called false gods and idols—into devils, and casting those of the Roman Empire the same way. This, of course, passed into Christian iconography. As Jeffrey Burton Russell writes, "medieval demons show traces of the leg wings of Hermes Psychopompos; the serpents associated with the Gorgons, Typhon, and Hydra; the goat-like or donkey-like features associated with Dionysos, Pan, the satyrs, and Charun; and the beaked nose, grimacing lips, and dark blue hue of Charun, as well as the weapon he carried" (170-172). He especially singles out Pan, whose influence, he says, was "enormous" (126). All of these classical mythic creatures now function as a pantheon of demons from which the figure of the devil can be drawn.

So it is little surprise that European imperialists cast the "heathen gods" in the New and Old Worlds as devils. At first some could take native reverence of their gods as acts of ignorance, but if conversion was resisted, it became deliberate devil worship. Take a description by Ludovico di Varthema in 1510 about his visit to Calicut (Kozhikode) in 1505. It had only been "discovered" by da Gama in 1498. He describes the chapel of the king where he "worships the devil."

Everything, in fact, highlights its Satanic and hellish character, says Partha Mitter, in *Much Maligned Monsters* (17-18). "In the midst of this chapel there is a devil made of metal, placed in a seat also made of metal. The said devil has . . . four horns and four teeth, with a very large mouth, nose, and most terrible eyes. The hands are made like those of a flesh-hook, and the feet like those of a cock; so that he is a fearful object to behold. All the pictures around the said chapel are those of devils, and on each side of it there is a Sathanas [a higher god=Satan] seated in a seat, which seat is placed in a flame of fire, wherein are a great number of souls . . . And the said Sathanas holds a soul in his mouth with the right hand, and with the other seizes a soul under the waist" (*The Travels of Ludovico di Varthema*, 1510, 137-138). This depiction of Sathanas might as well be drawn from Coppo di Marcovaldo's mosaic of hell at the Baptistery of Saint John in Florence, installed around 1301.

As far as I can tell Europeans never took such liberties as to add bat wings to the so-called pagan or demonic idols in India. Virtually everything else about Satan was. Affixing bat wings to indigenous deities was likeliest with regard to South and Central America since this is the location of the actual vampire bats, and hence of true "bat attacks." Bats also played an important role in some of the native cultures as art and in stories. Noteworthy as well was the fact that the bat was used in a few cultures in association with human sacrifice, like the Mochica in Peru.[50] A bat could be human-sized, holding a human head in its hand.

Artifact of the Moche culture, Lima, Peru Museo Larco[51]

---

[50] See David E. Brown 87-92; Elizabeth Benson 1991.
[51] Described in this catalogue as a "vampire demon or slayer bat;" named "Decapitator of the Dark and Deep World." https://www.museolarco.org/catalogo/ficha.php?id=11940

So consider the European attitude in the following three illustrations. An interesting woodcut can be found in Pedro Cieza de León's *Peruvian Chronicle*, first published in 1553 (Chapter 19). Satan appears with bat wings in the midst of these ceremonies on a pedestal as a god. He is said to be in the form of a native, thus human size. There are two different illustrations of the same thing in the 1553 edition (page 48) and the 1554 one (page 22).

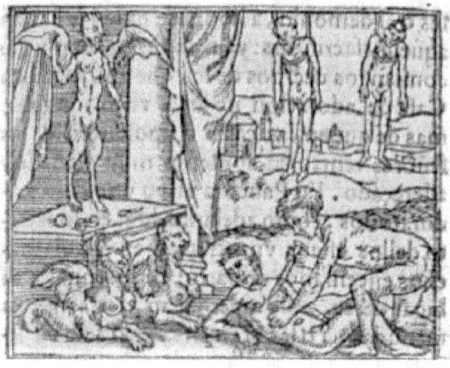

"On the rites and sacrifices which the Indians perform: and what kind of cannibals these butchers are."

We read the following in the 1553 edition: "Very great is the dominion that the devil, enemy of the human race, allowed by God to have over this people, by reason of their sins, and often is he visibly amongst them. . . . On the top of the platform they fastened the Indians whom they took in war by the shoulders, and cut out their hearts, which they offered to their gods or to the devil, in whose honour they made these sacrifices. . . . After they have performed these and other superstitious rites, the devil comes. They relate that he appears in the form of an Indian, with very bright eyes, and gives replies to the priests or ministers, to questions they ask him, concerning what they wish to know" (71-72).

The fourth illustration can be found in Alain Manesson Mallet's 1663 *Description de l'Univers*, of the Aztec god, Huitzilopochtli, a sun and war god (5: 311). The depiction is almost completely fabricated. It has many of the features expected by Europeans for the devil, including the bat wings, but little that would be recognizable to the Aztecs. Note the relative size.

There is little that is sensational, on the other hand, about the copy, except the mention of human sacrifice. The horror is mostly in the illustration. "[Mexicans] were formerly among the most idolatrous and superstitious of all the peoples of the world. . . . They used to have a number of . . . idols, the more remarkable of which are represented here as they depicted them. During certain ceremonies they sacrificed in a day a large quantity of people, free or slave" (5: 310).

Thus for the Old World Christians to look to the large and the ugly for the bleeding injuries on their Christian bodies inflicted by New World bats and to suppose that the same sanguivorous behavior extended to all such bats in the idolatrous Old World makes sense in this all-too-often overlooked religious worldview.

Conclusion

The first one to identify the true vampire was Felix de Azara in his 1801 *Essais sur l'histoire naturelle* (273-276), but his findings were ignored. It was Darwin's account, published in 1839, that took hold and began to change the field. But there were still a large number of naturalists and journalists that continued to identify the vampire with a large bat.

In the next two chapters I shall try, first from more a literary perspective, second from more a naturalist one, to demonstrate that the large vampire bat abounded during the nineteenth century as well. So Stoker was surrounded by sources where he could have picked up the idea. The only mystery is where, and that secret died with him. *Dracula*, then, represents the high point when a vampire monster could turn into a bat and it be recognized as a true vampire bat. If a vampire monster turns into one today, it is technically *sui generis*, unique unto itself. It is a vampire monster as a bat, not a vampire bat. The authentic vampire bat today is the microbat as will be demonstrated in the following chapters.

Much has been made of the fact that Stoker returned to the folklore vampire monster in his construction of Dracula. It is time now to recognize that he also dipped into a distinctively Western folklore for the bat as well.

Works cited

Aldrovandi, Ulisse. *Ornithologiae hoc est De auibus historiae libri 12*. Bononiae: Franciscum de Franciscis Senensem, 1599.

Azara, Felix de. *Essais sur l'histoire naturelle des quadrupèdes de la province du Paraguay*. 2. Paris: Charles Pogens, 1801.

Barber, Paul. *Vampires, Burial, and Death: Folklore and Reality*. New Haven: Yale University Press, 1988.

Basil. *Commentary on the Prophet Isaiah*. Trans. Nikolai A. Lipatov. Mandelbachtal: Edition Cicero, 2001.

Benson, Elizabeth P. "Bats in South American Folklore and Ancient Art." *BATS Magazine* 9: 1 (Spring 1991), 7-10.

Benzoni, Girolamo. *History of the New World*. Trans. W. H. Smyth. London: The Hakluyt acaSociety, 1857.v

Bontius, Jacobus. *Historiae Naturalis et Medicae. De Indiae utriusque re naturali et medica*. Guglielmo Pison. Amstelodami: Ludovicum et Danielem Elzevirios,1658.

Brown, David E. *Vampiro: The Vampire Bat in Fact and Fantasy*. Silver City: High-Lonesome Books, 1994.

Buffon, Georges-Louis Leclerc, Comte de. *Histoire Naturelle, générale et particulière, avec la description du Cabinet du Roi*. X. Paris: Imprimerie Royale, 1763.

Bunson, Matthew. *The Vampire Encyclopedia*. New York: Crown Trade Paperbacks, 1993.

Cabeza de Vaca, Álvar Núñez. "The Commentaries of Alvar Nuñez Cabeza de Vaca." *The Conquest of the River Plate (1535-1555)*. Trans. Luis L. Dominguez. London: Hakluyt Society, 1891.

Cassell's Popular Natural History. 1. London: Cassell, Petter & Galpin, 1865.

Cieza de León, Pedro. *Crónicas del Peru* 1. Sevilla: Martin de Montesdoca, 1553.

Cieza de León, Pedro. *The Travels of Pedro de Cieza de León, AD 1532-50, Contained in the First Part of His Chronicle of Peru*. Trans. by Clements R. Markham. London: Hakluyt Society, 1883.

Condamine, Charles Marie de la. *Relation abrégée d'un voyage fait dans l'interieur de l'Amérique méridionale*. Paris: Veuve Pessot, 1745.

Copper, Basil. *The Vampire in Legend and Fact*. New York: Citadel Press Book 1973.

Crawford, Heide. *The Origins of the Literary Vampire*. Lanham: Rowman & Littlefield, 2016.

Dante, *The Inferno of Dante Alighieri*. Ed. Israel Gollancz. London: J. M. Dent, 1904.

Dimic, Milan V. "Vampiromania in the Eighteenth Century: The Other Side of Enlightenment." *Man and Nature/L'Homme et la nature: Proceedings of the Canadian Society for Eighteenth-Century Studies*. 3. Ed. R. J. Merrett. Edmonston, 1984. 1-22.

Ditmars, Raymond Lee; Greenhall, Arthur M. "The Vampire Bat: A Presentation of Undescribed Habits and Review of Its History." *Zoologia: Scientific Contributions of the New York Zoological Society* 19: 2 (April 3, 1935), 53-76.

Dobrizhoffer, Martin. *Historia de Abiponibus Equestri, Bellicosaque Paraquariae Natione.* 3. Vienna: Josephi Nob. de Kurzbek, 1784.

Donahue, Michelle Z. "Turning Vampire Myths Upside Down (or Right Side Up)." *BATS Magazine* 3 (2016), 8-11.

Edwards, George. *A Natural History of Birds* 4. London: College of Physicians, 1751.

Fermin, Phillippe. *Description générale, historique, géographique et physique de la colonie de Surinam* 2. Amsterdam: E. van Harrevelt, 1769.

Fernández de Oviedo y Valdés, Gonzalo. *Sumario de historia natural o De la natural Historia de las Indias.* Toledo: For the author, 1526.

Frayling, Christopher. 1991. *Vampyres: Lord Byron to Count Dracula.* London: Faber and Faber, 1991.

Furnseth, Andrew. "The Open Shop." *The American Photo-Engraver* 13: 5 (April 1921), 204-210.

Groom, Nick. *The Vampire: A New History.* New Haven: Yale University Press, 2018.

Gumilla, Joseph. *El Orinoco ilustrado, y defendido: historia natural, civil, y geográfica de este gran río y de sus caudalosas vertientes.* Madrid: Manuel Fernandez, 1745.

Ito, Fernanda, Enrico Bernard and Richard A. Torres. "What is for Dinner? First Report of Human Blood in the Diet of the Hairy-Legged Vampire Bat *Diphylla ecaudata.*" *Acta Chiropterologica* 18: 2 (December 2016), 509-515.

Leatherdale, Clive. *Dracula: the novel & the legend: a study of Bram Stoker's gothic masterpiece.* 3rd edition. Westcliff-on-Sea: Desert Island Books, 2001.

Lee, Sarah. *Anecdotes of the Habits and Instincts of Animals.* London: Griffith, Faran, Okeden, & Welch, 1852.

Linnaeus, Carl. *Systema Naturae.* 10th ed. 1. Stockholm: Salvius, 1758.

Macmillan, Hugh. *Lessons from Life (Animal and Human).* New York: Fleming H. Revell, 1914.

MacNally, Raymond and Radu Florescu. "Vampirism: Old World Folklore." *The Vampire in Slavic Cultures.* Ed. Thomas J. Garza. San Diego: University Readers, 2009. 41-52.

Mallet, Alain Manesson. *Description de l'universe.* 5. Paris: Denys Thierry, 1683.

Martire d'Anghiera, Pietro. *De Orbe Novo: The Eight Decades of Peter Martyr D'Anghera.* 2 vols. Trans. Francis Augustus MacNutt. New York: The Knickerbocker Press, 1963.

Martyr of Angleria, Peter. "The Decades of the Newe Worlde or West Indies." Trans. Richard Eden. London: Guilhelmi Powell, 1555. *The First Three English Books on America.* Ed. Edward Arber. Birmingham: s.n., 1885.

Melton, J. Gordon. *The Vampire Book: The Encyclopedia of the Undead.* 3. Canton, Michigan: Visible Ink Press, 2011.

Miller, Elizabeth. "Bats, Vampires & Dracula." *The Night Flyer: News for the Friends of Florida's Bats* 3: 4 (Fall 1998). www.ucs.mun.ca/~emiller/bats_vamp_drac.html.

Miller, Elizabeth. *A Dracula Handbook.* s.l.: Xlibris, 2005.

Miller, Elizabeth. *Dracula: Sense and Nonsense.* Westcliff-on-Sea: Desert Island Books, 2000.

Miller, Elizabeth. "Getting to Know the Un-Dead: Bram Stoker, Vampires and Dracula." *Vampires, Myths and Metaphors of Enduring Evil.* Ed. Peter Day. Amsterdam: Rodopi Press, 2006. 3-19.

Mitter, Partha. *Much Maligned Monsters: History of European Reactions to Indian Art.* Oxford: Clarendon Press, 1977.

Noyers, Pierre des. [Untitled]. *Mercure Gallant.* May 1693. 62-69.

Oinas, Felix. "East European Vampires." *The Vampire: A Casebook.* Ed. Alan Dundes. Madison: University of Wisconsin Press, 1998. 47-56.

Oliphant, Samuel Grant. "The Story of the Strix: Ancient." *Transactions and Proceedings of the American Philological Association* 44 (1913), 133-149.

Pennant, Thomas. *Synopsis of Quadrupeds.* Chester: J. Monk, 1771.

Perkowski, Jan. *Vampires of the Slavs*. Cambridge, Mass: Slavika Publishers, 1976.
Perkowski, Jan Louis. *Vampire Lore from the Writings of Jan Louis Perkowski*. Bloomington: Slavika Publishers, 2006.
Pison, Guglielmo. *De Indiae utriusque re naturali et medica*. Amstelodami: Ludovicum et Danielem Elzevirios, 1658.
Pseudo-Orpheus. *The Orphic Argonautica*. Trans. Jason Colavito. s.l.: Lulu, 2011.
Rafinesque, C. S. *Analyse de la nature, ou tableau de l'univers et des corps organisés*. Palerme: Jean Barravecchia, 1815.
Russell, Jeffrey Burton. *The Devil: Perceptions of Evil from Antiquity to Primitive Christianity*. Ithaca: Cornell University Press, 1977.
Santacilia, Jorge Juan y and Antonio de Ulloa. *Relación histórica del viaje hecho de orden de su Majestad a la América Meridional*. 1.1. Madrid: Antonio Marin, 1748.
Schomburgk, Richard. *Travels in British Guiana, 1840-1844*. 1. Ed. Walter E. Roth. Georgetown: The "Daily Chronicle" Office, 1922 [1847].
Schutt, Bill. *Dark Banquet: Blood and the Curious Lives of Blood-Feeding Creatures*. New York: Three Rivers Press, 2008.
Skal, David J. *Vampires: Encounters with the Undead*. New York: Black Dog & Leventhal, 2001.
Skal, David J. *V is for Vampire: The A-Z Guide to Everything Undead*. New York: Plume, 1996.
Southey, Robert. *History of Brazil*. 1. London: Longman, Hurst, Rees, and Orme, 1810.
Stedman, John. *Narrative, of a Five Years' Expedition, Against the Revolted Negroes of Surinam, in Guiana, on the Wild Coast of South America; from the Year 1772, to 1777: Elucidating the History of that Country, and Describing Its Productions, Viz. Quadrupedes, Birds, Fishes, Reptiles, Trees, Shrubs, Fruits, & Roots; with an Account of the Indians of Guiana, & Negroes of Guinea* 2. London: J. Johnson and J. Edwards, 1796.
Stoker, Bram. *Dracula: A Norton Critical Edition*. Eds. Nina Auerbach and David J. Skal. London: W. W. Norton & Co., 1997.
Stoker, Bram. *Dracula. Scholar's Annotated Edition*. Ed. Christopher David. 2015.
Stoker, Bram. *Bram Stoker's Notes for Dracula: A Facsimile Edition*. Eds. Robert Eighteen-Bisang and Elizabeth Miller. Jefferson, NC: McFarland, 2008.
Stoker, Bram. *The New Annotated Dracula*. Ed. Leslie S. Klinger. New York: W. W. Norton & Co, 2008.
Stoker, Bram; *Dracula Unearthed*. Ed. Clive Leatherdale. Westcliff-on-Sea: Desert Island Books, 1988.
Stoker, Bram. *The Annotated Dracula*. Ed. Leonard Woolf. New York: Ballentine Books, 1975.
Tertullian. *Apologeticus. Ante-Nicene Christian Library* 11. Eds. Alexander Roberts and James Donaldson. Edinburgh: T. & T. Clark, 1869.
Varthema, Ludovico di. *The Travels of Ludovico di Varthema in Egypt, Syria, Arabia Deserta and Arabia Felix, in Persia, India, and Ethiopia, A.D. 1503 to 1508*. Trans. John Winter Jones. London: Hakluyt Society, 1863.
Voltaire. "Vampires." *A Philosophical Dictionary: From the French of M. de Voltaire*. Vol. II. Trans. Abner Kneeland. Boston: J. Q. Adams, 1836. 371-372.
Warren, George. *An Impartial Description of Surinam upon the Continent of Guiana in America*. London: William Godbid, 1667.
Zimmermann, E. A. W. *Geographische Geschichte des Menschen und der vierfüssigen Thiere*. Leipzig: Weygandschen Buchhandlung, 1780.

II.

The Vampire Bat and Monster

Francisco José de Goya y Lucientes
"El Sueño de la razón produce monstruos"
(The sleep of reason brings forth monsters)
from *Los Caprichos*, number 43

"Vampire spectre (*Vampyrus spectrum*) suçant le sang d'une jeune femme endormie."
(A vampire spectre sucking the blood of a young woman asleep)
In J. Regade's *La création naturelle et les êtres vivants: histoire générale du monde terrestre*
(1887), 705.

4.
"Blood Suckers Most Cruel:"
The Vampire and the Bat
in and before *Dracula*

Introduction

Study of the vampire as an artifact of popular, and even of high, culture in the nineteenth century is, in several ways, arrested.[52] It has its topoi, its familiar places, especially concerning vampires and bats, to which researchers regularly return and assume the validity of their consensus. I want, in this paper, to introduce three areas that need careful reconsideration. I will pose them as questions. Does the nineteenth century use the word "vampire" the way we use it today or do we project our ideas back on to it? How did the nineteenth century understand the vampire bat? Was it the microbat we designate today or was it something else entirely? Finally, how did it work out the relationship between the vampire monster and the vampire bat? Were the two commonly conflated, but awaited Bram Stoker's *Dracula* before they could transform into each other? Or was a blurring between them relatively rare, with mutual metamorphosis, equally uncommon, nonetheless preceding the book?

The Bat in *Dracula*

The vampire is a complex shapeshifter in Bram Stoker's *Dracula* (1897). There are four types in evidence: two are dispersive—to particulate matter and to vapor; two are concrete—to a wolf and, of course, to a bat.

The bat is the primary way Dracula approaches Lucy and may be the predominant way he feeds on her as well. There are ten mentions of a large bat in the context of Lucy, several times emphasizing the flapping, scratching, buffeting, and striking of its wings against the window, which at times appear to have an almost hypnotic effect (8.89-90; 9.103; 12.148-49). One reference is by Quincey Morris where he compares Lucy's precipitous decline with that of a horse he saw in the plains of South America drained of its blood "from those big bats that they call vampires." She dies with a great bat circling around outside.

Now part of the Pampas region referred to by Morris is within the range of the *Desmodus rotundus*, the real vampire bat, and therefore would be associated with bat attacks. But as Morris makes clear, the vampire bat in question is the large mythic one, which has no presence there. I therefore have no idea why Stoker might have chosen this area; he probably found reference to bat attacks in a travelogue. The large bat, by the way, was placed there in Thomas Carlyle's 1843 study "Dr. Francia" (564). and in Oliver Wendell Holmes' 1865 "Farewell to Agassiz" (584). Perhaps he got it from one of them.

---

[52] A shorter version of this chapter appeared as an article in *Athens Journal of Humanities and Arts* 6: 2 (2019), 107-132.

Afterward, disappearances of children are reported; they are found alive, but they have marks on their throats. Van Helsing prepares for his revelation that the postmortem Lucy is responsible by reminding his audience of vampire slayers about nocturnal bats that "open the veins of cattle and horses and suck dry their veins" and others which flit down on sleeping sailors and take their lives (14.179). The attending physician of one of the victims conjectures the child was bitten by a bat: "Out of so many harmless ones . . . there may be some wild specimen from the South of a more malignant species. Some sailor may have brought one home, and it managed to escape, or even from the Zoological Gardens a young one may have got loose, or one be bred there from a vampire" (15.182).

With the vampire Lucy dispatched, Van Helsing explains to the five that comprise the group as much information as he can about Dracula, including the fact he can appear as a bat. As discussion ensues, Quincey leaves and shortly thereafter a pistol shot rings out. Quincey had left the building and fired at a "big bat" that had perched on the window sill (18.224-25). Also, when Dracula makes his fifth metamorphosis to vapor after blood-raping Mina, a bat is seen to rise from Renfield's window. Following this, as the six pursue Dracula to his eventual demise, the fact that he can turn into a bat regularly enters into their calculations (25.312; 26.322, 328).[53]

Thus Stoker's is a large bat which drinks human blood, hovers and travels with purpose, surveils, sedates, mesmerizes, and feeds with an intention to kill. It is not called a vampire bat—just a vampire.

Scholarship and the Immense Bat

It is easy, when one is asked about the origin of a huge, deadly bat as the vampire to reference *Dracula*, but the real question is the reverse: How did Stoker pick up the notion of a gruesome bat to affix to his monster as one of several ways he can manifest himself outside the human form? Was it simply an act of imagination, of fictional innovation? Or was it more like dipping a ladle into a "cauldron of story," as J. R. R. Tolkien put it? In other words, were there already stories out there in the mix that he could draw out and combine with other elements in a novel way? Or was it ignorance or a misunderstanding? Did he misapprehend or not know various facts about the natural world and, by happy accident, fashion a fascinating tale in spite of or because of it? Or did he deliberately misrepresent something he knew to be the opposite? There is nothing mutually exclusive about some of these, but where should we place the emphasis?

At least from the 1970s, Stoker's imposing bat has presented a problem for vampire experts due to the fact that all three of the real vampire bats are small. It is only very recently that the hairy-legged bat (*Diphylla ecaudata*) has added human blood to its diet mainly of birds (see Ito, Bernard and Torres, "What is for

---

[53] Had the Icelandic version been the one originally released in England, Dracula would hardly be associated with bats. It hardly plays a role. See Bram Stoker & Vladimar Ásmundsson, *Powers of Darkness* (2017).

Dinner?" 2016), so when we refer to the vampire we still mean the common one (*Desmodus rotundus*), whose food source consists solely of mammals' blood. This "microbat" has a body about the size of an adult human's thumb, a wingspan of about 14-16 inches, and drinks up to one fluid ounce of blood in a feeding. It does not suck, but at the point of its small incision it laps up the blood. Its saliva contains an anticoagulant, called, tongue in cheek, "draculin," which inhibits the blood from clotting while it is feeding and causes bleeding to continue afterward.

So how have vampire historiographers dealt with the discrepancy? Of the four positions mentioned above, they have overwhelmingly embraced the first and the third. Elizabeth Miller was the first and probably still the only one who has faced this directly. She argued that "Stoker obviously did not know (or chose to ignore) the fact that the vampire bat is quite small," and thus could never do what is attributed to it in the book. By making it a transformation of a vampire, however, he created one "quite capable of attacking and draining humans."[54]

Others have noted it only in passing, if they mention it at all. Christopher David felt himself free to annotate a scholar's edition of *Dracula* without making a single comment on the bat. Leonard Wolf in 1975 ignored Stoker's immense vampire bat and educated the reader on the small one instead. Matthew Bunson, bordering on anachronism, did much the same, noting that Europeans named this microbat "vampire," because they were scandalized to learn it survived on blood (266). J. Gordon Melton (50-52) and Heide Crawford (50-52) recognized a long European history of vampire bats that went back to the sixteenth century but likewise treated it as if the name had always designated small ones. So too Felix Oinas (49). David Skal noted in passing that bats have had a rich place in folklore but then turned to the little vampire bat for the rest of his observations.[55] For all of them, it appears, Stoker simply made up the large bat. What mattered was not how he came up with the notion, but rather that the real vampire bat and its history was being misrepresented. This is important to bat conservation but not for the understanding of *Dracula*.

Christopher Frayling thought the origin of its size did need some explanation. He held that the ideas of a large bat and a vampire monster might have merged due to eighteenth-century theories of sexual generation and cross-breeding. "If everyone had heard of a child-calf and a child-wolf, why not a man-bat," that is, a bat with a human face (Frayling 36)? More substantively, Basil Copper diverted from his description of the small bat to note, in a single sentence, the fact that "vampire" was first attached to a large bat (48). Jan Perkowski included in his anthology Ditmars and Greenhall's significant study on the vampire bat, which introduced a short history of a large mythic vampire bat, but attached no importance to it in his enthusiasm to report on the microbat.[56] Finally,

---

[54] See Miller "Bats, Vampires & Dracula." Cf. Miller, *Dracula: Sense and Nonsense* 34; *A Dracula Handbook* 46; "Getting to Know the Un-Dead 15; *Bram Stoker's Notes for Dracula* 105 n. 220.
[55] Skal, *Vampires* 402; cf. Skal, *V is for Vampire* 19-21. In the latter Skal does reference Benzoni writing in 1565 but makes no distinction between the large bat he reports and the small vampire Skal is describing. Then he turns his attention to bats and demons as well as theatrical and film vampires and bats. It is a little strange that he does not recognize the large bat because the illustration he uses—from the 1865 *Cassell's Popular Natural History* (158-59)—features the Malagasy giant mastiff bat, called the Madagascar bat..
[56] *Vampires of the Slavs* (1976), 19-21. This may also be found in *Vampire Lore* (2006), 67-69.

Auerbach and Skal (*Dracula: A Norton Critical Edition*, 138) observed dismissively that "[n]o single vampire bat . . . is large enough to drain a horse, much less an adult woman;" for them it was a matter of fact, not of myth. So overall even if there was a tradition of linking a large bat with vampirism, it was of relative unimportance to vampire scholarship.

The goal of these professionals has been, therefore, primarily to set the record straight. The true vampire bat is small, therefore Stoker was either erring with his great bat or ignoring the little one and taking literary license. Miller, as we have seen, held, in 1998, that the size was important for the book mainly to explain the extent of blood loss in the victims ("Bats, Vampires & Dracula"). Miller has added to this its literary effect; it was an effective way "to make readers shudder" (qtd. in Donahue 10). So far as it goes, she is undoubtedly correct on both counts. Clive Leatherdale has guessed that Dracula must have been forced to conform to a "crude law of constant physical mass," so should he turn into a bat it would have to be a big one, whereas should he become an elephant, it must be a small one (*Dracula Unearthed*, 158).

Thus, there has been virtually no interest among authorities to locate an antecedent for Stoker's large bat. Miller is again an exception, but the best she has been able to do is locate a single source as a possibility (*Dracula: Sense and Nonsense* 34-35; "Getting to Know the Un-Dead" 15). She has written that since Stoker referred to Sarah Lee's 1853 book entitled *Anecdotes of Habits and Instincts of Birds* in his notes for *Dracula*, perhaps he also read her companion volume, *Anecdotes of the Habits and Instincts of Animals* (1852). There (28-30) Lee spoke of the vampire bat being of "monstrous size."

But in point of fact there is a good amount of material that connects a lust for human blood and large bats going back to the early sixteenth century. And it has not been hidden to vampire scholarship. It is much more Tolkien's image of the "cauldron of story." I noted above that Jan Perkowski in 1976 included Raymond Ditmars and Arthur Greenhall's 1935 study on the *Desmodus rotundus*, which included a short history of the mythic vampire bat, in his anthology on the vampire ("The vampire bat," 60, 70-71). In 1994, David E. Brown published his book *Vampiro* which also included brief overviews of myths surrounding the vampire bat. And in 2008 biologist Bill Schutt gave a more extensive, if still short, introduction (*Dark Banquet*, 33-39).

We can only conclude that historians, who have been so determined to reconstruct the development of the vampire myth in the West when it pertains to the monster, have given little attention to the other vampire, to the slow unfolding of the lore of the monstrous bat. The progress of this tale is equally as interesting as that of the monster. It spread quite quickly out from scientists, physicians, soldiers, explorers, missionaries, and settlers in Central and South America to the general population to become a tenacious piece of modern folklore. Long after the vampire monster was relegated to a creature of the imagination in Western Continental Europe, Britain, and the United States, belief in the mythic, dangerous vampire bat persisted—even into the twentieth century—despite Darwin's descriptions of the true one in 1839. In fact it does continue to this day, making vampire bat conservancy especially important.

The Mythic Vampire Bat in the nineteenth century

This contains a very short summary of the previous chapter; if the reader has already gone over that material, s/he can skip the opening part. For help in establishing the large bat in nineteenth-century culture, we can turn to the 1935 study on the bat by Ditmars and Greenhall ("The Vampire Bat," 70-71). They argued that when Cortez's followers returned "with tales of bloodsucking bats, founded on acquired knowledge of an actual blood-drinking creature," superstitions soon arose of such bats being in the Old World "where no sanguivorous bats have ever occurred." Early naturalists, then, working from legends and deductions from dead specimens rather than by observation, thought the "ugliest and largest bats . . . to be the vampire."

Early reports from South and Central America were no doubt a complex intermixture of experience, exaggeration, indigenous folklore and art, and sheer imagination, shaped by expectations drawn from Christianity, classical mythology, and bestiaries. Already in 1511, before Cortés sailed to the mainland, Peter Martyr d'Anghiera in his *De Orbe Novo* (1.179) wrote that bats as large as pigeons would bite them so that they became desperate and had to give way before them. In 1516 he added that they were dangerous, that rumors were that some have died from their wounds (355). Ulisse Aldrovandi in 1599 noted that in the hot regions of the world, like India, bats were reported to be savage. They are the size of doves and "attack the faces of people, by striking and wounding in such a way that they sometimes mutilate noses or ears or other parts" (579). Accounts have even surfaced, he says, of people being beaten down by their wings.

Joseph Gumilla, in *El Orinoco ilustrado* (1731), described a different function for their large wings: "if by misfortune a vein is opened, which happens not infrequently, [victims] slip from dream to death, so subtle is the penetration of their teeth, while their wings softly beat the air to cool and lull the sleeper, whose life, they intend to take" (406). In *Relation abrégée d'un voyage* (1745), Charles Marie de la Condamine described the bats as being "monstrous in size" (171), a phrase used repeatedly thereafter; it was first translated into English in 1751 as "of a monstrous Bigness" (*A Natural History of Birds* 201). Then in 1758 Carl Linnaeus in his *Systema Naturae* (31), in a fateful move, named the Malayan flying fox, a megabat with a wingspan of nearly five feet, *vampyrus*. Raymond McNally and Radu Florescu advance the ludicrous claim that Cortés himself named them vampire bats (*In Search of Dracula* 125; "Vampirism: Old World Folkore" 47).

In English, Thomas Pennant (*Synopsis of Quadrupeds*) mentioned in 1771 the vampire, which was enormous, fanning the air with its wings to create "a still sounder sleep" and "insinuat[ing] its aculeated tongue into a vein without being perceived, and then suck[ing] the blood till it is satiated (361-62)." John Gabriel Stedman in his 1796 *Narrative, of a Five Years' Expedition*, gave one of the most quoted descriptions in the nineteenth century (142-44). Therein he spoke of being bitten by a "*vampire* or *spectre* of Guiana." He described it as "a bat of monstrous size, that sucks the blood from men and cattle when they are fast asleep, even sometimes till they die." It does this by feeding to satiation, disgorging, and sucking again until it can hardly fly; it has a wingspan as wide as three feet.

The naturalist William Wood in the 1807 *Zoography*, extended the span to four feet (347-49). In 1825 Charles Waterton wrote a book (*Wanderings in South America*) that was reprinted throughout the century, describing several visits by these large "nocturnal surgeons" (11, 153, 174-79, 287-89). Always ready for a nice turn of phrase, he called them elsewhere, "sanguinary imps of night" (*Essays on natural history*, 70-72).

These reports were confirmed in 1847 by Richard Schomburgk in *Travels in British Guiana* (225-26) and in 1853 by Alfred Wallace in *A Narrative of Travels on the Amazon* (449-50), both naturalists. "Vampire" entered taxonomy with Linnaeus and it leaves a legacy to this day. The most prodigious bat in the Americas is named the *Vampyrum spectrum*. Linnaeus' vampire is known today as the *Pteropyus vampyrus*. There are the genera and subgenera *Vampyressa* (1843), *Vampyrops* (1865), *Vampyriscus* (1878), and *Vampyrodes* (1889). Many others became popularly known as vampires, although their scientific names today do not reflect it; they are now called "false vampire bats" (French 11-14). Johann von Spix in his 1823 *Simiarum et Vespertilionum Brasiliensium species novae* famously designated the *Glossophaga soricina* as "a blood sucker most cruel" (*Sanguisuga crudelissima*) (67); it was sometimes known as the "long-tongued vampire" (Lydekker 1: 303).

In the 1840s the descriptions of the bat began to be tempered by Darwin's direct observation of the *Desmodus rotundus* feeding on blood, the first sighting to be taken seriously (*Narrative of the surveying voyages of His Majesty's Ships* 3: 24-25). Before him, by the way, in 1801, Felix de Azara (*Essais sur l'histoire naturelle* 2: 273) described this blood-sucking bat with considerable care but he was immediately ignored. By Stoker's time, sources might deal with the mythic one by itself or some compromise between it and the proper one. For an extensive compromise, see Lydekker 1: 299-306. A few even dealt with the true vampire with no reference to the large one, for example, *Alden's Cyclopedia*'s (1893) "Vampire-Bat." In popular culture, it was strictly the legendary one that was used.

So Stoker had readily available to him a vampire that was very large, had predatorial instincts, and sucked blood to such a degree that it could take a life. It used its wings to sedate hypnotically, both while hovering and while feeding. Stoker did not invent it, by making it a human-like vampire monster in a transformed state, but utilized a bat that already existed, albeit in people's imagination, and affixing it to the monster. It is correct, then, that he may have ignored the *Desmodus rotundus*, but is not so in insinuating the mythic one to be hard to account for. And the language was most often of the vampire rather than the vampire bat.

The Conflation of Monster and Bat

Because the nineteenth century uses "vampire" to designate both the bat and the monster, we have to be careful when reading literature from the period. In fact, the latter half of the century seems to represent a shift away from a supernatural monster to a more normalized vampire, and the bat is part of this. For this we shall look at an article by Andrew Boylan ("Stoker and the Bat" 2014) that lists works he believes lead up to Stoker to see if a pattern emerges.[57] He

---

[57] See also Boylan, *Media Vampire* 183-84.

is a respected enthusiast and the only one I know to investigate the issue at any length. All the references are intended to designate a blurring of boundaries between the monster and bat, with the idea that Stoker might have got his idea of metamorphosis from one or more of the references.

Boylan notes first the 1888 entry in the *Encyclopedia Britannica* and an 1896 article from the *New York World* dealing with "vampirism" in New England. In each case both the monster and the bat are brought together in a single article. He goes on to reference Richard Burton's 1870 story *Vikram and the Vampire*, in which a creature, identified as a vampire, hangs from a bough, "like a flying fox;" a cartoon in *Punch* (1885) where the Irish National League is identified as the Irish "Vampire," and pictured as a bat, "replete with human face;" Goya's print *Las Resultas* (1810-20) which shows a bat "with a humanoid face suckling on the chest of a corpse;" Dumas' 1851 play where Ruthven, the vampire, is revived from death, spreads his "great wings and flies off;" A. Y.'s 1829 story, "Pepopukin in Corsica," of an invented vampire who sings of flying over the alps; Bruxas in William Kingston's 1863 short story "The Vampire," who are ordinary women during the day but become vampires at night and can transform into "gigantic bats;" Baring-Gould's 1884 "Margery of Quether" whose vampire has hands and arms "shrivelled and like those of a bat;" Christian iconography like the painting of St. Michael by Carlo Crivelli (c. 1476) where the devil has bat wings; and the 1896 short film, *Le Manoir du Diable*, by Georges Méliès, in which Mephistopheles turns from a large bat to a human.

Elizabeth Miller adds two others: first a "bat-like vampire appears . . . as a cover illustration in the novel *Varney the Vampire*, which appeared fifty years before *Dracula*" ("Bats, Vampires & Dracula").[58] Then, "'The Mysterious Stranger', as Count Klatka keeps company 'with the bat and the owl'" (*Dracula: Sense and Nonsense* 34). Boylan concludes his blog, "[W]hat we have seen is a rich pre-Stoker connection between bats and vampires . . . Certainly Stoker was not the first to suggest that a vampire could transform into a bat. The best that can be said is that he popularised the connection."

I will look at these chronologically, changing any problems with dating.

First is Crivelli's painting. Christianity picked up the notion of wings on its devils and angels early on. For instance, the early Latin father, Tertullian, *Apologeticus*, wrote in the late second century (197 CE), "Every spirit is possessed of wings. This is a common property of both angels and demons" (97). The first differentiation of them into feathered and bat like, albeit meant strictly metaphorically, is probably by the Greek Father, Basil of Caesarea (*Commentary on the Prophet Isaiah*), in the mid-fourth century: "The bat is indeed winged, yet it is not furnished with feathers, but flies through the air by means of a fleshy membrane. Such are demons as well" (110).

It does not seem to have occurred in earnest until the late high Middle Ages. The frescoes by Giotto, "The Exorcism of the Demons" [Scene 10] and "The Confession of the Woman of Benevento" [Scene 27] dated between 1295 and 1299 were quickly followed by Duccio Di Buoninsegna's "The Temptation of Christ on the Mountain" and "Descent to Hell" (1308-11). Dante in his *Inferno*

---

[58] Miller later wrote, "The first literary connection with vampires—I am not aware of any connection in the folklore—may be the cover illustration of an early edition of *Varney the Vampire*" (*Dracula: Sense and Nonsense* 34).

around 1314 insisted that the devil's wings were not feathered, "but were in form and texture like a bat's" (385). So Crivelli is just a later instance of this. Boylan is right insofar as it is a conflation of a monster and a bat, but it is a stretch to see it leading up to Dracula.

In fact I think it is the opposite, but this is pure conjecture. In prospect I believe one reason it took some time before the two vampires were brought together intimately was because the bat was already taken by Christianity's evilest figure. In retrospect, when Stoker had adopted the name for his monster, he may have made some interesting connections between the satanic wings, the vampire monster, and the vampire bat. After all Stoker may have understood "Dracula" to translate devil, following William Wilkinson (see *Bram Stoker's Notes for* Dracula 245). On the other hand, the vampire bat and Satan were already linked closely together by 1866 (Carlisle 118).

Goya's print adds nothing: it is merely his use of the mythic vampire bat sucking the life out of a victim while resting on his stomach as a symbol for the horror of war to a nation. He is probably working with the famous picture *Nightmare* by Henry Fuseli where the *mare* of folk stories sits upon the chest of a sleeping beauty giving her nightmares (1781). The nineteenth-century vampire bat in literature, whether or not dependent upon Goya, is henceforth likely to be sitting on the ribs or stomach sucking blood from the chest or throat.[59]

A. Y.'s 1826 story is significant. The vampire is a prank, but taken on its own terms, the monster is said to rise from its grave clothes and fly over the alps, dripping from its "blood-swol'n body" (53-54). Yet it does not tie together the monster either with the bat or with bat wings, but only with wings and flying. Heaven is promised to it and it attacks only sinners, so there is no reason its wings not be feathered.

Wachsmann's "Der Fremde" was published in German in 1844 and a translation into English as "The Mysterious Stranger" printed in 1854.[60] The passage in question—keeping company with the bat and the owl—simply means he is asleep during the day and awake at night. In the German it is *"ich mit Kauz und Uhu . . . niste*, "I nest with the screech and eagle owls" (167).

Next is Alexandre Dumas with *The Vampire: Drama in 5 Acts* (1851) and this does appear to be a genuine conflation of the two vampires. He has two supernatural vampire characters that are set in conflict with each other. He calls the female one "a ghoul" and links her with Arabs.[61] Ghouls are said to be coquettes, choosing handsome young men and then lying in wait for them. "They

---

[59] Goya has a much earlier etching that obviously uses vampire bats in the background: "There is Plenty to Suck" (c. 1798).

[60] 1860 was given by Montague Summers as the date of the English translation in his *Victorian Ghost Stories* 1934 and it was used in English sources thereafter. Recent critical studies place it in 1854. The research of Douglas A. Anderson and Thomas Honegger resulted in locating the original German and so the record was finally set straight by Mike Ashley, who credits them (33).

[61] The "ghoul" first appeared in "The Story of Sidi Nouman" in Antoine Galland's translation/ adaptation of the Arabian Tales (*Les Mille et Une Nuits*, Vol. 10, 1712; see the reprint, 1785, 35-56). It is most likely a creation of Galland himself. The ghoul was later "vampirized" by Collin de Plancy (104-16), who doubtless fabricated an "Arabic" story based on "Sidi Nouman." Dumas is simply pulling from this tradition. For an important perspective on the ghoul, see Al Rawi 291-306.

watch for the passing of their prey, lull him to sleep with the movement of their vast wings and when he is asleep in a mortal bliss, they aspirate his blood and his life" (Act 2, scene 2). There is no doubt about her being a preternatural monster, with vampire bat wings which sedate. Lord Ruthven, the other vampire, dead among the mountain rocks, is revived by moonlight. "Lord Ruthwen first sits up—then rises completely, . . . deploys great wings and flies off" (Act 3, scene 3). Dumas uses the same construction he does for the ghoul: *grandes ailes*—vast wings. Both are surely hybrids of the vampire monster and bat.[62]

Miller's reference to the illustration in *Varney the Vampire* also appears to be an actual conflation of the two.[63] The story was originally printed between 1845 and 1847 as a "penny dreadful." It was published in book form in 1847. What Miller is referring to is the cover of the 1853 edition.[64] A skeletonized Varney spreads his cloak to form bat wings and hovers over a sleeping beauty. He is surrounded by four demons complete with bat wings watching eagerly. So the illustration does seem to bring together the vampire monster and the bat. But because of the emphasis on the bat by the appearance of the four demons and of him hovering over her like a bat, the illustration is more about it than the monster. A similar picture, by the way, is painted by Charles Dickens in *Bleak House* (1852-3): Mr. Krook finds his tenant dead on the bed and calls for help, "with his lean hands spread out above the body like a vampire's wings" (97).

We turn to Burton's very free 1868 translation of *The Baital-Pachisi* or *Vetala Panchavimshati* entitled *Vikram and the Vampire*. It ends up being largely irrelevant to our study. "Vampire" is a misleading translation for *baital* or *vetala*, a Hindu impish and devious trickster spirit that can inhabit corpses in charnel grounds. "Vampire" refers to the spirit, whether incarnate or disembodied (409); it corresponds to the way the word became used by Spiritualism and Theosophy. Insofar as it inhabits a dead human body, there is a parallel with the monster. Here it animates an altered body that looks like a flying fox, i.e., a vampire bat. So "vampire" refers to neither the monster nor the bat as such, but to the spirit behind them both.

The eponymous Margery of Quether, over two hundred years before the story, used to sit in church and pray for everlasting life and her Christian God granted it, in Sabine Baring-Gould's 1884 story.[65] She now lives like a bat in the belfry of the church, shrunk to the size of an infant in mummified flesh. This is how George Rosedhu encounters her. She drops from the bell rope, scrambles on the ground "much as [he has] seen a bat scramble" (351), has hands and arms shrivelled "like those of a bat" (352), and when his heart goes out to her and he

---

[62] A vampire of a similar sort is also described in the anonymously written (male) adolescent novel, *The Vampire* (1885). It uses "bird" for "bat" throughout the story: "'Tain't a bird, . . . but a sort of a devil w'ot comes in the shape of a big bird; it's got the figger of a man, but the wings of a bird, a kinder hitched onto a man's arm, and the only thing it can live on is human blood." So too the famous picture by Albert-Joseph Penot, *La chauve-souris*, circa 1890. See Rossback 138.
[63] Some twenty years before this there is an illustration like this for Planché's play, *The Vampire: or, The Bride of the Isles*.
[64] See Pettit. Butler (37) avers that it is the 1847 edition.
[65] Baring-Gould is Christianizing classical myths which counsel human beings to avoid hubris and accept their mortality. Those who wish to be like the eternal gods live to regret it. The Sibyl of Cumae shrivels up with her increasing years like a cicada—so does Tithonus, Eos's favorite; both, in their withered condition, plead for their ever-elusive death.

decides he will protect her in his home, she clings to his chest clutching him with her "bat like hands and claws" (358) and sinks her one remaining tooth deep into his flesh. She is a bat situated on his breast and feeding.

Thus begins a strange relationship where George suckles her back to youth as he himself slips into decrepitude and old age. Her "vampirism" (the word "vampire" never appears) is imaged 100% as that of a bat; her transformation from being "bat like" to being "normal" is slow and in stages as was her change from human to being bat-like beforehand. The figure of a bat is superimposed on the human at one stage of her life; there is no conflation of a monster and bat, for there is no monster.

George Rosedhu suckling Margery of Quether.
Illustration from *Cornhill Magazine* by Harry Furniss, 357.

The 1888 entry on "vampire" in the *Encyclopaedia Britannica* follows. The two vampires are put together because they share the same name. The bat gets more space because it is the object of greater interest. Instead of conflation, it displays the bat's primacy. In fact, the author writes that the word vampire "originally applied in eastern Europe to blood-sucking ghosts, but in modern usage [is] transferred to one or more species of blood-sucking bats inhabiting South America" (Dobson 52).[66] In other words, usage for the monster is archaic; for the bat it is current. So too the 1896 article from the *New York World*; although it is only about the monster, the author devotes the final paragraphs to the bat, since it is "more recent" and is "founded on fact" rather than superstition (*Bram Stoker's Notes for Dracula* 186-93).

The illustration in the October 17, 1885 issue of *Punch*, "The Irish Vampire," is misunderstood if one holds "The Irish 'Vampire'" as meaning anything more than the bat. A huge bat, with the National League written on its wings, hovers over the sleeping body of Ireland (or "Hibernia," aka "Erin") ready to take her life.[67] *Punch* was a humor weekly which saw any nationalist movement, like the

---

[66] Cf. "They Burned the Vampire" (1893).
[67] It is preceded by a poem with the same name, wherein the luckless Erin (Ireland), beset by problems, has attracted yet new ones. She is counselled to wake up and put up her guard lest they take her life. She is facing the predatory National League which arose in her midst from her lack of vigilance.

Irish League, to be destructive of the British Empire. That is why superimposed on the bat's face is that of Charles Stewart Parnell, an "infamous" supporter of home rule and organizer of the National League (Tenniel, 198-199).[68] Parnell is a vampire to the staff at *Punch* only in the sense of the bat. *The Irish Plot* November 7, 1885 published a rejoinder to this entitled "The English Vampire," which celebrated the National League as protection against British imperialism. It has Erin with sword drawn and National League on her shield facing the swooping English vampire with a fearful look on its face.

Images like this were prevalent at the time. A particularly provocative one appeared in the January 28, 1893 issue of the *Worker* out of Brisbane, Australia, with the caption "Queensland and the Vampire." A vampire bat with Q. N. Bank on its wings is on the belly of a prostrate topless woman sucking blood and milk from her breast. On the head is the face of the general manager of the Queensland National Bank, Edward Robert Drury, who is extracting the assets of Queensland for the sake of outside investors. In the terms of the time, both are "human vampires."[69]

Along the same lines, at the beginning of Mary Elizabeth Braddon's 1896 "Good Lady Ducayne," a story in which a wealthy elderly woman hires lower middle class women in order secretly to have their blood transfused into her to extend her life at the threat of their own, is an illustration of an old woman in a fur coat with a huge imposing bat hovering behind her. She is acting like a vampire bat. The first instance of this kind of illustration of which I am aware features a frightful human face placed on the body of a vampire bat with a handsome mask dangling down on his chest ("The Vampyre (Psalmicantor Vehemens) 1851, 185). As the description that accompanies it makes clear, the vampire is to represent the sadistic hypocrite who seems a friend but secretly

"Good Lady Ducayne, 185"

---

[68] Dalby (11-12) comments how the face reminds him of Stoker's.
[69] A "human vampire" is used during the final decades of the nineteenth century at times to denote someone acting like a vampire. A good example is Napier's 1870 *The Book of Nature* (263-264). Cf. the "Death Watch" dinner put on by the Order of the Vampires, i.e., vampire bats, October 2, 1892, in New York. The program had a large vampire bat flying over a grave with the words "Homo Desmodus" streaming across its body. Homo Desmodus is translated in this context "Human Vampire Bat." It is also assumed in the song "Shriek" they sang: "By gravestone cold and white/ We spread our wings at night:/ Over the mounds we love to dance/ And wake a corpse right out of his trance./ His trance, trance, trace [*sic.*]."

slanders behind one's back. It is entitled "Vampire," and refers solely to the bat.

A most striking example comes from a review of Dion Boucicault's "The Phantom," an 1852 adaptation of Charles Nodier's 1820 play, "The Vampire." The notation is from a revival of it and appears in the January 20, 1875 *New York Times* by M. E. W. Sherwood: "Then somewhere along here, I think in a summer season, comes a vision of Boucicault playing the 'Vampire,' a dreadful and weird thing, played with immortal genius. That great playwright would not have died unknown had he never done anything but flap his bat-like arms in that dream-disturbing piece."

I must add one other literary piece that was not covered by Boylan: Anne Crawford's "A Mystery of the Campagna" (1887). She actually wrote under the pseudonym of Von Degen. Marcello finds a quiet villa to work on the score to an opera and his friends leave him alone until Detaille visits him and finds him gaunt and cold. A short time thereafter Detaille becomes seriously ill and fixates on Marcello, seeming to be linked to him in some way. Another friend, Robert, checks on Marcello as a favor to Detaille, hiding on the estate. He sees Marcello walk mechanically to a sepulchre and meet a woman there. He thinks he has simply witnessed a tryst until he finds out that at that same time Detaille, who was losing his mind, was extremely agitated. The following night Marcello is violent again and his friends even see Marcello in the doorway until he evaporates away.

His friends decide to go to the villa and talk to Marcello. When he turns up nowhere, they check the sepulchre and find him dead with marks on his chest. Robert sees an inscription that reads D. M. VESPERTILIAE *THC* ΑΙΜΑΤΟΠΩΤΙΔΟC *Q* FLAVIVS *IPSE *SOSPES *MON* POSVIT.[70] He interprets this to mean: "'To Vespertilia'—that was in Latin, and even the Latin name of the woman suggested a thing of evil flitting in the dusk [*Vespertilio* is Latin for a bat; *Vespertilia* (rarely used) for a female bat]. But the full horror of the nature of that thing had been veiled to Roman eyes under the Greek τῆς αἱματοπωτίδος, 'The blood-drinker, the vampire woman.' And Flavius—her lover—*vix ipse sospes*, 'himself hardly saved' from that deadly embrace, had buried her here, and set a seal upon her sepulchre, trusting to the weight of stone and the strength of clinging mortar to imprison for ever the beautiful monster he had loved." (155-156). They open the sepulchre and stake the vampire, so she can do no further harm. Thus there is a conflation of vampire and bat in her name and in her vocation of bloodsucking.

The Metamorphosis into a Bat

Nina Auerbach and David Skal in their *Dracula: A Norton Critical Edition* (1997) wrote that "the now-inevitable association of vampires with the bat" began with Dracula (90). Melton (52) and Crawford (41) aver much the same. In 1998, Elizabeth Miller ("Bats, Vampires & Dracula") declared more forcefully, "Stoker's major contribution to the association of vampires with bats was his introduction of the idea that a vampire could shapeshift into the form of a bat (as well as a wolf and mist)." Anthony Hogg, a particularly well-informed amateur,

---
[70] This is not in the original but is understood from his translation.

has asserted in his April 6, 2014 *Vampirologist* blog entry entitled "Bats Before Bram," "that Stoker invented one of the most popular 'folkloric' characteristics associated with vampires: they could change into bats." Hogg ("Bats Where They Don't Belong" January 25, 2011) also holds that finding a list that predates Dracula and includes a bat as something into which a vampire (monster) can turn would be "an exciting find." I have some inspiring news for him.

First, we must deal with the remaining sources to which Boylan refers. William H. G. Kingston's "The Vampire; or, Pedro Pacheco and the Bruxa (1863) is not an early instance of metamorphosis.[71] Ordinary women by day, bruxas become demon possessed by night and have orgies. The name *bruxa* means a witch, and witches are already associated with night orgies and demon possession. They can also shapeshift, so it is no surprise that following the orgy they turn into bats, ducks, or owls. As such they lead passers-by on a wild goose chase, leaving them lost, scratched, and humiliated, and finally they return home and with a "vampirish hunger," seize their children, fan them with their huge black wings, bite them, and "suck the life-blood from their veins." The vampire in the title refers only to the bat. There is no vampire monster, only a witch. Stoker might have read a highly abbreviated story similar to this, by the way (*Bram Stoker's Notes for Dracula*, 206-209). It is actually a single sentence in Isabella Lucy Bird's *The Golden Chersonese* from 1883: "A vile fiend called the *penangalan* takes possession of the forms of women, turns them into witches, and compels them to quit the greater part of their bodies, and fly away by night to gratify a vampire craving for human blood" (451-52).

Le Manoir du Diable by Georges Méliès (1896) has been called "the first vampire film" (Hardy et al. 17; Stuart 218). It features a monster, Mephistopheles, turning into a bat and vice versa. But Mephistopheles is an imp of the devil created in the sixteenth century along with the first Faust tales and thereafter a surrogate for the devil; he is never a vampire monster. It does demonstrate the interchangeability between a human-like devil and a bat (there is no evidence it is a vampire bat), but bats have been associated with the devil for a long time. Nonetheless transformation is important, even if it does not apply immediately to the vampire. So there are only two on Boylan's list that are germane: the two vampires in Dumas' play and the cover to Varney the Vampire.

There is nothing controversial about the folklore vampire being a shapeshifter. What is of significance, we are told, is the absence of the bat from any such list. In Edmund Veckenstedt's *Wendische Sagen, Märchen und abergläubische Gebräuche* (1880), however, which refers to the stories and rituals of the Western Slavs, there is a sentence on the issue: *Die Vampyre nehmen die Gestalt von Katzen, Fröschen, Kröten, Fliegen, Spinnen oder Fledermäusen an*—"Vampires take the form of cats, frogs, toads, flies, spiders, or bats" (354).

Another can be found a year earlier in a textbook entitled *Simple English Poems* (Part 2, 1879) edited by H. Courthope. In an explanatory footnote to Robert Browning's "The Pied Piper of Hamlin," which makes a passing reference to "Vampyre bats," we read that they are "huge bats found in the tropics, so called

---

[71] The same story was published in 1846 and 1863, albeit with different names for the lead character. The 1846 text is entitled "Gil Perez and the Bruxa: A Legend of Portugal." In 1863, however, an introduction was affixed and it is that alone which concerns us (see Kingston, "The Vampire" 73-74).

from the superstition about vampyres. A vampyre is supposed to be a dead man who returns in body and soul from the other world, and wanders about the earth doing mischief to the living. He sucks the blood of persons asleep, and these persons become vampyres in turn. He lies as a corpse during the day; but at night, especially at full moon, he wanders about in the form of a dog, bat, &c, biting sleepers on the back or neck" (42).

With regard to literature, there are at least two popular stories that feature a vampire monster turning into a vampire bat.[72] The strongest is entitled "Ein Vampyr" and is by Karl May, one of the best-selling German writers of all time.[73] May wrote his Orient Cycle between 1881 and 1888, and it was published in installments in the Catholic weekly, *Deutscher Hausschatz in Wort und Bild*. The fourth volume of the cycle, *In den Schluchten des Balkan*, appeared in the 1885-1886 issues. It was then revised and published in book form in 1892. The following is found in the seventh chapter.

Kara Ben Nemsi is traveling in the Bulgarian Mountains with his companions. They spend the night at the home of a poor Christian man, Kerpitschi. Kara learns that the man and his wife are fasting that night, so he goes outside to eat and notices there the grave of their daughter who recently had died. When he is finished and returning to the house, Kerpitschi stops him to ask whether he believes in ghosts. Kara says he does not, but Kerpitschi responds that he knows they exist for their daughter is a vampire; his wife and he fast in order to redeem her.

He is told that their daughter, who was already ill, cared for her fiancé's mother as she was dying of smallpox. She returned home after her death frightened—something had happened to her there—and she soon became delirious. In this state, she would say that Wlastan's son, her fiancé, must die. When she was near death the priest was gone so she made no confession and received no absolution; because she died of smallpox she could not be buried in the cemetery. So presently "she appears as a bat," knocks on their door, and then flies over to Wlastan's home and feeds on his son, who has started to waste away. "Now she is a vampire and she is keeping him for herself" (340). The priest has said the only way to stop her is to stake her, but they will not allow it. Thus Wlastan, who was once a dear friend, is now his enemy.

Kara decides to keep watch over the house, even though Kerpitschi tells him he must not, for no one can look at a vampire and live. That is the reason why they have never answered the door. Kara says he will do so anyway for he wants to see a "*gespensterhaften Blutsauger hinter die Flughäute*" (ghostly bloodsucker behind membrane-wings) (818). Kara sees a man come that night and make bat noises and knock on the door; he is eventually caught and confesses. It is Wlastan's servant who had slowly been poisoning Wlastan's son, so that he himself could become heir. Kerpitschi's daughter caught him, but he threatened to kill her parents if she ever told anyone. That is why she spoke as she did.

---

[72] The jury is still out on "The Vampire Maid" by Hume Nisbet. In *The Vampire Archives* (2009), Otto Penzler, writes that "The Vampire Maid" was first published in a magazine in 1890 and then reprinted in book form in 1900 (166). I wrote Penzler and he cannot recall where he found the datum after all these years. Mike Ashley, Douglas A. Anderson, James Doig, and I can find no evidence for the claim.

[73] I was first introduced to this short story in the wonderful 2012 anthology edited by Oliver Kotowski, *Lasst die Toten ruhen*.

There is another one dated later. It is *The Strange Story of Dr. Senex* (1891) by E. E. Baldwin. George Marsh is made executer of the eccentric Dr. Senex's estate and comes into possession of his journals. There he learns that Dr. Senex, as a young man, in the 1620s, became a disciple of an alchemist who was working on arresting the processes of decay in the human body and the rejuvenation of tissues and fluids to their youthful condition, in other words, longevity. When he tries the concoction himself, however, he dies and Senex inherits his wealth. Thus he is able to travel and he finds the real solution—a chemical compound plus a transfusion of blood from a young person, who will probably die in the process.

He decides, cruelly and egocentrically, to use his young associate as a guinea pig, but on the day the experiment is to be performed he is late. It is because of his wife's dream. "She dreamed that we were all together one night in your quarters, and that while discoursing upon some of the hidden mysteries of life, you said 'that the blood was not at all essential for the young, that youth possessed more than its fair share, and that the aged had the right to demand from the young a part of their supply.' As you were thus talking, your features underwent a change and you seemed to be transformed into a huge vampire bat, and without warning, and before she could even scream or give a sign, you struck me with your horrible wings, and seizing me in your claws, buried your fangs in my throat and sucked my blood. When you were through, I seemed to shrivel up until I became nothing but a heap of dust, and then, seizing her in your embrace and singing with joy and exultation you bore her away to your abode in some outlandish place" (125-26). Dr. Senex persuades him to partake in the experiment and he finally relents; it works; the young assistant dies; Senex's new blood carries the young man's love for his wife, so Senex woos her and marries her, only to ruin her life. Senex is a vampire turning into a bat. This is the first story I know where the vampire can drink blood that effects a change in her/him.

There is, by the way, yet another: "The Stone Chamber" by H. B. Marriott Watson. It is often dated 1898 or 1899, taken from the publication of the book in which it appears, but it was actually printed first in mid-1896. It clearly implies the turning of Priscilla, Lady Marvyn, dead some 150 years, into a bat which is currently feeding on occupants in the stone chamber but it is worked out only in 1898, after *Dracula* appeared; the 1896 version is too abbreviated.[74]

Conclusion

There does seem to have been an almost inevitable collision course between the two vampires—monster and bat—if for no other reason than they shared the same name and tended to have similar traits. That started when soldiers, naturalists, even taxonomists began naming bats with the name of the folklore monster and creating a list of lurid characteristics for them. In this way, many of the terrifying aspects of the monster were preserved but the "superstitious" elements could be removed—no more revenants, or ritualized desecrations and

---

[74] In the US, it appears on page 29 of the June 28, 1896 issue of the *New York World*. Mike Ashley seems to have located an earlier appearance on June 11 in *Vanity Fair*.

stakings, or the victims becoming vampire monsters, or theological problems about how such fit into the order of a benevolent, but just God's creation.

In the latter half of the century the monster seems to be in the process of being naturalized. If referred to at all and not the bat, the monster becomes a psychic vampire mesmerizing, a medical one transfusing, a scientist electrically magnetizing, a *femme fatale* or *homme fatal* seducing; a killer murdering; a necrophile desecrating, etc. All draw the life force, resources, dignity from their victims. At the same time the unreconstructed monster becomes largely the property of folklorists, early psychologists, and love poets. After Dumas and Boucicault, Lord Ruthven, the most famous vampire of the nineteenth century, begins slipping into the shadows of redundancy or parody.

Nonetheless, the monster does still live on at the margins of the late nineteenth-century literature. Most of the authors of these stories, however, prefer to keep their options open between coincidence, illusion, trickery, and reality, as May and Baldwin do. A world like ours where the monster can operate unapologetically becomes rare. Yet a few masterpieces still arise like J. Sheridan Le Fanu's *Carmilla* (1871) in English; Marie Nizet's 1879 *Le Capitaine Vampire* in French; and in 1885 Heinrich Ulrichs' "Manor" in German, but these, for the most part, were overlooked at the time of their publication.

Dracula should have joined them here at the fringes, but instead it broke out and has become one of the best-selling novels to this day. Stoker's use of the contemporary large and menacing bat—to spy, to sedate, to hypnotize, to prey upon, to escape—as one weapon in an arsenal to be wielded by a relentless, foreign, imperial monster bent on conquest in the very heart of the British Empire at the time is quite staggering. In comparison, the previous literary associations of a corpse and a bat are quite anemic.

This is where we must see the significance of the book. It does not lie in its being the first to utilize the bat as something into which the monster can shapeshift. Nor is it the climax of a mainstream movement in its direction. Rather it plays a key role in reasserting the primacy of the monster over the bat that typified the first half of the century. In the latter half, if one used the word "vampire" seriously, chances were one meant the bat. Today we mean by it the monster alone and if we refer to the bat, it is merely an adjective.

Finally, the twentieth century saw the victory of the microbat over the macrobat as the true vampire, so when a monster turns into a large bat, it is not technically into a vampire bat anymore. *Dracula* is the greatest example of an era when that was not the case, when the monstrous bat still reigned as the vampire.

Works cited

Alden's Cyclopedia of Natural History 2. New York: John B. Alden, 1893.

Aldrovandi, Ulisse. *Ornithologiae, hoc est de avibus historiae libri XII*. Bologna: A Sienese Franciscan, 1599.

Al-Rawi, Ahmed K. "The Arabic Ghoul and its Western Transformation." *Folklore* 120: 3 (December 2009), 291-306.

Anghiera, Pietro Martire d'. *De orbe novo, the eight Decades of Peter Martyr d'Anghera*. 1. Trans. Francis Augustus MacNutt. New York, London: G.P. Putnam's Sons, 1912.

Ashley, Mike. *Vampires: Classic Tales*. Mineola: Dover Publications, 2011.
Azara, Felix de. *Essais sur l'histoire naturelle des quadrupèdes de la province du Paraguay*. 2. Paris: Charles Pogens, 1801.
Barber, Paul. *Vampires, Burial, and Death: Folklore and Reality*. New Haven: Yale University Press, 1988.
Baring-Gould, Sabine. "Margery of Quether." *The Cornhill Magazine* April & May 1884, 337-60; 466-85.
Basil of Caesaria. *Commentary on the Prophet Isaiah*. Trans. Nicolai A. Lipatov. *Texts and Studies in the History of Theology* 7. Eds. Kinzig Wolfram and Vinzent Wolfram. Mandelbachtal/ Cambridge: Cicero, 2001.
Belwood, Jacqueline J. & Morton, Patricia A. "The truth about the bats people love to hate is even more fascinating than the myths..." *BATS Magazine* 9:1. Spring 1991.
Benson, Elizabeth P. "Bats in South American Folklore and Ancient Art." *BATS Magazine* 9:1. Spring 1991.
Benson, Elizabeth P. "Bats in South American Folklore and Ancient Art," *Andean Past* 1 (1987), 165-90.
Benzoni, Girolamo. *History of the New World*. Trans. W. H. Smyth. London: Hakluyt Society, 1856.
Bird, Isabella Lucy. *The Golden Chersonese and the Way Thither*. New York: G. P. Putnam's Sons, 1883.
Bowen, H. Courthope, ed. *Simple English Poems: English Literature for Junior Classes. In Four Parts*. London: C. Kegan Paul and Co., 1879.
Boylan, Andrew. *Media Vampire: A Study of Vampires in Fictional Media*. Lulu.com., 2012.
Boylan, Andrew. "Stoker and the Bat." *Vamped* April 1, 2014. vamped.org/2014/04/05/stoker-bat/.
Braddon, Mary Elizabeth. "Good Lady Ducayne." *The Strand Magazine: An Illustrated Monthly* 11 (February 1896), 185-199.
Brown, David E. *Vampiro: The Vampire Bat in Fact and Fantasy*. Silver City: High-Lonesome Books, 1994.
Buffon, George-Louis Leclerc, Comte de. *Histoire Naturelle, générale et particulière, avec la description du Cabinet du Roi*. Vol. 10. Paris : Imprimerie Royale, 1763.
Bunson, Matthew. *The Vampire Encyclopedia*. New York: Crown Trade Paperbacks, 1993.
Burton, Richard F. "Vikram and the Vampire; or, Tales of Indian Devilry." *Fraser's Magazine for Town and Country*. 77 (April-June 1868), 407-432; 560-576; 700-716. 78 (August, October-December), 230-248; 480-497; 584-602; 748-761.
Butler, Erik.*The Rise of the Vampire*. London: Reaktion Books Ltd, 2013.
Carlisle, Thomas. "Natural History: Bats." *The Juvenile Instructor and Companion*. 17/5 (New Series). London: William Cooke, 1866. 114-119.
Carlyle, Thomas. "[Dr. Francia]." *The Foreign Quarterly Review*. 31 (July 1843). 544-589.
de la Condamine, Charles Marie. *Relation abrégée d'un voyage fait dans l'intérieur de l'Amérique méridionale*. Paris: Veuve Pessot, 1745.
Copper, Basil. *The Vampire in Legend and Fact*. New York: Citadel Press Book, 1973.
Crawford von Rebe, Anne. "The Mystery of the Campagna." *The Witching Time: Tales for the Year's End*. Ed. Henry Norman. New York: D. Appleton and Company, 1887. 107-160.
Crawford, Heide. *The Origins of the Literary Vampire*. Lanham: Rowman & Littlefield, 2016.
Dalby, Richard. *Dracula's Brood*. New York: Dorset Press, 1987..
Dante. *Inferno*. Trans. Carlyle John Aitken. London: J. M. Dent & Co., 1904.
Darwin, Charles. *Narrative of the surveying voyages of His Majesty's Ships Adventure and Beagle between the years 1826 and 1836, describing their examination of the southern shores of South America, and the Beagle's circumnavigation of the globe. Journal and remarks. 1832-1836*. 3. London: Henry Colburn, 1839.
"Death Watch." New-York Historical Society. October 28, 2011. DOI=blog.nyhistory.org/early-vampire-celebrations/.
Dickens, Charles. *Bleak House*. London: Bradbury & Evans 1853.

Ditmars, Raymond Lee; Greenhall, Arthur M. *The vampire bat; a presentation of undescribed habits and review of its history.* Zoologia: Scientific Contributions of the New York Zoological Society 19:2. New York: New York Zoological Society, 1935.

Dobson, G. E. "Vampire." Encyclopaedia Brittanica. Vol. 24. New York: Henry G. Allen and Company, 1888. 52.

Dumas, Alexandre. Maquet, M. Auguste. *The Vampire: A Drama in Five Acts.* Trans. Frank N. Morlock. Top of Form

The Return of Lord Ruthven the Vampire. Ed. Frank N. Morlock. Tarzana: Hollywood Comics, 2004 [1851].

Edwards, George. *A Natural History of Birds.* London: College of Physicians, 1751.

Estournelles, P. d'. "The Superstitions of Modern Greece." *The Nineteenth Century: A Monthly Review.* 11: 62 (April 1882), 586-603.

French, Barbara. "False Vampires and Other Carnivores: A glimpse at this select group of bats reveals efficient predators with a surprisingly gentle side . . ." *BATS Magazine* 15:2. Summer, 1997.

Frayling, Christopher. *Vampyres: Lord Byron to Count Dracula.* London: Faber and Faber, 1991.

Galland, Antoine. "Histoire de Sidi Nouman." *Le Cabinet de Fées, ou Collection Choisie des Contes de Fées et Autres Contes Merveilleux,* 11. Paris, 1785 [1712].

Greenhall, Arthur M., Gerhard Joermann and Uwe Schmidt. "Desmodus rotundus." *Mammalian Species* 202 (8 April 1983), 1-6.

Gumilla, Joseph. *El Orinoco ilustrado, y defendido: historia natural, civil, y geográfica de este gran río y de sus caudalosas vertientes.* Madrid: Manuel Fernandez, 1745.

Hardy, Phil, Tom Milne, and Paul Willemen, Eds. *Overlook Film Encyclopedia: Horror.* Woodstock, NY: Overlook Press, 1995.

Hogg, Anthony. "Bats Before Bram." *The Vampirologist.* April 6, 2014. thevampirologist. wordpress.com/2014/04/06/bats-before-bram/.

Hogg, Anthony. "Bats Where They Don't Belong." *Diary of an Amateur Vampirologist.* January 25, 2011. doaav.blogspot.com.au/2011/01/bats-where-they-dont-belong. html.

Holmes. Oliver Wendell. "A Farewell to Agassiz." *The Atlantic Monthly A Magazine Of Literature, Science, Art, And Politics.* 16: 97 (November 1865), 584-585.

"The Irish 'Vampire.'" *Punch, or The London Charivari,* 39. 17 October 1885.

Ito, Fernanda, Enrico Bernard, and Richard A. Torres. "What is for Dinner? First Report of Human Blood in the Diet of the Hairy-Legged Vampire Bat *Diphylla ecaudata.*" *Acta Chiropterologica* 18: 2 (December 2016), 509-515.

Kingston William H. G. "Gil Perez and the Bruxa: A Legend of Portugal." *The New Monthly Magazine and Humorist* 3: 78 (January 1846), 90-94.

Kingston, William H. G., "The Vampire; or, Pedro Pacheco and the Bruxa." *Tales for all Ages.* London, Bickers and Bush, 1863. 72-80.

Lee, Sarah. *Anecdotes of the Habits and Instincts of Animals.* London: Grant & Griffith, 1852.

Lee, Sarah. *Anecdotes of the Habits and Instincts of Birds, Reptiles, and Fishes.* London: Grant & Griffith, 1853.

Le Fanu, J. Sheridan. "Carmilla." *The Dark Blue.* December 1871. 434-448.

Link, Luther. *The Devil: A Mask Without a Face.* London: Reaktion Books, 1995.

Linnaeus, Carl. *Systema Naturae.* 10th ed., 1. Stockholm: Salvius, 1758.

Lydekker, Richard, ed. *The Royal Natural History* 1. London: Frederick Warne & Company, 1893-94.

McNally, Raymond and Radu Florescu. *In Search of Dracula: The History of Dracula and Vampires.* Boston: Houghton Mifflin Company, 1994.

McNally, Raymond and Radu Florescu. "Vampirism: Old World Folklore." *The Vampire in Slavic Cultures.* Ed. Thomas J. Garza. San Diego: University Readers, 2009. 41-52.

May, Karl. "Ein Vampir." *Lasst die Toten ruhen: Deutsche Vampirgeschichten aus dem 19. Jahrhundert.* Ed. Oliver Kotowski. Stolberg: Atlantis Verlag, 2012.

May Karl. "Giölgeda padiśhanŭn: Der Letzte Ritt." *Deutscher Hausschatz in Wort und Bild.* 1886. 337-40; 817-20.

Melton, J. Gordon. *The Vampire Book: The Encyclopedia of the Undead.* Michigan: Visible Ink Press, 2011.

Miller, Elizabeth. "Bats, Vampires & Dracula." *The Night Flyer: News for the Friends of Florida's Bats* 3:4. Fall 1998. ucs.mun.ca/~emiller/bats_vamp_drac.html.

Miller, Elizabeth. "Coitus Interruptus: Sex, Bram Stoker, and Dracula." *Romanticism on the Net* 44. 17 November 2006. ronjournal.org/articles/n44/coitus-interruptus-sex-bram-stoker-and-dracula/

Miller, Elizabeth. *A Dracula Handbook.* Bloomington: Xlibris, 2005.

Miller, Elizabeth. *Dracula: Sense and Nonsense.* Southend-on-Sea: Desert Island Books, 2000.

Miller, Elizabeth. "Getting to Know the Un-Dead: Bram Stoker, Vampires and Dracula." *Vampires, Myths and Metaphors of Enduring Evil.* Ed. Peter Day. New York: Rodopi Press, 2006. 3-20.

Napier, Charles Ottley Groom. *The Book of Nature and the Book of Man.* London: John Camden Hotten, 1870.

Nisbet, Hume. "The Vampire Maid." *The Vampire Archives: The Most Complete Volume of Vampire Tales Ever Published.* Ed. Otto Penzler. New York: Vintage Books, 2009. 170-173.

Nizet, Marie. *Captain Vampire.* Trans. Brian Stableford, Encino: Black Coat Press, 2007.

Oinas, Felix. "East European Vampires." *The Vampire: A Casebook.* Ed. Alan Dundes. Madison: University of Wisconsin Press, 1998. 47-56.

Pennant, Thomas. *Synopsis of Quadrupeds.* Chester: J. Monk, 1771.

Penzler, Otto, Ed. *The Vampire Archives.* New York: Vintage Books, 2009.

Perkowski, Jan. *Vampires of the Slavs.* Cambridge, Mass: Slavika Publishers, 1976.

Pettit, Edward. "Varney the Vampire by James Malcolm Rymer," 2008. bibliothecary.squarespace.com/in-print/2008/4/29/varney-the-vampire-by-james-malcolm-rymer.html.

Pison, Guglielmo. *De Indiae utriusque re naturali et medica.* Amstelodami: Ludovicum et Danielem Elzevirios, 1658.

Plancy, Jacques Collin de. *Histoire des Vampires.* Paris, 1820.

Platts, John Tompson. *The Baitāl Pachchīsī, or, The Twenty-five Tales of a Sprite.* London: Wm. H. Allen, 1871.

"Queensland and the Vampire." *The Worker: Journal of the Associated Workers of Queensland* 3: 90. 28 January 1893. trove.nla.gov.au/newspaper/article/70863652/6652203.

Rossback, Susanne. *Des Dandys Wort als Waffe: Dandyismus, narrative Vertextungsstrategien und Geschlechterdifferenz im Werk Jules Barbey d'Aurevillys.* Tübingen: Max Niemeyer, 2002.

Schomburgk, Richard. *Travels in British Guiana During the Years 1840-1844.* 1, Leipzig: J. J. Weber, 1847.

Schutt, Bill. "The Curious, Bloody Lives of Vampire Bats." *Natural History Magazine* 117: 9 (November 2008). naturalhistorymag.com/features/31700/the-curious-bloody-lives-of-vampire-bats.

Sherwood, M. E. W. [Review of Boucicault's "The Phantom"]. *Actors and Actresses of Great Britain and the United States: From the Days of David Barrick to the Present Time* 5. Eds. Brander Matthews and Laurence Hutton. New York: Cassell & Company, 1886. 87-88.

Skal, David J. *V is for Vampire: The A-Z Guide to Everything Undead.* New York: Plume, 1996.

Skal, David J. *Vampires: Encounters with the Undead.* New York: Black Dog & Leventhal, 2001.

Spix, Johann von. *Simiarum et Vespertilionum Brasiliensium species novae ou Histoire Naturelle des espècies nouvelles de singes et de chauves-souris observées et recueillies pendant le voyage dans l'interieur du Brésil exécuté par ordre de S M Le Roi de Bavière dans les années 1817, 1818, 1819, 1820.* Munich: Typis Francisci Seraphi Hybschmanni, 1823.

Stedman, John. *Narrative, of a Five Years' Expedition, Against the Revolted Negroes of Surinam, in Guiana, on the Wild Coast of South America; from the Year 1772, to 1777: Elucidating* the *History of that Country, and Describing Its Productions, Viz. Quadrupedes, Birds, Fishes, Reptiles, Trees, Shrubs, Fruits, & Roots; with an Account of the Indians of Guiana, & Negroes of Guinea* 2. London: J. Johnson and J. Edwards, 1796.

Stephens, Henry L., *The Comic Natural History of the Human Race*. Philadelphia: S. Robinson, 1851.

Stoker, Bram. *Dracula*. New York: Grosset and Dunlap, 1897.

Stoker, Bram; Ásmundsson, Valdimar. *Powers of Darkness; The Lost Version of* Dracula. Trans. Hans Corneel de Roos. New York: Overlook Duckworth, 2017.

Stoker, Bram. *Dracula: A Norton Critical Edition*. Eds. Nina Auerbach and David J. Skal. London: W. W. Norton & Co., 1997.

Stoker, Bram. *Dracula: Scholar's Annotated Edition*. Ed. Christopher David. s.l: s.n., 2015.

Stoker, Bram. *Bram Stoker's Notes for Dracula: A Facsimile Edition*. Eds. Richard Eighteen-Bisang and Elizabeth Miller. Jefferson, NC: McFarland, 2008.

Stoker, Bram. *The New Annotated Dracula*. Ed. Leslie S. Klinger. New York: W. W. Norton, 2008.

Stoker, Bram. *Dracula Unearthed*. Ed. Clive Leatherdale. Westcliff-on-Sea: Desert Island Books, 1988.

Stoker, Bram. *The Annotated Dracula*. Ed. Leonard Wolf. New York: Ballentine Books, 1975.

Stuart, Roxana. *Stage Blood: Vampires of the 19th Century Stage*. Bowling Green, OH: Bowling Green State University Popular Press, 1994.

Tertullian. *Apologeticus. Ante-Nicene Christian Library* 11. Alexander Roberts and James Donaldson. Edinburgh: T. & T. Clark, 1869.

"They Burned the Vampire." *Healdsburg Tribune, Enterprise and Scimitar*. June 22, 1893. cdnc.ucr.edu/cgi-bin/cdnc?a=d&d=HTES18930622.2.25.

Ulrich, Heinrich. "Manor." *Lasst die Toten ruhen: Deutsche Vampirgeschichten aus dem 19. Jahrhundert*. Ed. Oliver Kotowski. Stolberg: Atlantis Verlag, 2012.

Valdés, Gonzalo Fernández de Oviedo y. *Sumario de la natural historia de las Indias*. Toledo, 1555.

The Vampire, or, Detective Brand's Greatest Case. Old Cap Collier Library 2, 1885.

Veckenstedt, Edmund. *Wendische Sagen, Märchen und abergläubische Gebräuche*. Graz: Leuschner and Lubensky, 1880.

"Vikram and the Vampire; or, Tales of Indian Devilry." Trans. Richard F. Burton. *Fraser's Magazine for Town and Country* 77 (April 1868), 407-432; 560-576; 700-716.

Vikram and the Vampire, or Tales of Hindu Devilry. Trans. Richard F. Burton. London: Longmans, Green, and Company, 1870.

Wachsmann, Karl Adolf von. "Der Fremde." *Erzälungen und Novellen*, 3:7. Leipzig: Carl Jocke, 1844.

[Wachsmann, Karl Adolf von.] "The Mysterious Stranger." *Chambers's repository of instructive and amusing tracts* 4. Edinburgh: William and Robert Chambers, 1854. Tract 62.

Wallace, Alfred Russel. *A Narrative of Travels on the Amazon and Rio Negro: With an Account of the Native Tribes, and Observations on the Climate, Geology, and Natural History of the Amazon Valley*. London: Reeve & Co., 1853.

Waterton, Charles. *Essays on natural history, chiefly ornithology*. London: Longman, Orme, Brown, Green and Longmans, 1838.

Waterton, Charles. *Wanderings in South America, in the North West of the United States, and the Antilles, in the Years 1812, 1816, 1820, and 1824*. London: J. Mawman, 1825.

Watson, H. B. Marriott. "The Stone Chamber." *New York World*. 28 June 1896. 29.

"Weird New Facts about Vampires: Winged and Human." *The Spokesman-Review* 46 (22 November 1927), 16.

Wood, William. *Zoography; Or, The Beauties of Nature Displayed: In Select Descriptions from the Animal, and Vegetable, with Additions from the Mineral Kingdom Systematically Arranged*. 1. London: Dadell and Davies, 1807.

A. Y. "Pepopukin in Corsica." *The Stanley Tales*. 1. Ambrose Marten ed. London: W. Morgan, 1826. 45-71.

5.
"That Demonical Face with Staring Fixed Saucer Eyes:" The Other Nineteenth-Century "Blood-Sucking Vampire"

Introduction

In my precursor to this chapter, "An Evil Kind of Animal," I reached certain conclusions about the large blood-sucking bat in the sixteenth through the eighteenth centuries. Many commentators in the sixteenth and seventeenth centuries stressed the bat was capable of killing a person in one's sleep if its bite was not treated, although some dismissed it as little more than a nuisance. The bite was generally painless and unnoticed, until blood shed during the night alerts one upon awakening, if one wakes at all, what has happened. Descriptions of the bat were not plentiful. From the beginning, it was as large as a medium-sized bird—a pigeon or dove. A few placed them in the East Indies, but most describe them only in terms of the New World. Their wings, when mentioned, were frightening, flapping around in one's face, or used to beat people and probably even disfiguring a victim from time to time.

The bat in the eighteenth century, was no longer just deadly, it became sinister. It was not indigenous simply to Latin America but spread out into the East Indies. It was enormous and had an insatiable thirst for blood, so much so it could fell a cow or horse. Not only was its bite indiscernible, but it now fanned its victim with its gigantic wings to sedate one into an ever deeper sleep or to obtain consent for drawing blood. No longer did it kill as a consequence of its need for blood, but it actually seemed to intend to bring about one's death. Its sucking might be due to the normal procedure of suction from the mouth, or to the manipulation of the tongue. Stedman at last explained how it could drain victims much larger than itself of their blood: they drank until satiated, vomited it up, and then started again.

In this essay I will break down this creature, this *Vampyrus sanguisuga* or blood-sucking vampire, by looking at it through the eyes of naturalists, soldiers, and travelers including popularizers; journalists and newspaper reporters; poets; authors; illustrators. We then attempt to show how engrossed the nineteenth century was with the vampire bat. It is absurd to think that with this amount of attention that Bram Stoker was somehow unexposed and unaffected. An overview of secondary sources was done in the previous chapter.

Naturalists, Soldiers, Travelers, and Popularizers: Educational Studies

It was only one year into the nineteenth century that the true vampire was identified by Félix Manuel de Azara, a soldier and engineer stranded in Paraguay for some twenty years (*Essais sur l'histoire naturelle*, 1801). His description of the *Desmodus rotundus*, aka *Vampire d'Azara* or *Rufous Vampire*, is uncannily accurate. Its body is about 3 inches in length, he wrote, and its wingspan around 16 ½ inches. It removes a small amount of flesh, just enough to expose the capillaries it feeds from; it does not reach veins or arteries. It "attacks" human beings only when other food is unavailable and for Azara the blood lost beyond what is fed upon is about ½ ounce. He spoke from experience for he was bitten four times. The wound is tender but not dangerous. He conjectured that it sucks and licks the blood. It is, as a matter of fact, licking alone. "As for what they said concerning the monstrous size and the manners of this bat, they are excessively exaggerated and full of falsehoods" (see Azara 2, 273-276) Today, as a matter of fact, it is known as a microbat.

The problem with Azara's depiction was that it was almost completely ignored, although he was well respected as an amateur naturalist elsewhere. Darwin, for example, read him carefully and referred to him in his writings.[75] But Darwin did not reference him when he described his own encounter with the bat (*Narrative* 3, 24-25). He wrote, "The whole circumstance has lately been doubted in England; I was therefore fortunate in being present when one was actually caught on a horse's back. We were bivouacking late one evening near Coquimbo, in Chile, when my servant, noticing that one of the horses was very restive, went to see what was the matter, and fancying he could distinguish something, suddenly put his hand on the beast's withers, and secured the vampire" (25). He identified it as the *Desmodus*.[76]

Unlike Azara's, Darwin's account became very well known and was rehearsed throughout the century.[77] Thus it is surprising that the imposing bat of the sixteenth-eighteenth centuries not only survived but flourished. In fact, it was so pervasive that it overshadowed the small true vampire of Azara and Darwin. We can start with the aforementioned John Stedman, probably the most quoted person on the topic in the nineteenth century and whose popularity continued into the twentieth.[78] He was a British-Dutch soldier and he depicted his encounter with the "bat of monstrous size." He said the bat knows by instinct when its victim is in a sound slumber, it alights near the feet and begins to fan the person with its enormous wings, bites off a very small piece out of the big toe

---

[75] He was alluded to some 30 times in the third volume of Darwin's *Narrative of the surveying voyages of His Majesty's Ships Adventure* (1839) and about 60 times in Darwin's *Birds: Part 3 of The zoology of the voyage of H.M.S. Beagle* (1841).
[76] Darwin, *Mammalia* (1838), 2.1: 3. After Darwin, Azara is occasionally referenced but it is rare. For example, in "The Vampire Bat," published in *The Lancaster Gazette* (July 29, 1843), 4. Here he is singled out as "a good describer." But the author references the large bat: "This species, the Andira-Guacu of Piso, is a native of South America; its total length is about six inches." That is the size of the *Vampyrum spectrum*, not the true vampire bat.
[77] Running through the century, there are, for example, Lord Brougham, *The Penny Cyclopædia of the Society* (1843), 106; George Mivart, "What are Bats?" (1876), 533-35; W. J. Gordon, *Popular Natural History for Boys and Girls* (1894), 64. "Bats that Suck Human Blood," *St. Louis Globe-Dispatch* (November 10, 1895), 25. One of the best is one of the earliest, for it tracks the whole discussion: Edward Blyth, "Notice of the predatory and sanguivorous habits of the Bats" (*Journal of the Asiatic Society of Bengal*, March 1842), 255-62.
[78] For example, Brougham 22-23.; Buffon 2: 76-77; "Attacked by Vampires" 7; "The Blood-Sucking Vampire" 3.

and begins to suck the blood until it is scarcely able to fly and the sufferer is left to die, if that be his/her fate.

Stedman was referring to the largest bat in the Western hemisphere: the *Vampyrum spectrum*.[79] This was not, however, the first to be named so; in 1758, Carl Linnaeus named the large flying fox "Vampyrus" (referred today as *Pteropus vampyrus*). These are the two that appear most often in naturalist studies and popularizations. One or the other was labeled, besides "large" and "monstrous," "tremendous" in G. Shaw's 1800 *General zoology* (144), "very formidable" in W. Wood's 1807 *Zoography* (347) and "enormous" (Humboldt and Bonpland 240). Elsewhere it is said to be about the size of a magpie, which compared to the average European bat is basically huge (Cuvier 126). William Carpenter, in the 1848 *Zoology*, compared its wingspan of "two or three feet across" (188) to the British *Vespertilio noctula*'s fifteen inches and the continental *Vespertilio murinus*' sixteen, both big bats in their regions (see Cuvier 126).

Over the eighteenth and nineteenth centuries a number of bats would be named "vampire;" they are known today as false vampires (see French, "False Vampires and Other Carnivores"). There are, for example, in addition to the two mentioned above, the Asian false vampire bats (*Megaderma lyra* and *M. spasma*), the African one (*Cardioderma cor*), the Australian one (*Macroderma gigas*), and other Latin American ones (*Chrotopterus auritus* and *Glossophaga soricina*). And there are the genera and subgenera *Vampyressa* (1843), *Vampyrops* (1865), *Vampyriscus* (1878), and *Vampyrodes* (1889). But these seldom appear in expositions on the vampire bat. What *is* there is the general conjecture that vampire bats are not limited to a single species.

Most of the time two bats are chosen, following J. Gumilla's 1741 account in *El Orinoco ilustrado* (427). Geoffroy-Saint-Hilaire says in his "Sur Les Phyllostomes et les Mégadermes" that Gumilla meant the *andira-guaca* of Brazil and the *andira* of Jamaica (172). Gumilla himself is unclear. In *Reise nach Brasilien* (1821), Maximilian Prince of Wied discerns them to be the *Vampyrum spectrum* and the *Vampire des Azara* (241n). Charles Waterton, the author of *Wanderings in South America* (1825) probably more influential in the nineteenth century than Stedman on the topic of bats, concluded that there were two in Guyana; one larger than the other: "The larger sucks men and other animals; the smaller seems to confine himself chiefly to birds" (176). The large one is the *Vampyrum spectrum*; the smaller appears to be the *Chrotopterus auritus* or the *Phyllostoma hastatum*. "I could only find two species of bats in Guiana," he continues, "with a membrane rising from the nose. Both these kinds suck animals and eat fruit; while those bats without a membrane on the nose seem to live entirely upon fruit and insects" (70).

The two for Edward Blyth, writing in his "Notice of the predatory and sanguivorous habits of the Bats of the genus Megaderma" (1842), are the *Megaderma lyra* and Darwin's *Desmodus*. The reason for the former is that he witnessed it preying on a smaller bat and on inspecting the smaller one, he believed he saw marks on it that demonstrated the *Megaderma* had been sucking the blood of the bat before intending to devour it (see 255-262). Finally, there is

---

[79] We have already noted that it was originally named "Vampyrus" in Rafinesque 54. More information on its name can be found in Gardner 299-300. Both studies refer back to E. Geoffroy-Saint-Hilaire but, while he refers to the *spectrum* as vampire, he does not dub it *Vampyrus* (see Saint-Hilaire 157-198).

Richard Lydekker in his *The Royal Natural History* (1893-94), who wanted to look at a portion of the bats called "vampires" (299). He could not examine them all: "The number of genera and species of vampires is so great that only the more remarkable types can be even mentioned in this work" (302-303). He was of the opinion that in addition to Darwin's bat and the *Diphylla ecaudata*, which had only recently been discovered as sanguivorous, there was the javelin bat or *Phyllostoma hastatum*. He based his decision with regard to the last on experts: "the testimony of several observers inclines us to believe that the indictment is true" (303).

Ironically, there is an interesting tendency among several writers to use Darwin's small bat in order to bolster the claims of a large vampire. Darwin's observations are integrated into the discussion of the big one by eliminating talk of the species of bat he described and its size. John George Wood noted in *The Illustrated Natural History* (1859) that until Darwin captured one, naturalists had dismissed the vampire as a "traveler's tale" (116-117). Now it is known to exist and it is the huge *Vampyrum spectrum*.[80] Sarah Lee, writer of important works on nature for juveniles, began (in her 1852 *Anecdotes of the Habits and Instincts of Animals* 1852) by surveying statements of large bats and then added that Darwin caught a bat on the neck of a horse. She then returned to describe Stedman's experience (29). This was mid-century.

In the last decade of the century, there was the case of Alfred H. Miles, who (in the 1895 *Natural History in Anecdote*) also brought Darwin into the discussion followed by Stedman's description of the "monstrous" bat (36-37). Achilles Daunt (in *Frank Redcliffe. A Story of Travel and Adventure* published in 1889), made clear what the others insinuated. Darwin's servant caught a vampire, he explains; "The species of which we had secured a sample is called *Phyllostoma* [i.e. *Vampyrum spectrum*]" (51-52).

As far as the fanning of the victim goes, it endured throughout the century, usually with Stedman lurking somewhere in the background, although doubts were expressed (e.g., Carpenter 188). Almost always the fanning was to cool the object of its hunger, but once it was conjectured to act like a cradle, to lull one to sleep by its steady rhythm (Munro Smith 67). With reference to drinking blood, some even asserted that drinking blood was common to most bats.[81] That at least one did was seemingly incontrovertible, because so many averred it to be the case by experience. It is true that many of the bats that were held to be vampires turned out not to be so, but the evidence in Latin America seemed irrefutable. At the same time, however, the disappointment registered at finding that most so-called vampires shunned blood and natural skepticism of tall tales led a number to doubt the existence of a blood-sucking bat at all and not just some of its most outlandish qualities.[82]

---

[80] In the first edition of the work, it is a straightforward account and he includes the fanning of the victim, which is part of the "traveler's tale" in the second edition. The first edition is from 1853 (see 26-27).
[81] See Shaw 144; Gregory 853. "Natural History of the Vampyre Bat" 145-146. The last directly follows an article on Polidori's *The Vampyre*.
[82] E.g., de Vere 362-363. Charles Waterton in 1838 was on the defensive that it was not a fable. So was Charles Darwin, as we have seen. On doubts expressed of the Indian vampire bat, see Heber 2: 36, 59; and Timbs 274. Concerning the arrival of the latter in England, see "Vampire Bat" 29.

There is something that Stedman did not touch upon: the use of the tongue. The tongue had two purposes in the nineteenth century. One dates back to Buffon in *Histoire Naturelle*. It is the agent that draws the blood. It does it in two ways. First, Buffon saw its function this way: "this tongue is pointed and bristled with hard, very fine and very sharp papillae which are directed backward; these points which are very thin are able to insinuate themselves in the pores of the skin, enlarge them, and penetrate enough in order that the blood acquiesces to the constant suction of the tongue" (64-65).

Second, Thomas Pennant, whose 1771 *Synopsis of Quadrupeds* is by far the most quoted work on the subject in this century although almost never directly cited, puts it this way: "The Bat is so dexterous a bleeder as to insinuate its aculeated tongue into a vein without being perceived, and then suck the blood till it is satiated" (2: 361-62). So one way is for the tongue to lie upon the surface and suck through the pores; the other is to penetrate the skin and insert itself into a vein.

In the early part of the century the notions of the tongue's use were quite popular, but they wane after the 1850s, although they continued to surface. The longest depiction was by W. E. B. Webster in his *Narrative of a Voyage to the Southern Atlantic Ocean* (1834): "[H]e scarifies you very gently with his tongue; and the retroverted spines or knobs, or papillæ, are peculiarly suited to this; because as he applies his tongue, he keeps hold of the part by this very means, and they gently drag the orifices open, and the labial pouches enable him to suck extremely well; and I believe this is all that is necessary for the perfect art of cupping. . . . [He] take[s] half a pint of blood at a time" (356-357).

This brings up the second purpose: the scarification. It is not the teeth that makes the small incision but the tongue. Alfred Wallace, another influential naturalist along with Waterton and Darwin, some forty years later than both (in *Tropical Nature, and Other Essays* from 1878), writes "The motion of the wings fans the sleeper into a deeper slumber, and renders him insensible to the gentle abrasion of either by teeth or tongue. . . . They . . . have a tongue with horny papillae at the end; and it is probably by means of this that they abrade the skin and produce a small round wound" (120).

So there is a debate about how the bat gets to the blood. In his *Explorations of the highlands of the Brazil* (1869) Richard Burton, explorer and scholar extraordinaire, delineated it succinctly: "Prince Max. [Maximilian, Prinz von Wied] asserts before the doubting days, 'Ce vampire (Phyllostomus) fait avec ses dents un grand trou dans la peau des animaux' ('This vampire makes a large hole with its teeth in the skin of animals'). Gardner [George Gardner, *Travels in the Interior of Brazil*] believes the puncture is made by the sharp hooked nail of the thumb. Lieutenant Herndon [*Exploration of the valley of the Amazon*] thinks that the tusks bite, whilst the nostrils are fitted for a suction apparatus. Others trace the wound to the papilla of the tongue, an organ of action" (108).

Alfred Wallace, had a couple of unusual ideas of the vampire feeding that never caught on. The first, recounted in *A Narrative of Travels on the Amazon and Rio Negro* (1853) is based on the opinion of his brother: "the bat applied one of its long canine teeth to the part, and then flew round and round on that as a centre, till the tooth, acting as an awl, bored a small hole; the wings of the bat serving, at the same time, to fan the patient into a deeper slumber" (449-450). The second (expressed in 1878 in *Tropical Nature, and Other Essays*) has to do with dining while on the fly. Blood flows from the aperture in the skin "which is sucked or lapped up by the hovering vampyre" (120). I know of only a few quotations of either one, but more of the latter than the former. Another conjecture that was not repeated in any of my sources was that of the vampire bat being drawn to an individual by body odor (see Marcoy 71).

Finally, it is indescribably ugly. Here we are talking solely of the *Vampyrum spectrum*. The usual way to do this is by comparing it to the mythological harpy. It was used first in 1511 to describe its terrible behavior and that is the way it was again by Richard Schomburgk in 1847 (*Travels in British Guiana* 225). But it was applied to appearance by George W. Bennett in 1866 in *An Illustrated History of British Guiana*: "it resembles the harpies of old in its hideous and disgusting appearance" (149-150). And again by John McClintock and James Strong, in their *Cyclopædia of Biblical, Theological, and Ecclesiastical Literature* (1867; they typify it as "of the harpy or goblin family" and add that it is "repugnant to the senses" (1: 692). Darwin, in *Journal of researches into the geology and natural history of the various* (1839), describes a snake whose face was hideous and fierce; "I do not think I ever saw anything more ugly, excepting, perhaps, some of the vampire bats" (114). So Darwin actually named another bat "vampire" than his *Desmodus* and he clearly meant the *Vampyrus spectrum*.

It is Richard Burton, however, who, in 1869, gives the most memorable sentence on the subject and it is where we get the title of the chapter: "It must be like a Vision of Judgment to awake suddenly and to find upon the tip of one's nose, in the act of drawing one's life-blood, that demonical face with deformed nose, satyr-like ears, and staring fixed saucer eyes, backed by a body measuring two feet from wing-end to wing-end" (108).

Journalists and Newspaper Reporters

Reports can be accurate, exaggerated, fantasized, or metaphorical. Accurate does not mean that it is factual, but that it conforms to the depictions above: a large bat that gingerly penetrates the flesh of an animal or human being to imbibe the living blood of the victim all the while fanning the body to pleasure it and to keep one asleep. Or that it is a faithful account of a large bat's actual behavior or characteristics. Under real reporting, there is an 1868 story of flying foxes or vampires in Australia, denuding orchards and then migrating to other locations, even some twenty to thirty miles away ("The Oamaru Times" 2). In 1872, in "Voyage à la Nouvelle-Grenade," Doctor Saffray reports that domestic animals—poultry, cattle, mules, horses—were attacked by vampire bats (2: 116). True to their name, they went after blood. Those that were freshly put out to pasture were especially delectable. He finally found a repellent with lemon juice applied to their hides and combs.

Another concerns the steamship *Nevada* (in 1873). A flying fox, "a veritable vampire," was found on board and captured. ("A Veritable Vampire" 1). Then there is an 1889 account from Venezuela that corrects the notion of the "fabled vampire bat." It is real, but "only attacks a man's big toe, and while he may lose considerable blood the attack is not fatal nor especially serious." ("The Varied Vermin of Venezuela" 2).

Concerning the standard picture, the opening paragraphs of Edward Blyth's monograph on his two vampire bats, the *Megaderma lyra* and Darwin's *Desmodus*, are reprinted in newspapers, journals, and books ("What are Bats?" from September 1876). There is an 1888 story that in Chile explorers and their animals grow weaker daily, until one of their party stays up all night and discovers giant vampire bats undulating their wings and feeding upon them either from the air or on the ground ("Mysteriously Attacked" 2). There was no telltale blood to clue them in sooner. Finally—also in 1888—we are told that as the vampire hovers over the toe of its victim, fanning him, it applies its needle-sharp teeth to it with such quickness and dexterity that there is no pain: "The lips are then pressed against the wound and the blood sucked until the vampire is saturated. In a few moments he returns to the attack, and he works through the night until the sleeping victim perishes from sheer loss of blood" ("A Load of Vampires" 2). As with so many other commentators, vampire bats have lips.

The following might as well be exaggerations. In 1846, Johann Jakob von Tschudi reports how an Indian servant falls asleep in a plantation inebriated and a vampire bat sucks from his nose so much blood that it cannot fly away. The bite set off an inflammation so terrible that the man's face became unrecognizable (*Peru* 2: 244). In a story from 1851, a Mexican man was bitten as he lay in the open and several days thence, he was still unable to walk ("The Vampire Bat" 2). In 1863, a servant was said to have received an enormous bite on his nose and his heels were found full of holes, "the animal having fanned him to sleep with its wings" ("Things Worth Knowing: The Bloodsucking Vampire" 85). Big bite, many holes, making someone go to sleep rather than stay asleep are all unusual features.

A young woman in Venezuela was a somnambulist and wandered one night miles from home, according to an article from 1890. Her parents eventually found her dead with a big bat, having a wingspan of over six feet from tip to tip, attached to her throat. The vampire was too full of blood to fly so it was easily shot; the girl's face was placid indicating that she died in her sleep lulled further in by its wings ("Killed by a Vampire" 8). The following year, another young lady was found stretched out on the ground, apparently sleeping but actually dead, with a large vampire drinking from her jugular vein ("No Peace on the Roof" 6). Finally, in 1895, Mrs. Brown-Potter was performing Lady Macbeth's sleep-walking scene in India when a vampire flew in the window and began sucking from her arm ("Topics of the Week" 4). The crowd became agitated but she was so engaged with her role she did not realize it until she went backstage. It flew away and she fainted.

Over against the actual is the metaphorical. Anxieties are like vampires ("The Pain of Anxiety" 1). At night they brush up against you while flittering about, they land upon you and suck your blood, and when you think they're gone they return to haunt you again. Elsewhere we read the true vampire (*Vampyrum spectrum*) has "a nose in the form of the point of a lance" and the wish is expressed that all human cutthroats had such a distinguishing feature:

"The vampires resemble the priests who have so long 'sucked the juices of the state,' and so know well how to soothe 'the national conscience' to sleep, as they draw its substance" (Napier 263-264).

A deeply sarcastic letter was written to the editor "praising" General Adam Badeau in *The Hutchinson News* of April 1, 1888. He is compared to a vampire, fanning his victims "like a nurse, soother, and friend" all the while sucking their blood ("A Letter to Gen. Badeau" 8). A politician who is overpaid and surrounds himself with a formidable array of servants has become a "a hydra headed vampire sitting on the body politic like a nightmare of Erebus, and drawing the very life blood from the people" ("Mr Morgan at Upokongaro" 2).

The vampire is the legacy of capitalists. The ironmasters of Merthyr in Wales left behind for the town and laborers a deficit of liberty according to *The Merthyr Telegraph and General Advertiser for the Iron Districts of South Wales* of September 17, 1870. As the recent celebrations of these masters demonstrated, their agents "are evidently still suffering from the bad old system, and have not yet shaken off the fatal vampire so completely as to breathe with perfect freedom" ("Our 'Noble Old' Ironmasters'" 2).

War is a vampire. A news report in "The Latest War News" (*Oamaru Times* October 21, 1870, 2) appeared less than two months after the beginning of the Franco-Prussian War. In 1865, the *Brecon Reporter and South Wales General Advisor* reported that "The war-fiend has spread his baleful wings like a huge vampire over Western Europe, and . . . there is blood! blood! blood! on every hand." A war economy in a time of peace is likewise a vampire ("Vox Populi" 8.) Britain ought to "cut off this war vampire which has fixed itself on the vitals of the country," for there is no bellicose threat even on the horizon.

Interestingly bats are said in *The Citizen-Examiner* of November 16, 1893, to suck blood "after the fashion of mosquitoes" ("Nocturnal Creatures" 4). What then do they do? Suck through the teeth? And in an article on the suburbanization of a small country town we read "Vampire-like its wings are spreading wider and wider. All those peaceful lanes and sweet rural nooks will soon be in its greedy clutch ("Man About Town" 2)." Wings with clutches. The strangest one is comparing a vampire's fanning more favorably than the experience of acute [male] pleasure. "But experienced travelers say that next to the fanning of the vampire bat, the most delicious sensation experienced by mortals is traveling on a hot summer day on a hand car, not too closely crowded, and seated by the side of a handsome young lady" ("The Jackson Railroad" 1).

Then there is exaggeration. A visitor to the zoo in East London, we are told by *The Abbeville Press And Banner* of April 27, 1892, encountered a vampire bat and was told how, with "deadly purpose" and "diabolical thirst," it hovers over the unsuspecting, sleeping victim swishing its wings to lull one into a deeper sleep, and then settles at the foot and "draws the blood, drop by drop, from the flesh" (("Wild Animals: Visit to a Noted London Establishment" 6). From George Gardner's 1846 *Travels in the Interior of Brazil* we learn that vampire bats, which puncture the skin with its claws and draw blood from the combination of tongue and lips, "nearly destroyed the first establishment of the Europeans in the New World" (388).

A vampire bat skeleton was found in Fort Scott, Kansas according to the *Fort Scott Daily Monitor* of August 4, 1897. We are told that "vampire bats are very large and are poisonous" ("A Bat's Skeleton" 3). Poison was occasionally associated with them in the sixteenth through eighteenth centuries, but is almost unheard of in the nineteenth. It is much the same with lethal intent, until *Dracula* and that is not a news report.

Consumption elicits a reflection on hope and resignation: "the vampire surrounds its victim with perfumed air while it gorges itself with life blood" ("Lena Davis" 3) Another report, this time from *Greensboro Watchman* (June 23, 1887), reads that "the vampire is said to settle beside his victim, fluttering his wings gently while sucking the blood. This action fans the wound so it is not felt" ("Vampire Bats" 1). Two unique ways of using the wings: perfumed air and numbing the wound.

An autobiographical account tells how a traveler in Mexico slept outdoors and a vampire began circling around him at regular intervals "analogous to the well-timed passes of a mesmerist" ("Blood-Sucking Bats" 5) He slipped into a semiconscious state in which he felt several vampires on him but was indifferent to them, for he was dreaming "the air was heavy with the breath of countless rare and beautiful flowers." He was near death when he was awakened and it took five weeks to recuperate enough to continue his journey.

According to *Rural New York* (May 24, 1879) sucking itself is portrayed in an unexpected manner, i.e. with no bite or abrasion at all. "The blood is obtained by suction from the capillary vessels, and not by any wound made by the teeth" ("The Naturalist: The Flying Fox or Roussette Bat" 325). The blood is sucked, apparently by the mouth, directly from the skin. In Brazil "[l]arge vampire bats often fly in one's face at night. They are four times the size of our bats. Many natives bear scars from their teeth" ("Life in Brazilian Forests" 5). One seldom hears of such widespread scarring. Vampire bats return to the same individuals, but there is a story in the *Arizona Republic* of September 26, 1894, that even if one moves ten to twenty miles away, "no immunity is gained thereby, as the bat is sure to follow him and keep up his bloodthirsty attack" ("The Vampire Bat: A Dread Creature That is Common in India" 2).

Finally there is a bizarre story in *Chamber's Edinburgh Journal* of June 12, 1847, from a merchant in Trinidad. While he was resting a large vampire bat flew into his apartment and he decided to conduct an experiment by baring his chest. The bat flew back and forth until it hovered noiselessly above him, fanning him, which he found most soothing. It lighted upon his chest, continuing to fan, and when he felt a bite like a leech he reached out, snatched it, and strangled it to death ("The Vampire Bat" 384).

The largest category is the fanciful. The first pertains to wings. A collector of nightmares shared with the author one of the most memorable in *The Ottawa Journal* of August 1, 1896. A gentleman had a dream around three times a year "of a red-hot vampire bat, which used to fan him with her wings until the heated air began to suffocate him" ("A Collector of Nightmares" 6). Searing the victim rather than cooling. Another is a woman's dream where the vampire opposes women's rights related by Eva Horton in the *Douglass Tribune* on December 21, 1894. A vampire is drinking blood from a beloved giant and the men are divided between wanting to kill it, preserve it, or just ignore it. The women all want it dead but they cannot enter the fray because they are shackled in their houses by the chains of custom and law. The dreamer calls to the men to liberate the women but they shout back that they must not for what would happen to the home? The women would become so independent they would not want to marry. They would become too masculine. The vampire "lifted its ugly head and shot its red tongue out spitefully" ("A Dream" 1). In the ensuing cacophony of voices she woke up.

In the forests of Darien are found vampires which are "numerous, large, and very troublesome" ("Pests of Darien" 7). No pain is felt from their bite and "with their large feathery wings they fan the sleeping victim to a state of delightful coolness." Henderson, North Carolina, sells itself as the "pearl of mountain towns" according to the *Henderson Gold Leaf* (August 4, 1887). One of its most attractive features is that "sleep, when the time comes, [brings] our sweet mountain slumbers—for it takes no vampire to fan the foot of the weary traveler that he may sleep under the bright twinkle of our stars." It is almost as if there were no other way to fall asleep when on a journey.

There are two fanciful ones that are especially significant for they draw together the vampire and the devil. One is didactic and the other more literary. A Christian juvenile monthly, *The Juvenile Instructor and Companion*, had a regular feature by Thomas Carlisle entitled "Natural History." In that issue the subject was bats and we read "Satan, is much like the vampire. He matures his plan in the deep darkness, and flying on noiseless wing to his intended victim, he tries to lull him to sleep, and then seeks to draw from the soul everything that is good, leaving nothing but evil behind" (118-119). The vampire becomes a visible symbol of the spiritual enemy of Christians.

Next is one masquerading as a news story and it poses the question "What is it? Vampire or Devil?" The day before children started disappearing from their beds, a huge human-sized monster with gigantic black wings was spotted by two boys fishing near the desolate region known as "Briar Patch" ("A Demon of the Night" 2). Then as the children continued to vanish, a gentleman, hunting hogs in the Briar Patch, came across some human bones. As he examined them he saw an enormous face peering at him, "the face of the common bat, but magnified more than a hundred fold." It was blinking in the sunlight as if it was having difficulty seeing and this gave the man the opportunity to escape. The gigantic vampire and a devil look enough alike as to be confused.

In an article from *Reading Times* (May 3, 1876) upholding the righteousness of the Republican party against the "ex-Confederate House" or the Democrats, we run into this comparison of the vampire bat to the latter. "It is said that the vampire which has once tasted human blood, has often been known to beat out its life in vain efforts to strike down the iron window bars that intervene between it and another feast" ("Political Pinkertons" 1). In a short news bulletin entitled "Killed by Vampire Bats" (*The Buffalo Commercial* August 15, 1882), we find "It is reported that 600 cattle were killed in a single night at Peru Expagna by vampire bats" (1). There was a report of a California brakeman, John Santine, whose sleep was interrupted almost nightly by what seemed to be a ghost ("Pursued by a Vampire" 7). Sometimes he would find himself covered with strange insects that died when exposed to the light; he would sleep with his windows open and on many an occasion awaken with stomach pains, so he concluded it was a vampire. He wanted his story to be told in case others were suffering from the same thing.

And then there is this one buried in an ode to Labor Day comparing capitalists to vampire bats: "Under the foliage of the mighty trees of the Brazilian forests there lives the vampire bat. The aborigines tell of this animal, that it follows and watches the traveler, waiting to catch him in his sleep to suck his blood. They say that when men go to sleep, protected, as they think from the rays of the sun by the foliage above them, this animal sits quietly waiting until the sun, changing its position, strikes the sleeper, who, in pain caused by the heat, tries to move or awake. The bat comes along, and, using its wings as fans, it gives coolness and rest. It alights on the sleeper's breast, still fanning, it moves toward his throat, still fanning; it sinks its fangs in the jugular, still fanning. The sharp pain almost awakes the sleeper, but those quietly moving wings, giving such relief from the heat, keeps him sleeping still. If the two are left undisturbed the sleeper will awake only to sleep again and forever" ("Labor Day Epic" 217). All this in the daylight. This same story is picked up in the twentieth century by Andrew Furnseth ("The Open Shop" 210).

An article on vampire bats in the *Greensboro Watchman* (June 23, 1887) includes the story of a South American man who once "remarked that he could not understand how some people were always getting unaccountably bitten by bats. At the very moment when he made the statement, a bat was sucking one of his toes, unperceived by him in the dusk. As he moved, the creature fluttered away, and the toe was found to be bleeding" ("Vampire Bats" 1). When Claes Larsen did not come home one evening the citizens of Lake View were convinced a vampire had attacked him ("Vampire of Lake View" 25). The Lake View Historical Society prepared a paper entitled "Vampires as Agents of Mysterious Disappearances" and a group of boys calling themselves "Vampire Hunters" began scouring a nearby park for the creature. His coat was found which rendered proof of the contention because bats are very particular about clothes, never touching them. "It is on record that in Galicia during the middle ages a vampire which counted its prey by the thousand happened to swallow the waistcoat button of a substantial farmer and immediately expired." After several days of this, Larsen returned home, sobering up after a drinking binge.

There are absurder ones. After comparing bats to an intoxicated human we get this story in the *Galesburg Enterprise* of July 6, 1888: A vampire flew in and Col. Ochiltree was pretending to be asleep. "The vampire alighted at Col. Ochiltree's feet, and carefully untying the strings of the Colonel's shoes, which were tied in several hard knots, removed his stockings preparatory to sucking his blood, when the Colonel unexpectedly awoke and buried his glittering falchion in vampire's vitals" ("The Bat" 6). Untying shoes and pulling off socks! A favorite amusement for US Americans in Mexico was to catch a vampire in a room and to put a cigarette in its mouth around which its soft mouth contracted. "Every time the bat breathes it draws in the smoke and then exhales it. . . The smoke generally kills the bat before the cigarette is all smoked up" ("Smoking Vampires" 4).

There are unique species and hybrids. In 1892, *The Sun* ran a story about mosquitoes which had a head on both ends and could grow to such a size that one end could bite under the right eye and the other under the left. A comparison is drawn to a vampire seen one time: Mr. Dodder's father "described a vampire to him once and this . . . sucks blood at both ends. It is only about as large as a sparrow, and, therefore, Mr. Dodder is probably right. It is a new species of vampire" ("Twin Screw Mosquitoes" 21).

Now for hybrids. We have already seen the human-sized vampire or devil with "the face of the common bat, but magnified more than a hundred fold." There was "a cross between a vampire and a catamount which dropped, out of a tree upon the shoulders of a possum hunter and proceeded to smother, scratch, bite, and otherwise devour the unfortunate man" (*Evergreen Star* October 11, 1888, 3). It is said in the *Sacramento Daily Union* of July 7, 1883, that: "Santa Barbara claims to have on exhibition a genuine blood-sucking vampire. It has the head of a kitten, the body of a gopher and the wings of a bat" ("Pacific Coast Items" 8).

Finally, there is a weird article, "Vampires Not Vicious, After All," in *The Daily Democrat* of January 12, 1889, which features an advocate of sympathy for the vampire bat. The occultist Mrs. Lawrence Oliphans said that when a mystically sensitive person, in waiting upon the powers of healing, "finds himself in company with a Vampire, if he will only go in for sympathizing with him he will find, instead of the drain he expected, a new life coming through him from a source that is inexhaustible. He could yield power to a thousand men and be stronger for the yielding." This could be assumed to be the monster, not the bat, but it is not the case. The author immediately presents the testimony of Col. Stedman. Because Stedman killed the vampire, the author concludes "The gallant Captain, I suppose, was not a 'sensitive,' except as regarded his great toe" ("Vampires Not Vicious" 7).[83]

Literature: Poetry

First we shall examine poetry and then prose. Because the vampire is most often used metaphorically in poetry in order to compare it to something else, we will start with those examples. Some of the poets will be renowned, others amateurish.

The vampire monster first appeared in art—i.e. poetry—with Heinrich August Ossenfelder's *Der Vampir* (1748). The first breakthrough for the bat, so far as I know, was forty years later: in Robert Burns' 1788 "The Poet's Progress. A Poem in Embryo" published in *Poems, chiefly in the Scottish dialect* (183).[84] It begins with a complaint. Nature has provided its animals with defenses—the bull, lion, ass, wasp, fox, poisonous toad—and most stations of civilized life—statesmen, courtiers, merchants, priests, and even "silly women." But the poet has been left defenseless and with no sense of smell to track money ("mammon;" "the root of all evil"). There is no context for the monster in the poem; the vampire, like everything else in the poem, is an animal.

---

[83] Another article on her does take the vampire for the monster and not the bat (in *Omaha Daily Bee* November 28, 1888, p. 4). Mrs. Oliphans cannot be alluding to the American "B-flat" vampire which is a bed bug but to the Slavonic vampire monster, which cannot leave Slavonic soil. Sensitives who encounter the American vampire "usually burst into vigorous Saxon, strike a match, light the gas, turn over the pillows, and commence a strenuous pursuit which usually ends in a gory but odoriferous massacre."

[84] It was written independently under this title in 1788, but became embedded in the *Second Epistle to Graham of Fintry* dated October 5, 1791. It was then published in 1797.

> No nerves olfact'ry, true to Mammon's foot,
> Or grunting, grub sagacious, evil's root:
> The silly sheep that wanders wild astray,
> Is not more friendless, is not more a prey;
> Vampyre-booksellers drain him to the heart,
> And viper-critics cureless venom dart.

The second is a stronger image: Sir Walter Scott's 1813 *Rokeby; A Poem*. Therein Wilford is in love with Matilda, but being a poet and not a lover, is too shy to tell her, so he lives his love in his fancy. But imagination acts like a vampire (43).

> 'Tis Fancy wakes some idle thought,
> To gild the ruin she has wrought;
> For, like the bat of Indian brakes,
> Her pinions fan the wound she makes,
> And, soothing thus the dreamer's pain,
> She drinks his life-blood from the vein.

Then there is John Polidori, the father of the modern vampire monster novel. He also knew how to use the vampire bat in his writings. Thomas Chatterton was a famous figure to the Romantics, and in the poem entitled "Chatterton to his Sister," in his *Ximenes, the Wreath, And Other Poems*, Polidori imagines him, at 17 years old, writing to a fictitious little sister his suicide note. Polidori, by the way, may have killed himself two years after publishing this, at 25 years old, and he did have a younger sister.[85] In any case, Chatterton, in this 1819 poem, projects forward his young sister becoming a woman, and facing men, who are mostly like vampire bats, with the prospect of marriage.

> What dangers then beset my dear,
> When most the men shall flatter, fear —
> When most the men shall softly smile,
> They fondly hope they may beguile,
> And hope to hurt when most they please,
> As vampire bat excites a breeze
> Soft, cooling, lulling to repose
> The child whose life's blood quickly flows,
> Feeding the filthy beast with all
> A mother's fondest name may call. (138)

Percy Shelley creates a narrator who is spectator to the grand triumphant pageant of time. The lead car is bright with light but is icy cold. It is driven by a blind charioteer and is leading wildly dancing captives. When it has passed, he encounters Jean Jacques Rosseau, who then takes over the narration. Rousseau explains about the pageant and then tells his own story. The chariot returns with its throngs and Rousseau is swept away into its crowd. His journey brings him to a grove which becomes a tropical jungle peopled with shadows.

> The earth was grey with phantoms, & the air
> Was peopled with dim forms, as when there hovers

---

[85] There is some question about this. See Viets 1773-1775.

> A flock of vampire-bats before the glare
> Of the tropic sun, bring ere evening
> Strange night upon some Indian isle . . . (Shelley 202)

In 1834, an author celebrates the inevitable forward march of Justice and Mercy. The following stanza glories in the fall of the tyrant, King Miguel of Portugal, just as the previous one had done so with regard to Charles X of France. They, and all despots like them, were vampires in the branches of the trees of state.

> . . . Every bird of prey
> Lodg'd in its branches, and hideous
> Vampire, half bird half beast.
> The canker-worm is gnawing at the heart—
> The worm that never dies—till it
> Hath slain its victim,—
> And let all nations say—Amen. (Sydney 4)

The experience of losing a loved one at an untimely age brings the realization that memory is like a vampire ("To —, At Parting," *Mississippi Palladium* (August 29, 1851), 3). Perhaps the worst thing is that death eludes the survivor.

> But e'en this boon's denied me, for Death himself doth flee,
> As if he feared contagion of the woes that burden me!
> And while unto the very dregs I quaff life's bitter cup,
> The cruel vampire, Memory, doth drink my spirits up.

Friedrich von Heyden's 1852 poem entitled "Der Vampyr und die Camarilla" compares the two.[86] A Camarilla is a group of unaccountable advisers to a ruler; they have no official government position but they have an undue amount of influence on policy. We might call them cronies today. When disaster hits, usually due to their counsel, they move on to another court. The work starts off with a description of the vampire.

> Places sunbaked as hell,
> Where north winds do not blow,
> The vampire chooses to dwell,
> And its malice to show.
> It flies out and returns
> To the sleeper asleep in his room,
> On him it descends and turns,
> But the man wakes not to his doom.
> Upon his breast it settles
> As lightly as a swan
> The movement of wings is gentle
> To cool and to calm.
> As that one lies obliviously
> Lost in a dream's desire
> The vampire sucks at him vigorously
> Warm blood from his breast to acquire.

---

[86] See Heyden 200-201. The translation from the German is my own so it should not reflect upon Heyden.

> And the vampire it hastens
> And flies away when done
> Meanwhile the sleeper awakens
> Finding he's weary and wan.

The vampire bat is also used as an image for a lover that has chosen another suitor. In a bitter poem entitled "To a Stolen Fan," appearing in *The Courier-Journal* of 9 July 1882, the rejected one described his reaction to his ex-girlfriend's "deceit."

> See! a message here is written,
> Carrier-dove, beneath thy wing,
> And a name—not mine—another's!
> Vampire bat, 'tis thus I'll fling
> From me one whose deadly art
> Fanned my cheek and drained my heart!

Josephine Pollard published a very popular temperance poem, "The Price of a Drink," on March 3, 1883 in the *Saturday Evening Mail*, that was soon turned into a song. Here, interestingly enough, the vampire is not the alcoholic beverage, the bartender, or the establishment, but the disease bred by the poverty that drunkeness ushers in.

> The price of a drink! if you want to know
> What some are willing to pay for it, go
> To that wretched tenement over there
> With dingy windows and broken stair,
> Where foul disease like a vampire crawls
> With outstretched wings on the mouldy walls,
> Where poverty dwells with her hungry brood,
> All wild-eyed as demons for lack of food . . .

Then there are some poems that simply refer literally to the vampire bat. Two do it *en passant*. For example, Robert Browning's "Pied Piper of Hamelin" (1842). Hamelin was overrun by rats and the elders interviewed a piper in colorful clothing who promised that he could rid the town of the vermin the way he had other places.

> In Tartary I freed the Cham,
> Last June, from his huge swarms of gnats;
> I eased in Asia the Nizam
> Of a monstrous brood of vampyre-bats . . .

The Battle of Wyoming was part of the Revolutionary War, pitting the US American Patriots or Whigs against the British and the Iroquois. Some three hundred Revolutionaries died compared to just three of their adversaries. Jesse Harding wrote an ode to the massacre on its 100th Anniversary ("Wyoming Massacre" 217). In it he declares that with so much bloodshed it would be an invitation to vampires. It is interesting that they are depicted as "blood-snuffing." Some naturalists above saw the leaf-like structure of the nose as a suction device.

> The roaring of muskets, the plunging of spears,
> The yells and the scalps, and the last groan of lives—
> The regent of terrors and monarch of fears

Are holding their revel till no Whig survives—
The blood-snuffing vampires, drawn out of their lair,
With the gluttons of carnage are rioting there.

Finally, there is a poem by Morgan Hawkes entitled "The Vampire Bat," appearing in the *Adelaide Observer* December 11, 1886, where the vampire bat is a subject. This is unique for several reasons. One is that the bat is an object of the story not just a terror confronting the main character(s). Second, the tale is comical. Other instances, poetry or not, are serious, even if the effect is amusing, like the bat untying shoes and removing stockings. Another is that the vampire is affected by what is in the blood it drinks. This is the first, so far as I know, that this is explored.[87] Then there is the dexterity of the bat; it can open wine casks and drink. Lastly, this is a lighthearted Anglican dig at Roman Catholicism, with its winebibbing and selfishness.

A vampire bat has a secret nest in an Italian monastery and from there it flies down to the town and imbibes on the peasants there until they are beside themselves. The monks decide on a plan to stop it from feeding on blood; they use the cellar man, who is perpetually drunk, as a lure. The bat gets drunk on his blood and stops visiting the village; the monks rejoice until they notice that their wine casks are losing their precious contents. With this realization, they wish the bat would return to the village.

And the peasants grew rosy and plump and hale,
And the wine in the cellars still shrunk and shrunk,
And the monks grew skinny and pinched and pale,
And the Vampire Bat got drunk and drunk.
Till one sultry morn by a blessed mistake
On the holy water he chanced to light,
And he took but a drop his thirst to slake
And it killed him dead on the spot outright!

Literature: Prose

Now we turn to prose. We have three that mention vampires merely in passing. In "A Ride in a Hurricane Through the Sugar-Cane," *Fraser's Magazine* March 1850, 292-94, Reginald Hardy volunteers to cross the island of Trinidad to run an errand when no one else will, because of an anticipated hurricane. Once he hits the forest the winds break forth so that the horse bolts in the midst of wind that bends the trees nearly to the ground and constant lightning in otherwise complete darkness. Somehow during this drenching, hammering ride he can hear "a horrid assemblage of sounds, composed of the hideous gibberings and squeakings of the monkeys, accompanied by the most ludicrous grimaces and contortions, the hootings of the owls, the shrieks of the vampire-bats, the hissing of the serpents, and the cries and howlings of the other wild animals."

There is a story of intrigue between two European traders on the mythical island of Falesá in the South Seas told by Robert Louis Stevenson in his 1893 book *Island Nights' Entertainments*. John Wiltshire is the hero and he has settled

---

[87] There is only one other of which I am aware: E. E. Baldwin's *The Strange Story of Dr. Senex* (1891).

in a village near a cape of woods and married a native woman. He describes the nearest bay: "Many birds hovered round the bay, some of them snow-white; and the flying-fox (or vampire) flew there in broad daylight, gnashing its teeth" (92). Flying in the day, gnashing teeth. Elsewhere the vampire is a metaphor. For example, one is invited to imagine the perfect funeral for one's loved ones in "Churchyard and Funerals in the Year of Our Redemption," published in 1872 in *The Churchman's Shilling Magazine and Family Treasury*. There will be grief and sorrow, of course, but "horror and despair should cast no gloom on the sacred spot—those Vampire wings should never hover there."

There is one that really features a vampire as metaphorical. It centers around the life of young Herbert Montague who, at the beginning of this earnest story, signs a pledge of abstinence ("The Vampyre by the Wife of a Medical Man" from 1858). He is forced by his uncle to renounce it and take a drink with him, thus leading him to a life of debauchery at the local bar, The Vampyre Inn. The Vampyre Inn is said to be named after the Vampyre Bat which is described as "the most expert blood-sucker in the world" (18). It flies in the window, fastens itself on a sleeper's body, and sucks, often ending the person's life. The reason its bite is not felt is because of the "refreshing agitation of the Vampyre Bat's wings, which contributes to increase the sleep."

Herbert does have a few months of sobriety. He is nursed back to health by his longsuffering mother. At the beginning of withdrawal he is so crazed that he has to be restrained and visions ever crossed his distempered brain of the Vampyre. "They fly—they bite—they suck my blood—I die. That hideous 'Vampire!' Its eyes pierce me through—they are red—they are blood-shot. Tear it from my pillow. I dare not lie down. It bites—I die! Give me brandy—brandy—more brandy" (37) He goes back to drinking and finally dies, dragging down his mother, his uncle, the landlord of the bar, and a bar patron with him.

Five others follow in which the vampires play a substantive role and three of those have similar plots. They are literal. The first is "Battling with Bats" with a subtitle of "How a Man Drove Away a Horde of Hungry Vampire Shaped Creatures" published in *The Auckland Star* on 26 March 1892. Dr. J. J. Kite was exporing a cave when a boulder dislodged and he was plunged into darkness and attacked by bats "of remarkable size and fierceness." "So vicious did they become that he was forced to fight them off by swift movements of his hands. . . . Stunned and only partly aroused from their stupor, thousands precipitated themselves against the jutting rocks and fell upon the floor dead or flapping awkwardly about in their wounded agony." "They swarmed on the doctor's back and neck like huge bees. They dashed against his face and clung to his clothes, his hair and his beard . . . He struck savagely and hurled hundreds of the squeaking harpies upon the earth and trampled them under his feet. The cavern's rocky bottom became so slippery with the blood and scattered entrails of mangled bats that he could scarcely keep his footing. He set his coat aflame and they backed off into other areas of the cave. He then was able to dig himself free" ("Battling with Bats" 3).

Sidney Bertram's "With the Vampires" (*Phil May's Illustrated Winter Annual* 1899) tells the story of Charlie Grant who was exploring a cave when something brushed against him.[88] A couple more passes and he slipped and found himself

---

[88] This tale was rescued from oblivion by Mark Ashley in *Vampires: Classic Tales* (231-240).

on a small ledge surrounded by darkness with an injured leg and three vampires at his feet. "No detail of their loathsome bodies could he now fail to distinguish. The candle only intensified the horror of the two sharp incisor teeth in front, and the lancet-shaped fangs at the sides of their mouths; but worst of all, the split leaf-like appendage with which they suck the blood of their victims." He lost the candle and he finally gave up his frantic movements. Due to his immobility the vampires ranged themselves on the injured leg and started to suck.

"The flesh of the victim began to shrink on the bones it covered, as the blood was drawn out; and vitality ebbed through the punctures made by the sharp teeth of the assailants. Half an hour passed, and one of the creatures fell off, wallowing on the slimy ground. A few moments after it returned again to its loathsome work. In turn each of the vampires left the body, but only to return. Suddenly one of the legs of the victim moved convulsively. The three creatures tried to fly, but their loathsome bodies refused to move. They were too full of the blood of their victim, and the wings were not powerful enough to lift them." Suddenly the lanterns of his friends, who had been off hunting, appeared and he was rescued, to the irritation of the bats, who rolled over the ledge and sunk heavily into the darkness.

Then there is a story from the Philippines (P. I. D., "At a Hemp Farm in Luzon," *Youth's Companion* 15 May 1899). The adventure is set after the Spanish-American War and just at the commencement of the Philippine-American War. The owner of a small hemp farm came back from a trip and went to the shed to inspect his 4-horse-power, steam-driven machine for stripping hemp fiber. The safety valve was rusted shut and when he finally released it the steam shot up to the roof. This dislodged a good number of "'flying foxes,' the great fruit-eating vampire of the Philippines." "Nasty, clammy hands seemed to buffet my face! Claws clutched my hair. Teeth chattered in my ears!" Something bit his left wrist and clung there and it took all his strength to shake it loose. He swung a poker at them and knocked down around twenty-nine and fully as many escaped out the door when it was opened.

There was a ship which was eponymously named *The Maelstrom* and the small crew of which had nearly been wiped out described in *The Royal Magazine* (March 1899). There was only one survivor. A ship ran across an exsanguinated man on the beach and brought him to *The Maelstrom* for identification and there the sailors learned the story from the unfortunate man. A Spanish woman was on board and whosoever became the focus of her attention died. First the captain, then the first mate, finally the man on the beach. The survivor pointed out that on two occasions he heard swishing noises from the room where they died.

Two members of the crew boarded the ship to solve the mystery. They entered a room and were immediately set upon by a giant bat; it drew blood but in the end was killed. They found the woman dead with a suicide note nearby. Therein she explained that she had a pet vampire who was domesticated and would do her bidding. The captain "trod her into the dirt" so she had him killed; the first mate turned his affection toward her but she hated him and he died as well. She loved the man found dead on the beach, but as they slept together, the bat got out and attacked him on the toe. He finally broke free, ran across the deck, and disappeared in the ocean.

Illustrations

1. Bat Attacks

The story of traveling through Venezuela is told by a young man of 20 years. He and his companions were surrounded by bats of the *Vampyrum Spectrum* variety which are designated as vampires in Daunt Frank Redcliffe's *A Story of Travel and Adventure in the Forests of Venezuela* (1899). They all flew away except one who seemed intent on making them its banquet. They shot it, it bit one of them, they crushed its head and measured it. It was two feet across its wings. In the midst is Stedman's account of the vampire bat. The illustrator takes some liberties with the story. Although the sky is full of large bats, the ones actually feeding on the men are small (see Redcliffe 53).

This is drawn by Émile-Antoine Bayard and entitled "Les Chauves-Souris Vampires" ("The Vampire Bats"). It is an illustration from the 1872 "Voyage dans les Vallées de Quinquinas (Bas-Pérou)" by M. Paul Marcoy. Liberties are taken again from the text but they are not due to the illustrator, for the drawing is "after a water color by the author." The text precedes the picture by some fourteen pages and it relates an episode with a native guide in which a bat bit his toe. "Questioned by us about what he had felt during his sleep, the man responded that the only impression he believed he recalled was a sensation of freshness much more agreeable than the march and the heat of the day which rendered his feet red-hot." The illustration, however, is of a general vampire attack.

The Other Nineteenth-Century "Blood-Sucking Vampire"

In the tale that this picture depicts entitled "The Stone Chamber," from *New York World* (28 June 1896), Warrington was engaged to be married and was restoring Marvyn Abbey to be their home.[89] He slept in the Stone Chamber during the renovations and there was attacked by a bat which left a wound on his throat. Instead of being worn out by it, he became ill-tempered and aggressive, eventually losing his fiancée due to his unpredictable fits. A friend of his stayed behind when Warrington left, ashamed of himself, and he too was attacked and became cantankerous and belligerent with the same wound upon his neck. He finally explored the ancestral crypt of the Marvyns and found the bat down there and inadvertently killed it.

2. Vampires with Exaggerated Bat Faces

This is plate 72 of Francisco de Goya's *Los Desastres de la Guerra: Las Resultas* or *The Disasters of War: The Consequences*. It appears that the collection of 82 prints was in response to the circumstances in Spain and France, especially two periods of fighting between them: the Dos de Mayo Uprising of 1808 and the Peninsular War (1808–14). The vampire in the foreground is followed by a horde of others in the background. The position of sitting on the stomach sucking from the chest of a supine figure (here, the people of Spain) will become a favorite of artists.

---

[89] One day prior it was advertised as "The Stone Chamber of Death: The Vampire's Home." *New York World*. A fuller text appeared in 1898 that directly tied Lady Marvyn, who died some 150 years before, with the vampire: *The Heart of Miranda and Other Stories* (140-224).

This is an illustration by Walter Crane, an avowed socialist: "The Capitalist Vampire" (*Justice* 22 August 1885; reprinted in *Cartoons for the Cause, 1886–1896*). It stands alone with no text assigned to it. The supine figure has "Labour" written across it and he is lying, exhausted, next to the tools of his trade. He is being attacked by the huge vampire bat of capitalism with its respective wings of religious hypocrisy and political parties. Into this scene enters the angel of socialism with its clarion call of freedom and liberation. Walter Crane wrote a poem, "On The Suppression of Free Speech at Chicago" appearing in *Renascence, A Book of Verse* from 1891, which is connected to it: "Doth Freedom dwell where ruthless Kings of gain, Like stealthy vampires, still on Labour feed, Still free—to toil or starve on plenty's plain? Then what of Labour's hope—the will to be Equal, fraternal, knowing want nor greed, Shrined in a peoples' heart when states are free?"

The text to this picture, altered from the original by Otto Marcus, is "The Working Man and his Vampire (But is the Vampire Rightly Labeled?" on the frontispiece of W. T. Stead's *Chicago To-day: The Labour War in America* (1894). In the background of this illustration is the Pullman Strike of 1894. The thesis is expressed thus: "In the frontispiece I reproduce a German cartoon representing Labour, preyed upon by the vampire of Capitalism. The worst vampire that preys upon Labour in America is not Capitalism, but the fatal lack of that spirit of loyal brotherhood, which is the indispensable foundation of all effective co-operation" (263). This means government, capitalism, and labor must be run by honest people who share each other's burdens, i.e., are part of the renewal of civil religion. The original is Otto Marcus, "Der Vampyr," *Der Wahre Jacob*. Here the neck of the vampire has "Kapitalismus" written on it and the angel, wearing a revolutionary Phrygian or liberty cap, carries a book with the title "Wissenschaft" or "Science," referring to scientific socialism. The worker, exhausted, has dropped his hammer and is Capitalism's helpless victim. So the initial picture is basically the same as Crane's image, albeit with a different meaning.

The Other Nineteenth-Century "Blood-Sucking Vampire"

This is by George Frederick Keller entitled "The Vampire or the Landlords of San Francisco" (*The San Francisco Illustrated Wasp* 2 September 1882). To the left is a landlord vampire squeezing a laborer in a press drawing from his pockets a stream of coins. Wrung from the worker's face is an equal quantity of blood, sweat, and tears. In the back is a store with two stereotypical Chinese waiting to exploit him further. To the right of center is a landlord vampire sitting in opulence and grandeur with two bags labeled $500,000 and an open ledger with rents on one side and receipts on the others. A Chinese cook is bringing in a meal, indicating again that the Chinese are acting as servants to the vampires. At the bottom is a landlord being pulled from his money by death to be forced to join his companion landlords in the molten fires of hell.

With the discovery of the Comstock Lode of gold in 1859, San Francisco went from 57,000 inhabitants in 1860 to 233,000 in 1880. The financing to develop the Lode came from the new stock exchange in the city and gambling on it soon became a passion. The illustration by G. F. Keller ("The Curse of California," in *The Wasp* of 14 July 1877) is fairly straightforward. The barnyard animals gather before the vampire stockbrokers who rake in their savings with promises of large dividends on their investments. When the price of the stocks falls, the same vampires, loaded now with the animal's life savings (the bag of $10,000 has written on it "Poor People's Money"), send them away destitute and ruined. The words on the large desk that divides the winners from the losers are "California Stock Exchange, Vampire and Co. President."

"Cardiff's Vampire" appeared in the Welsh daily newspaper, *The Evening Express* (8 May 1895), a paper which represented a conservative outlook on politics and economics and which circulated in the district of Cardiff. Here the illustrator is pillorying the city for scaring away manufacturing plants and the jobs they can bring with the vampiric qualities of "high rates" surrounded by high taxes, expenses, extravagance, prices, and waste. In the 1890s the city had already begun its close association with steel production, but the illustrator obviously wants more than that. The caption reads of the industries ready to locate there: "Would-be Residents: 'O lor, we ain't a-going to settle in a town where there's a monster like that!'"

The caption reads "The English Vampire: Reply to Punch's 'Irish Vampire' October 24th." Above is the name of the publication, *The Irish Pilot*, and the date, November 7, 1885. The *Punch* illustration, which appears here, since it has a human face, depicts Erin, or Ireland, asleep with a vampire bat with the face of Charles Parnell and the name of National League on its wings swooping down to destroy her. She must wake up and face the threat. This rejoinder has a defiant Erin with National League emblazoned on her shield and her sword drawn standing firm and defending herself against a vampire bat with a frightened look on its face and British Rule written across its chest. The nineteenth century was a time of great unrest by the Irish against English domination. Ireland was predominantly Catholic while England was Protestant, so landholding was the domain of an English minority who were often absent and the Catholics were dispossessed and the Roman Church disestablished. In the wake of the Great Irish Famine (1845-51) the English landlords began a mass eviction of tenant farmers. The National Land League was formed in 1879 under the presidency of Charles Parnell to protect the rights of tenant farmers. When the league was suppressed, Charles Parnell founded the National League in 1882 with that same goal, but with extended objectives such as home rule and economic reforms.

Human-Faced Vampires: General

Daniel Compère has named this picture "Vampires Lunaires" (Lunar Vampires) and it is found in his essay "Paul Féval et les vampires" (*Paul Féval, romancier populaire* 59-67). It is usually entitled "The Ruby Amphitheater" or "Lunar animals and other objects Discovered by Sir John Herschel." It is part of what has come to be called "The Great Moon Hoax." In August of 1835 *The New York Sun* ran a series of six articles under the title "Great Astronomical Discoveries Lately Made by Sir John Herschel" alleging that the astronomer Sir John Herschel had discovered life on the moon. In the fourth installment (August 28, 1835) these creatures were found. "We could then perceive that they possessed wings of great expansion, and were similar in structure to this of a bat, being a semitransparent membrane expanded in curvilineal divisions by means of straight radii, united at the back by the dorsal integuments.... We scientifically denominated them as Vespertilio-homo, or man-bat; and they are doubtless innocent and happy creatures." Hardly vampires.

Albert Joseph Pénot: *La Femme Chauve-Souris* or *The Bat Woman* (c. 1890). The caption according to Wikimedia Commons reads "Oil painting of a nude woman with long dark hair flowing behind her and bat wings in front of a dark cloudy sky." One can add that a full moon is seen in the background peeking through the clouds and that the bat woman draws the viewer in by her mesmerizing gaze. It is not a picture of a human vampire bat but it has been put on the covers of the 2009 Valancourt Classics edition of Francis Marryat's *The Blood of the Vampire* (1897) and Jean Marigny's 2009 *La fascination des vampires*, so it will be considered to be one for years to come. Apart from these it is occasionally advertised as "The Flying Vampire."

THE POLITICAL VAMPIRE

Politics and the railroads went hand in hand. Politicians granted land, determined the railroad's routes, and issued corporate charters. Eugene Debs, the famous union organizer, wrote in the *Locomotive Firemen's Magazine* of December 1885, the same year as this cartoon, "When legislatures meet, the first thing in order is to see that every member has a railroad pass. The Kings [the railway owners] see to it that their decrees in this regard are obeyed to the letter, the theory being that a legislator with a railroad free pass in the pocket is going to vote the way he rides. From the moment he accepts the pass he is secure. . . . [T]hey assume that government ought to be of the railroads, by the railroads, and for the railroads." It is, in other words, a bribe. Thus the human skull on the vampire bat with "free pass" inscribed on its wings by Thomas Nast, "The Political Vampire" (*Harper's Weekly*, April 1885).

This is labeled "The Commercial Vampire;" it is by Leon Barritt from the July 20, 1898 issue of *Vim*, a short-lived satirical weekly and reprinted in Vincent Virga, *Eyes of the Nation: A Visual History of the United States* (237). It was a vampire bat labeled "Greed" seated on its nest entitled "Department Store" ringed with human skulls and bones. The cartoon saw the department store as a bloodthirsty predator of small independent businesses. The skulls and bones are named: butcher, jeweler, clothier, hardware merchant, gents furniture dealer, milliner, piano dealer, bookseller, hatter, druggist, dry goods merchant, grocer, shoe dealer, bicycle dealer. As Sara Libby Robinson in her *Blood Will Tell: Vampires as Political Metaphors before World War I* has put it: "The department store was to shopping what the sweating system was to more skilled methods of manufacturing: it took small, decentralized stores specializing in a limited number of consumer goods and brought them together into enormous, efficient conglomerates, where the widest variety of goods could be found under a single roof" (86). And it is an unmistakenly Jewish face. Jews were forced into usury because medieval Catholicism would not let Christians charge interest when lending money to each other, so Christians needed middlemen to do it. Then Jews were confined to professions such as tailoring, peddling, and banking, including usury. So some Jews naturally moved into retail sale and were pilloried for doing so.

The Other Nineteenth-Century "Blood-Sucking Vampire"

VAMPYRE.

Vampires are identified as the worst kind of hypocrites as they are in this illustration by Henry L. Stephens, "The Vampyre (Psalmicantor Vehemens)" in *The Comic Natural History of the Human Race* published in 1851. As social ones, they treat one with kindness and respect to one's face while engaged in defamation behind one's back. In particular are those who cloak their scandals with religious piety. There are also political ones, e.g. the contributors or editors of journals which ostensibly take the moral high ground. They circulate rumors which spread like wildfire and then offer retractions few read. They love to latch on to talented women, threatening them with slander if they do not grant them access to their bodies. They wear a deceiving mask; pull it off and you find the face of a fiend, hence the illustration.

The Vampire That Hovers Over North Carolina.

"Negro Rule" is the "Vampire that Hovers over North Carolina," by Norman Ethre Jennett in *News and Observer* (27 September 1898). This cartoon by Norman Jennett, an outspoken white supremacist working for the equally prejudiced newspaper, depicts the Democratic strategy to wrest control of state and local governments from the "Fusionists," a union between Black Republicans and the People's Party, a radical agrarian coalition. Thus the ballot box. The plan of the Democrats was to pillory the Fusionists for supporting "Negro Rule" or "Negro Domination." It depicted Black male sexuality as endangering white women, hence the predominance of women running from its claws. The result of this was the Wilmington race riot of 1898, which occurred some six weeks after the appearance of this cartoon. A mob of white men destroyed the property of the Black citizens and killed dozens of them, essentially carrying out a coup d'état against the duly elected government of Wilmington, the only successful one in US history. For more information see Kirschenbaum's essay "The Vampire that Hovers Over North Carolina:' Gender, White Supremacy, and the Wilmington Race Riot of 1898."

Human-Faced Vampires: Specific

A CADMAN TO THE RESCUE.

This is actually more on a vampire slayer. This is called "A Cadman to the Rescue," *The New Zealand Observer and Free Lance* (19 June 1897). The caption reads "The Government has resolved to appeal against the amendment of the Cyanide Patent—the vampire that threatens to drain the life blood out of the mining industry." "A Cadman" is pictured as coming to the rescue with "Liberal Govt" on his shield and his sword drawn. Alfred Jerome Cadman was the minister of Mines in New Zealand so he worked for the interests of the mine owners. The vampiric cyanide syndicate was the MacArthur-Forrest Company which owned the patent on using potassium cyanide to dissolve gold ore and then adding zinc to extract the gold from the resulting sludge. This made mining gold much more profitable than previous methods. The problem was that the company charged such high royalties on the process. Thus the mine owners turned to the government for help—to annul the patent.

THE IRISH "VAMPIRE."

This illustration by John Tenniel, "The Irish Vampire" in *Punch, or The London Charivari* (17 October 1885), is accompanied by a poem. A luckless, supine young woman ("Poor Erin") is warned to awaken. Sleep will bring no relief; with her defenses down, she will be attacked by a vampire. The picture shows us Ireland (Hibernia) and the vampire The National League. The League was founded by Charles Stewart Parnell in 1882, thus the bat's head is his. The League worked for land reform, home rule, more enfranchisement, and economic reforms in Ireland. Conservatives, such as the staff at *Punch*, where this appeared, saw any compromise of London's power over Ireland as creating a domino effect that would effectively end the British Empire, for others would agitate for home rule as well. Parnell and The National League were dangerous agitators, sapping the life of the country, in their estimation. We have already seen the rejoinder to this: "The English Vampire."

The Other Nineteenth-Century "Blood-Sucking Vampire"

QUEENSLAND AND THE VAMPIRE.

The bat's proboscis emerges from the mouth and chin of the face of the general manager of the Queensland National Bank (Q N Bank on the wings), Edward Robert Drury, and is biting the breast of the immobilized Queensland drawing milk and blood therefrom. It appeared as "Queensland and the Vampire," in *The Worker: Journal of the Associated Workers of Queensland* (28 January 1893), with the caption: "'The directors of the Queensland National Bank announce that the net profits for the six months, after making the usual provision for rebate, interest, and bad debts, amount to more than £47,000' (*Courier*)—sucked of course from Queensland's deposit of Two Millions sterling." The vampire is raping Queensland for its pleasure and gain. The bank, at the time, was run primarily for the sake of outside investors, who received regular dividends, and therefore judged its success according to interests other than those of the state.

Humorous

This is simply making fun of women's fashion. The caption reads "They thought it was a vampire for sure but—it wasn't," *Los Angeles Herald* (21 July 1895). It is from the German illustrated humor and satire magazine, *Fliegende Blätter* or *Flying Leaves* as "Das vermintliche Gespenst," *Fliegende Blätter*, number 2596, year 1895, 162 by Eugen Kirchner In the original the heading reads "The Putative Ghost" and the caption, "Kathl [Katharina], It's over now! Here comes a Vampyr! . . . Geez, it's only our gracious Lady!" By having peasants use "Lady" the emphasis is more on class differences rather than fashion. But either way, the reference is to the vampire bat.

This final one is from *La mode illustrée, Journal de la famille*, (2, 1887) and is entitled "Travestissement chauve-souris" (A Bat Costume). The title is all there is. It was reprinted on page 49 of *Masquerade and Carnival: Their Customs and Costumes* (1892) by Jennie Taylor Wandle. The copy there reads: "Gown of black gauze made over a black foundation. Mantle of black satin, made double and whaleboned to represent huge wings cut similarly to an umbrella top. Fichu of black gauze fastened with an artificial bat, and bat head-dress. Long black gloves, black stockings and slippers with bats upon the latter. A bat-wing mask may be worn if desired." There is no reference to a vampire so its inclusion is just for a lark, brought on by the previous illustration.

Works cited

Ashley, Mark. ed. *Vampires: Classic Tales*. New York: Dover Publications, Inc., 2011.
"Attacked by Vampires." *Marshall County Republican* 18, 26 February 1874.
Azara, Felix de. *Essais sur l'histoire naturelle des quadrupèdes de la province du Paraguay*. Paris: Charles Pogens, 1801.
Baldwin E. E. *The Strange Story of Dr. Senex*. New York: Minerva Publishing Company, 1891.
Barritt, Leon. "The Commercial Vampire." *Vim*. 20 July 1898. 10-11.
"The Bat." *Galesburg Enterprise*. 6 July 1888. 6.
"A Bat's Skeleton." *Fort Scott Daily Monitor*. 4 August 1897. 3.
"Bats that Suck Human Blood." *St. Louis Globe-Dispatch*. 10 November 1895. 25.
"Battling with Bats." *The Auckland Star*. 26 March 1892. 3.
Bennett, George W. *An Illustrated History of British Guiana*. Georgeton, Demerara: Richardson & Co., 1866.
Bertram, Sidney. "With the Vampires." *Phil May's Illustrated Winter Annual* 10, 1899.
"Blood-Sucking Bats." *The Buffalo Commercial*. 28 April 1890. 5.
"The Blood-Sucking Vampire," *The Wyalong Advocate and Mining, Agricultural and Pastoral Gazette*. 27 July 1912. 3.
Blyth, Edward. "Notice of the predatory and sanguivorous habits of the Bats of the genus Megaderma, with some Remarks on the blood-sacking propensities of other Vespertilionidae." *Journal of the Asiatic Society of Bengal*. March 1842. 255-262.
Brougham, Henry Peter. ed. *The Penny Cyclopaedia of the Society for the Diffusion of Useful Knowledge*. London: Charles Knight & Co., 1837.
Brougham, Henry Peter. ed., *The Penny Cyclopaedia of the Society for the Diffusion of Useful Knowledge*. London: Charles Knight & Co., 1843.
Browning, Robert. *Dramatic Romances and Lyrics: and Sordello*. London: W. Scott, 1897.
Burns, Robert. *Poems, chiefly in the Scottish dialect*. (New ed.) 2. Edinburgh: T. Cadell, 1797.
Richard Burton, *Explorations of the highlands of the Brazil; with a full account of the gold and diamond mines* 1. London: Tinsley Brother, 1869.
Buffon, Georges-Louis Leclerc, Comte de. *Histoire Naturelle, générale et particulière, avec la description du Cabinet du Roi* 10. Paris: L'Imprimarie Royale, 1763.

Buffon, Georges Louis Leclerc Comte de, et al. *A Natural History of Man, the Globe, and of Quadrupeds from the Writings of Buffon, with Additions from Cuvier, Lacépède, and Other Eminent Naturalists.* New York: Leavitt & Allen, 1857.

"A Cadman to the Rescue." *The New Zealand Observer and Free Lance.* 19 June 1897. 1.

"Cardiff's Vampire. *The Evening Express.* 8 May 1895. 1.

Carlisle, Thomas. "Natural History: Bats." *The Juvenile Instructor and Companion.* May 1867. 114-121.

Carpenter, William Benjamin. *Zoology, A Systematic Account of the General Structure, Habits, Instincts, and Uses of the Principal Families of the Animal Kingdom* 1. London: Wm. S. Orr and Co., 1848.

"Churchyard and Funerals in the Year of Our Redemption 1872." *The Churchman's Shilling Magazine and Family Treasury.* February 1872. 565-74.

"A Collector of Nightmares." *The Ottawa Journal.* 1 August 1896. 6.

Crane, Walter. "The Capitalist Vampire." *Justice.* 22 August 1885. Rpt. *Cartoons for the Cause, 1886–1896.* London: Twentieth Century Press, 1896. 6.

Crane, Walter. *Renascence, A Book of Verse.* London: Elkin Matthews, 1891.

Cuvier, Georges. *Le règne animal distribué d'après son organisation, pour servir de base à l'histoire naturelle des animaux et d'introduction à l'anatomie comparée.* Paris: Deterville, 1817.

D., P. I. "At a Hemp Farm in Luzon." *Youth's Companion.* 15 May 1899. 250-51.

Darwin, C. R. ed. *Birds Part 3 of The Zoology of the Voyage of H.M.S. Beagle by John Gould.* London: Smith Elder and Co., 1841.

Darwin, C. R. *Journal of Researches into the Geology and Natural History of the Various Countries Visited by H.M.S. Beagle.* London: Henry Colburn, 1839.

Darwin, C. R. ed. *Mammalia Part 2 No. 1 of The Zoology of the Voyage of H.M.S. Beagle. By George R. Waterhouse. Edited and superintended by Charles Darwin.* London: Smith Elder and Co., 1838.

Darwin, C. R. *Narrative of the Surveying Voyages of His Majesty's Ships Adventure and Beagle between the Years 1826 and 1836, Describing their Examination of the Southern Shores of South America, and the Beagle's Circumnavigation of the Globe. Journal and Remarks. 1832-1836* 3. London: Henry Colburn, 1839.

Daunt, Achilles *Frank Redcliffe. A Story of Travel and Adventure in the Forests of Venezuela; A Book for Boys.* London: T. Nelson and Sons, 1889.

Debs, Eugene V. *Locomotive Firemen's Magazine.* December 1885. 723-26.

"A Demon of the Night." *Hinds County Gazette.* 23 April 1887. 2.

Elliot, Daniel Giraud. *The Land and Sea Mammals of Middle America and the West Indies* 4.1. Chicago: Field Columbian Museum, 1904.

Evergreen Star. 11 October 1888. 3.

French, Barbara. "False Vampires and Other Carnivores: A glimpse at this select group of bats reveals efficient predators with a surprisingly gentle side. . ." *BATS* 15: 2 (Summer 1997).

G., P. "Natural History of the Vampyre Bat," *The Imperial Magazine, or, Compendium of Religious, Moral, and Philosophical Knowledge* 1, 1819.

Gardner, Alfred L. *Mammals of South America* 1. Chicago: University of Chicago Press, 2006.

Gardner, George. *Travels in the Interior of Brazil, Principally Through the Northern Provinces, and the Gold and Diamond Districts, During the Years 1836-1841.* London: Reeve, Brothers, 1816.

Geoffroy-Saint-Hilaire, Étienne. "Sur Les Phyllostomes: Et Les Mégadermes, Deux Genres de la Famille des Chauve-Souris." *Annales du Muséum d'Histoire Naturelle.* 15. 1810. 157-198.

Gordon, W. J. *Popular Natural History for Boys and Girls.* London: The Religious Tract Society, 1894.

Goya, Francisco de. *Las Resultas*, Etching, 6 7/8 × 8 11/16 in; 17.5 × 22.1 cm. New York: Metropolitan Museum of Art, 1863 (after 1814–15).

Gregory, G. "Verpertilio," *A new and complete dictionary of arts and sciences: including the latest improvement and discovery and the present state of every branch of human knowledge* 2. London: Tegg, 1813.

Gumilla, J. *El Orinoco ilustrado, y defendido: historia natural, civil, y geográfica de este gran río y de sus caudalosas vertientes*. Madrid: Manuel Fernandez, 1741.
Harding, Jesse. "Wyoming Massacre." In *Wyoming, A Record of the One Hundredth Year Commemorative Observance of the Battle and Massacre, July 3, 1778-July 3, 1878*. Ed. Wesley Johnson. Wilkesbarre: Beardslee & Co. 1882.
Hare, March (Morgan Hawkes). "The Vampire Bat." *Adelaide Observer*. 11 December 1886. 26.
Heber, Reginald *Narrative of a Journey Through the Upper Provinces of India* 1. London: John Murray, 1828.
Henderson Gold Leaf. 4August 1887. 2.
Herndon, W. M. Lewis. *Exploration of the valley of the Amazon made at the direction of the Navy department* 1. Washington: Robert Armstrong, 1854.
Heyden, Friedrich von. "Der Vampyr und die Camarilla." *Gedichte von Friedrich von Heyden mit einer Biographie des Dichters*. Ed. Theodore Mundt. Leipzig: Friedrich Brandsetter, 1852.
Horton, Eva. "A Dream." *Douglass Tribune*. 21 December 1894. 1.
Houghton, Walter E., Ed. *The Wellesley Index to Victorian Periodicals 1824-1900*. Toronto: University of Toronto Press, 1972.
Humboldt, Alexander de, and A. Bonpland. *Personal Narrative of Travels to the Equinoctial Regions of America, During the Years 1799-1804* 4. Trans. Helen Maria Williams. London: Longman, Hurst, Rees, Orme, and Brown, 1819.
Humboldt, Alexander de and Bonpland, *Voyage aux régions équinoxiales du nouveau continent, fait en 1799, 1800, 1801, 1802, 1803, 1804*, 6. Paris: N. Maze, 1820.
"The Jackson Railroad." *The Times-Picayune*. 12 September 1865. 1.
Jennett, Norman Ethre. "The Vampire that Hovers Over North Carolina." *News and Observer*. 27 September 1898. 1.
Keller, George Frederick. "The Curse of California." *The Wasp*. 14 July 1877. 548.
Keller, George Frederick. "The Landlord Vampires of San Francisco." *The San Francisco Illustrated Wasp*. 2 September 1882. 560.
"Killed by a Vampire." *The St. Paul Globe*. 8 December 1890. 8.
"Killed by Vampire Bats." *The Buffalo Commercial*. 15 August 1882. 1.
Kingsley, John Sterling. *The Riverside Natural History*. 5. Boston: Houghton, Mifflin and Company, 1888.
Kirchner, Eugen. "Das vermeintliche Gespenst." *Fliegende Blätter* 2596. 162.
"Labor Day Epic." *American Federationist*. November 1899. 217.
"The Latest War News." *Oamaru Times*. 21 October 1870. 2.
Lee, Mrs R. *Anecdotes of the Habits and Instincts of Animals*. London: Griffith, Farran, Okeden, and Welch, 1852.
"Lena Davis." *Essex County Herald*. 24 September 1897. 3.
"A Letter to Gen. Badeau." *The Hutchinson News*. 1 April 1888. 8.
"Life in Brazilian Forests." *The Dallas Daily Herald*. 4 October 1887. 5.
"A Load of Vampires." *The Times Picayune*. 9 November 1888. 2.
Lydekker, Richard. *The Royal Natural History*. London: Frederick Warne and Co., 1893-94.
"The Maelstrom." *The Royal Magazine*. March 1899. 412-21.
Marcoy, M. Paul. "Voyage dans les Vallées de Quinquinas." *Le Tour du Monde: Nouveau Journal des Voyages* 23. Paris : Lahure, 1872. 65-176.
"Man About Town." *South Wales Echo*. 8 September 1894. 2.
Marcus, Otto. "The Working Man and his Vampire." *Chicago To-day: The Labour War in America*. Ed. W. T. Stead. London: William Clowes and Sons, 1894. Frontispiece.
Marcus, Otto. "Der Vampyr." *Der Wahre Jacob* 203. Mai 1894. 1692.
Maximilian, Prinz von Wied-Neuweid. *Reise nach Brasilien in den Jahren 1815 bis 1817*, 2. Frankfurt a. M.: H. L. Brönner, 1821.
Maximilian, Prinz von Wied-Neuweid. *Voyage au Brésil, dans les années 1815-1817*, 3. Trans. J. B. B. Eyriès. Paris: Arthus Bertrand, 1822.
McClintock, John; Strong, James. *Cyclopædia of Biblical, Theological, and Ecclesiastical Literature* 1. New York: Harper and Brothers, 1867.

Miles, Alfred H. Ed. *Natural History in Anecdote*. New York: Dodd, Mead and Company, 1895.
Mivart, George "What are Bats?" *The Popular Science Monthly* 9, September 1876. 523-539.
"Mysteriously Attacked: Frightful Experience of Travelers up the Santiago River in Chile." *The San Francisco Examiner*. 22 December 1888. 2.
Napier, Charles O. Groom. *The Book of Nature and the Book of Man*. London: John Camden Hotten, 1870.
Nast, Thomas. "The Political Vampire." *Harper's Weekly*. April 1885. 224.
"The Naturalist: The Flying Fox or Roussette Bat." *Rural New York*. 24 May 1879. 325.
"No Peace on the Roof." *The Inter Ocean*. 22 July 1891. 6.
"Nocturnal Creatures." *The Citizen-Examiner*. 16 November 1893. 4.
Omaha Daily Bee. 25 November 1888. 4.
"The Oamaru Times, and Waitaki Reporter. Tuesday, May 5, 1868." *The Oamaru Times and Waitaki Reporter* 10: 308 (5 May 1868), 2.
"Our 'Noble Old' Ironmasters.' *The Merthyr Telegraph and General Advertiser for the Iron Districts of South Wales*. 17 September 1870. 2.
"Pacific Coast Items." *Sacramento Daily Union*. 7 July 1883. 8.
"The Pain of Anxiety." *Wyoming Democrat*. 4 June 1897. 1.
Pennant, Thomas *Synopsis of Quadrupeds* 2. Chester: J. Monk, 1771.
"Pests of Darien." *Chicago Tribune*. 23 April 1883. 7.
Peters, W. C. H. "Systematische Stellung der Gattung Mormoops Leach und über die Classification der Phyllostomata Savie über eine neu Art der Gattung Vampyrus von Welcher Hier ein Kurzer Bericht Gegeben Wird." *Monatsberichte der Königlichen Preussichen Akademie der Wissenschaften zu Berlin*. 1856.
Polidori, John. *Ximenes, the Wreath, And Other Poems*. London: Longman, Hurst, Rees, Orme, and Brown, 1819.
"Political Pinkertons: The Democratic Spy System." *Reading Times*. 3 May 1876. 1.
Pollard, Josephine. "The Price of a Drink." *Saturday Evening Mail*. 3 March 1883. 7.
Pollard, Josephine. "The Price of a Drink: A Descriptive Song." Music by Geo. F. Root. Cincinnati: John Church Co., 1887.
"Pursued by a Vampire." *Buffalo Evening News*. 16 July 1897. 7.
"Queensland and the Vampire." *The Worker: Journal of the Associated Workers of Queensland*. 28 January 1893. 1.
Rafinesque, C. S. *Analyse de la nature: ou, Tableau de l'univers et des corps organisés*, Palerme, 1815.
"A Ride in a Hurricane Through the Sugar-Cane; fragment from the unpublished memoirs of Reginald Hardy, Esq." *Fraser's Magazine*. March 1850. 292-294.
Robinson, S. L. *Blood Will Tell: Vampires as Political Metaphors before World War I*. Boston: Academic Studies Press, 2011.
Saffray, M. Le Docteur. "Voyage a la nouvelle—Grenade." *Le tour du monde nouveau journal des voyages*. 2nd half year, 1872. 98-144.
Schomburgk, Richard. *Travels in British Guiana During the Years 1840-1844*. 1. Ed. Walter E. Roth. Georgetown: The "Daily Chronicle" Office, 1922 [1847].
Scott, Walter. *Rokeby: A Poem*. Edinburgh: John Ballantyne and Co., 1813.
Shaw, G. *General zoology, or, Systematic natural history*. London: G. Kearsley, 1800.
Shelley, Percy. *Shelley's The Triumph of Life: A Critical Study*. Ed. Donald H. Reiman. Champaign: University of Illinois Press, 1964 [1822].
Smith, G. Munro. "Sleep and Dreams." *Proceedings of the Bristol Naturalists' Society*. Bristol: James Fawn, 1888. 62-83.
"Smoking Vampires." *Stevens Point Journal*. 19 June 1899. 4.
Stedman, John. *Narrative, of a Five Years' Expedition, Against the Revolted Negroes of Surinam, in Guiana, on the Wild Coast of South America; from the Year 1772, to 1777: Elucidating the History of that Country, and Describing Its Productions, Viz. Quadrupeds, Birds, Fishes, Reptiles, Trees, Shrubs, Fruits, & Roots; with an Account of the Indians of Guiana, & Negroes of Guinea* 2. London: J. Johnson and J. Edwards, 1796.
Stephens, Henry L. *The Comic Natural History of the Human Race*. Philadelphia: S. Robinson, 1851.

Stevenson, Robert Louis. *Island Nights' Entertainments.* London: Cassell and Company, Limited, 1893.
Sydney. "Letter to the Editor of the Cambrian." *The Cambrian.* 28 June 1834. 4.
Tenniel, John. *The Irish Vampire, Punch, or The London Charivari* 89. 17 October 1885. 199.
"They thought it was a vampire." *Los Angeles Herald.* 21 July 1895. 5.
Things Worth Knowing: The Bloodsucking Vampire." *The London Journal, And Weekly Record of Literature, Science, and Art.* 8 August 1863. 85.
Timbs, John. "The Vampyre Bat, At 'The Surrey Zoological Gardens.'" *The Literary World: A Journal of Popular. Information and Entertainment.* 27 July 1839. 273-275.
"To —, At Parting." *Mississippi Palladium.* 29 August 1851. 3.
"To a Stolen Fan." *The Courier-Journal.* 9 July 1882. 8.
"Topics of the Week." *Rhyl Record and Advertiser.* 20 April 1895. 4.
"Twin Screw Mosquitoes." *The Sun.* 6 March 1892. 21.
Tschudi, Johann Jakob von. *Peru, Reiseskizzen aus den Jahren 1838-1842* 2. St. Gallen: Scheitlin und Zollikofer, 1846.
"The Vampire Bat." *Chamber's Edinburgh Journal.* 12 June 1847. 384.
"Vampire Bat." *Edinburgh Journal of Natural History, and of the Physical Sciences.* September 1839.
"The Vampire Bat." *The Lancaster Gazette.* 29 July 1843. 4.
"The Vampire Bat." *Richmond Weekly Palladium.* 11 June 1851. 2.
"The Vampire Bat: A Dread Creature That is Common in India." *Arizona Republic.* 26 September 1894. 2.
"Vampire Bats." *Greensboro Watchman.* 23 June 1887. 1.
"Vampire Bats in India: They Suck the Victim's Blood and Afterward Devour the Body." *International Gazette.* 8 April 1893. 6.
"Vampires Not Vicious, After All." *The Daily Democrat.* 12 January 1889. 7.
"The Vampyre by the Wife of a Medical Man" London: A. W. Bennett, 1858.
"The Varied Vermin of Venezuela: How the Vampire Attacks its Victims," *Daily Telegraph.* 7 December 1889. 2.
Vere, M. Schele de. *Modern Magic.* New York: G. P. Putnam's Sons, 1873.
"A Veritable Vampire: A Strange Beast Secured in the Middle of the Pacific." *Daily Alta California.* 23 February 1873. 1.
Viets, Henry R. "By the Visitation of God": The Death of John William Polidori, M.D., in 1821." *The British Medical Journal.* 30 December 1961. 1773-1775.
Virga, Vincent. *Eyes of the Nation: A Visual History of the United States.* New York: Knopf, 1997.
Wallace, Alfred Russel. *A Narrative of Travels on the Amazon and Rio Negro, With an Account of the Native Tribes, and Observations on the Climate, Geology, and Natural History of the Amazon Valley.* London: Reeve and Co., 1853.
Wallace, Alfred Russel. *Tropical Nature, and Other Essays.* London: Macmillan and Co., 1878.
Waterton, Charles. *Essays on natural history, chiefly ornithology.* London: Longman, Orme, Brown, Green, and Longmans, 1838.
Waterton, Charles. *Wanderings in South America, in the North West of the United States, and the Antilles, in the Years 1812, 1816, 1820, and 1824.* London: J. Mawman, 1825.
Watson, H. B. Marriott. *The Heart of Miranda and Other Stories, Being Mostly Winter Tales* London: John Lane, 1898.
Watson, H. B. Marriott. "The Stone Chamber." *New York World.* 28 June 1896. 29.
"Wild Animals: Visit to a Noted London Establishment." *The Abbeville Press and Banner.* 27 April 1892. 6.
Webster, William Henry Bayley. *Narrative of a Voyage to the Southern Atlantic Ocean, In the Years 1828, 29, 30* 2, London: Richard Bentley, 1834.
Wood, J. G. *The Illustrated Natural History.* London: George Routledge and Co., 1853 [1851].
Wood, J. G. *The Illustrated Natural History.* London: Routledge, Warne, Routledge, 1859.
Wood, W. *Zoography; or, The beauties of nature displayed* 1. London: Cadell and Davies, 1807.

III.

Gender and Sexuality

SO HALF-WAY FROM THE BED SHE ROSE,
AND ON HER ELBOW DID RECLINE
TO LOOK AT THE LADY GERALDINE.

"Christabel" in Andrew Lang's *The Blue Poetry Book* (321).

6.
"With Whom Do You Think You Have Been Dealing?"
Making Love to Evil: Woman, the Devil, and the Nineteenth-Century Vampire

Introduction

The tale of making love to evil was first about a particular male viewpoint on women, promulgated and justified by numerous Western institutions, not least of all the mainstream Christian church. Women were held responsible for males being attracted to them and thus were detested by some and distrusted by others. Especially women who were strangers.

This male vigilance points to a deep-seated uneasiness about the female body and a woman's intentions. It was easy for early Christianity, for example, to read the temptation narrative in Genesis as an explanation of woman's proximity to Satan. The serpent (i.e., the devil) worked upon Eve because she was intellectually and volitionally weaker than Adam. She succumbed to his wiles and ate the forbidden fruit; she then tempted Adam, adopting the role of the devil with him. After their sin they discovered they were naked and covered themselves. Thus, there was a progression: devil-woman-sin-nakedness. She made nakedness dirty and acted like Satan to the man.

The great Greek father of the church Clement of Alexandria wrote in about 198 CE: "[B]y no manner of means are women to be allowed to uncover and exhibit any part of their person, lest both fall—the men by being excited to look, they by drawing on themselves the eyes of the men" (2.2: 246). In other words, women start it.[90] St. John Chrysostom, one of the so-called Three Hierarchs of the Eastern Christian Churches said around 391: "[M]any are the circumstances in society which have the power to upset the balance of the mind, and to hinder its straightforward course; and first of all is his social intercourse with women. . . . [T]he eye, not only of the unchaste, but of the modest woman pierces and disturbs the mind" (6.8: 79). Therefore it is the female eye that evokes the male gaze.

This paper will begin by investigating one set of stories in Western, particularly French, literature that start off with a woman being the devil incarnate and then adapts that theme to her being a vampire. As such, a man makes love to her; or at least she tries to make him to do so. With regard to the vampire, there long had been a tradition with the European revenant, the precursor to the vampire, that unless the dead body had returned to confess, to compensate for one's wrongdoings, or to exhort the listeners to piety, it was probably a vehicle for the devil.

---

[90] The context is temperance, so it is not all because of women. But he does single them out, for wine also brings immodesty as well as irrationality. "For nothing disgraceful is proper for men, who is endowed with reason; much less for woman, to whom it brings modesty even to reflect of what nature she is."

The ease with which the switch was made between the devil and the vampire between the eighteenth and nineteenth centuries indicates that the relationship between the two had become even more intimate. Instead of the devil possessing a human body, the devil has given way to a surrogate who is already incarnate. This may account, in part, for the fact that mid-century the vampire made inroads into taking on more characteristics of the devil than it previously had, like having bat wings, which had been the sole property of demons for centuries.

We will look, in this study, at a very early example of the story (thirteenth century) and then chart how it divided into three variations in the seventeenth century. Two advanced into the nineteenth century where they displaced the devil with the vampire, which was considered to be a vampire at the time.

But secondly the idea of the devil seducing a man in the form of a woman took another influential form in the late eighteenth century. This was when the devil represented a more secular male fantasy: a powerful woman who wants to give herself wholly and for all time to a particular man. She was then vampirized into two separate patterns in the nineteenth. We shall examine both. There is a final example, Baudelaire, that has elements of the second tradition, but represents more a reversion to the first.

The Early Tale

Our journey begins in the thirteenth century with the compendia of the lives of the saints. This is not particularly unusual. For example, material that would become precursors to the Faust stories is found therein as well: for example, in tales of St. Basil; St. Peter the Apostle; St. Justina; the Virgin Mary—her nativity and her assumption.

The text in question is Icelandic, the *Maríu saga,* likely dated before 1238 assembled by Kygri-Björn Hjaltason in 1871 (1.2.14, 507-10). The story found therein is "Af Petro þræl" or "On Peter the Slave." The following is a much fuller account than appears in chapter two. Peter of Grationopolis, in gratitude to the Virgin Mary and St. Hippolytus healing his lame leg, has taken up a small room in a hermitage to devote himself entirely to God. The devil is envious so he takes the form of a naked woman and enters his cell through the cesspool beneath. This succubus flatters and reveals her body to him in order to provoke a lustful response but she fails. The devil, then, with "unbridled rage and venomous anger," attacks him, to force him into fornication. Every night they are locked in a wrestling match. Word spreads and thus "many came from afar to the church to ascertain the truth concerning these matters."

Finally Peter calls to his observers to bring him a consecrated stole. When he receives it, he wraps it around the neck of his adversary and she chokes to death. "[T]he carcass then withered and was destroyed, since its occupant was defeated. It was the body of a woman the enemy had entered, which now lay there still." The roof is removed and the corpse of what is now an old woman is hauled out. It is dragged away, burned, and the ashes thrown into water. "Later, in the filth from under the hermit's hut, they found old rags, which the devil had torn from the woman's body."

A later variation leaves no uncertainty about the corpse. It is a "genuine human body" and emits an almost unendurable stench (2.1157-60). Jacobus de Voragine picked it up[91] and added it to his *Legenda sanctorum* or *Legenda aurea*, commonly translated as *The Golden Legend* (*circa* 1260).[92] It is reduced to a couple of sentences. Peter wraps a consecrated stole around her neck "and straightway the devil departed and left lying there a stinking and rotten corpse. So great a stench issued from it that there was none that saw it but said that it was the body of some dead woman which the devil had taken."[93]

This is a particularly grotesque narrative. It is bad enough to break a vow of chastity with a normal woman but add to this having sexual intercourse with the devil. At least, however, Peter knows who his adversary is. But he knows nothing about the nature of the body, so the story shifts perspective at the end by compounding Peter's struggle with the element of necrophilia—and not with a freshly buried body but one old and in advanced decay. So had Peter made love to the woman, he would have suffered a double indignity—knowingly having sex with the devil and unknowingly doing so with a putrid body the devil robbed from its grave. At the end of sexual intercourse, the body would have obviously become a stinking corpse.

Three Trajectories

The telling of this type of narrative went in three different directions. We have moved away from literature aimed primarily for the edification of and use by the clergy and their congregations, so the good no longer will be absolute, but flawed in some way. And the power of Christianity shall be more limited, relegated mainly to individual piety, confession, and last rites. But these are still very religious perspectives. Interestingly in just two years all three examples would be published.

The first is found in a pamphlet by François du Carroy, *Histoire prodigieuse d'un gentilhomme* (1613). This has already been covered in the first chapter. A young Parisian gentleman returns from town to find a well-dressed and well-mannered lady sheltering from the rain at the entrance to his home. She explains she is waiting for her servant to return with her coach and apologizes for any inconvenience. He insists that she join him indoors to watch for the coach's arrival. He finally overcomes her resistance and they settle down inside.

Her servant never comes and so he yields his bed to her; he will sleep in the other room. He begins to flirt with her and finds not only that she is adept at such language but that she responds readily to him. Encouraged, he later enters her room to inquire about her comfort and works slowly until he eventually lies down with her and "enjoyed pleasures he considered to be perfect" (100).

In the morning he quickly vacates the room and then sends his servant in to wake her so there be no sign of impropriety. She explains that she would like

---

[91] He may have accessed the story elsewhere, although I know of no earlier instance in Europe. It does fit a certain pattern in Nordic stories of a Nordic hero wrestling a revenant, so that may have been the origin.
[92] The tale may not have been in the first edition but was added at least by 1476. I do not have access to earlier texts.
[93] In current English script: Jacobus de Voragine. *Legenda aurea sanctorum*, Early English Books Online 2020 (1483), 251-252. Original translation: Voragine, *The Golden Legende* 1483, folios 251-252, images 516-17. Latin: Voragine *Legenda aurea de Sanctis* 1486, q 3., image 250.

to stay in bed longer since she did not sleep during the night. The young man spends a while outdoors and when he returns he discovers her dead. Judges and doctors come and recognize her to be a woman hanged some time before. They conclude that some demon must have inhabited the body to deceive the poor gentleman. At that point a cloud of smoke arises from the bed and when it dissipates the body is gone, leaving in its wake a horrible stench. There is no indication what becomes of the man thereafter as Carroy immediately draws his lesson that men should control their passions. That the body is a human one commandeered by the devil is shown by the malodor.

The next is located in a short story by Simon Goulart in his 1614 *Thrésor d'histoires admirables et mémorables* (638-641) by the name of "Imposture horrible & du tout estrange."[94] Goulart, a respected Reformed theologian, tones down the tale simply to be about sex with the devil. There is no way to know for sure whether the body used has been created by the devil or pulled from a grave for it to inhabit, thus there is no scene of the young man finding his lover dead.

François is on a business trip when a woman, disheveled and weeping, stops him and begs for his protection. She has been robbed and nearly raped by some brigands but escaped and is afraid they are in pursuit. She explains her father's castle is a day's journey away so she needs to find lodging for the night. It is too late for him to continue so he finds a place for her that is to her liking and arranges to stay there as well. She then pleads with him and their hosts to be allowed to sleep in the same room as he, for she is too fearful to sleep alone. She importunes until finally he and the hosts agree that she may. That night, pretending she thinks him asleep, she takes off her clothes and begins to perform in front of him. Unable to resist any longer he moves over to her bed and she receives him.

The following morning she is gone, and after waiting a long time for her, he rides off. In the open country, a knight rides at him to attack, but he, as an accomplished soldier, repels him. The knight then faces him and lifts his visor. The young man sees the woman with whom he had lain. She chides him for having slept with the devil and he returns home desolate, takes to his bed, repents, confesses, and dies trusting in the mercy of God.

François de Rosset's tale "D'un demon qui apparoist in forme de Damoiselle," also published in 1614, is the final one.[95] This is a more comprehensive telling of the tale than appears in chapter one. La Jaquière, a lieutenant in Lyon's city guard, widely known to visit prostitutes, declares one night to his friends that he feels on fire: "if at this moment I met the devil, he would never escape my grasp until first I had had my way with him." Just seconds later, he sees a finely dressed woman walking hurriedly down the street; he dismisses all but two of his companions, and meets the stranger, offering her his services. She accepts him willingly, explains how unhappy she is with her husband, and lets him and his friends inside upon arriving home, for her husband is away. He makes advances to her, swearing oaths that he will never reveal a thing. She yields. Afterward he declares that his friends have not made such vows so she will need to have sex with them as well. She threatens suicide but he seduces her a second time. After further cajoling she makes love to the other two.

---

[94] It is not in the 1610 edition.
[95] It is the eighth chapter in the 1614 edition; the tenth in 1619. This story has already been told in chapter one.

When finished they are praising her every feature when she rises and turns toward them. "You believe to have accomplished something great by having obtained from me the fulfillment of your desires. It is not nearly so great as you think. With whom do you think you have been dealing?" She then removes her clothing to reveal "the most horrible, ugly, stinking, and revolting carcass in the world" (341). The house disappears and they are thrown unconscious upon ruins which are filled with manure and garbage. Everything was an illusion. One dies immediately, the other two return to their senses in the morning and their groans bring help. La Jaquière lives only long enough to confess; the last has time to relate the story before his death.

Goulart's story did not make it into vampire literature, as far as I know. Carroy's tale continued to be retold, for example, by Nicolas Lenglet Dufresnoy "Histoire prodigieuse" (1751) and was summarized in 1818 by Jules Garinet in his *Histoire de la Magie en France*. It was included in Collin de Plancy's 1820 *Histoire des Vampires*, basically *verbatim* from the original and then adapted in Washington Irving's 1824 "The Adventure of the German Student." De Rosset's book was quickly translated into German by Martin Zeiller ("Von einem Schaarwächter Leuten-Ampt zu Lyon in Franckreich wie ihme der Teuffel in einer Sdelichen Dame Gestalt erschienen," 1628) where the story was moved from the tenth chapter to the first and carried forward in 1687 by Eberhard Werner Happel, in "Die Stinckende Buhlschaft." In 1804, Jan Potocki reworked the tale in his *Manuscrit trouvé à Saragosse*, claiming it to be from Happel, and set it in the context of vampires.[96] Potocki heightened its every major detail and transformed the woman from a modest wife to a curious virgin. His version was then retold as "Les Aventures de Thibaud de la Jacquière" in 1822 in a popular book by Charles Nodier, a short collection of stories entitled *Infernaliana*.

The Alternative

This other way of portraying women was not to play on male anxiety, but on the fantasy of male desire—a beautiful, well-to-do woman passionately and irreversibly falls in love with him. More occurs with the change from devil to vampire here than where the vampire is simply a substitute. In this new trajectory, things become more ambiguous. Evil and good are not so clear cut, not so clearly separate. The Christian moorings start to unravel and the devil/vampire becomes more sympathetic. The setting becomes more secular. Women are no longer typified solely by their sinful bodies and are now more complex. It all starts with Jacques Cazotte's *Le Diable amoureux* (1772/1776).[97]

Alvaro, captain in the king's guard in Naples, is no saint; he lived "after the manner of young men, that is, gaming and womanizing, as long as [their] purses could bear it" (29). This is not enough for him, however; presently he has a Faustian urge to employ a spirit, assumed to be the devil, as his servant. When his conjuring is successful, the spirit appears in a hideous form, so he has it turn into a spaniel to lick his feet. He notices it is female, so he asks that it turn into a male

---

[96] Potocki 1990 (1804), 132-142. Only in 2006 were definitive editions of his 1804 and 1810 versions of his work published. Both have virtually identical tellings of this story. Potocki 2006 (a), 125-34; Potocki 2006 (b), 101-110. The tale is told on the tenth day.
[97] The earliest is from 1772. The earliest English translation is *The Enamoured Spirit* (1798).

page. It does so but it still maintains feminine features. Later, thinking his pious mother would disapprove, he desires to release the page from his service, but he pleads with Alvaro not to do so; it has risked a great deal in becoming human, especially a "person of my sex" (44), and the only thing that can make her safe is for him to give her his protection. He capitulates and does so, because he has promised his mother to serve women all his life, admitting that she is a woman.

Thus begins the adventure. He refuses to treat the spirit as an actual female and so demands it appear in male form with the name of Biondetto, even though all evidence points in the other direction; he does not believe the spirit really is human but instead the horrible beast he saw at first, so he is cruel to him and dismissive of his feelings. He desperately wants to be close to him, but he keep him at arm's length, although in truth he is attracted to him. He sees his every overture as a "demonic attack." It is only when he is stabbed and on the verge of death that Alvaro finally expresses his true feelings. "I am overwhelmed with love; I am persuaded that you are not an imaginary being, and I am convinced that you love me, despite my outrageous conduct towards you until this moment" (69). She eventually recovers.

Events now take a Wizard-of-Oz turn. He refuses to take her as his mistress but wants to marry her properly. He therefore begins a quest to return home and ask for his mother's blessing, but he keeps on hitting obstacles and Biondetta, as she is now called, is at the center of each. Finally, a day's journey from his home, he can keep his passions in check no longer and he makes love to her. She declares herself now truly happy and she wants to raise him to the height of greatness, for she is the devil and she loves him. The devil wants him to pronounce his feelings in as tender words as its feelings are to him: "my dear Belzebub, I adore you" (101). Their relationship is now binding, he declares, and with that he turns into the hideous form Alvaro originally saw. Alvaro dives under the bed and faints.

In the morning s/he is gone and he finishes his journey alone. His mother believes his story must be the product of a dream, but her venerable doctor is convinced it has been real. "Your enemy has withdrawn, so much is clear. He seduced you, it is true, but he did not succeed in corrupting you; your will power and your remorse have preserved you, together with the supernal aid you have received" (108). He advises Alvaro to marry a woman his mother chooses, for then "never would you be tempted to take her for the Devil" (109). In the end the doctor appears to be correct. The devil had given him the opportunity to enter into a Faustian pact with him acting as Helen of Troy and Alvaro turned from it.

Ambiguities abound here, such as whether this all has been a dream or reality. And there is the issue of extensive gender bending. But it is the love story that concerns us and its relation to the three trajectories from Peter of Grationopolis. De Rousset's rendition can be felt in Alvaro's dissolute lifestyle and the terrifying apparition at the end. But Alvaro also proves to be an honorable man particularly after he declares his love to Biondetta. He has never tried to seduce her, either before or after he comes to terms with his feelings for her. He tries to do what is right by her, as the young man does in Goulart's tale. He offers his protection to Biondetta like the main characters in both Goulart and Carroy. Carroy's appropriation is most present at the end. The devil is gone in the morning; he is not presented with a fetid carcass, for her body is manufactured; Alvaro lives through the ordeal.

Still the story is much more complicated, for the devil certainly seems to be in love; it is not just an appearance to lure him to humiliation or death. Biondetta is relentless in trying to have sex with him and it seems this is the diabolical equivalent to marriage: "Now, Alvaro, our bond is indissoluble," she says after their intimacy. She genuinely wants him to be happy, but her subterfuge has to end so they can be properly united. Thus she reveals herself as she really is, hoping that he can return her love. She offers him grandeur and dominion, but she is just too terrifying for him. Also he is tethered to his mother's piety so he could never pledge an allegiance of affection to the devil.

Without making too much of this, strange romance stories with the devil and revenants long precede Cazotte. Here is one of each concerning a dead wife told by Robert Burton in *The Anatomy of Melancholy* (1638). A man, long mourning his wife's death, is visited by a devil in her form who says to him that in order for her to return he must marry her again and stop blaspheming (!) otherwise she will disappear. They marry and have children, but one day he swears. She vanishes and is never seen again (Burton 434). A young man buries his wife and mourns her for a long duration according to *Master Walter Map's book, De nugis curialium* (c. 1182). One night he finds her dancing among a throng of phantom women; he grabs her and she rejoins him in marriage, bearing him many children (Map 97-98; 218).

Its Legacy in Vampire Lore

The story continues in Théophile Gautier's 1836 "La Morte Amoureuse" or "Clarimonde."[98] This tale investigates much more fully than anything before, including such classic early experiments as John Keats' *Lamia* (1819) and Ernst Raupach's 1822 *Lasst die Toten ruhen*,[99] the consensual love affair between a mortal and a vampire. It concerns, therefore, unapologetic necrophilia. The dream motif in Cazotte moves from a possibility to the reality of a man apparently with dissociative identity disorder, but more likely, with an actual double existence. The vampire he makes love to is found in her grave beautiful and untouched by decay with a drop of his blood on her lips, so their affair appears to be real.

The devout, spiritually eager Romuald, at his ordination, sees the ideally beautiful Clarimonde standing nearby and she starts telepathically communicating with him in endearing blasphemies: "If you will be mine, I will make you happier than God Himself in His heaven . . . I am beauty, youth, life, come to me, and together we shall be love. What could Jehovah offer you in exchange?" (95). He finishes the ceremony now only by inertia and afterward he struggles so terribly that Father Serapion enters his cell and warns him that he is under attack by the devil: "[A]rm yourself with prayers, make a shield of mortifications, and wrestle valiantly with the enemy; you will defeat him" (98). The following day, Father Serapion accompanies him to his country parish and on the way he sees Clarimonde's palace. Serapion tells him that awful things happen there, but Romuald longs to be there with her nonetheless.

He takes up his pastoral duties, but his mind continues to turn to

---

[98] It was first advertised as *Les Amours d'une morte* before appearing as *La Morte Amoureuse* (1836) and was later published in 1850 under the title of *Clarimonde*.
[99] The first English translation (1823): Raupach, "Wake not the Dead" 233-291.

Clarimonde. A year after he takes the post he is called upon to give last rites to "a very great lady" (102) and after a long, but preternaturally fast ride on horseback with his swarthy guide, he ends up alone before the corpse of Clarimonde, for he arrived too late. Facing the object of his passion, he weeps for, he adores, and he kisses her. At the last, she gently breathes, opens her eyes and puts her arms around him, declaring her love to him and her pleasure that with the kiss they are betrothed and she can come to see him. Her head then drops back and she is dead again. A few days after returning home, Father Serapion visits. "There have always been strange stories going round about this Clarimonde . . . It has been said that she was a ghoul, a female vampire, but I am convinced that she was the Devil in person. . . . My son, I must warn you, your foot is poised over an abyss, beware or you shall fall. Satan has a long arm, and the grave is not always secure. Clarimonde's tomb should be triply sealed, for they say it is not the first time she has died" (107).

Sometime thereafter everything changes: she starts coming to him in his sleep. As a priest, each night he dreams that he is with Clarimonde; in the other reality, each night, as her lover, as an exquisite young lord and libertine, he dreams he is a priest. This is because he cannot love her solely; he loves God equally, but only equally, so his life is divided. He confesses that with Clarimonde he is second only to Satan in pride and insolence. Despite this, he is totally faithful to her and she to him; she is so adept at pleasure that having her alone is more like having twenty mistresses.

But then tragedy strikes; Clarimonde's health begins to deteriorate and no one can treat it. One morning Romuald cuts himself and she pounces on the wound and sucks the blood with delight. Her health is restored. She begins each night to prick him in his sleep and take a few drops for herself; when he discovers it, he says nothing. He begrudges her not the tiny amount and feels like offering this "vampire," as he calls her, as much as she wants: "Drink! And may my love enter your body with my blood!" (115). But he says nothing and they continue to live in perfect bliss.

Clarimonde feeding from the sleeping Romuald[100]

[100] Aifiando Colucci 2016. https://www.alejandrocolucci.com/carmilla?lightbox=dataItem-j9h0aniy.

Meanwhile the bifurcated life is wearing on both of him. One has to go. Father Serapion says desperate times require desperate measures, and suggests they disinter the body so he can show him her true self, a decomposed body. Romuald goes along with it but is inert through the process. Serapion does everything. Romuald sees in the determination of the man something demonic and he wishes lightning would strike him. When the Father opens the coffin she is perfectly preserved with a little drop of blood at the corner of her lips. In a fury Father Serapion throws holy water on her making the sign of the cross and she instantly turns to dust. She had never sought Serapion's destruction as he did hers; she simply exhorted Romuald to turn from his influence. She persuaded. He destroyed.

He confesses that he has regretted this often to this day, at 66 years old. He counsels young clergymen never to look upon a woman, and "walk always with your eyes upon the ground, for chaste and sober as you may be, a moment can suffice to make you lose eternity." This is also the way he started the narrative: "One weak and indulgent glance at a woman nearly caused the destruction of my soul" (117).

The introduction and conclusion are insincere, of course. It is the eroticism of his affair with Clarimonde, not his vocation as a priest, that occupies him for the remainder of his life. There is no doubt now that although diabolical, although a vampire, she does not need nor want to send him to his death, for she loves him. So we have the introduction in this tradition of vampirism without killing the victim and with the victim complicit. It is not coincidental that this short story is named "La Morte Amoureuse." She drinks only so much of his blood as she needs from her monogamous source. He suffers no ill effects and is willing to yield to her more out of his own self-sacrificial love. And she was herself; her own soul animates her own dead body, which Romuald makes love to. Her body is foul only to Father Serapion and he is hardly cast as someone unambiguously good.

The next move falls to Alexandre Dumas *père*. The most recognizable vampire of the nineteenth century was Lord Ruthven or Ruthen. He made his first appearance in John Polidori's 1819 *The Vampyre: A Tale*. This story was quickly translated into a wildly popular French play by Charles Nodier (*Le Vampire*, 1820) and returned to England that same year as an adaptation of that play by James Planché (*The Vampire: or, The Bride of the Isles*). Ruthwen was presented on the German stage in 1821 by Heinrich Ludwig Ritter with Der Vampyr (in 1821 and 1828 two German operas featuring him opened with the same name, Der Vampyr, one by Heinrich Marschner and the other by Peter Josef von Lindpaintner.[101] He kept on reappearing in one way or another through the rest of the century. Doubtless the finest story he ever starred in was Alexandre Dumas and August Maquet's *The Vampire: A Drama in Five Acts*.

What concerns us with the story is a subplot featuring a female vampire or ghoul. It could easily be entitled "La Vampire Amoureuse" ("The Vampire in Love" or "The Amorous Vampire"). It unmistakably belongs to this tradition and leads it in another unique direction. This is the only story that does not have sexual intercourse since Peter of Grationopolis. She offers the same things as

---

[101] Lindpaintner's libretto has no settings, directions, or context. Some background can be found in "Im Königlichen Hof- und National-theater" 25 October 1828, 25-30; 1 November 1828, 33-36; 8 November 1828, 41-43.

Biondetta and Clarimonde—wealth and power—but Gilbert rejects them in a much more forceful way than Alvaro.

The vampire first appears as a Moorish woman staying at a Spanish inn. She is attracted to a handsome visitor, Gilbert, a native of Brittany, but has just learned that there is an attractive man alone in the nearby ruins of a castle, so she takes flight with her bat wings, arrives there just minutes later, and drains him of his blood. She exclaims before she abandons the body: "He was young! He was beautiful! I've become young and beautiful again" (Act 2, Scene 2). She flies away saying she intends to meet Gilbert again.

She disappears from the narrative for a while, but in the intervening time we learn more about her kind: the ghoul (which is a female vampire) is "evil doing, murderous, the spectral woman, wearing the appearance of beauty, the forms of youth to better conceal her snares and attacking especially young men, the handsomer, the fresher, the better" (Act 2, Scene 2). "[T]hey lie in ambush in some solitary place. They watch for the passing of their prey, lull him to sleep with the movement of their vast wings and when he is asleep in a mortal bliss, they aspirate his blood and his life. They are invisible, they assist in the sorrow of the fiancée, whose tears they drink with a voluptuousness equal only to that of drinking his blood."

A year later, Gilbert is returning to Brittany to attend his sister's wedding. Near his destination, a poor old woman (the vampire in disguise) pulls him from his horse just as a musket is fired, saving his life. The marksman is Lord Ruthwen who is the one engaged to his sister in order to kill her by drinking her blood. He wants Gilbert out of the way, for he is the only one that can stop the marriage. Thereafter she enters Gilbert's dream and reveals everything Ruthwen plans to do. In the meantime, Ruthwen discovers and confronts the vampire, demanding to know why she is interfering with his business. She explains that she is in love with Gilbert and she wants no harm to come to him. Ruthwen refuses not to hurt him and exclaims "You shall learn what I can be when I hate" to which she responds "You shall learn what I can be when I love" (Act 3, Scene 4). Ruthwen ends up being successful with Gilbert's sister, but Gilbert himself does escape injury.

We next encounter her in the last act as Ziska, a Circassian beauty, helping Antonia, Gilbert's fiancée, to arrange things in the palace the lovers have just purchased. They are awaiting the arrival of Gilbert, who has now finished the mourning period for his sister. When he arrives and Ziska and Gilbert are alone she declares her love to him and offers him immortality and dominion over the world. But he cannot accept—he is in love with Antonia and part of her preciousness to him is her mortality. Just then Ruthwen arrives with malicious intent toward Antonia. Gilbert throws himself on Ziska's mercy and says he will marry her if only she will save Antonia, but she declares she cannot.

So in desperation he plans that he and Antonia poison themselves and die in their love together, foiling Ruthwen. When Ziska sees they are serious, she stops them and tells Gilbert how to kill Ruthwen, thus violating the rule of supernatural beings, and sacrificing her life for him and his happiness. "[A]s you have refused my immortality I am giving you my death" (Act 5 Scene 9). As consolation she dies holding his hand. He is thus able to kill Ruthwen. When that happens Ziska, although a vampire under the rule of Satan and with a train of victims, rises up from the ground and joins the hosts in heaven.

The potential has been there for this kind of self-sacrifice since the beginning of the female vampire, as will be seen. The early stories feature a traditional Christian devil—a creature motivated by the single desire to damn believers. But because it operates in the context of God's providence, it can also punish evildoers to effect final contrition and repentance against its will. Either way, the devil itself is irredeemably evil. Love is simply an appearance, a lure from hell. Yet if the context changes, a demon can develop a more complex inner life than merely taking a body to destroy a Christian man. This is what Cazotte opened up with his small book.

When this becomes vampirized, this deepened narrative unites with another movement in the same direction that had been working specifically with the female vampire. The lamia, like the succubus, had operated as an irremediably evil being in classical mythology—a creature, a metamorphized snake, bent on killing handsome young men and babies. It is antinuptial and antimaternal. Its seminal transformation occurred with Robert Burton, in *The Anatomy of Melancholy* (1621), who tells of a lamia falling in love with a man and making herself vulnerable in order to fulfill his dream of marriage; her devotion is never questioned (434). She is discovered, but before she is destroyed, she weeps, apparently at her loss.[102] This rendition of the lamia with a soul was there within the scope of the literary female vampire from the start. It was in Goethe as love,[103] in Samuel Taylor Coleridge as regret,[104] in John Keats as romantic vulnerability.[105]

The Death of Ophelia (1880), sculpted in marble by Sarah Bernhardt.

---

[102] The original has none of this; she is simply luring the young man to his death. Philostratus. *Life of Apollonius of Tyana* First Half of Third Century CE.
[103]"From my grave to wander I am forc'd,/Still to seek The Good's long-sever'd link,/ Still to love the bridegroom I have lost,/ And the life-blood of his heart to drink" (Goethe "The Bride of Corinth", 187). She actually asks to be burned with her lover, in part, so she does not have to seek other victims after his death.
[104] Deep from within she seems half-way/ To lift some weight with sick assay,/ And eyes the maid and seeks delay" (Coleridge, "Christabel"). The point is she hesitates from feeding upon her friend. By the way, these lines were not in the first printing of 1816.
[105] "I was a woman, let me have once more/ A woman's shape, and charming as before./ I love a youth of Corinth—O the bliss!/ Give me my woman's form, and place me where he is" (Keats, "Lamia" 10). Lamia is a serpent and wants to be restored to her female shape to court a man she has fallen in love with but who has never met her.

So here, far surpassing Cazotte, we have self-sacrificial love—a vampire as savior. She is a leech living off human blood, so she is a monster. She is not like Gautier's vampire, where a small amount of blood suffices to quell her hunger. Feeding is lethal, so she exists only by human death. Yet out of love, she refuses to feed upon Gilbert although he is young and handsome. Like Cazotte's devil, she offers him dominion and immortality if he unites himself to her. But when he refuses her offer she does not disappear but remains. She accepts the fact that she shall never couple with the man she loves. When the human pair faces immanent death, she sacrifices herself for his life and happiness. By this messianic move, she assures herself redemption and a place in heaven.

A Reversal

Charles Baudelaire represents a return to the traditional story, albeit run through Cazotte and Gautier, with his "Les Métamorphoses du Vampire" (1857). A woman tells the poet, writhing like a snake (lamia), her breasts bulging in her corset, that she knows how, with her kiss, to make men lose their conscience, how, with her breasts, to make old men laugh like children. Her naked body, she continues, replaces for them the heavens and all therein. In her arms and upon her bed, while making love, the angels would damn themselves to be with her.

"When she had sucked out all the marrow from my bones And I languidly turned toward her To give back an amorous kiss, I saw no more Than a wineskin with gluey sides, all full of pus!" (Baudelaire 137). He faints and, when he recovers, he sees in the morning light a skeleton and hears from it the sound like a moaning weather vane or a creaking sign above an inn, blown by the winter winds.

As with Rosset's La Jaquière, the narrator acts on his passions. After coercing a demure woman, La Jaquière finds out he has made love to a decomposed corpse, as does this man. The woman's erotically blasphemous speech parallels that of Gautier's Clarimonde. The early devils, of course, would never do anything so brazen; it would tip off the victim. But they do manipulate the man in a similar way. Goulart's woman strips and starts role playing in front of him. She seems "more beautiful than anything ever presented to his eyes before." The others play hard-to-get and thereby lead their suitors on. Like with Alvaro and La Jaquière, he faints at the revelation of her true self.

The points which are germane here are the reduction of the woman to her body again and with it, to her raw, animal sexuality and promiscuity; the the poet rendered as hostage to his passions, as greedy for her body, and as victim of her seductive blasphemies; the aftermath of the sexual intercourse leaving the narrator exhausted by her vampiric powers; his new perception of the woman as decomposing body, as repulsive and nauseating; her final state as bones rattling in the early light of dawn. The last lines point in two directions. In his post-coitus state he finds her dispensable, as dead to him; as a vampire, she is displaying to him her reality. A vampire is, after all, a living corpse unable to endure the sunlight in the tradition he is following.

Conclusion

> When God was on the point of making Eve, He said: "I will not make her from the head of man, lest she carry her head high in arrogant pride; not from the eye, lest she be wanton-eyed . . . I will form her from a chaste portion of the body," and to every limb and organ as He formed it, God said, "Be chaste! Be chaste!" Nevertheless, in spite of the great caution used, woman has all the faults God tried to obviate.
> Louis Ginzberg, *Legends of the Jews* I (1909), 66.

> "[Men] riveted us between two horrifying myths: between the Medusa and the abyss. That would be enough to set half the world laughing, except that it's still going on. . . . You only have to look at the Medusa straight on to see her. And she's not deadly. She's beautiful and laughing."
> Hélèn Cixous, "The Laugh of Medusa" (1976), 885.

The first literary line has to do with a woman exercising power over the man by her sexual prowess alone. She wants to defeat him, to bring him to ruin; under the appearance of love she is full of a simmering hatred and resentment. She suffers no loss to her power in the narrative—actually, she may enhance it—while he loses his social standing: soldier, businessman, gentleman—and in two cases, his life. She represents the male fear of an independent woman, in charge of her body. But she is simple, defined by one desire and consumed with a single goal—an impulse for his destruction. She is void of the power to create.

The second works in a very different way. The context is, of course, the fulfillment of a male fantasy. The woman is genuinely expressing herself in love and devotion to the man. She is aware that she is more powerful than he in much more than her sexuality, for she originates in supernature. She does not want to destroy him, although she is fully capable of doing so, but rather to lift him up to her level, to make him her equal.

Biondetta announces at the end before Alvaro faints, "I shall intoxicate [you] with delights, I shall fill [you] with knowledge; I shall raise [you] to the heights of greatness." Clarimonde declares to Gilbert, a lowly country priest, "[Y]ou will come with me; you will follow me whithersoever I desire. . . . You shall be the proudest and most envied of cavaliers; you shall be my lover! To be the acknowledged lover of Clarimonde, who has refused even a Pope!" Ziska explains to Gilbert, "I can make [you] a god . . . I can make [you] the king of the world and terrestrial creatures." There is something of a male desire to be offered by a powerful woman to be her kept man, to be that attractive to her, especially sexually. And there is something of the self-humbling of her love rather like the Christian myth of the divine Word becoming flesh in the person of Jesus to save humanity.

They both empower woman in different ways, as we have seen, but they both degrade her as well. Each measures a woman in terms of the man of her interest, in terms of what use she is to him. Worst of all is Baudelaire, however. Woman is reduced to her body again, but without the power of a demon or the strength of a vampire behind her. She appeals to man's passions when he is most vulnerable; she is left as a rotting piece of meat and then as bleached bones when he is done. She exhausts a man with her sexual vampirism. But the sucking of his blood brings her no benefit. If she be a prostitute, there is no empowerment.

This was a time in France when being a prostitute of a certain class, especially a kept woman, could lead to a level of upward mobility, social freedom, and respectability surpassing any wife. There is nothing of that here.[106]

As far as switching to the vampire from the devil is concerned, it offered more flexibility than Satan could. There was the vampire that acted as a simple substitute for the devil, that only followed in its wake. But there was also the branch that derived from the complex lamia of Burton and Keats. Little was made of Cazotte's female devil in the nineteenth century and her love for Alvaro tended to be understood as a cynical attempt to damn him. In other words, she appears to have been seen through the eyes of the first lineage. But the woman vampire could be developed, and she was in the second tradition. So the switch to the vampire provided opportunities for Cazotte's idea that simply would not have been there otherwise.

Works cited

Baudelaire, Charles. *The Flowers of Evil*. Trans. William Aggeler. Fresno: Academy Library Guild, 1954 [1857].

Burton, Robert (Democritus Junior). *The Anatomy of Melancholy, What it is: With all the Kinds, Causes, Symptomes, Prognostickes, and Several Cures of it*. 5th ed. Oxford: Henry Cripps, 1638.

Carroy, François du. *Histoire prodigieuse d'un gentilhomme auquel le diable s'est apparu et avec lequel il a conversé soubs le corps d'une femme morte, advenue à Paris le premier de janvier 1613*. Paris: François du Carroy, 1613.

Cazotte, Jacques. *The Devil in Love*. Trans. Judith Landry. Sawtry: Dedalus, 1991 [1776].

Cazotte, Jacques. *Le Diable amoureux*. Naples, 1772.

Clement of Alexandria. *The Instructor*. Trans. William Walker. *Ante-Nicene Fathers*. 2. Eds. Alexander Roberts & James Donaldson. Grand Rapids: William B. Eerdmans Publishing Company, 1956.

Coleridge, Samuel Taylor. *Christabel. The Poetical Works of S. T. Coleridge*. 2. London: William Pickering, 1828.

Chrysostrum. "On the Priesthood." *A Select Library of the Nicene and Post-Nicene Fathers of the Christian Church*. 9. Ed. Philip Schaff. New York: The Christian Literature Company, 1889.

Cixous, Hélèn. "The Laugh of Medusa." Trans. Keith Cohen & Paula Cohen. *Signs* 1: 4 (Summer 1976), 875-893.

Decottignies, Jean. "Variations sur un succube—Histoire de Thibaud de la Jacquière." *Revue des Sciences humaines* 111 (1963), 329-340.

Dufresnoy, Nicolas Lenglet. "Histoire prodigieuse, D'un Gentil-Homme auquel le Diable s'est apparu, et avec laquel il a converse sous le corps d'une femme morte, advenue à Paris, le premier de Janvier 1613." *Recueil de dissertations anciennes et nouvelles*. 1.2. Avignon: Jean-Noel Leloup, 1751.

Dumas, Alexandre; Maquet, M. Auguste. *The Vampire: A Drama in Five Acts. The Return of Lord Ruthven the Vampire*. Trans. Frank J. Morlock. Tarzana: Hollywood Comics, 2004 [1851].

Garinet, M. Jules. *Histoire de la Magie en France*. Paris: Foulon et Compagnie, 1818.

Gautier, Théophile. "The Dead in Love." *Demons of the Night: An Anthology*. Eds. & Trans. Joan C. Kessler. Chicago: University of Chicago Press, 1995. 91-117.

---

[106] There is a lot of material on Baudelaire's misogyny or, at least, ambivalence toward women. A helpful starting point, because of the comparisons drawn with feminist Delmira Agustini, is Smith Rousselle 29-46.

Gautier, Théophile. "La Morte amoureuse." *Oeuvres complètes de Théophile Gautier.* 13. Paris: Charpentier et Cie, 1884. 261-295.
Ginzberg, Louis. *Legends of the Jews.* 1. Baltimore: Johns Hopkins University Press, 1998 [1909].
Goethe, Johann Wolfgang von. *The Poems of Goethe.* Trans. E. A. Bowring. London: John W. Parker & Son, 1853.
Goulart, Simon. "Imposture horrible & du tout estrange." *Thrésor d'histoires admirables et mémorables.* Paris: Jean Houze, 1614.
Happel, Eberhard Werner. "Die Stinckende Buhlschaft." *Grösste Denkwürdigkeiten der Welt, oder so genannten Relationes Curiosae.* 3. Hambourg: Thomas von Wiering, 1687.
Hjaltason, Kygri-Björn. *Maríu saga: legender om Jomfru Maria og hendes jertegn: efter gamle haadsckrifter.* Ed. C. R. Unger. Christiania: Brögger & Christie, 1871.
"Im Königlichen Hof- und National-theater: Der Vampyr." *Münchener Musikzeitung.* 2. 25 October 1828. 25-30; 1 November 1828. 33-36; 8 November 1828. 41-43.
Irving, Washington. *Tales of a traveller, by Geoffrey Crayon, gent.* 1. Paris: L. Baudry, 1824.
Keats, John. *Lamia, Isabella, The Eve of St. Agnes, and Other Poems.* London: Taylor & Hessey, 1820.
Lindpaintner, Peter Josef von, and Cäsar Max Heigel. *Der Vampyr. Romantische Oper in drei Aufzügen.* Stuttgart: C. Eichele, 1828.
Map, Walter. *Master Walter Map's book, De nugis curialium (Courtier's trifles)* Trans. Marbury Bladen Ogle & Frederick Tupper. London: Chatto & Windus, 1924 [*c.* 1182].
Marschner, Heinrich. *The Vampyr.* Trans. Jutta Romero. 1997 [1828].
Nodier, Charles. "The Adventures of Thibaud de la Jacquière." *Infernaliana: Anecdotes, stories, and tales of ghosts, phantomes, demons, and vampires.* Trans. Sarah Archer. 2012 [1822]. Kindle.
Nodier, Charles. "The Vampire." *Lord Ruthven: The Vampire.* Ed. & Trans. Frank J. Morlock. Encino: Black Coat Press, 2004 [1820].
Nodier, Charles. *Der Vampyr, oder Die Todten-Braut, romantisches Schauspiel in drei Acten.* Trans. Heinrich Ludwig Ritter. Braunschweig: G. C. E. Meyer, 1822.
Philostratus. *Life of Apollonius of Tyana.* 1. Trans. F. C. Conybeare. London: William Heinemann, 1912 [3rd century CE].
Planché, James Robinson. *The Vampire: or, The Bride of the Isles.* London: Cumberland, 1820.
Plancy, Collin De. *Histoire Des Vampires et Des Spectres Malfaisans, Avec un Examen du Vampirisme.* Paris: Masson, 1820.
Polidori, John. "The Vampyre." *New Monthly Magazine.* 11: 1 (April 1819), 195-206.
Potocki, Jan. *Manuscrit trouvé à Saragosse (version de 1810). Oeuvres 4.1.* Eds. François Rousset & Dominique Triaire. Louvain: Peeters, 2006 (a). 125-134.
Potocki, Jan. *Manuscrit trouvé à Saragosse (version de 1804). Oeuvres 4.2.* Eds. François Rousset & Dominique Triaire. Louvain: Peeters, 2006 (b). 101-109.
Potocki, Jan. *Tales from the Saragossa Manuscript (Ten Days in the Life of Alphonse Van Worden).* Trans. Christine Donougher. Sawtry: Dedalus Limited, 1990 [1804].
Raupach, D. Ernst. "Wake Not the Dead." *Popular Tales and Romances of the Northern Nations.* Trans. Anonymous. 1. London: W. Simpkin & R. Marshall, 1823 [1822].
Rosset, François de. "D'un demon qui apparoist en forme de damoiselle au Lieutenant du Chevalier du Guet de la ville de Lyon." *Les Histoires memorables et tragiques de ce temps.* Paris: Pierre Chevalier, 1619 [1614].
Rousselle, Elizabeth Smith. "The (New) Decadent Woman: Delmira Agustini's Tête-à-Tête with Charles Baudelaire." *L'Érudit Franco-Espagnol.* 6 (Fall 2014), 29-46.
Voragine, Jacobus, de. *The Golden Legend.* Trans. Wyllyam Caxton. Westminster: Wyllyam Caxton, 1483.
Voragine, Jacobus, de. *Legenda aurea de Sanctis.* Lyons: Matthias Huss, 1486.
Voragine, Jacobus, de. *Legenda aurea sanctorum, sive, Lombardica historia.* Early English Books Online. Trans. Wyllyam Caxton. 2020 (1483). https://quod.lib.umich.edu/e/eebo/A14559.0001.001/1:155.1?rgn=div2;view=toc.
Zeiller, Martin. *Theatrum Tragicum, Das ist: Newe, warhafftige, trawrig, kläglich und wunderliche Geschichten.* Tübingen: Philibert Brum, 1628.

7.
"A Person of My Sex:" The Transgendered Vampire of the Nineteenth Century

Introduction

Scholarship, predictably, has been preoccupied with contemporary works of fiction when considering the vampire and gender relations. If one pushes back, one will find a concentration on *Dracula*. There are a plethora of studies on this tale, almost always equating the vampire bite with the act of sex, and not without reason, although it can be taken to extremes. There is no finer study than Miller's "Coitus Interruptus" (2006) on the preoccupation with sex in studies on *Dracula*. Moving backward from today like this to *Dracula* means the topic changes from "sleeping" with a vampire[107] to being "kissed" by one.[108] If a longer arc is taken the temptation is still to start in earnest with *Dracula* and move on from there.[109] Looking for the origins of *Dracula*'s gender interstitiality, one finds attention shifts to homosexuality, mainly lesbianism, and in particular *Carmilla* with a sideward glance to Coleridge's incomplete poem, *Christabel*. So here we move from transgenderism into specific studies of nineteenth-century vampire homosexuality and that, while related, is a separate issue.

The nineteenth century was a time of changing attitudes toward what male and female meant. Pre-Enlightenment thought saw men and women as similar beings in a hierarchy where the latter was a pale reflection of the former. With the Enlightenment, discussion shifted to two natures, separate but complimentary. In the latter half of the century with more women entering the labor force, pursuing an education, and agitating for change—not only for the vote and equality of station, but for more comfortable and useful attire—professional attitudes started to change again. Interest was shown in designating cross-dressers in history and homosexuals as masculine women and feminine men. Both were designated as "inversions."

Scientists developed competing theories about why inversion was the case. One turned to the environment and the other to biology. Both, however, used the notion of a spectrum to define genders; human beings were in essence bisexual and fell on a continuum between masculinity and femininity. There is a nice thumbnail sketch of this in Joanne Meyerowitz's *How Sex Changed* (2002), 14-15; 21-23.

---

[107] I am, of course, lifting the phrase from Agata Łuksza, "Sleeping with a Vampire" (2014).
[108] The reference is to the title of the popular article by Christopher Craft "'Kiss Me with those Red Lips" (1984). "As the primary site of erotic experience in *Dracula*, [Dracula's] mouth equivocates, giving the lie to the easy separation of the masculine and the feminine" (109). Craft sees the female vampire mouths as subordinate to his and therefore carrying the same gender ambiguity. See also Tom Pollard, *Loving Vampires* (2016). He has a chapter on gender that starts with Dracula.
[109] Milly Williamson, *The Lure of the Vampire* (2005). She makes a few passing asides to Polidori's *The Vampyre* and a couple of its adaptations; a remark or two on Varney the Vampire; a few paragraphs on Carmilla and lesbianism. This is typical.

Needless to say public attitudes were contradictory. There was, on the one hand, a strong reaction against any blurring of distinctions between men and women, going so far as a good number of US cities judging cross-dressing to be illegal starting in 1848 (Stryker 31-33). In Victorian London male cross-dressers were frequently arrested and, because it was not illegal, were charged with other crimes. In Paris, women wearing male clothing was prohibited in 1800 and stayed on the books for 213 years. On the other hand, in the latter half of the nineteenth century, some of the most popular entertainers were female and male impersonators. For example in England and the United States there were Ella Wesner, Annie Hindle, Vesta Tilley, Ernest Boulton, and William Horace Lingard.

In this context the notion of the vampire flourished. Through it people could deal with issues ranging from serial killers to religion; from pestilence to gender. Tom Pollard is correct when he writes today, "vampire metaphors, instead of enshrining traditional gender roles, depict a variety of 'gender schema'—including heterosexual, gay, lesbian, bisexual, and transgender orientations" (61). So too, *mutatis mutandis*, in the 1800s.

In this essay, I am interested in investigating the issue of transgenderism in the nineteenth-century vampire. I will consider first cross-dressing.[110] This will clue the reader in that I am using "transgender" in its broadest sense. The female-to-male change seldom pertains to the vampire. It is typical of adjuncts to vampire hunters. I know of only one instance where it is of a female vampire. The male-to-female, on the other hand, almost exclusively pertains to the vampire. From there we will turn to transsexuality. I am aware of six instances of this and will arrange them according to the extent of the transformation rather than by chronology in spite of the fact they span well over a century.

Cross-dressing

The least controversial is the narrative of a young woman passing as a man. After all, it was a regular feature of ballads and comedies and it represented upward mobility rather than downward, even if it was not countenanced in real life. While present in vampire tales, it is seldom used with the vampire itself. For example, in an adolescent boy's book by Colonel Prentiss Ingraham, *The Ocean Vampire; or, The Heiress of Castle Curse* (1882), a young man joins the crew of the nefarious pirate, the "Ocean Vampire" (this is modeled after the bat not the monster, which is dismissed as superstition), and works with the hero, who has been forced to serve aboard, in order to bring the vampire to justice. In the end the pirate is hanged, and the young man is revealed to be the villain's wife who had been trying to put an end to his violence and her shame. She quickly gets married to a heroic man.

In another, *Dashing Duval* (c. 1889), a male adjunct to the hero is about to be executed but narrowly escapes due to the daring rescue mission performed by his lover dressed as a man. Thus, the hero and he can continue to pursue the vampire

---

[110] Susan Stryker (16-18) follows the consensus in her glossary and distinguishes transvestitism from cross-dressing by its application only to male-to-female dress and its association with erotic pleasure. The former term lacks them, as do the following examples.

and stop his outrages. Both women slip back contentedly into their proper roles when their aim is accomplished.[111]

There is one that stands out, however: Richard Marsh's "The Mask" (1892).[112] Mr. Fountain is on a train when a gentleman enters his compartment, sits down, and offers him a drink. Afterward, he dozes off but is awakened by a monster robbing him, scratching at his chest with its claws, and then drinking his blood. His companion is nowhere to be seen. Later he learns that this might have been Mary Brooker who is a recently escaped lunatic and a cruel killer and who purposely deformed herself. She had been incarcerated for one murder but was likely guilty of several more.

Having disembarked the train, he meets a beautiful young woman, Mrs. Jaynes, at the hotel meal and she talks to him about the possibility of making masks as realistic as wigs. Then he runs into the man on the train who explains he had also been accosted by the beast but fled. Later he is invited into Mrs. Jaynes' hotel room and while she is in the other room her mother brings him some tea and confides in him that her daughter worries her, for she talks of a lot of murdering men in disguise.

She leaves and the man in the train appears who describes Mary Brooker as a misunderstood genius who has been acting solely to gratify her taste for killing. Meanwhile Fountain has discovered that he is paralyzed by the tea. Mrs. Jaynes then enters, after the man departs, and explains that although he is clearly attracted to her it is only a mask he sees and she removes it to show him the disfigured face of Mary Brooker, the monster on the train. She declares "I scratched you yesterday. I bit you. I sucked your blood. Now I will suck you dry, for you are mine" (Marsh 561). He had only sipped the tea so he has gotten his mobility back by this time and he suddenly grabs her by the throat. She throws him off as if he were a child and begins to strangle him, but the commotion draws other patrons to the room. She is apprehended and returned to prison. Mr. Fountain hangs between death and life for several days but lives to tell the tale.

This is a woman who enjoys outwitting, overpowering, and killing men by using techniques of deception which include cross-dressing. She is criminally insane, but she is also an evil genius, unconstrained by morality, unconcerned with social welfare, driven only by technical mastery and her individual interests, not unlike many industrialists of the day. In her pursuits she is patient, diligent, careful, capable of long-term planning and short-term self-denial. So her love of killing is bounded by her interests in mastering methods of disguise; her enjoyment of taking the life of her victims is necessarily linked with the cruelty of betraying their trust.

The examples from the male side are similar to the previous ones; I shall give three. Charlotte Brontë's 1847 *Jane Eyre* (published under the pseudonym of Currer Bell) has a scene where Rochester, husband to Bertha, the vampire of the

---

[111] Steve Holland, in a blog written on January 18, 2010 writes: "Dashing Duval is dated by James/Smith as c. 1875 but it describes itself as the "most interesting and thrilling story ever presented to the boys of Albion." The short-lived magazine, Boys of Albion was launched by Palmer in 1888, hence the likely date for Dashing Duval is 1889."

[112] Marsh is a pseudonym for Richard Bernard Heldmann. There has been a renewed interest in him in recent years, aided substantially by Minna Vuohelainen's studies, which include her 2007 Ph.D. dissertation, *The Popular Fiction of Richard Marsh: Literary Production, Genre, Audience*, her 2009/10 *Victorian Fiction Research Guide 35: Richard Marsh*, and her 2015 *Richard Marsh*.

story, dresses as a gypsy woman to read Jane's fortune and draw her closer to him (88-103). In another, Paul Féval's *The Vampire Countess* (1860), there are two shady characters—one is said to be an oupire or cannibal and the other, a vampire.

Rochester dressed as a female gypsy. Illustrated by F. H. Townsend. Brontë 1897, ch. 19.

The first is tall and speaks in a baritone voice; the second is short and is a tenor. We encounter them at the beginning posing as an investigator and a priest as they tell a wealthy audience who are taking up a collection for persecuted Christians, about two 400-year-old brothers—one large, the other short. After the brothers, years ago, had related a story to a father and daughter of great wealth of two gypsy brothers of the same size differential who survived their public beheading, they abducted the daughter, and ruined them in part by the exorbitant ransom. The investigator and priest presently warn the guests that these brothers are expected to show up at the party this very night and may be disguised as "an old man and a young woman, a husband and his wife, or a father and his daughter" (81). They are there to arrest them.

There is no surprise to the audience of such a gender-bending description of the brothers' disguises because also in their opening monologue, the investigator clued his listeners that the younger, small one had cross-dressed before. The tall one explained that the brothers had recently stolen all the valuables, including the crown jewels, from the nobility celebrating the baptism of the Prince Royal of Wurtemburg. They were present as the *Infante* and *Infanta* of Spain—she being "noble, gracious, and charming" (66).

While everyone is looking out for the scoundrels, the two steal the offering and escape unnoticed. But they lose something of immense value there, a property deed, and they are able to trace it to one of the guests—a young man—who was probably going to return it to the rightful owners, the very same father and daughter mentioned above, for it is to their estate. They plan to throttle the young man, take back what they consider to be theirs, and kidnap the daughter again. To do the latter, the vampire proposes finding out where they live, visit them disguised as a 50-year-old dowager, flatter the young girl into her carriage, and put an end to the masquerade in order to reveal his design of marrying her.

This has to be abandoned, but the two do set up watch at the residence of the father and daughter as a beggar and elderly woman. They viciously attack the young man when he comes to visit and leave him for dead, but their search turns up nothing. The young man survives and ends up marrying the girl himself. The two thieves are discovered later in their graves, to which they must return yearly, and are scorched to ashes. In the conclusion, the young man receives a note reading "See you soon! And by way of signature: The tall one and the short one" (162).

In the third tale, *The Vampire, or, Detective Brand's Greatest Case* (1885), five wealthy men have been found dead and the police are baffled. All they know is that the assailant has portrayed himself as a vampire bat and the victims have been found stabbed to the heart with a stiletto and have two marks on their necks. The dead men were known to have visited high-end establishments and spend their money freely, so Detective Brace takes this social status as his disguise.

Being a bachelor, he is interested when a woman looks at him in a rather flirtatious manner. "The lady was young and good-looking, dark-eyed and dark-haired . . . She was dressed in the most exquisite taste, . . . and it was plain that she was a lady by birth, breeding, and station" (9-10). This pretty woman was a widow so Brace knows if he plays his cards right, he will marry into a fortune. He hears her story, follows her home, and disappears. Several days later, he is found with his heart pierced and the two neck wounds.

Meanwhile Victor Lee has learned that a young orphan woman is sailing to New York and that, unbeknownst to her, she will inherit a fortune. He is "slender in build and short in stature . . . ; [his] face was smoothly shaven and appeared effeminate" (3). He boards the ship before it docks, makes the girl's acquaintance, and then abducts her in a small boat; he identifies himself to the pursuers as a vampire, which is immediately taken by them as a compound of the bat and the monster. A storm commences and the boat capsizes. Both survive but go in different directions when they leave their respective saviors.

Detective Brand takes over the case from Brace and follows the same art of deception his predecessor did and he too runs into an attractive woman—a "stunner" as a clerk describes her. Brand is invited to her room, but soon learns his mistake; she spikes his drink with opium. In his state of apparent incapacitation she reveals herself to him as the murderer of "many a strong man" and as one who craves blood. She then thrusts her dagger at his heart, but it snaps as it hits his protective vest. He has a tolerance to opium so he can stop putting on the act and subdue her. Nonetheless she escapes.

Lee is home relaxing when the detective enters and discloses that the place is surrounded so he might as well go peacefully to his fate. Caught, Lee says,

> I have played a bold game, haven't I? It was easy enough in my disguises to entrap my victims. They entered the house on one street, met their doom, then, they were carried to the stable in the rear on another street, placed in the coach, and their bodies thus easily disposed of. . . . I have preyed upon my fellow men as mercilessly as any wild beast. (48)

He commits suicide before Brand can incarcerate him. He had finally kidnapped the young woman so she is now liberated, gains the fortune, and marries the man who has been trying to rescue her ever since she was taken from the ship. In both cases the cross-dressing men are doing so to enrich themselves by deception and in one case, by murder.

Transsexuality and Transgendering

There is more than cross-dressing in vampire tales, so we will move on to the transsexual ones now. I will arrange them not by chronology but by the extent of the transformations, although they span over a century. This means that stories representing different time periods will necessarily be jumbled together.

The first is Jacques Cazotte's *The Devil in Love* (1772/76). This will focus on something not in the previous synopsis. While not exactly a vampire story, it was directly influential on several high-profile vampire tales in the nineteenth century. Alvaro decides he wants to have a spirit as a servant and so conjures one up. The recitation of a short formula works. But it is a monster that appears and when he overcomes his fear he demands that it turn into a spaniel and lick his feet. When the dog turns on its back, he notices it is a "little bitch," so he commands that it change genders and he names his servant Biondetto. (36). He is a most attractive man.

He begins to think better of his wish, afraid that he will "pay a price for it" (41), thus he tries to dismiss him, but he begs him to stay, saying it would be scandalous to abandon a woman on the streets unprotected. He finally relents; his servant tries to show his love to him but he only responds with cruelty, even though he is attracted to him. Although Alvaro does long for him, he continues his charade, holding she is a man and refuses his advances. Alvaro eventually does abandon him, and unprotected he is stabbed and hovers between life and death. This provokes a confession of love from Alvaro and an admission that she is a woman. He renames her Biondetta.

When she recovers she tells him she is a sylph, an elemental spirit of the air. By taking the form of a woman she has forfeited her natural rights of her kind. She did this from respect for him and this became love when she incarnated. Since becoming a woman she has longed for sexual union with him, but Alvaro wants to get his mother's blessing and marry her before he does. One day's journey from home she showers him with questions why they must wait and he finally succumbs to his desires and has intercourse with her.

She declares herself now truly happy. But then she makes a surprising announcement: she is actually the devil and yet she truly loves him. The devil wants him to pronounce his feelings in as tender words as its feelings are to him: "my dear Belzebub, I adore you" (101). She turns back into the monster he initially encountered. Alvaro crawls under the bed where he faints. In the morning s/he is gone and he finishes his journey alone.

Where things change from a basic transgenderism to transsexual is at the manifestation of the devil at the end. Until that point it seems to be a female spirit that had been made to dress like a man. But with the revelation of its true nature the pronoun changes. The male devil had become a female spirit manifested as a woman who must dress as a man. Before they make love Alvaro tells how he is moving close to Biondetta's sweet mouth and how her indescribable arms, her whiteness, softness, and shapeliness create a bond that he cannot endure losing. Afterward, as she reveals herself to him, he explains "I was defenseless in the face of my enemy: *he* seized *his* advantage and I was wholly at *his* mercy. . . . 'The die

The devil revealing itself illustrated by Édouard de Beaumont. In Jacques Cazotte, *Le diable amoureux* (1871 edition), 271.

is cast,' *he* told me, without noticeably altering the tone to which *he* had accustomed me. 'You sought me out. I followed you, served you, obliged you; in the end I did as you wished.'" (italics added (101). He is now a male speaking in a female voice.

What makes this a minor incident of transsexuality, however, is that this is the way of all female incarnations of devils. Denizens of hell are overwhelmingly pictured as male in their natural state, so it is a sexual transformation whenever they enter the world as women or succubi. One can see this early in Christianity. In the depiction of the great Egyptian anchorite, Anthony the Great described by the great church father, Athanasius, the devil manifests itself to attack him with every form of temptation. "And the devil, unhappy creature, one night even took upon him the shape of a woman and imitated all her acts simply to beguile Antony."[113] Becoming a woman and tempting in this way was the lowest and most degrading means taken by the devil to lead him astray. It is mentioned at the end of his lures to sin as a last resort.

Along the same lines, but stronger, is *The Manuscript Found in Saragossa* (1804). Here the text is an issue. At last a critical edition has been prepared and it demonstrates that two versions were consciously prepared by the author—an 1804 one and another in 1810—as different works rather than as partial aspects of a reconstructable original text. The first fourteen chapters are essentially the same. The two start to diverge significantly at fifteen and at forty-two they

---

[113] Athanasius. "Life of Anthony" (1907), 197. For the Greek and Latin see Athanasius "Vita S. Antonii" (1857), 847-48.

become two very different books. What interests us is the first 14, because they are basically the only ones that feature the vampires.[114]

Officer Alphonse van Worden is crossing through the nearly desolate Valley of Los Hermanos; the expanse begins with two brothers hanging on a gibbet. He stops at an abandoned inn but at midnight it is vacant no longer; he is awakened by two exotic sisters who say they have waited for him, because they are his cousins. Although they have lived a cloistered life and have never until now even seen a man, they are adept at the art of making love, having practiced on each other.[115] He is chastely but passionately entertained through the night, falls asleep between them, and awakens under the gibbet with the bodies of the dead men on either side.

That day he finds shelter with a monk and hears the story of a young man, Pacheco, who had gone to the same empty inn and at midnight found himself with his aunt, with whom he had fallen in love, and his stepmother. He "drank the cup of criminal passion to the last drop," fell asleep, and likewise woke under the gallows with the two brothers. The third day van Worden is arrested and finds his two cousins have been as well; on the fourth all three are rescued. He stays with his benefactors for the next four days.

The fifth night the sisters enter his room with chastity belts and they dally through the night. He does not wake up under the gallows this time. Nor does he the next night when the same thing occurs. But on the seventh night they enter without their chastity belts, close the bed curtains, and consummate their love. Interestingly this is witnessed by Pacheco before he is chased away, and he sees something completely different: Alphonse caressing two men before they seclude themselves behind the curtain. The morning of the eighth he finds himself back under the gibbet, but this time both brothers are lying on one side of him and another man is on the other. He is a rabbi and cabbalist who was betrothed by his father to two immortal sisters. With diligence, patience, and persistence he finally mastered the techniques to call them forth. The place for conjuring was the inn and at midnight they came. He will say nothing beyond his lying down next to them.

Alphonse learns from him that the two brothers are vampires, but of a special variety. Eastern European vampires are corpses that arise at night to suck blood, but the Spanish ones are "foul spirits which assume the first dead body they come across, turn it into any imaginable shape and—" At that point Alphonse walks away, knowing what he was getting at. It is the fourteenth day that Alphonse, now affixed to a band of wandering gypsies, who have told him that the brothers often vacate the gallows at night, sees the cabbalist's sister between the two brothers on the ground. She too had been promised to a pair of immortal demi-gods. Like her brother, she had to call them forth in the inn. They appeared ready to seduce her when she muttered a secret name and they disappeared. She fainted and found herself between the two dead bodies.

Dropping the talk of demons for a moment, we are faced with two brothers whose corpses do not seem to decompose, for they have been around a long time,

---

[114] On the 25th day in the 1804 version we do get another story, but it is very much the same as what we have already encountered, although this time with a mathematician. Potocki, *Manuscrit trouvé à Saragosse* (version de 1804), *Oeuvres* 4.2. *The Manuscript Found in Saragossa* translated by Ian Maclean is of a reconstructed text that never existed, but, as said above, days 1-14 are generally accurate for both versions, so I have used his text here.
[115] This is really the art of making oneself attractive and desirable to another, perhaps with a little foreplay.

The Transgendered Vampire of the Nineteenth Century

who turn themselves into women, seduce, and have sex with men (or they stay men to have sex with women). They are not interested in sucking blood or human energy, but in humiliating and confounding their prey. They are not in love with their victims as the devil was above, but are promiscuous and doing this largely to enjoy themselves. But they are still technically succubi to the men, devils appearing as women. It is not a coincidence that these first two stories are by far the earliest of our examples. Transsexuality initially must be mediated through Satan.

Next is "A Kiss of Judas" by Julian Osgood Field (1893). On the boat ride to Turkey, Richard Rowan innocently insults a passenger. In a rage the man, who is unbelievably ugly, threatens him, but nothing comes of it at the time.[116] In Turkey he hears of the Children of Judas, a loosely knit band of supernatural assassins in direct lineage from Judas. These people, generally horribly disfigured, move among ordinary people looking for acts of personal indignity at which to become angry; they punish the perpetrators by committing suicide, gaining the tools in hell necessary to ensure their success, and being reincarnated so as to kill them. In the process, genders are irrelevant. One can be reincarnated as a virus, insect, animal, a male or female human being, etc.; howsoever they kill the victim is called the kiss of Judas, the sign of Judas' betrayal. If the kiss is from a human, the victim will have XXX left on their bodies, representing the sum of money Judas received to sell Jesus to the Romans.

Shortly thereafter the awful man attacks him with a knife and Rowan knocks him out, picks up the knife, and drives it through his hands into a tree. There he can either escape or die. That evening Rowan sees him again. He lunges toward Rowan shouting "I am really—glad; for I shall come to you now and you cannot escape me!" (354) He takes the knife and sinks it deep into his chest.

Rowan moves on to Moldavia and the incident is forgotten in the midst of other concerns. One night he hears a woman sobbing outside his door. When Rowan opens it and sees her, he is struck by how much she looks like the Virgin Mary as Mater Dolorosa. His heart is moved by compassion and in the many languages he knows he tries to comfort her, but she appears to be deaf and mute. She responds very little. Then he speaks passionately to her: "You're . . . the most beautiful woman I think I ever saw . . . What language can you speak, I wonder? Only the language of love, perhaps!" (364-365) He begins to speak it and as he increases his ardor, she sheds her sorrow and begins to respond. Her face, that "ideal type of womanly purity," becomes lit by joy (365). He opens his arms wide and she rushes into them and kisses his neck, leaving behind a small scar of XXX.

Illustration from Julian Osgood Field, "A Kiss of Judas," 366.

---

[116] Montague Summers sees this as vampiric (*The Vampire: His Kith and Kin* 183).

Here the talk of the devil recedes, but it is still there. The whole is an inversion of Christianity: Judas, the archetypal traitor, betraying Jesus for 30 pieces of silver is the focus; the hands of an evil man driven into wood by a good one; suicide in hate rather than sacrifice in love; resurrection in vengeance instead of reconciliation; the image of the Mater Dolorosa, pure innocence, for the sake of murder. When the stranger went to hell after his suicide he had to consult with the devil as to how best to kill him. The point is, however, that this is a single soul, first in a man's body as a deformed villain and then in a woman's, the very incarnation of heavenly beauty. It is now unencumbered by the succubus.

A step further is *Princess Daphne* by Edward Heron-Allen and Selina Delaro (1888) which has to do with a psychic vampire according to Brian J. Frost (49). In London's artistic district "Princess Daphne" resides. She is stately, beautiful, intelligent and independent. She is unwilling to compromise her freedom so he has no lovers. In the US, where "all men are equal and none of the women" (Heron-Allen and Delaro 36), specifically in New York City, lives Mahmouré, an attractive actress and bohemian, who is equally independent. Unexpectedly both fall in love, Daphne with Eric and Mahmouré with Paul.

Mahmouré's lifestyle has taken a toll on her and for five months she has been near death. Paul begins, by mesmerism, to turn her into "his charming vampire;" he willingly gives her his energy and so weakens himself. However, Paul becomes interested in more than empowering her; he wants through the hypnosis for Mahmouré to make contact with someone far away. She does—with Daphne. And it turns out Paul is related to Daphne and is now, under false pretenses, living on her inheritance. This makes him even more obsessed with the experiments.

Paul starts projecting Mahmouré into Daphne's body, causing her confusion as she both does and does not recognize her surroundings and herself for the duration of the habitation. Mahmouré also appears to her as a ghost. Daphne acclimates to this but Eric becomes increasingly concerned. Meanwhile Paul is becoming seriously enervated yet will not stop, for he is driven now to perfect the science of mesmerism. Strangely, as Paul transfers his energy to Mahmouré, he is simultaneously sending part of his soul, his "psychic energy," through her to Daphne. When he dies, he channels the rest of his soul to her. This proves too much for her and she dies at the same time. She revives however . . . but no longer as Daphne *per se*, rather as a hybrid of Paul and herself.

Mahmouré is now heading to Spain and stops in London where she has a little business to do with Daphne about the inheritance. When they meet, both are immediately drawn to each other. Before business is even discussed, they seat themselves close together on the lounge. Daphne has found it difficult to compose herself: she "felt under the influence of Mahmouré's presence, of her gaze, of her kiss. It seemed a new obsession . . ." (203). They caress each other tenderly.

It is not long, however, before the narrative distances itself from this mutual attraction. It explains that Mahmouré is intoxicated with Paul inside Daphne and Daphne with her because of Paul's love for Mahmouré within; that the mesmerism had caused the good to die out in Daphne and be replaced by the amorality of Paul (making her attraction to Mahmouré bad); that her male lover, Eric, a good man, takes an instant dislike to Mahmouré and soon leaves Daphne; that they are allegedly suffering from hysteria. They will have to be separated from each other, we are told, but it cannot be imposed from without, otherwise it will cost them their lives. It will have to come naturally, through a quarrel. After weeks of intimacy together they do fight and Mahmouré strangles Daphne in a fit of passion.

This has same-sex attraction through transsexuality. It is not compromised by notions of succubi, yet it is, of course, by the supersedure of heterosexuality. But we have to be careful if we call this lesbianism, but we shall deal with that in a separate chapter. The nineteenth century had another option that is not present today: romantic friendship. Here deep intimacy and attachment was openly shown and encouraged, utterly eclipsing any relationship with a male, but with no sexual expression. If lesbianism is about a woman-oriented woman then this is a lesbian narrative; if it refers to a sexual relationship this is almost certainly not the case.[117] But the point is that it is a transsexual narrative with consensual same-sex allure.

This is followed by J. T. Sheridan Le Fanu's *The Haunted Baronet* (1870).[118] Sir Bale Mardykes, whose "temper and conduct were uncertain, and his moods sometimes violent and insulting" has a personal assistant, Philip Feltram, a relative of his whom he treats "worse than a dog" (81). Feltram suffers under an ignoble heritage. Ninety years before, his great-grandmother, Mary, had two children with Sir Jasper Mardykes and insisted that she was properly married to him. Nonetheless she was turned out of the house along with her children, whom he declared to be illegitimate, so he could marry another. She and her youngest apparently drowned in the lake abutting the Mardykes estate; Philip is the grandson of the one child who survived.

Lately Feltram has suffered from dreams in which Mary appears to him, demanding that he claim the name of Mardykes for himself and assert his rights. But he is a gentle man and wishes only to have the family name cleared and to be treated with dignity; he is not rapacious and so does not desire any of the wealth. It is not long after the dreams start that Bale declares Feltram *persona non grata* and is ready to jettison him from the house despite a prophecy that if Feltram go in weakness, he shall return in power. Feltram leaves of his own accord a few hours before the deadline and is dragged into the lake, which he had to cross, by an arm that reaches up to him, and drowns. As his body is being prepared for burial he revives a new man, stern and aloof.

It is largely unknown but to his personal assistant that the Baronet is heavily in debt. Feltram announces he will stay on two years to get him out of his indebtedness and then will leave. He soon offers to act as a mediary between him and a benefactor who will provide him the names of horses to bet on at the races on the condition that he cross the lake (which he despises, having received a warning that what he hates most will come from it) and meet with him. The two mysterious persons he encounters turn out later to be Mary's mother and father. His estate does become solvent again and he courts and then marries one of Feltram's distant relatives, Janet. When she moves in, she brings her elder cousin, Gertrude, with her.

---

[117] The subject of romantic friendships will be dealt with more extensively in the following two chapters on male and female homosexuality.
[118] M. R. James gave a lecture at the Royal Institution of Great Britain in March of 1923. In it he referred to this story as exemplifying the "Vampire-idea." http://www.users.globalnet.co.uk/~pardos/ArchiveLeFanu.html.

Over a year later, just after Philip has left, William, who had fallen in love with Gertrude, shows up, just having gained enough wealth to ask for her hand. They marry and settle down in a farm house on the estate. But Bale takes a dislike to William, thinking of a prophecy he had received that his estate would belong to a Feltram, and under his pressure the two begin to plan to leave the estate. Mary's mother, however, identifying herself simply as a relative, visits Gertrude in a dream and tells her she must not go. So they stay several years more until Sir Bale dies. Because Janet never produced an heir eventually William takes over the estate and assumes the name of Mardykes for himself and his progeny.

This is a particularly important instance of transsexuality because it is not about romance or sex; it is about a woman who was wronged taking over the male body of a descendent, who is advantageously placed, in order to bring about justice, for he lacks the desire to do it on his own. She could never do so by killing and inhabiting the corpse of a female no matter how well placed she may be, because of the unequal status of men and women at the time. So this is about dominance and control over the future, making sure that this very generation will take back what was robbed from her three generations previously, including getting it operating in the black.

Finally, we turn to Paul Féval, *Vampire City* (1875), which I consider to be the strongest and most bizarre instance. Brian Stableford has written that this is the "ultimate literary ancestor" of *Buffy the Vampire Slayer* (8), but the latter takes few of the risks represented here. The plot is complex, so we will look at it through the prism of its most prominent vampire: Otto Goetzi. He appears to be human and so he can walk among us undetected. But when seen in his natural state he "shone brightly green, and his lower lip burned as red as a hot iron. His hair stood on end, flowing and trembling like a flaming punch-bowl" (75). He stinks like a she-cat in heat, attracting amorous tomcats to him.

He exsanguinates his victims and can drink them "like a glass of lemonade," but we see him merely using a gold pin to puncture behind a woman's left ear and "suckling" on the wound, as well as turning into a large green spider and feeding on the left breast of a young female. We are informed that male vampires are powerful but rather effeminate and the females tall and bold, yet we must be careful here, for gender distinctions are problematic. Interestingly, they can have children—half demons, half phantoms, sterile, and "deprived of the blessing of death" (121).

The young Anne [sic] Radcliffe reads that her close friends, Ned and Cornelia, who are engaged to be married, are in trouble abroad, so she and an old servant go to Holland, as she is directed. When they reach their destination they travel to an inn where they confront a faceless man with hair and a beard, a parrot perched on his shoulder, a small boy propped up on a hoop, a monstrous flesh-colored dog whose form was nearly human, and a bald, rotund woman, all in suspended animation. We learn that vampires for an hour every day freeze in position. At the striking of the hour the five begin to move again and who should enter the inn but Ned's valet followed by exact duplicates of those five already noted in pursuit.

We discover that along with a duplicated Monsieur Goetzi, they are all he. They are victims of his, changed and incorporated into his being. After a vampire passes its apprentice stage and becomes a master, it begins to incorporate its prey and can reach upwards of a hundred such servants (151). So we have our first level of transgenderism: Goetzi, while looking to be a single sex, is actually composed of both. It is not that he has their characteristics but rather he *is* a community of them, thus the bald woman is he.

In a subsequent conflict between the three humans and Mr. Goetzi's "vampiricules" (112), they happen to behead the "Goetzi-in-chief" and all of his members lose their heads as well. As soon as the second Mr. Goetzi finds his head they lock him in a trunk so that when the original finds his and reassembles, he is incomplete and the three have a captive. It turns out that the second Goetzi must become a servant to his captors and answer truthfully whatever questions they pose to him. He explains that Goetzi has now become powerless. He is going to stay nearby them but he must return to Vampire City to be healed. Every vampire has a key hole on the left side of the breast where it can be wound up to regain its power. This is what he needs.

The second Goetzi also reveals that after the original had passed its apprentice level, his first victim was someone Anne actually knew: Polly Bird. Now we reach a second level of transgenderism, indeed transsexuality. It is not just that his prey is entering a collective being still maintaining their own sex, but that a female has actually become male. This is not a male or female spirit or soul taking over a body of the opposite sex, but is the exact same person whose body is physically transformed.

They follow Goetzi into Vampire City and find him during the hour of suspended animation; they burn his heart, putting an end to him. Now they must find Cornelia and rescue her. They have already liberated Ned in the fight at the Inn. The only vampiricule left is Polly Bird and she has become a member of their team. However when Polly enters the castle where Cornelia is being held to fetch her, she betrays them, for with the removal of the original she has "fully usurped the personality of Monsieur Goetzi" (171) and wants to complete his goal. "In spite of her native sex, she had resolved to marry Cornelia."

Anne is chained in a fearful dungeon, where a victim of this chamber centuries before, a Countess, appears to her and finishes the story. Mr. Goetzi is actually the latest incarnation of an infamous woman. So what we end up with is a woman who changes her sex to a male, who then absorbs a female transforming her into a man, and becomes comprised of a female. She is then is reduced to his female/male second, and subsequently wants to marry a woman. This is about as gender-bending a narrative as one could hope for from the nineteenth century and far outstrips anything in *Buffy the Vampire Slayer*.

Conclusion

It should come as no surprise that cross-dressing has nothing to do with eroticism nor is it concerned about identity or gender. Rather it is considered as utilitarian, a means to an end. It is used to escape detection so as to rescue someone, to bring about restitution, to spy, to rob, or to kill. It is still utilizing the idea of a vampire—real or metaphorical—for the purpose of transgressing standard gender boundaries.

Looking over the six examples of transsexuality one thing stands out. Until the last one we have a kind of "cross-sexing." One changes sex for a purpose. It is cross-dressing writ large. The first two are for the act of sex. The male devil falls in love with a man; he transforms himself into a woman who wants just one thing, to have sexual intercourse with the man. At the end, after consummating their love, he reveals himself as male and still with Biondetta's voice wants to make the relationship permanent. The second is much the same, except it is promiscuous. Two dead males, their bodies apparently demon possessed, transform themselves into women at midnight, seducing and having sex with men. Afterward they turn back into males. There is another possibility and that is that they give the illusion of being females and their prey is actually having sex with a male. Be that as it may, they have also another goal—embarrassment or humiliation. The problem with both is the proximity of the devil, who can masquerade as a woman.

The third follows this but in a richer way. The primary purpose now is revenge. Sexual change assumes a stronger role and sexual intercourse a weaker one. The children of Judas are Judas' progeny so they were at one time human beings. They have become supernatural through the mediation of the devil but their actions and the change are their own. Nonetheless everything is very temporary.

The fourth substitutes the "science" of mesmerism for the devil. Through its mediation a man is able to channel his energy to one woman and his soul to another. The soul in the second woman is only partially his, yet the change might have been permanent had the two women simply quarreled and gone their separate ways. This deepens the connection to female mutual attraction in the sex change. No matter in which direction Daphne might have developed her desires, part of her would always be drawn to the same sex, for she was internally double-sexed. And this is the only story where homoeroticism is consensual.

The fifth jettisons the notion of sexual attraction altogether and makes the sex change about power and restitution. The great grandmother kills her male descendent and thereby becomes a male. S/he thereby has intimate access to the estate that should have been hers and can work everything out for the eventual transfer of a solvent estate to her progeny. The transformation is temporary but lasts years.

The final one is permanent; it is the nineteenth century equivalent both of a sex change operation and true transgenderism. The postmortem soul of a woman incarnates herself as a man, who then duplicates himself by incorporating a woman into himself, and both parts of her/him, as one being, internalize within him/herself victims of both sexes and manifests her/himself accordingly. Finally the woman part of the vampire takes over and as a man wants to marry a woman. In every transformation she identifies herself not with her own sex but the other, when appropriate.

There were, therefore, a whole range of gender and sexual experiments going on in the nineteenth century. As entertainment they could touch on a number of serious topics with regard to identity and orientation without the scandal of being actual cases. For this the vampire was a perfect vehicle. All of the preceding instances predate *Dracula*. They ought no longer to be ignored.

Works cited

Athanasius. "Life of Anthony." *A Select Library of the Nicene and Post-Nicene Fathers of the Christian Church* 4. Trans. H. Ellershaw. New York: Charles Scribner's Sons, 1907 [c. 360].

Athanasius. "Vita S. Antonii." *Patrologia Graeca*. 26. Ed. J. P. Migne. Paris: Apud Garnier Fratres et J.-P. Migne Successores, 1857.

Brontë, Charlotte (Currer Bell). *Jane Eyre*. London: Smith, Elder, and Co., 1847.

Brontë, Charlotte. *Jane Eyre: An Autobiography*. London: Service & Paton, 1897.

Cazotte, J. *Le Diable Amoureux*. Paris: Henri Plon, 1871.

Cazotte, Jacques. *The Devil in Love*. Trans. Judith Landry. Sawtry: Dedalus, 1991 [1776].

Craft, Christopher. "'Kiss Me with those Red Lips:' Gender and Inversion in Bram Stoker's Dracula." *Representations*.8 (1984), 107-133.

Dashing Duval; or, The Ladies' Highwayman. London: Palmer & Co., c.1889.

Faderman, Lillian. *Surpassing the Love of Men: Romantic Friendship and Love Between Women from the Renaissance to the Present*. New York: William Morrow & Company, Inc.

Féval, Paul. *Knightshade*. Trans. Brian Stableford. Encino: Black Coat Press, 2003 [1860].

Féval, Paul. *Vampire City*. Trans. Brian Stableford. Encino: Black Coat Press, 2003 [1875].

Field, Julian Osgood. "A Kiss of Judas." *Pall Mall Magazine*. July 1893: 339-366.

Heron-Allen, Edward, and Selina and Delaro. *Princess Daphne*. Chicago: Belford, Clarke & Co., 1888.

Holland, Steve. "Yesterdays Paper: A Tale of Two Roberts." January 18, 2010. http://john-adcock.blogspot.com/2010/01/tale-of-two-roberts-by-steve-holland.html.

Ingraham, Prentiss. *The Ocean Vampire; or, The Heiress of Castle Curse*. Beadle and Adams' "The Dime Library." 172. New York: Beadle & Adams, 1882.

James, M. R. "M.R. James on J. S. Le Fanu." *Ghosts and Scholars*. 7, 1985 [1923].

Le Fanu, J. T. Sheridan. "The Haunted Baronet." *Belgravia: A London Magazine*, July-November 1870. 69ff.

Łuksza, Agata. "Sleeping with a Vampire: Empowerment, submission, and female desire in contemporary vampire fiction." *Feminist Media Studies*, 15: 3 (2014), 429-443.

Marsh, Richard. "The Mask." *The Gentleman's Magazine*. December 1892. 541-561.

Meyerowitz, Joanne. *How Sex Changed: A History of Transsexuality in the United States*. Cambridge, MA: Harvard University Press, 2002.

Miller, Elizabeth. "Coitus Interruptus: Sex, Bram Stoker, and Dracula." Romanticism on the Net. 44, November 2006.

Pollard, Tom. *Loving Vampires: Undead Obsession*. Jefferson, NC: McFarland & Company, Inc., 2016.

Potocki, Jan. *The Manuscript Found in Saragossa*. Trans. Ian Maclean. London: Viking, 1995.

Potocki, Jan. *Manuscrit trouvé à Saragosse* (version de 1804). *Oeuvres* 4.2. Ed. François Rousset & Dominique Triaire. Louvain: Peeters, 2006 (1804).

Stryker, Susan. *Transgender History*. Berkeley: Seal Press, 2008.

Summers, Montague. *The Vampire, His Kith and Kin*. London: K. Paul Trench, Trubner, 1928.

The Vampire, or, Detective Brand's Greatest Case. Old Cap Collier Library. 2. Issue 161. New York: N. Munro 1885.

Williamson, Milly. *The Lure of the Vampire: Gender, Fiction and Fandom from Bram Stoker to Buffy*. London: Wallflower Press, 2005.

8.
"A Yearning Drove Me Here to You:" The Male Homosexual Vampire of the Nineteenth Century

Introduction

> I grieve for you, Jonathan my brother; you were very dear to me. Your love for me was wonderful, more wonderful than that of women.
> 2 Samuel 1:26, New International Version.

> To the query, "What is friendship?" [Aristotle's] reply was, "A single soul dwelling in two bodies."
> Diogenes Laertius *Lives of Eminent Philosophers* 5:20, 463.

Both of the quotes above have to do with close friendships between men that are nonsexual and non-erotic in orientation. The nineteenth century was rife with such intimate but platonic relationships. David Deitcher (*Dear Friends: American Photographs of Men Together*, 2001) writes in his book on photographs in the late Victorian United States "men posed for photographers holding hands, entwining limbs, or resting in the shelter of each other's accommodating bodies, innocent of the suspicion that such behavior would later arouse" (50). Elizabeth Howie, ("Bringing Out the Past," 2014) makes a similar observation: "In twenty-first-century American culture, such touches signify sexuality. In the nineteenth century . . . conventions of articulating affection between devoted friends, male or female, make expressions of intimate romantic friendship difficult to distinguish from declarations of erotic desire" (46).

A major reason for the development of such "romantic friendships," which could span from the platonic to the rare, homosexual, was because of changes in the relationship between men and women. Pre-Enlightenment thought saw men and women as similar beings in a hierarchy where the latter was a pale reflection of the former. Much of the attitude can be summarized in *Generation of Animals*: by Aristotle: "the female is, as it were, a deformed male" (175).

With the Enlightenment, discussion shifted to two natures, separate but equal. Here women were compartmentalized and domesticated. She had her own sphere of influence and her own education. As Rousseau wrote in *Emile* (1762): "[W]here sex is concerned man and woman are unlike; each is the complement of the other. . . . When once it is proved that men and women are and ought to be unlike in constitution and in temperament, it follows that their education must be different" (326).

Men were designed for the public sphere, where they would be in constant and close contact with other men—as competitors and colleagues. And their education, if available, was typified by comradery and friendly combat as well. In light of the fact that there was little contact between men and women outside of courtship and marriage, with the exception of relatives, men turned to other men for the close companionship and intimacy they needed. In his 1849 *A Week on the Concord and Merrimak Rivers*, Thoreau wrote of male friendship using a sample letter from one to the other: "This is what I would like,—to be as intimate with you as our spirits are intimate,—respecting you as I respect my ideal" (282).

Derek M. Bolen and John Marc Cuellar put it this way in their 2016 "Romantic Friendships: "Many men formed intimate, lifelong bonds in the context of professional mentorships. Such relationships also arose in situations where men worked closely alongside each other toward common goals, often developing deep levels of trust. When these bonds were formed, men often displayed behaviors that modern viewers might associate with sexual attraction, such as sharing beds, kissing each other on the lips, holding hands, professing undying love for one another, exchanging love letters, and cuddling" (971).

So we have to be careful starting off a paper on a subject like this. All "romantic friendships" can be treated today as erotic, because it is not clear to us where one ends and the other begins, and standards of what constitutes the erotic have changed. But perceptions were different in the nineteenth century and that also must be taken into consideration. And they cannot count directly as homosexuality, although there is little doubt that a few were. Also since some homosexuality, by which I mean here as sexual desire, intent, and/or action toward another man, is not erotic and vice versa, one category cannot be inclusive of the other. Rather the two overlap. So they have to be kept conceptually separate.

I should note in passing that before the construction of distinct sexual-identity categories became popular in the late nineteenth and the early twentieth centuries, "same-sex sexual acts were viewed as unacceptable, but they were not considered to be indicative of any sort of enduring personality trait. Yet with the new categorizations, an individual came to be categorized as homosexual or heterosexual, and the focus shifted from same-sex acts to homosexual individuals" (Bolen & Cuellar 971).

As we would expect, the vampires most analyzed for their homosexuality are the twentieth and twenty-first century ones. When the nineteenth-century one is reviewed it is usually as lesbian: Coleridge's "Christabel" at the turn of the century and Le Fanu's *Carmilla* in 1871-72. The "gay" vampires examined are usually "Manor," "The Sad Story of the Vampire," and *The Picture of Dorian Gray*,[119] although there is at least one scholar who asserts the nineteenth century had none.[120] I, however, shall treat two of the above as homoerotic, not as homosexual. Still, many of those included here, when part of a study on the author or the work itself, are identified as homosexual vampire stories. Since they all have not been collected and studied together, nor have they been separated from the homoerotic, there is need of a paper like this. I am going to avoid the

---

[119] Benshoff 132-33 combines the first and last; Auerbach 84 the second and last; Robinson 185-186 the first and second; Dyer 47-72, all three. Dyer also mentions the names of de Sade and Lautréamont but gives no reference even to which books, much less how the vampire was used. When *Dracula* is placed on the list it is usually based on a misunderstanding, i.e., that Dracula is saving Harker for himself rather than simply using him and then leaving him to his wives. E.g. Pollard 31; Hanson 325.

[120] Melton 347-348 cites *Christabel* and *Carmilla* and then denies there were any male ones.

trope that vampires represent forbidden or hidden sexual desires or actions, like homosexuality. Although there is no doubt this is true at times, it can quickly become speculative and diversionary.[121]

Homoeroticism

Remember this is homoerotic to us, not to them. The first has a slight amount of homoeroticism, but it concerns the vampire slayer, not the vampire *per se*. The Greek lamia was often treated as a vampire in the nineteenth century so I am treating it as such here.[122] Plus this story has been identified as one by at least one vampire scholar (Bane 89). The story in Antoninus Liberalis's *Metamorphoses* (the second century CE, eighth chapter) is that outside of Delphoi "a great and immense monster" called either Lamia or Sybaris, dwelt in a huge cave, whence it emerged daily to feed on the flocks and sometimes people. The inhabitants consult the oracle to find a suitable place to relocate, but they are told that the menace will end if they abandon in the cave a youth they have chosen. By lot, they choose Alcyoneus, the only son of his father, remarkably beautiful. As they are leading him to his fate, a partially divine young man sees him.

"Stricken by love for him (πληγεὶς ἔρωτι), and asking why they were so proceeding, he thought it dreadful not to defend him to the utmost and just allow the youth to perish wretchedly. . . . [H]e . . . gave orders that he himself should be led forward instead of the youth. As soon as the priests had led him up to the cavern, he ran in and hauled out Sybaris from her lair, carrying her into the open and hurling her from the crags. Tumbling down, she struck her head . . . Because of this wound she faded from sight."

On the subject of homoeroticism, this is, of course, too short to make out what exactly is being said. Yet such passion is definitely present as is indicated by the choice of the word for love, for there were several from which to choose in Greek. "Eros" (ἔρωτι above) was used for passionate love and that is what appears here. There is nothing, however, in this text about any relationship beyond this event. So it will have to remain ambiguous whether love was acted upon beyond attraction and an act of substitution.

Dracula implies Dracula biting a man, Renfield, but Renfield is introduced into the story already in a sanatorium in England and in thrall to Dracula. So any homoeroticism between the two is left completely to the reader's imagination. The first encounter between the two to which we are privy has Renfield very obsequious to his "Master." "I am here to do your bidding, Master. I am your slave, and you will reward me, for I shall be faithful. I have worshipped you long and afar off. Now that you are near, I await your commands, and you will not pass me by, will you, dear Master, in your distribution of good things?"[123] No eroticism here. Any homoeroticism there may be here seems to await the 1931 film.

---

[121] For example, I find the notion that Polidori's *The Vampyre* and Byron's *Fragment* are homoerotic to be a simple case of eisegesis. See, for examples of this, Rigby's "'Prey to some Cureless Disquiet'" and Lau 5-7. Nor is there anything homophobic to be read from the texts. In fact it is no romantic friendship.

[122] Schmidt 246. In the body of the study is a rendition in German that omits the episode (142: "The Arachobans and the Lamia"), but it is included in Greek in the appendix. I am using the translation of Francis Celoria: *The Metamorphoses of Antoninus Liberalis* (1992), 58-59.

[123] Stoker 1897, 96.

The Male Homosexual Vampire of the Nineteenth Century

Frame from *Dracula* directed by Ted Browning in 1931

The first few pages of *Flames: a London phantasy* by Robert Hichens (1897) describe an intense male friendship somewhat like Thoreau pictured above. Valentine Cresswell is popularly called the Saint of Victoria Street, not so much for what he does, but for what he does not. He seems constitutionally unable to be tempted by the vices of the age; he is a gentleman of complete refinement. His best friend is cut from a very different cloth; Julian Addison would give himself virtually to all sins and passions if it were not for the influence of Valentine upon him by his friendship and example. It is always a fight and struggle for Julian but none for Valentine.

Interestingly, Valentine, in the comfort of his drawing room, often stares at the painting by Sir Edward Coley Burne-Jones done in 1863 entitled "The Merciful Knight" in which Jesus, close to naked, bends down from his cross to kiss the knight on the forehead. "[Julian] loved this Christ, . . . roused into life by an act of noble renunciation, bent down and kissed the armed hero who had been great enough to forgive his enemy. He loved those weary, tender lips, those faded limbs" (17).

The Merciful Knight by Edward Burne-Jones

Valentine had ever been, and still remained, to [Julian] a perpetual wonder, a sort of beautiful mystery. He actually reverenced this youth who stood apart from all the muddy ways of sin . . . Valentine was to Julian a god . . . Valentine [too] was apt to look up to Julian with admiration . . . And Julian loved Valentine for looking up to him, finding in this absurd modesty of his friend a crowning beauty of character. He had never told Valentine the fact that Valentine kept him pure, . . . was the wall of fire that hedged him from sin, the armour that protected him against the assaults of self. (5-6)

Soon, unfortunately, Valentine's soul is jettisoned by a vampire who takes up residence in his body. He then turns subtly upon Julian and begins to degrade, humiliate, and torture him. He exalts himself by diminishing him. Yet before that occurs the intimacy and mutual attraction are palpable.

Julian remains enamored by him until the end. Early after the transformation there is this exchange, which could almost be seen as sublimated foreplay.

> "How extraordinarily strong you look to-day, Val."
> Valentine spurred his horse into a short gallop.
> "I feel robust," he said. "I think it is my mind working on my body. I have attained to a more healthy outlook on things, to a saner conception of life. For years you have been learning from me, Julian. Now I think the positions are reversed. I am learning from you."
> Julian pressed his knees against his horse's sides with an iron grip, feeling the spirited animal's spirited life between them. . . .
> [Valentine] sent his horse along at a tremendous pace for a moment, then drew him in, and turned towards Julian.
> "We are learning the lesson of the spring," he said. (124)

In the spiritualist novel by Robert Ford, *Born Again* (1893), where there are two types of vampires—the benign, who extracts life-energy with no damage and the malevolent, who intends harm—there is a passing scene that is homoerotic in our estimation today (231). This was a time when paintings featuring adolescent boys by male artists were pervasive. An older gentleman, a painter, the sympathetic vampire, cannot marry a young neighbor girl and so he mentions to her, "If I can't be your husband, I will be your son." Somehow, she sees nothing strange about this remark. Soon after he dies, a celestial child appears to her and to her prospective suitor, and directs them to court and marry. They do and have a son, René, that looks just like their spiritual cupid, the benign vampire *redivivus*. At eleven, he starts taking painting lessons from a former student of the older man, Mr. Hart. At one lesson we read this exchange between pupil and teacher.

> [T]hen as if something striking on René's canvas attracted his attention, he said: 'You have a fine little bit of water there, René. I could hardly better it myself.'
> René blushed a little, which added greatly to the comeliness of his face. Mr. Hart's discerning eye catching it caused him to say, 'I wish René, that color in your cheeks would remain about five minutes, and

I would try to match it.' At this the color became a couple of shades deeper and René said: 'Don't Mr. Hart, my cheeks don't feel good.'

'All right,' said the teacher of painting. 'Let us get on to this rock in the foreground. We'll enliven the scene with a figure. We'll have it a boy disrobing for a bath.'

Thus the morning's lesson passed lightly.[124]

It is difficult to read this today without sexualizing it and either chuckling or cringing, whereas at the time it would have been quite unremarkable.

The Picture of Dorian Gray needs some background on attitudes toward homosexuality in England. 1886 appears to be the year in which Oscar Wilde, the author, recognized and began following his inclination for homosexuality. There were, at that time, two laws against male homosexuality: The 1861 Offences against the Person Act, which required life imprisonment for a conviction on the charge of sodomy, or "buggery" as it was called, which survived until 1967 (before 1861 it was a capital crime and had been referred to legally as the "nameless offense of great enormity" in 1836); the 1885 Criminal Law Amendment Act which mandated up to two years in jail for acts short of sodomy, i.e. "gross indecency." In 1895 Wilde was found guilty of the second in a court trial that included this book as evidence.

The novel was submitted to *Lippincott's Monthly Magazine* in 1890. The editor unilaterally censored material that he felt to be too controversial—some 500 words. It still provoked a storm of criticism for its sexual content and Wilde was forced to defend it. Meanwhile he diluted the homoeroticism for the 1891 publication of his story in book form. So there are three versions. A critical edition of his original manuscript (*The Picture of Dorian Gray: An Annotated, Uncensored Edition*) has been published (2011) and that is the original one to which I shall refer.

Basil Hallward and Lord Henry Wotton admire the picture of Dorian Gray. Illustrated by Eugène Dété. Oscar Wilde 1908, frontispiece.

---

[124] Julia F. Saville, "The Romance of Boys Bathing" (1999). On page 253 we read that the motif of boys bathing provides the potential for "displaying and admiring the male body as in itself an object of beauty and eros."

The homosexuality or eroticism the text presents is in two ways. One is direct: the homoerotic reactions of Basil Hallward, a painter, to Dorian Gray's young beauty. Although erotic, it was mainly due to reasons of art. According to Timothy D'Arch Smith, *Love in Earnest* (1970), poets and artists who dealt with such subjects at the turn of the century were primarily interested in the aesthetic appreciation of male adolescents (xx-xxii.). Stephanie Newell, in *The Forger's Tale* (2006), wrote that "their passions remained largely aesthetic and textual" (80). We are, therefore, dealing more with romantic friendships between older gentlemen and adolescent boys.

Directly, then, Basil confesses to his friend Henry that when he first encountered Dorian at a gathering he was afraid that if he spoke to him he would become "absolutely devoted to him" (79). He does and tells Henry the result: "I couldn't be happy if I didn't see him every day. Of course sometimes it is only for a few minutes. But a few minutes with somebody one worships mean a great deal" (83).

He keeps this to himself, but later he shares it with Dorian candidly, albeit in the past tense. "It is quite true that I have worshipped you with far more romance of feeling than a man should ever give to a friend. Somehow, I had never loved a woman.... I quite admit that I adored you madly, extravagantly, absurdly. I was jealous of every one to whom you spoke. I wanted to have you all to myself.... One day I determined to paint a wonderful portrait of you.... It is my masterpiece.... There was love in every line, and in every touch there was passion.... You must not be angry with me, Dorian, for what I have told you. As I said to Harry, once, you are made to be worshipped" (172).

The second way will be dealt with below under "Homosexuality."

Now we move into a more serious story because the homoerotica is much closer to the heart of the story. Still we have to remember the observations of D'Arch Smith and Saville on adolescent beauty at this time and I think this is where the following story belongs. It is "The Sad Story of a Vampire" by Eric Stanislaus Stenbock (1894), which was originally titled "The True Story of the Vampire."[125] Count Vardalek is stranded at the train station and so is brought by Mr. Wronski to his castle where he meets his two children, Carmela and Gabriel. Carmela, the narrator, late in life, admits that at 13, she was a little wild, but holds that her younger brother, whom she adored, was very much so—climbing, running barefoot, fond of wild animals, bringing home strays. Yet when Gabriel first sees the Count, he runs upstairs and dresses in his finest clothes. From that point on Gabriel is completely devoted to him and gives up his untamed lifestyle.

At the same time, however, his health begins to wane as Vardalek's improves. His father is for a long while oblivious to this, for he is so enchanted by his visitor's knowledge. He is intelligent and as cultured as his age would dictate—well read, well traveled, well versed in music, multilingual.[126] So her father is preoccupied. When he does notice his son's health, he sends for the doctor, but he could find nothing physically wrong to explain his wasting away.

---

[125] The first appearance of the story under "The Sad Story of a Vampire" that I can find is in *The Dracula Book of Great Vampire Stories* edited by Leslie Shepard (1977).
[126] In contrast is the Twilight trilogy which features vampires who are surprisingly ignorant, misinformed, and unaccomplished despite their years and experience.

When Gabriel takes to his bed, Vardalek nurses him with the utmost tenderness. One day the count cries out that a priest must be sent for, kisses his lips, and, by the time the priest arrives and Gabriel dies, is nowhere to be found. A short time later her beloved father follows her brother.

The vampire is a psychic one; he does not touch his victim when extracting his life. He has the power of mesmerism which he exerts on the whole family, but particularly on Gabriel. He is attracted to young boys for his nourishment. This is further demonstrated by a short exchange at their first dinner: "[W]hen my father was relating some of his military experiences, he said something about a drummer boy who was wounded in battle. His eyes opened completely again and dilated: this time with a particularly disagreeable expression, dull and dead, yet at the same time animated by some horrible excitement" (135). He had the same sort of pupil dilation when he first saw Gabriel. He displays little interest in Carmela or the governess.

Carmela one time overhears his sad, erotic talk to Gabriel when the latter is in a trance and the Count plays a moving song on the piano: "My darling, I fain would spare thee; but thy life is my life, and I must live, I who would rather die. Will God not have any mercy on me? Oh! oh! life; oh the torture of life! . . . O Gabriel, my beloved! my life, yes life--oh, why life? I am sure this is but a little that I demand of thee. Surely thy superabundance of life can spare a little to one who is already dead" (143).

Like *Carmilla*, the most famous "lesbian" vampire story of the nineteenth century, it is set in Styria; it is experienced by similarly named teenagers but told at a more advanced age here; neither of the survivors holds any rancor against the perpetrator; both vampires are strangers invited to stay with a family; each has similar homoerotic speeches made to their victims. While the speech is less passionate here than in *Carmilla*, this has a much more advanced notion of the tragic vampire. The "sad" in the title is both an objective and subjective genitive: it is not only the sadness caused by the vampire but his own sorrow as well. When he was asked to prolong his visit the first night, he smiled a smile which was "bitter, very bitter." In other words, he knew it would be the same deadly routine again to his regret, but made necessary by his biology.

Stenbock's superimposition of a love of adolescents—"pederasty" is far too strong a word—onto the vampire has captured the attention of several of his commentators. John Adlard has included in his book on Stenbock a short article, "A Study in the Fantastic," penned in 1869 by his acquaintance, Arthur Symons, which said, "Stenbock fed his furious imagination on vampires." Francis King has noted in his 2004 book *Megatherion* that perhaps Stenbock "made an attempt to understand his homosexuality in terms of traditional occultism, eventually coming to view his condition as an aspect of vampirism and lycanthropy" (18). James Machin has said of his use of the vampire: "It is of course possible that Stenbock was distancing himself from his own troubling impulses by making them other and monstrous" (97). In *Love in Earnest* (1970), Tmothy D'Arch Smith has argued that his interest in the vampire was more than literary; it was a "serious self-comparison with the vampire legends of his childhood to which he had linked his own lust for young boys and his morbid desire for death as a release from psychological distress" (37).

The previous year Stenbock wrote a poem, "The Vampire," that might have served as a template for "The Sad Story of a Vampire." Since it is virtually never referenced I will give it in full. The homoerotica is strongest in this piece and it may be better placed in the homosexual section, for it is very physical. Stenbock was fascinated by snakes so its image below may mean no more than just this symbol, but it could also refer to the lamia, indicating either that the vampire is being feminized or the lamia masculinized.

> I would seek thee in secret places
> In the darkest hour of night,
> Embrace thee with serpent embraces,
> Delight thee with strange delight.
>
> In a serpent's coils entwine
> Thy supple and exquisite form,
> And drink from thy veins like wine
> Thy blood delicious and warm.
>
> With slow soft sensual sips
> Draw the life from the tender spray,
> And brush from thy soft lithe lips
> The bloom of thy boyhood away.
>
> I would breathe with the breath of thy mouth
> And pang thee with perfect pain;
> And the vital flame of thy youth
> Should live in my limbs again.
>
> Till thy vital elastical form
> Should gradually fade and fail,
> And thy blood in my veins flow warm,
> And glow in my face, that was pale. (37)

Homosexuality

In this section we shall rank the stories by the bond forged between homosexuality and homoeroticism.

Our first selection here has no homoeroticism and the homosexuality is only an accusation. It is a true account of a metaphorical vampire's victim. What this news story does is establish again some of the context in which homosexuals had to operate, since acting on their impulses was criminalized. That the accused here turned out to be innocent changes nothing. It shows how serious even the accusation was.

Austin Kirby was arrested in May of 1896 for extorting money from John Herman in 1882. This is depicted in the newspaper article "The Kirby Case" (19 August 1896). Kirby was at the time of the crime an officer in Timaru, New Zealand, and was accused of going to Herman's tobacconist shop and telling him he held a warrant against him for "an infamous crime," for which he would face ten years in jail and the confiscation of all his property. Technically homosexuality was a capital crime at the time, but no one was ever executed for it in New Zealand. To keep it quiet, he demanded a total of £700 and a gold watch.

Herman had to sell his shop; he left New Zealand and did not return for thirteen years. Upon his arrival back, he informed a friend of the incident and his friend, in turn, alerted the government. Kirby was found guilty of fabricating the warrant for the purpose of blackmailing Herman; he was sentenced to three years "in penal servitude" (Gary Wotherspoon, "1896, Austin Kirby and William George Bassett").

In the *article*, we read these words: "An officer of the law, sworn to be as much a protector of the innocent, as a detector and punisher of the guilty, he deliberately entered upon a scheme for the plundering of Herman, a scheme in the carrying out of which he displayed the greatest audacity, combined with a greed of spoil, which made him resemble a vampire more than a human being. The fear of being publicly charged with a peculiarly odious offence, an offence of which there is not the slightest ground to believe he was ever guilty, made Herman for a time at any rate an easy victim to his bloodsucking enemy." Although it is never spelled out, it is obvious that homosexuality was the alleged crime. It is referred to in the code words: "an infamous crime" and "a peculiarly odious offence."

In literature, we are faced first with the most offensive example, one that is actually antierotic for the vast majority of readers. Marquis de Sade crafts a story about his eponymous victim, Juliette in 1791. She is an orphan girl turned out on the streets. She tries to live a pious and pure life but is thrown from one situation of abuse to another always with increased violence, particularly by sexual predators. In her world no good deed goes unpunished; no act of wickedness unrewarded, or, as she states it, "I become a whore from kindness, a libertine through virtue" (173). She is finally rescued from her torments only to face her final outrageous rape, being impaled by God's celestial penis, the lightning bolt.

In one episode, based on the tale of "Bluebeard," who became known as a vampire in the nineteenth century, she is forced into an orgy arranged by a corpulent Count, who coerces Juliette and tortures his wife for his sexual pleasure and that of the two young men who are his companions. He scratches his wife's buttocks deeply until they bleed and sucks on the wounds. He later lances her so the blood will drip and at the end opens the veins in both her arms and has an orgasm watching her blood spurt out.

But there is a long period building up to that climax, which involves the boys. It starts with them having anal intercourse with the Countess and pulling out in time to ejaculate in the Count's mouth. He has the boys indulge each other in fellatio as he watches or he performs simultaneous oral sex with one after the other. He has Juliette suck on the accomplices and then deliver the "incense" into his mouth. He has them engage in anal intercourse with his wife and immediately upon their withdrawal suck them or lick the anus of the boy engaged with his wife.

All of this explicit homosexuality has nothing erotic in it. It is largely the cruelty and humiliation that leads the Count to satisfaction. This is the case with the final scene of debauchery in the novel as well, which includes explicit acts of pederasty and the shedding of blood—the suturing together of Juliette's anus and vagina, and then forcing them open with the penis. There is nothing consensual about any of this for Juliette; it is rape and personal violation to the ultimate degree. As a licentious and cruel monk declares: "[T]o make this sort of pleasure as intense as it is capable of being, it is . . . absolutely essential for the man to pleasure himself at the expense of the woman" (139). Sade's male homosexuality thrives on this.

Non-erotic is the way *Dorian Gray* depicts homosexuality. It is indirect, by insinuation, indicative of actual acts of "buggery." Some eighteen years after the scene delineated above with Basil speaking in such an endearing way of Dorian, he confronts Dorian, who has not aged a day, in a very different manner; all eroticism is gone. "I hear all these hideous things that people are whispering about you . . . Why is it that every young man that you take up seems to come to grief . . .? There was that wretched boy in the Guards who committed suicide. You were his great friend. There was Sir Henry Ashton, who had to leave England, with a tarnished name. You and he were inseparable. What about Adrian Singleton, and his dreadful end? . . . What about the young Duke of Perth? What sort of life has he got now? What gentleman would associate with him? Dorian, Dorian, your reputation is infamous" (215).

When Dorian kills Basil in an act of sudden passion that very night, he sends a message to Alan Campbell, a chemist, with whom he had once been "great friends" (231). When he arrives, filled with obvious contempt for Dorian, Dorian appeals to him to dispose of the body chemically. Campbell responds that he would never do anything to help him, especially destroy the body of this victim. So Dorian writes something on a piece of paper and pushes it across the table. Alan turns deathly pale when he reads it and agrees to do it. Nicholas Frankel writes of this passage in his 2011 edition of *The Picture of Dorian Gray*: "Dorian is blackmailing Campbell. In the wake of Section 11 of the 1885 Criminal Law Amendment Act . . . practicing homosexuals were frequently blackmailed" (236n21). Alan performs the task and then commits suicide.

To discern the vampirism of the tale we must turn briefly to the plot. Basil paints a portrait of Dorian and gives it to him. Dorian, upset that he will have to age while the picture does not, prays for the opposite. In the subsequent 18 years, with the picture cleverly hidden to all but himself, Dorian lives a life of licentiousness; his cruelty, indifference, and signs of aging are registered on the picture, while he remains beautiful and untouched. In a final act of desperation, fearful that the painting be discovered, which now displays the evidence of his crime of murder as well, he stabs it. The following day he is found dead with a knife in his chest and horrible features on his face, near the portrait of a beautiful young man, the way Dorian had looked the night before.

Like Lord Ruthven, the most famous vampire of the nineteenth century, his ageless life is littered with dead bodies and lost reputations. Dorian dies, having been staked in the heart. He has lived according to the dictates of a "new hedonism," where novelty is the goal of life and boredom its bane, so like a vampire, he cannot help but use people to feed himself and throw them away, ruined, when he is done. Toward the end, for instance, he tries to do a good deed to see if that will change the picture for the better. It makes it worse, because he was just doing something he had not tried before.[127] So he becomes a little tragic.

---

[127] The arguments that this is a vampire tale are more subtle than what is here. Anderson 57-59, Eastham 46-60, and Twitchell 171-178) call Dorian an aesthetic or artistic vampire, which is the usual designation. George 36-78 compares Dorian to Dracula and David Reed's vampire painting. Paglia 526 interestingly portrays the picture itself as a vampire feeding on Dorian.

The next is like it in that it is also non-erotic: Lautréamont's *Maldoror* (1868-1869). Here we shall use extensive quotes to capture some of the explicitness. It is not easily summarized. The language denying his vampirism is insincere; Lautréamont utilizes scenes from Gilles de Rais and Sergeant Bertrand in his book who were well known as vampires at the time of his writing. But that is the point: he defines vampire only in the literal sense whereas he is a metaphorical one like de Rais and Bertrand. And elsewhere he actually accepts the designation for himself. The thought of sperm evokes here the vampire for the eponymous Maldoror—as one who extracts (sucks), exudes (drools), and ejaculates (vomits) blood.

> Oh incomprehensible pederasts, I shall not heap insults upon your great degradation; I shall not be the one to pour scorn on your infundibuliform anus. . . . [Y]ou, young adolescents, or rather young girls, explain to me how and why (but keep a safe distance, for I, too, am unable to control my passions), vengeance has so sprouted in your hearts that you could leave such a crown of sores on the glands of mankind. . . . I kiss your faces, I kiss your breasts, I kiss, with my smooth lips. . . . But (I must stress this), do not forget to wash your lower parts with hot water every day, for if you do not venereal chancres will infallibly grow on the commissures of my unsatisfied lips.
>
> Oh! If, instead of being a hell, the universe had only been an immense celestial anus, look at the motion I am making with my loins: yes, I would have thrust my verge into its bleeding sphincter, shattering with my jerking movements, the very walls of its pelvis! . . . I should have discovered the subterranean place where truth lies sleeping and rivers of my viscous sperm would thus have found an ocean into which they could gush. . . . Meanwhile, let him who burns with ardour to share my bed come and find me; but I made one condition for my hospitality: he must not be more than fifteen years old. . . . I do not like woman! . . .
>
> Bitter saliva is flowing from my mouth, I do not know why. Who will suck it for me, that I may be rid of it? It is rising—it is still rising! I have noticed that when I suck blood from the throats of those who sleep beside me (the supposition that I am a vampire is false, since that is the name given to the dead who rise from their graves; whereas I am living), I throw up part of it on the following day: this is the explanation of the vile saliva. . . .
>
> I even murdered (not long ago!) a pederast who was not responding adequately to my passion; I threw his body down a disused well, and there is no decisive evidence against me. Why are you quivering with fear, young adolescent reading me? Do you think I want to do the same thing to you? You are being extremely unjust— You are right: do not trust me, especially if you are handsome. My sexual parts perpetually offer the lugubrious spectacle of turgescence; no one can claim (and how many have approached!) that he has ever seen them in the normal flaccid state, not even the shoeblack who stabbed me there in a moment of ecstasy! The ungrateful wretch! . . .

> A final word—it was a winter night. While the cold wind whistled through the firs, the Creator opened his doors in the darkness and showed a pederast in. (194-198)

Although it uses erotic language, it does not intend to be taken that way. Maldoror sees himself as an enemy of God and humanity, so he is being provocative; he is illustrating the hell of the world through the depravation and degradation of pederasty. He evokes homoeroticism only to turn away to oral venereal disease, sucking blood at the mouth, adolescent murder, and genital mutilation. There is nothing positive in this picture. And afterward, he turns on God. God, in the depth of winter darkness, when any potential observers would be too chilled to surveil, lets in a pederast for a night of sodomy and oral sex. It is an attack on God by God's association with what is lowly and shunned. This shows how negatively homosexuality is being assessed.

We turn now to *The Manuscript Found in Saragossa* (1804).[128] Officer Alphonse van Worden is crossing through the almost desolate Valley of Los Hermanos, which starts with two brothers hanging on a gibbet. In the early days of the story, for it is divided into days as chapters, the two dead brothers haunt the narrative, but they slip into obscurity after the fourteenth day. The two hanged men are Spanish vampires meaning that they are demons who inhabit dead bodies and can change them into anything they want. They seem to know what each of their victims want, are able to lure them into a trap, alter their forms to become the people whom they desire, and then have sex with them. These vampires are not interested in blood or life energy, but in humiliation. Once they have had their way with their victims they charm them to sleep lying between them. The suitors wake up perplexed the following day as they lie under the gallows with the brothers' dead bodies on either side. All but one of the victims are men.

Because we are getting everything from Alphonse's perspective, the encounters he has are with two beautiful women. Alphonse has three meetings with the exotic sisters, Emina and Zubeida, who tempt him under the guise of being his amorous cousins, before their love is consummated. Sexual intercourse occurs on the seventh day. On this day, instead of wearing their chastity belts, they enter with them in hand. They ask him to remove the religious relic from his neck and when he refuses, they cut it off, tossing it aside, and replace it with a necklace of their woven hair.

> Then Emina pulled out a gold pin which held her hair in place and used it to close up the curtains around my bed tight together. I shall do as she did and draw a veil over the rest of this scene. You need only know that my charming companions became my wives. There are doubtless cases where it is a crime violently to shed innocent blood, but there are others where such cruelty enhances innocence by making it appear in all its lustre. That is what happened to us. (90-91)

On the eighth day, however, he runs across an acquaintance who happened to witness the same event. He tells the story in the third person.

> He was in his bed and beside him were two very beautiful girls ... These two young persons first caressed him, then removed from

[128] See the previous chapter for the information about the two editions of this work.

his neck a relic that was round it. As soon as they did this, their beauty vanished before my eyes and I saw them to be the two hanged men from the valley of Los Hermanos. But the young gentleman still took them to be beautiful young creatures and called them the most affectionate names. Then one of the two hanged men took the rope from around his neck and put it round the neck of the gentleman, who showed his gratitude by renewed caresses. In the end they shut the bed-curtains, and I do not know what they did next although I imagine that it was some horrible sin. (95)

Potocki, the author, was Polish by nationality. From the latter half of the eighteenth century until 1815, Poland was typified by "the fluid attitude toward sexuality that was favored by the Enlightenment's tolerance and secularism" (Stanley). Also Potocki wrote in French and post-Revolutionary France was the first modern Western European country to decriminalize homosexual acts, including sodomy, as long as they were conducted in private between consenting adults. It remained so throughout the century and up to today. So there were no impediments to him making an explicit reference to private acts of homosexuality in 1804 when he finished the first version of the story. Sade was an exception to such toleration, however; he was arrested in 1801 explicitly because of *Justine* and spent the rest of his life in an asylum.

There is no coercion here but there is deception. It seems the intimacy he had with his two cousins was an illusion, and he made love instead to two men. Homosexuality is put in a bad light but its actual expression is gentle and affectionate. Alphonse does not become apoplectic when he hears the other perspective; instead he chooses to ignore it and continue to view them as women.

We turn finally to what in my opinion is the most tender and touching vampire story in the nineteenth century: Karl Heinrich Ulrichs's "Manor" (1885). Fifteen-year-old Har and his father are fishing when their boat capsizes in a sudden storm. A sailor, Manor, sees it happen from the shore and is able to save Har, but not his father. From that moment on, Har is happy only when he is with Manor. He loves his embrace and will steal out of the house if Manor shows up outside his window at night. Manor goes out to sea in his capacity as a sailor and near port, after being gone two months, the ship is wrecked on the reefs in another storm and the crew drowns. When Manor's body washes ashore, Har is there. He admires his handsome body even in death, and then throws himself on the body he loved. "For one moment, sobbing, he savored the joy of a last embrace."

Yet that night a wet form enters his room, lies down with him icy cold, strokes his cheek, kisses his lips, and sighs "A yearning drove me here to you. I have found no peace in my grave." The next night he returns to embrace him, kiss his cheeks and lips, and place his head on his chest, which pounds with terror and joy. That night Manor begins to suck at his nipple "filled with yearning and thirstily, like an infant at its mother's breast." After he leaves, Har feels as if an animal had sucked him dry. Each night he comes back; "Every time, Manor's lips would explore the tender mound above his heart" (40). In the morning Har would notice a little blood there, but simply shrug it off. "Har was tormented the whole day long and pined. But he waited impatiently for night to come and yearned for the blissful thrill of the midnight embrace."

Twelve days pass and Har's mother goes to a witch to find out what the matter is with her son, for he is now white as a ghost yet will not share with her why. The woman reveals that he is being visited by the dead. Har's mother gathers up men from the village and with Har and the witch present, they dig up Manor. Har throws himself on the body again. He is torn away and a stake over 5 feet high and as thick as a man's arm is driven into his chest. Har is inconsolable that night but Manor still enters his room—this time with a gaping hole in his chest. "He lay beside Har, embraced him and began to suck. He sucked thirstily and with a greater ardor."

His mother has heard the goings on in the night and asks if "it" had been there. Har affirms "it" was. Anyway, the bed was "smeared with the dead man's blood that had drained from his deep wound." She rallies the men again and they return to the grave, this time without Har, for he has become emaciated. They replace the stake with a sturdier one that is twice as thick at the top than it is for the rest of its length, like an old-fashioned nail. That evening his mother explains to Har that he will no longer be bothered by Manor but he responded, "Mother, dear mother, he didn't torment me . . . I've nothing to live for. . . . I can hear him calling me" (42). A month after the shipwreck he declares to his weeping mother that he shall not last the night and requests that he be buried with Manor. "'Indeed,'" he said, 'I can't wait until I join him in his grave'" (43).

> Midnight struck. Suddenly transfigured, he raised his head slightly as if listening intensely. His eyes shining, he looked toward the window and the branches of the lilac bush.
>
> "'Look, mother, there he is.'"
>
> Those were his final words. His eyes rolled back. He sank into his pillow and passed away.
>
> And they did as he requested. (43)

Karl Heinrich Ulrichs was different from all the authors above. Despite the repressive atmosphere in Prussia, he was openly homosexual and was actively working for homosexuality's social normalization, with its community accorded the same opportunities and protections under the law as heterosexuals. Thus he is acknowledged by many today as the "first gay activist." In "Manor," he was not shy displaying the humanity of homosexuals and the humanizing qualities of their love.

I am reminded of Friedrich Hebbel's aphorism here: "All the dead are vampires, except those who are unloved" (73).[129] and the refrain of "Nature Boy:" "The greatest thing you'll ever learn is just to love and be loved in return." Manor loves; he is loved. "So what," Ulrichs is saying, "if they are same-sexed." Manor is a vampire because of both loves. "A yearning drove me here to you." His desire and Har's. Their love is monogamous. The vampire is never a threat to others; he only wants his young male lover to share his grave. Until that wish be fulfilled, no stake can hold him back; after Har is buried with him, no stake is needed to keep him down. And it is overtly homoerotic; it is not reluctant to display it. Unlike all of the above, the love affair is fully consensual and mutually fulfilling. No one is using the other as a means to an end and there is no sense that life is hardly worth living in this hell of a world. The world is made meaningful by love.

---

[129] The entry date in Hebbel is January 31, 1844.

Conclusion

Homosexuality and the nineteenth century vampire cannot be properly analyzed simply by citing a couple of examples uncritically. Homosexuality has to be distinguished from homoeroticism and both from romantic friendships. Although *The Picture of Dorian Gray* and "The Sad Story of the Vampire" are currently treated as homosexual, they probably are better seen as examples of platonic romantic friendships, except for the non-erotic homosexual passages of the first. From today's perspective, *mutatis mutandis*, they can be treated as homoerotic. This means that two of the three most used examples of homosexuality are really not what vampire scholars designate them to be. It also signifies that there is a substantial distance from the two and "Manor," so it is quite inappropriate to group them together without qualifications.

There is also the issue of range. Under the rubric of homosexuality, there is spectrum from the antierotic to the highly erotic. Concerning homoeroticism one can discern a progression from the ambiguous to the strong. Stenbock's poem, "The Vampire," which I include in the first category, might belong to the second in its combination of eroticism and physicality, depending on how it is read. First is it voluntary and informed? It does not appear to be. But to what does "Delight thee with strange delight" refer? Second, how closely ought we to align sucking blood with having intercourse? This can be and often is overstated. But it does seem to apply to "Manor" with the suckling at the teat. This brings it quite a distance from the intimacy of friendship. It is the most erotically charged same-sex relationship of the era, regardless of how one reads Stenbock's piece.

So although homosexuality and homoeroticism were hardly thriving subjects for nineteenth-century depictions of vampires, there are more of them than scholars seem to believe and they are more nuanced than they grant.

Works cited

Anderson, Melanie R. "Wilde's Dorian Gray as Aesthetic Vampire." *POMP: Publications of the Mississippi Philological Association*, 2005, 12 ed. 157-159.

Aristotle. *Generation of Animals*. Translated by A. L. Peck. Cambridge, MA: Harvard University Press, 1942.

Auerbach, Nina. *Our Vampires, Ourselves*. Chicago: University of Chicago Press, 1995.

Bane, Theresa. *Encyclopedia of Vampire Mythology*. Jefferson, NC: McFarland & Company, Inc., 2010.

Benshoff, Henry M. "The Monster and the Homosexual." In *The Dread of Difference: Gender and the Horror Film*, edited by Barry Keith Grant. Austin: Universityof Texas, 2015.

Bolen Derek M.; Cuellar, John Marc. "Romantic Friendships." *The SAGE Encyclopedia of LGBTQ Studies*. 3. Ed. Abbie Goldberg. Los Angeles: SAGE Publications, Inc., 2016.

D'Arch Smith, Timothy. *Love in Earnest: Some Notes on the Lives and Writings of English Uranian Poets from 1889 to 1930*. London: Routledge, 1970.

Deitcher, David. *Dear Friends: American Photographs of Men Together, 1840-1918*. New York: Harry N. Abrams, 2001.

Dyer, Richard. "Children of the Night: Vampirism as Homosexuality, Homosexuality as Vampirism." *Sweet Dreams: Sexuality, Gender, and Popular Fiction.* Ed. Susannah Radstone. London: Lawrence & Wishart, 1988. 47-72.

Eastham, Andrew. *Aesthetic Afterlives: Irony, Literary Modernity and the Ends of Beauty.* London: Coninuum International Publishing, 2005.

Ford, D. N. *Born Again: Or, The Romance of a Dual Life.* Falmouth, MA: Succanesset Press, 1893.

George, Sam. "'He make in the mirror no reflect': Undead aesthetics and mechanical reproduction--Dorian Gray, Dracula, and David Reed's 'vampire painting.'" *Open graves, open minds: Representations of vampires and Undead from the Enlightenment to the present day.* Eds. Sam George and Bill Hughes. Manchester: Manchester University Press, 2013. 36-78.

Hanson, Ellis. "Undead." *inside/out: Lesbian Theories, Gay Theories.* Ed. Diana Fuss. New York: Routledge, 1991, 324-340.

Hebbel, Friedrich. *Tagesbücher.* Vol. 2. Berlin: G. Grote'sche Verlagsbuchhandlung, 1887.

Hichens, Robert. *Flames: A London Phantasy.* London: William Heinemann, 1897.

Howie, Elizabeth. "Bringing Out the Past: Courtly Cruising and Nineteenth-Century American Men's Romantic Portraits." *Love Objects: Emotion, Design and Material Culture.* Eds. Anna Moran and Sorcha O'Brien. London: Bloomsbury, 2014. 43-52.

King, Francis. *Megatherion: The Magical World of Aleister Crowley.* London: Creation Books, 2004.

"The Kirby Case." *The Marlborough Express* 31: 194 (August 1896), 2.

Laertius, Diogenes. *Lives of Eminent Philosophers.* Translated by R. D. Hicks. Vol. 1. Cambridge, MA: Harvard University Press, 1959.

Lau, Kimberly J. "The Vampire, the Queer, and the Girl: Reflections on the Politics and Ethics of Immortality's Gendering." *Signs: Journal of Women in Culture and Society* 44 (2018), 3-24.

Lautréamont, Comte de. *Maldoror and Poems.* London: Penguin Books, 1978 [1868-1869].

Liberalis, Antoninus. *The Metamorphoses of Antoninus Liberalis.* Trans. Francis Celoria. Abingdon: Routledge, 1992.

Machin, James Fabian. *'Determined to be Weird': British Weird Fiction Before Weird Tales.* London: Birkbeck, University of London, 2016.

Melton, G. Gordon. *The Vampire Book: The Encyclopedia of the Undead.* 3rd ed. Canton, MI: Invisible Ink Press, 2011.

Newell, Stephanie. *The Forger's Tale: The Search for Odeziaku.* Athens: Ohio University Press, 2006.

Paglia, Camille. *Sexual Personae: Art and Decadence from Nefertiti to Emily Dickenson.* New Haven: Yale University Press, 1991.

Pollard, Tom. *Loving Vampires: Our Undead Obsession.* Jefferson, NC: McFarland & Company, Inc., 2016.

Potocki, Jan. *Manuscrit trouvé à Saragosse (version de 1804).* Oeuvres 4.2. Edited by François Rousset & Dominique Triaire. Louvain: Peeters, 2006.

Potocki, Jan. *The Manuscript Found in Saragossa.* Translated by Ian Maclean. London: Viking, 1995.

Rigby, Mair. "'Prey to some Cureless Disquiet': Polidori's Queer Vampyre at the Margins of Romanticism." *Romanticism on the Net.* 2004, 36-37. https://www.erudit.org/fr/revues/ron/2004-n36-37-ron947/011135ar/.

Robinson, Sara Libby. *Blood Will Tell: Vampires as Political Metaphors before World War I.* Boston: Academic Studies Press, 2011.

Rousseau, Jean-Jacques. *Emile.* Trans. Barbara Foxley. London & Toronto: J.M. Dent and Sons, 1911 [1762].

Sade, Marquis de. *Justine, or the Misfortunes of Virtue*. Trans. John Phillips. Oxford: Oxford University Press, 2012.

Saville, Julia F. "The Romance of Boys Bathing: Poetc Prescedents and Respondents to the Paintings of Henry Scott Tuke." *Victorian Sexual Dissidence*. Ed. Richard Dellamora. Chicago: University of Chicago Press, 1999. 253-277.

Schmidt, Bernhard. *Griechische Märchen, Sagen und Volkslieder.* Leipzig: B. G. Teubner, 1877.

Shepard, Leslie. *The Dracula Book of Great Vampire Stories*. Secaucus: Citadel Press, 1977.

Stanley, John D. "Poland." In *An Encyclopedia of Gay, Lesbian, Bisexual, Transgender, and Queer Culture*, edited by Claude J. Summers. 2004.

Stenbock, Eric Stanislaus. *Myrtle, Rue, and Cypress, A Book of Poems, Songs, and Sonnets*. London: Hatchets, 1883.

Stenbock, Eric Stanislaus. "The Sad Story of a Vampire." *The Shadow of Death; Studies of Death*. New York: Garland Publishing, Inc. 1984 [1894].

Stoker, Bram. 1897. *Dracula*. New York: Grosset and Dunlap, 1897.

Symons, Arthur. "A Study in the Fantastic." *Stenbock, Yeats and the Nineties*. Ed. John Adlard. London: Cecil & Amelia Woolf, 1969.

Thoreau, Henry D. *A Week on the Concord and Merrimak Rivers*. Boston: James Munson & Company, 1849.

Twitchell, James. *The Living Dead: A Study of the Vampire in Romantic Literature*. Durham: Duke University Press, 1981.

Ulrichs, Karl Heinrich. "Manor."*Sailor Stories*. 2nd. Trans. Michael Lombardi-Nash. Jacksonville, FL: Urania Manuscripts, 1990 [1885].

Wilde, Oscar. *The Picture of Dorian Gray*. Paris: Charles Carrington, 1908.

Wilde, Oscar. "The Picture of Dorian Gray." *Lippincott's Monthly Magazine* 46 (July 1890), 1-100.

Wilde, Oscar. *The Picture of Dorian Gray*. London: Simkin, Marshall, Hamilton, Kent & Co., 1891.

Wilde, Oscar. *The Picture of Dorian Gray: An Annotated, Uncensored Edition*. Ed. Nicholas Frankel. Cambridge, MA: The Belknap Press of Harvard University Press, 2011.

Wotherspoon, Gary. "1896, Austin Kirby and William George Bassett" *Unfit for Publication* 2014. http://www.unfitforpublication.org.au/trials/1800s/582-1896-austin-kirby.

9.
"Now I Know What Love Is!:"
The Lesbian Vampire of the Nineteenth Century

Introduction

> To me it seems to have been a closer union than that of most marriages.
> We know there have been other such between two men and also between two women. Love is spiritual, only passion is sexual.
> *Mary Grew on the death of her lifelong friend.* (Carroll Smith-Rosenberg, "The Female World of Love" 1975, 27).

> As I put on my cloak and set off to school I used to hug myself and think, "now I know what love is!" And anything Dr Robertson offered seemed timid and colourless in comparison.
> *Louisa Lumsden to Constance Maynard after turning down Dr. Robertson's marriage proposal.* (Holly Furneaux, "Female Romantic Friendship" 2009, 28).

Romantic friendships in the nineteenth century ran the spectrum from the nonerotic to the homosexual. What interests us in this introduction is the asexual, for it was by far the most common at the time, was encouraged by Victorian male culture, and can be confused today with homoeroticism or homosexuality. "[W]omen might kiss, fondle each other, sleep together, utter expressions of overwhelming love and promises of eternal faithfulness, and yet see their passions as nothing more than effusions of the spirit" (Faderman, *Surpassing* 16).

With the Enlightenment a new relationship between men and women began. Instead of both being of one essence but ordered as superior and inferior, they were now equals in complimentary spheres. In 1865, John Ruskin in his *Sesame and Lilies* argued the case: "Each has what the other has not: each completes the other, and is completed by the other: they are in nothing alike, and the happiness and perfection of both depends on each asking and receiving from the other what the other only can give" (146).

So this set up a division of labor. "Men saw themselves as needing the assistance of other men to realize their great material passions, and they fostered 'muscle values' and 'rational values,' to the exclusion of women. Women, left to themselves outside of their household duties, found kindred spirits primarily in each other. They banded together and fostered 'heart values.'" (Federman, *Odd Girls* 18).

The result was that "[d]aughters were born into a female world. Their mother's life expectations and sympathetic network of friends and relations were among the first realities in the life of the developing child. . . . It was within this closed and intimate female world that the young girl grew toward womanhood" (Smith-Rosenberg 17). Her bonds with her siblings could be especially close.

Consider Christina Rossetti's "Goblin Market." Lizzie is witnessing her dear sister, Laura, dying, while she pines for the goblin fruit she had tasted once but of which she can have no more, for the goblins no longer appear to her. They do, however, to Lizzie, so, in desperation, she tries to buy some fruit from the goblins for Laura. Because she will eat none herself, they will not sell her any, but instead smear her face with the fruit in an attempt to get some in her mouth, so she may die as well. They finally give up in disgust and she returns home and has her sister kiss it off her face, thereby saving her.

> "Did you miss me?
> Come and kiss me.
> Never mind my bruises,
> Hug me, kiss me, suck my juices . . .
> Eat me, drink me, love me . . ."
> [Laura] clung about her sister,
> Kissed and kissed and kissed her . . .
> She kissed and kissed her with a hungry mouth. (25-26)

In her monograph *Between Women* (2007), Sharon Marcus writes of this: "The fact that the speaker of these lines is a woman addressing her sister did not faze Victorian readers. Though in the twentieth century the poem has inspired lesbian tableaux in softcore pornography, Victorians included the poem in an anthology for schoolgirls" (15).[130]

When a girl or young woman began developing friends of her own, one would expect the relationships to be equally intense and intimate. And for them to be liberating as well. "Counseled to be passive in relation to men, women were allowed to act with initiative and spontaneity toward female friends, and friendship enabled women to exercise powers of choice and expression that they could not display in relation to parents or prospective husbands" (Marcus 56).

Men approved of these relationships and did not see them in competition with marriage. In fact they could be quite supportive of them. Think of William Haley in 1789. In his 1789 book, *The Young Widow*, he has Lucy write to comfort her sister-in-law. Her brother, dwelling with Lucy's family, has fallen in love with an Italian woman staying there and the family considers it to be a good match. "[I]f one of our family had been tempted to sleep with her, it would have been your humble servant Lucy, and not the innocent Edmund . . . [A]s I am absolutely in love with her myself, and have not alas the power of metamorphosing myself into a husband, I should most vehemently wish for Edmund's success" (118-119).

Some eighty years later in 1868, William Alger wrote *The Friendships of Women* and tells a true story related by Bettina von Arnim of her friendship with Karoline von Günderrode. He called it "a unique treasure" and approved of this kind of intimacy when female friends were faced with the prospect of separation. Günderrode, given to depression, shortly before her suicide, showed Bettina the spot "beneath her beautiful breast" where she planned to stab herself. "I broke into loud crying, I fell on her neck, I dragged her down to a seat, and sat upon her knee, and wept, and kissed her on her mouth, and tore open her dress, and kissed her on the spot where she had learned to reach the heart. I implored her, with tears of anguish, to have mercy upon me; and fell again on her neck, and kissed her cold and trembling hands" (311).

---

[130] Another example is a picture in Andrew Lang's *The Blue Poetry Book* (323). The illustration is of Christabel watching Geraldine undress in what strikes many today as a lesbian prelude. The collection, on the other hand, Lang avers, was seeking to "put before children, and young people, poems which are good in themselves and especially fitted to live, as Theocritus says, 'on the lips of the young'" (vii).

In nineteenth-century vampire studies, lesbianism seems well covered territory. Scholarship is agreed that there are two examples of lesbian vampires in the nineteenth century. J. Gordon Melton speaks for this consensus first by singling out Coleridge's "Christabel" at the turn of the century. It portends, he writes, "a theme that would reappear in vampire literature—lesbian vampire relationships" (Melton 347-348). He then turns to "Carmilla" (1872) by Sheridan Le Fanu, "in which the sexual element was even more pronounced." Other lesbian vampires appeared in succeeding decades, he continues, but he gives no further examples from the nineteenth century. Most modern scholarship likewise mentions only these two.

Yet there are other vampire texts that have been tagged as lesbian when a writer is dealing with them specifically. In the anthology *Dark Angels: Lesbian Vampire Stories*, a chapter from the book *Sardia* is lifted and in another, *Blood and Roses: The Vampire in nineteenth century Literature*, attention is given to the short story, "The Glass of Blood," which is considered to be lesbian. Interest in Florence Marryat's *The Blood of the Vampire* has been growing, but largely for its treatment of race, eugenics, spiritualism, and hysteria, not for any lesbianism. Yet there is sometimes some passing mention of it. This paper will bring them all together for the first time to try to make sense of the lesbian vampire of the nineteenth century. I will treat the six contributions in chronological order. I will quote extensively because context is very important, especially in light of the controversial conclusion.

The Texts

The task before us is not to declare definitively whether a text is both vampiric and lesbian, but to use the material above to help us decide whether a romantic friendship or ardent homosociality is the more likely explanation for the depictions of female intimacy below or a truly sexual orientation of one or both parties involved. There is no doubt that today we read this kind of closeness between women to be at least homoerotic, but that expresses more about our highly sexualized culture than about the original intentions of the author and the early expectations of and reception by the story's audience.

1. "Christabel" (1798; 1800)

Samuel Taylor Coleridge's "Christabel" always would have had a privileged place in vampire literature simply because of the "*Christabel* incident," (see Frayling 15) where verses from it were recited by Lord Byron to Percy Shelley, Mary Godwin, John Polidori, and "Claire" Clairmont, and Shelley ran from the room imagining a woman's nipples turned to eyes. In that gathering, the writing of the most famous vampire story of the nineteenth century, *The Vampyre*, had its beginnings.

"Christabel," as has already been noted, is almost always considered to be lesbian by vampire scholars and enthusiasts, when the issue of sex is brought up. (By the way, Geraldine is technically a lamia not a vampire: see Twitchell 40-41.) We have seen that J. Gordon Melton, author of the most important and exhaustive vampire encyclopedia, *The Vampire Book*, has held this view. It is the same in the seminal study of vampires by Nina Auerbach, *Our Vampires, Ourselves* (see Auerbach 51), just to mention two distinguished cases. Of course, it is mentioned in many studies specifically on the vampire and gender issues, like those of Richard Dyer ("Children of the Night") and Trevor Holmes ("Coming out of the Coffin"), and sometimes on homosexuality in more general literature— for instance, Christine Coffman's *Insane Passions* (168-269), Andrew Elfenbein's *Romantic Genius* (177-202),[131] and Camille Paglia's *Sexual Personae* (332-339). Finally lesbianism in "Christabel" comes up in works on Coleridge himself: examples are Calin Thomas Grajko (*'Christabel' and the Politics of Fragmentation*), Benjamin Scott Grossberg ("Making Christabel;" see 145-165), and Richard Holmes (*Coleridge: Darker Reflections* ; see 438-440).

It is rare that lesbianism is denied to this poem in vampire studies, but one such case is James Twitchell, who argues that Christabel is a substitute for a young man, even the author, being seduced by an older woman, possibly his mother (39-48). While there is precedent in Coleridge scholarship for this interpretation, especially as between a young woman and a mother substitute, it appears to have had little influence on the study of vampires.

One contemporary reviewer, William Hazlitt, "effectively destroyed" the poem's original reception by judging it to be impertinent, destitute of value, void of any genius (see Holmes 438; Hazlitt 58-67). Other reviewers did the same thing: but they attacked it mainly on literary grounds (Karen Swann "Literary Gentlemen and Lovely Ladies") or by personal attacks on the author (J. Percy Smith "Critic and Christabel"). They made little direct mention of the relationship of the two women to each other beyond that between a sorceress, even a vampire, and her victim. Karen Swann (407) does find behind early reviewers' "disgust" of the poem an implied reference to lesbianism but evidence is in short supply. For example, a pamphlet published in 1818 referred, in passing, to the poem as sinning as "heinously against purity and decency as it is well possible to imagine" (*Hypocrisy Unveiled* 50). Coleridge associated this with a rumor begun by a vengeful, erstwhile friend, whom he took to be Hazlitt, that Geraldine "was a man in disguise" (see Beer 40). It became rather popular thereafter (Smith 15-16; cf. Patrick 17-22). In that case, however, the scandal would be fornication not lesbianism.

It was not until 1948 that a piece of scholarship discovered lesbianism therein (see Grossberg 146-147), but even then, the issue lay mostly dormant thereafter until an article by Camille Paglia, "Christabel" in 1986 (reprinted in *Sexual Personae*), where she declares "Probably no poem in literary history has been so abused by moralistic Christian readings. Its blatant lesbian pornography has been ignored or blandly argued away" (Paglia 331). So the alleged lesbian affair between the two women posed no scandal to Coleridge's contemporaries, nor was it registered by readers for generations afterward.

Young Christabel slips out of her castle to pray for her fiancé when she hears someone moaning nearby. It is a beautiful woman, Geraldine, who is in distress so Christabel invites her in to spend the night in her bed until she can introduce her to her father in the morning. They creep back in softly so as not to wake anyone. "Christabel actively courts Geraldine," we are told by one commentator,

---

[131] He holds that the most original achievement of the poem was the "unyoking of lesbian representation from its patriarchal contexts" (195). Elfenbein is a classic case of "begging the question," he assumes the lesbianism that he must first prove exists.

"and invites, leads, and even carries her over the threshold as if she were her bride" (Taylor 64). Another writes that the women "appear to have journeyed not just from the forest to Christabel's room but from a place of fear to a place of security, completing a metaphorical movement from the heterosexual sphere to the homosexual" (Grajko 6). The reason for such language is, of course, what happens in the bedroom.

Christabel, so far as we know, has had no close female companionship her entire life. Her mother died in childbirth; there is no nurse or girlfriend identified, so there is no doubt this is the first time she has shared a bed with a woman. Christabel admires Geraldine's beauty and Geraldine tells her to disrobe and crawl into bed. From there she watches Geraldine undress. "Then drawing in her breath aloud,/ Like one that shuddered, she unbound/ The cincture from beneath her breast:/ Her silken robe, and inner vest,/ Dropped to her feet, and full in view,/ Behold! her bosom and half her side—/ A sight to dream of, not to tell" (1816, 18) Later we are told what that sight is: "Again she saw that bosom old./ Again she felt that bosom cold."

In a later addition to the poem, revised in 1828, Geraldine now wishes she did not have to do what she must: she "eyes the maid and seeks delay" (54). But she quickly collects herself, crawls into bed with Christabel, takes her in her arms, and presses her breasts against her naked back.[132] Thereby she casts a spell on her so that from that point on she will be like a dove enthralled by a deadly snake and therefore silent to any misgivings. With this Geraldine falls asleep with Christabel in her arms "as a mother with her child," while Christabel's eyes tear up as she dreams fearfully of that which is sorrow and shame, yet maintaining an attitude of prayer throughout.

Christabel awakens to find Geraldine already up, looking fairer than the night before and her breasts full. Yet she has a sense that something is wrong. "Sure I have sinned!" she says and prays to Jesus that he "might wash away her sins unknown" (1828, 61). Beyond this we need not go. Whether this episode in the bed chamber adds up to lesbianism will be considered in the conclusion.

2. *Carmilla* (1871-72)

Le Fanu"s 1871-72 *Carmilla* is the most well-known and most celebrated of the lesbian vampire stories of the nineteenth century. In fact, "Christabel" is usually registered simply as a precursor to and probably an influence on it.[133] Also, as we have seen, the two are almost always listed together as the only named examples of nineteenth-century vampire lesbianism. Like "Christabel" it seems to have caused little consternation initially because of its same sex intimacy (Haefle-Thomas 106-107). It only became a lesbian classic in the 1950s when it was listed in the top twenty readings of interest by the Daughters of Bilitis, an underground lesbian group in the US (*The Ladder* July 1957, 19). And while it is true today that "*Carmilla* is typically read as a tale of lesbian desire" (Killeen 99), there is

---

[132] My reading is at odds with the usual interpretation that Christabel faces her, reaches out and touches her breasts.
[133] Nethercot's "Coleridge's 'Christabel' and Lefanu's 'Carmilla'" (1949) is the first article I know to concentrate on the parallels in the two tales, with the idea that "Christabel" may have influenced *Carmilla*.

a minority that interprets the characters Carmilla and Laura, like Christabel and Geraldine, in terms of a surrogate mother and her daughter (e.g., Gordon 45-46). After all Carmilla is Laura's ancestor.

If read as lesbian fiction, current scholarship often concerns itself with the question of function. For example, is Le Fanu questioning the sexual politics of the Victorian period? (Sabriye 144). Is the tale about social anxiety concerning female sexuality considering it contagious? (Graham). Does it provide a cryptic reflection on menstrual blood? (Grenfell). Is it meant to rescue patriarchy from female power by staking the homosexual vampire? (Major; Gelder 58-64; etc.) Is illicit sex being used to emphasize the unnatural in his supernatural tale? (Tracy 66). Does it express the marginal experience of the Protestant Anglo-Irish? (Killeen 99-109). These are just some of the questions but we need not address them. They demonstrate that to call this a lesbian narrative can mean more than simply designating two young women's attraction to each other. The question that does remain for us is whether the attraction is lesbian? And that again will be dealt with in the conclusion.

This is, of course, a well-traveled road. It is the old tale of girl meets girl; girl loves girl; girl tries to drain the life out of girl; men kill girl. Laura, who identifies with her father's English heritage rather than that of her Austrian mother, lives with her father in Styria in an isolated castle. She lost her mother in infancy and is taken care of by a governess and a finishing governess. She says she has never had a friend (Le Fanu *Carmilla: A Critical Edition* 25) and lived "rather a solitary life," although she also notes that she has "two or three lady friends . . . who were occasional visitors" (6).

A carriage accident occurs in front of her castle, which results in an extended stay of a young lady, Carmilla. Throughout the narrative Laura keeps repeating how beautiful she finds Carmilla—"she was certainly the most beautiful creature I had ever seen" (25)—and how attracted she is to her. But Carmilla is *mysterium repellens et fascinans*: a mystery that at once repels and bewitches. So Laura also finds her to be cold and closed—she will share nothing

Carmilla. Illustrated by D. H. Friston. Le Fanu 1872, 704-75.

of her past although she promises all will be known soon enough. It is in the context of this that she makes her oft-quoted remarks.

> She used to place her pretty arms about my neck, draw me to her, and laying her cheek to mine, murmur with her lips near my ear, "Dearest, your little heart is wounded; think me not cruel because I obey the irresistible law of my strength and weakness; if your dear heart is wounded, my wild heart bleeds with yours. In the rapture of my enormous humiliation I live in your warm life, and you shall die—die, sweetly die—into mine. I cannot help it; as I draw near to you, you, in your turn, will draw near to others, and learn the rapture of that cruelty, which yet is love; so, for a while, seek to know no more of me and mine, but trust me with all your loving spirit."
>
> And when she had spoken such a rhapsody, she would press me more closely in her trembling embrace, and her lips in soft kisses gently glow upon my cheek. . . .
>
> In these mysterious moods I did not like her. I experienced a strange tumultuous excitement that was pleasurable, ever and anon, mingled with a vague sense of fear and disgust. . . .
>
> Sometimes after an hour of apathy, my strange and beautiful companion would take my hand and hold it with a fond pressure, renewed again and again; blushing softly, gazing in my face with languid and burning eyes, and breathing so fast that her dress rose and fell with the tumultuous respiration. It was like the ardor of a lover; it embarrassed me; it was hateful and yet over-powering; and with gloating eyes she drew me to her, and her hot lips traveled along my cheek in kisses; and she would whisper, almost in sobs, "You are mine, you *shall* be mine, you and I are one for ever.". . .
>
> "Are we related," I used to ask; "what can you mean by all this? I remind you perhaps of someone whom you love; but you must not, I hate it; I don't know you—I don't know myself when you look so and talk so.". . .
>
> Respecting these very extraordinary manifestations I strove in vain to form any satisfactory theory . . . What if a boyish lover had found his way into the house, and sought to prosecute his suit in masquerade, with the assistance of a clever old adventuress. But there were many things against this hypothesis, highly interesting as it was to my vanity. (29-30)

They often hold hands and sometimes walk with their hands around each other's waists. Once when taking a turn around the castle in the moonlight and Laura is again captivated by Carmilla's beauty, she utters these oft-cited words.

> "I have been in love with no one, and never shall," she whispered, "unless it should be with you." . . .
>
> Shy and strange was the look with which she quickly hid her face in my neck and hair, with tumultuous sighs, that seemed almost to sob, and pressed in mine a hand that trembled.

> Her soft cheek was glowing against mine. "Darling, darling," she murmured, "I live in you; and you would die for me, I love you so."
> I started from her.
> [T]he remainder of that evening passed without any recurrence of what I called her infatuations. I mean her crazy talk and looks, which embarrassed, and even frightened me. (40-42)

The last such exchange which is recorded is more remote and ambiguous.

> "Do you think," I said at length, "that you will ever confide fully in me?"
> She turned round smiling, but made no answer, only continued to smile on me. . . .
> "You were quite right to ask me that, or anything. You do not know how dear you are to me, or you could not think any confidence too great to look for. . . . The time is very near when you shall know everything. You will think me cruel, very selfish, but love is always selfish; the more ardent the more selfish. How jealous I am you cannot know. You must come with me, loving me, to death; or else hate me and still come with me, and *hating* me through death and after." (44)

One time the family discovers her missing and go into a panic at her loss. When she returns with a plausible excuse—we learn she has been attacking villagers some miles away about whom she does not care: "I do not trouble my head about peasants" [31] and lying in her coffin—Laura runs to her "in an ecstasy of joy; I kissed and embraced her again and again" (56).

Contrary to the villagers, to Laura her vampirism could be seductive and pleasurable. Even the bite in her sleep initially could be so, although inevitably it would become terrible. "Sometimes there came a sensation as if a hand was drawn softly along my cheek and neck. Sometimes it was as if warm lips kissed me, and longer and longer and more lovingly as they reached my throat, but there the caress fixed itself. My heart beat faster, my breathing rose and fell rapidly and full drawn; a sobbing, that rose into a sense of strangulation, supervened, and turned into a dreadful convulsion, in which my senses left me and I became unconscious." (52) This is not ultimately orgiastic, as some have said; it is suffocation. There is pleasure in the foreplay but not the act.

In the end, when Carmilla has been revealed to be a vampire and before she could turn Laura into one, and when her coffin has been located and she has been staked and beheaded, she still haunts Laura. After a thoroughly cynical assessment by Baron Vordenburg of Carmilla and her seduction of Laura, voiding it of any real need for loving companionship, Laura regains her own voice. "[T]o this hour the image of Carmilla returns to memory with ambiguous alternations—sometimes the playful, languid, beautiful girl; sometimes the writhing fiend I saw in the ruined church; and often from a reverie I have started, fancying I heard the light step of Carmilla at the drawing room door" (96).[134]

---

[134] As Jamieson Ridenhour puts it: "the status quo wins, asserting accepted norms and 'saving' Laura, who spends the rest of her life hearing Carmilla's footstep at the door" (175).

3. *Princess Daphne* **(1888)**

Heron-Allen's 1888 book is listed on several bibliographies as a psychic vampire story, but apart from that its contents appear to have escaped notice altogether by "vampirologists." Mahmouré has hovered near death for five months when Paul seduces and marries her. Paul immediately begins to make her "his charming vampire" and mesmerizes her to transfer some of his vital force to her. In the process, he learns she is a "highly magnetic woman" and begins to send her spirit from New York across the ocean to London, specifically to Daphne, the "princess" of a closely-knit community of artists. Mahmouré first enters her body, causing no small amount of trauma to Daphne as she both knows and does not know her surroundings, her fiancé, Eric, and herself.

Mahmouré soon protests that he is dangerously weakening himself and that she herself is feeling that intruding in Daphne's life this way is dishonest and shameful. But by this time Paul is dedicated to the experiments no longer just for Mahmouré's benefit but for the sake of science. And he has also been inadvertently sending part of his psychic force into Daphne through these visitations. So he dismisses Mahmouré's misgivings and extends the research to include her appearing as a phantom to Daphne.

"[O]n clearing from her eyes the mists of sleep, she had seen before her the figure of a lithe, supple, but withal beautiful woman who looked at her out of great soft brown eyes, which, so far from frightening the Princess, rather attracted and soothed her than otherwise; and Eric felt almost alarmed at the importance she ascribed to these visitations, and almost annoyed at the quasi-affectionate interest she took in what she playfully called 'her ghost'" (150).

Paul dies and transfers the residue of his soul to Daphne, which kills her. He has, in essence, been vampirizing her; removing what makes her unique and replacing it with some of himself. So when she revives she is no longer herself but a composite of Paul and her. Eric finds her to be "less womanly, but more female," that is, less stately and more common. Mahmouré calls on Daphne when in London to work out the details of Eric's estate, since he and Daphne were distantly related, and they find themselves inexplicably attracted to each other.

Inexplicable to them but not to the male perspective taken by the book. Among the reasons given for their intense relationship are that Mahmouré is intoxicated with Paul inside Daphne and Daphne with her because of Paul's love for Mahmouré within; that they are allegedly both suffering from hysteria due to the experiments; that Mahmouré is seeking another energy source like Paul. Yet all the women know is that they find each other alluring and fascinating. Eric, on the other hand, takes an instant dislike to Mahmouré when he meets her and he eventually leaves Daphne because of her.

> This strange sympathy that took possession of Daphne was the more absorbing from the fact that it was quite new to her for she was not given to what is called "gushing" over women. Though she liked them very well, she never made nor needed "greatest girl-friends." The affection which seems to be such a necessity, such an all-absorbing lien, between some women had always been a matter for wonder to

her. . . . She would submit in a gracious manner to being kissed; it seemed to please the other girl, and didn't hurt her but why? but why? she would question. . . .

Therefore was she the more amazed to find herself drawn irresistibly to this little woman, whose big eyes were fixed on her with a strange, far-off look. . . . She roused herself and advanced a little, stretching out both hands so as to take Mahmouré almost in her arms . . . and for the first time in her life offered her lips to be kissed by a woman, impelled by a fascination which was stronger than herself . . .

They were seated close together on the lounge, and though an ordinary observer would not have seen anything strange in the appearance of the two women, one of them at least had by no means recovered her self-possession. It was Daphne who could not reconcile her own conflicting sensations she could find no reason for the intense, soft satisfaction that she felt under the influence of Mahmouré's presence, of her touch, of her gaze, of her kiss.

It seemed like a new obsession. . . .

[After tea and some chatter Daphne says] "You cannot think how strangely happy I am that chance should have thrown us together like this. Our friendship, though sudden, must be lasting; promise me, Mahmouré, that it shall be."

And Mahmouré, lying among the cushions, looked up into Daphne's beautiful eyes and said: "I promise you!"

For answer Daphne bent and kissed the beautiful lips that had framed the words, as if to thank them. (200-204)

On a slightly later occasion Eric makes a visit to his fiancée.

> As Eric stood motionless in the doorway of the studio he saw Daphne lying in a lazy, languorous attitude upon the lounge, whilst Mahmouré du Peyral sat by her side, her arms twined round her, looking into her eyes. Daphne was playing lazily with the masses of Mahmouré's hair, which she had unbound, and which were floating in tawny billows all over her as she lay among the cushions. Neither woman spoke, but the silence was far more eloquent than words . . .
>
> "Ah! Eric. Is that you? I didn't suppose you would come in again to-night."
>
> At the sound of her voice and her words Mahmouré started away, but Daphne, restraining her by winding her arms about the supple little figure, said:
>
> "Don't go away, dear. He isn't going to stay. Eric, *mon cher*, come in the morning, will you? Madame du Peyral is staying here with me to-night. We did not get through our work till it was too late for her to think of going home alone." (231)

We hear no more details like this. After several weeks together, they quarrel and Mahmouré murders Daphne . . . and with her, Paul.

4. *Sardia* (1891)

Sardia by Cora Lynn Daniels has been largely ignored. It, like *Princess Daphne*, is found in exhaustive bibliographies, but, in contrast, it has actually been cited a few times outside them. The twenty-second chapter, entitled "A Vampire," has been lifted by Pam Keesey for her 1995 anthology, *Dark Angels: Lesbian Vampire Stories*. She calls the Countess "a classic vamp" and a "serpentine woman who unscrupulously and unrepentantly uses her sexuality to destroy both men and women" (15-16). In the encyclopedic *Gay and Lesbian Literary Heritage* Catherine Geddi's 2002 essay "Ghost and Horror Fiction," this vampire story is mentioned as having "homosexual attachments" and the annotated bibliography *Uranian Worlds* (1990) by Eric Garber and Lyn Paleo speaks of Sybil as using her vampiric mesmerizing power on women as well as men and as having a "lesbian attachment" to another woman. Other than these three examples, I am unaware of any further citation that brings together vampire and lesbian.

This sentimentalist, spiritualist novel pits two archetypal women against each other: Helen Fielding who is transcendently good and willing to sacrifice her own happiness for that of Ralfe, and Sybil Visonti who is pictured as a soulless, egocentric vamp trying to seduce Ralfe for his wealth. The latter is described as a vampire. "She eats one up body and soul" (15; cf. 68). There are mitigating circumstances to her behavior but the book is not interested in them; her purpose is to act as a foil for Helen's altruism and to demonstrate the fate of such a woman as she—she goes mad and tries to kill her son to murder the moon. In the midst of this, there is an affair between Sybil and another woman, Lulu.

At a country villa a select group of friends are gathered for the summer. When Sybil reaches a low point and is standing on a cliff wishing for another life, Lulu finds her and by her naïve effervescence reanimates her. They walk back to the house arm-in-arm and Sybil invites her up to her room. Lulu is enchanted by her culture and the grace she demonstrates with her body after she takes off her heavy dress. With her lost in admiration Sybil asks if she loves her. Lulu turns away when she steps on her shawl and it falls to the floor. Sibyl, unaware that Lulu is not looking, ties it up at her waist, still displaying her naked body, and asks Lulu if she remembers a sex scene in Grammaticus Musaeus's *Hero and Leander* that uses the phrase, "With that soft leave he loosed her virgin zone" (65), but the move does not work the way she expected. Lulu simply remembers discussing the poem with her mother. Sybil soon renews her advances by embracing her, gazing into her eyes, kissing her forehead. Lulu submits to it all until she moves in to kiss her lips. Lulu refuses.

Later, as Lulu is enthralled by her fiancé's wisdom, he exclaims "Avoid her! Never touch her! Do not permit her to kiss you!" (139). Through his wise simile, she realizes that Sybil is a spider catching both Ralfe and herself in her web. Nonetheless the very next day she returns to Sybil, drawn by her kindness. Time passes and one day, Guy, her fiancé, is shaken from his reverie while watching the two women walking together on the lawn by Sardia, a male parallel to Helen but more advanced and studied; he is an adept of Spiritualism. He helps Guy to notice how Lulu has lost her *joi de vivre* since she revived her friendship with Sybil.

Guy calls to her to come to him, but Sybil says she also needs her and she stays. He retreats to the house angry and frustrated.

Meanwhile Lulu and Sybil become closer still, eventually sharing a room.

> [Lulu] began to know the charm of being sought, sought persistently, patiently, humbly. She began to feel that her love and friendship to this one woman at least was invaluable, possessing an exceptional preciousness. She felt that she possessed the key to a thousand times richer nature than her own. . . .
>
> "You cannot get rid of me," Sybil softly whispered, winding a sunny lock of Lulu's bright hair about her fingers. "Nothing shall drive me away. I will hang on until you love me whether you want me or not. I will have you love me in spite of yourself," . . . Lulu did love her, agree with her, appreciate her and delight in association with her. . . .
>
> "Let us prove to ourselves if to none others, that there can exist between two women a love, holy, pure, exalted, which no change of circumstance can alter, no selfishness or jealousy can make less true. Let us enter into a sweet secret together of undying faith and mutual help . . ." Lulu with all her sweet soul tossed by varied emotions, sprang into Sybil's arms and sealed the compact with a long, clinging kiss, the first that she had voluntarily tendered to her woman-lover. . . .
>
> With the enthusiasm of youth which had been so gradually yet surely awakened, she longed to do anything, to give anything, to be anything to show the intensity of her devotion, the unadulteration of her friendship. . . . [S]he abandoned herself mentally and physically to the fascinating pleasure of giving that joy which thrilled the Visonti [Sybil] with visible emotion. . . . "I feel as if I were floating on white clouds, dearest, when you touch me. My body is light as air, and my soul seems to drift into a fairy realm. What magic lies in these precious finger-tips to give me such an unknown happiness!" . . .
>
> [I]f, with an occasional access of her original tendencies, Lulu deserted Sybil for a whole day, or went away with Guy to spend delicious hours of chat and fun, regaining in his wholesome presence, the strong, fresh vitality, which was her constitutional condition, she would soon be made to feel how lonely, how sad, how longing for her had been the time for Sybil, although occupied with her own affairs, protested that in her heart all was dreariness without the light of Lulu's smile. . . .
>
> Sybil had often with pricking pleasantry scorned in a general way, the idea of masculine intrusion. . . .
>
> The young girl felt her brain whirl with a sense of her subjugation of this woman. She assumed an expression which infinitely amused Sybil, while it pricked her to sudden wrath. Murmuring her promises and assurances as a mother soothes a nervous child, "Why, dear Sybil," she said, "are you so fearful that my noble Guy could not understand your tenderness for me? . . . [Y]our love and mine is something totally different, so impossible to contain the same elements that are in his

love and mine, that they are quite distinct, quite unapproachable by any comparison." And with all the loyalty of her soul aflame, she determined to let nothing so much as cast a shadow over so high and fine an union. (181-86)

It is shortly after this that Sybil begins her rapid descent into madness and Lulu returns to her old carefree self, fully restored to Guy as they tease each other and plan for their upcoming marriage. No residue from the affair here.

5. "The Glass of Blood" (1893)

It was Brian Stableford who brought this short story by Jean Lorrain to the attention of the English-speaking world, particularly of vampire scholars. In his book of Lorrain translations, *Nightmares of an Ether-Drinker* (2002), he asserts that this is "a pioneering tale of vampiric lesbian paedophilia" (ix).[135] And in an article, "Sang for Supper" (1997) he writes "[g]iven that 'Le verre de sang' is one of the very few tales of lesbian pedophilia ever penned, it is perhaps unsurprising that it proceeds in an unexpected and rather implausible direction" (71). Stableford is the only one I know who makes this claim.

A world-renowned opera singer, La Barnarina, at the peak of her career, recently got married and gave up her profession along with its fame. She did not marry out of love for the man, a widower, but for his 14-year-old daughter, Rosario. Rosario had become her pupil and she came to regard her almost as a daughter. When the marquis was offered a position in a remote region of the East, he made plans to relocate and take his daughter with him. Neither the actress nor the daughter could bear to be separated, so she married him, and he left alone with Rosario in her care.

Since then Rosario has begun to lose her health. The first diagnosis was that her stepmother loved her too much and vice versa, and that this was sapping her strength. But removing her signs of affection did nothing to heal her. The other physicians could find no cause, but finally one suggested she "join the ranks of the consumptives who go at dawn to the abattoirs and drink lukewarm blood freshly taken from the calves which are bled to make veal" (41). Since the place makes her ill, La Barnarina makes sure Rosario is accompanied there by her governess. Each day La Barnarina waits eagerly for her return. "[S]he anticipates the first kiss which the child will place upon her lips, as soon as she returns: a kiss which always carries an insipid trace of the taste of blood and a faint hint of the odour which perpetually defiles the rue de Flandre, but which, strangely enough, she does not detest at all—quite the contrary—when it is upon the warm lips of her beloved Rosario" (42).

We will have to wait on a verdict whether this is pedophilia but the language is strong at points. The diva "falls in love" with the girl; she is amused, seduced and conquered by her so as to give her lessons; when threatened with separation she observes that the child had become part of her—her own soul and her own flesh. But then there are statements like La Barnarina coming to regard Rosario almost as a daughter, her being a mother who had never given birth but now having an ardent passion for the child of another's loins, and her being called directly Rosario's mother ("but her mother understood").

---

[135] The story was originally part of a collection, *Buveurs d'âmes* (1893), 95-106.

And where does the vampirism come in? The first diagnosis proved to be wrong; she was not sucking the life out of Rosario by her affection. So if there is a vampire it must be Rosario herself, drinking animal blood. Starting in the 1870s it became popular enough for the sick—especially those suffering with consumption—to visit abattoirs to drink the fresh blood of oxen that there were a number of articles written on the subject. In fact, there was even a stated fear displayed in the coverage that the taste for oxen blood could easily turn to one for human blood, thus producing real vampires.[136] So the direction of the narrative may be unpredictable, but it is not implausible.

5. *Blood of the Vampire* (1897)

The issue of vampirism in this work is embedded in discussions of imperialism, reverse-colonization, race, inheritance, eugenics, miscegenation, class structure, transgressive heterosexuality, hysteria, and the occult in Florence Marryat's book. So same-sex desire is entangled in these other issues, resulting in contemporary assertions of lesbianism or bisexuality often being made only *en passant*. But that is only to be expected because the short episodes that reference it are at the furthest borders of the narrative.

The remarks from authors today focus on different aspects of the so-called "lesbian danger." Signorotti 611 wants to say it offers insight into stereotypes of female sexuality and gendered identity at the turn of the century; Depledge xxii talks of Harriet's staying with her friend as possibly a "coded reference to lesbian activity;" her "overt desire" toward another woman as indicative of "primitive bisexuality (Davis 44-45);"[137] Anatol 109-110) notes that while seven of her ten victims are women, they are chosen less by homoerotic impulses than by greed and availability.

Willburn 440 talks of the lesbianism as "unsophisticated and practically incidental;" Macfie 62-63 observes that the book conflates "close female bonding and lesbianism" with notions of the "unhealthy draining of female vitality." So its function in the book is in its presentation: is the lesbianism used to say something about prevailing sexual ideologies at the time or is it about how it itself is described or carried out? Only books specifically on the topic of homosexuality spend any time with it (for instance, Haefle-Thomas 96-119).

The blood of the vampire can be understood both as a subjective and objective genitive: the vampire's blood and the infected blood caused by the vampire. Normally the objective genitive would not pertain, but in this case it does and it applies to the primary vampire in the story, although its role encompasses but a few sentences. It is a vampire bat, which was often just called a vampire in the nineteenth century, who taints the blood of the maternal side of the family and turns them into vampires.

Marryat commences her story with Harriet, the featured vampire, the second in line of descendents with the contaminated blood. As Dr. Phillips instructs

---

[136] There are quite a few of articles on the subject of drinking ox blood. One that references the practice in France is "The Vampire versus the Phoenix" (1874), 431. It continued in France into the late 1890s as is demonstrated by the popular painting by Ferdinand Joseph Gueldry in Marion Harry Spielmann's "The Paris Salons" (1898), 496. Concerning the fear of people turning to human blood, see "Human Vampires" 4.
[137] In the second quote, she is quoting Davis 44-45.

us: "She possesses the fatal attributes of the Vampire that affected her mother's birth—that endued her with the thirst for blood, which characterised her life—that will make Harriet draw upon the health and strength of all with whom she may be intimately associated—that may render her love fatal to such as she may cling to!" (132, cf. 115; 262; 272; 273).

Her grandmother was bitten by a vampire bat and died in childbirth; her mother inherited it: "[S]he thirsted for blood, she loved the sight and smell of it, she would taste it on the tip of her finger when it came in her way" (115). Harriet picked up this contagion as well, but it is psychic. It could not be otherwise. As Dr. Phillips sagely observes: "'When the cat is black, the kitten is black too!' It's the law of Nature!" (130).

But the vampirism does not explain her sexual assertiveness and deviance from Victorian norms; there is something more in her blood and the aphorism stated above goes a long way to introduce it; she is a Jamaican quadroon, a product of miscegenation. Her grandmother was a slave who was raped by her white owner. Her mother, then, was a "half-breed." She never married but she had an illicit, long-term affair with a white man, a vivisectionist, who was a systematic killer of animals and people.

Dr. Phillips again: "She was not a woman, she was a fiend . . . A fat, flabby half-caste, who hardly ever moved out of her chair . . . I can see her now, with her sensual mouth, her greedy eyes, her low forehead and half formed brain, and her lust for blood" (115). Although breathtakingly beautiful now, Harriet will soon be fat like her mother, he prophetically tells us, and although fair-skinned, she shares her mother's mouth and smoldering eyes.

She is irresistible to two adult men and a young one in the story. Two die from her uncontrollable psychic vampirism. That it is unvolitional makes her one of the most tragic vampires of the nineteenth century. But she is also drawn to two women, one of whom responds to her a little. We must mention first that she has been housed the last ten years in a convent where there was no privacy and no toleration for friendships. She has only now been released and has spent most of her first days on board a ship.

She has been traveling with a younger companion from the convent, Olga Brimont, and the two have been sharing a room. Olga became deathly ill on the voyage. As Harriet relates it, "I stayed with her all the time. I used to sit up with her at night, but it did her no good" (19). Since they have landed, however, and Harriet has been out and about, Olga has been on the mend. We have seen already that at least one commentator has conjectured that the reference of sitting with her may be a "coded reference to lesbian activity."

After knowing Mrs. Margaret Pullen for a very short time, Harriet declares her intentions. She liked her immediately, "[a]nd I want you to like me too—so much! It has been the dream of my life to have some friends" (27). As they continue talking in the café, Harriet creeps closer to Margaret, encircles her waist with her arm and leans her head on her shoulder. Margaret feels uncomfortable, but allows it this one time for she seems so friendless. She begins to feel faint as if she has been "scooped hollow," when Harriet lays her head on her breast, and tries to extricate herself but Harriet "seemed to come after her." She finally does manage to get up and she hobbles into a friend, whom she asks to take her to her room. Harriet stands there feeling desolate. "She liked her so much—so very much—she had so hoped she was going to be her friend—she would have done anything and given anything sooner than put her to inconvenience in any way" (32).

The following morning, late because Mrs. Pullen slept poorly, they breakfast together with two others. "Margaret Pullen, glancing up once, was struck by the look with which Harriet Brandt was regarding her—it was so full of yearning affection—almost of longing to approach her nearer, to hear her speak, to touch her hand! It amused her to observe it! She had heard of cases, in which young unsophisticated girls had taken unaccountable affections for members of their own sex, and trusted she was not going to form the subject for some such experience on Miss Brandt's part. The idea made her address her conversation more to Mademoiselle Brimont, than to her companion of the evening before" (38-39).

There is nothing more beyond these two episodes, in part because Harriet turns her affections to Margaret's infant daughter. Margaret again notices Harriet's eyes, but they are turned in affection to her child, not to her.

"[T]hey were underlaid by smouldering fires which might burst forth into flame at any moment, and which seemed to stir and kindle and then go out again, when she spoke of anything that interested her. There was an attraction about the girl, which Mrs. Pullen acknowledged, without wishing to give in to. She could not keep her eyes off her! She seemed to hypnotise her as the snake is said to hypnotise the bird, but it was an unpleasant feeling, as if the next moment the smouldering fire would burst forth into flame and overwhelm her. But watching her play with, and hearing her talk to, her baby, Margaret put the idea away from her, and only thought how kindly natured she must be, to take so much trouble for another woman's child" (58).

Conclusion

Lesbianism—by which I mean sexual desire, intention, or action between women—cannot be ruled out in any of the cases. The question is whether it is the best and most persuasive explanation. With Christabel, there is evidence to suggest that in some way an image of mother and child is at play. This would cover the image of the old, saggy breasts and the exact analogy that is drawn ("as a mother with her child"). Regardless, the best way to understand them sleeping in bed together is back to front as a mother does with a child, not front to front or side to side. Her breasts, then, are pressed against Laura's naked back; Christabel does not reach out to touch them. If it were different, one would expect some sign of sexual awakening. Also, Geraldine would be dependent on Christabel touching her, which is not at all in the story. She is utterly independent.

There is nothing here that would rule out a pseudo-romantic friendship—false because it is not arrived at naturally but rushed and, of course, it is meant to destroy an innocent, not provide a safe place for her. This might explain Christabel's sense of sin and violation, i.e., the intimacy is founded on carelessness. To whatever this sense pertains, however, Christabel is said later to be "devoid of guile and sin," so her feeling is subjectively real but does not have an objective basis. And Christabel does not know what her sin may be anyway. If lesbianism, she did so unwittingly, which is very unlikely.

This interpretation also best suits the lack of critical attention to any homosexual content until the mid-twentieth century when sexual or Freudian interpretations of texts were in full swing. Lesbianism seems to be a case of eisegesis not exegesis; reading into a text rather than deriving something from it.

Renée Fox is the first and only one, so far as I am aware, to draw into the discussion of our readings, specifically *Carmilla*, the notion of romantic friendships. "Intimate, even passionate friendships between women pepper the most canonical Victorian texts . . . none of which the Victorians viewed as 'homosexual' or 'lesbian.'"[138] There is no doubt that *Carmilla* is homoerotic by our standards, but it is doubtful it was when it was written or for many decades thereafter. It is true that Laura makes advances to Carmilla too, so the relationship is not just one-sided, but when Carmilla talks erotically to her, she is confused and repulsed. From her side, a consensual, physical relationship would be rejected out of hand. As we saw, the bite was ultimately horrible. If it was lesbian, it was lesbian rape.[139]

The point, however, is that all that is exchanged between them can be chalked up to a pseudo-romantic friendship.[140] Again it violates the experience of a real one. There is no mutual sharing or even mutual understanding. Carmilla speaks intimately, even seductively, only in cryptic terms which are bewildering to Laura and, therefore, not experienced as intimate, much less alluring. And like "Christabel," one party, experienced and mature, is deliberately planning to hurt the other, naïve and inexperienced.

As I indicated above *Carmilla* was not considered lesbian until 1957 when it was listed as number nineteen in the top twenty lesbian stories by the Daughters of Bilitis. This is one reason I dismiss the whole discussion about this being seen as a threat to patriarchy by the men involved. Another is that the men would have to be privy to the intimate exchanges between the two girls. There is no indication of this in the text. The General is motivated by vengeance; Carmilla's father by protection.

With *Princess Daphne*, one of its unique features is that it is consensual; insofar as that can apply when Mahmouré has already shared Daphne's body and Paul is, in some manner, currently inside her. Also, with the reader given a male gaze in the book, it is important that the behavior is not thought of as uncommon or problematic: "an ordinary [male] observer would not have seen anything strange in the appearance of the two women" (203). It is so only to Daphne, who is unaccustomed to being "obsessed" with someone, particularly another woman. There is nothing here to point beyond a romantic friendship.

So too with *Sardia*, except for one scene which appears to have real lesbian intent, the most explicit of any text. Sybil removes not only her heavy dress but everything, one garment at a time, thinking she is going to make Lulu into

---

[138] See Fox 113-114. Agnieszka. Lowczanin's essay, "Damsels and Demons" (2013) holds that "The lesbian magnetism between the women is . . . of a highly ambiguous nature. . . . Laura's accounts of Carmilla's lesbian practice are never verified and take the form of innocent whispers and nudges during the day" (197). She continues that the only account of her nightly activities is of a large ill-defined object moving to a female's throat and becoming a "great palpitating mass the shape of which is far from phallic." David Skal (*V is for Vampire* 1996) writes "[t]he lesbianism in the story is surprisingly pronounced, as the girls spend languorous hours kissing, fondling, and gazing into each other's eyes" (53). Although well overstated, as Lowczanin points out above, this is still exactly what one would expect in a romantic friendship.
[139] I must take issue, therefore, with Sue-Ellen Case ("Tracking the Vampire,"1991) who says of Carmilla that she desires and is desired by her victim as if there was a parity between her and Laura's yearnings (Case 7). Tracy ("Loving You All Ways," 1990) is worse by identifying them both as "sexually aggressive women" (Tracy 40).
[140] "Fanu's 1872 character Carmilla . . . uses the guise of friendship to seduce and drain her victim" (Hobson 11-12).

someone like herself. She then "draped about her a light, large shawl of *crêpe du chine* which clung to the voluptuous figure as if in love with it and seemed to caress with its soft folds the person it but half concealed" (63). She uses it to captivate Lulu apparently with something of an imitation of Loïe Fuller.

> "No wonder you can make any one love you whom you please."
> "And do you love me, little one?" approaching so swiftly that the shawl became entangled about her feet. Lulu turned her head away and did not answer. "When I let my draperies go," Sybil remarked coolly, gathering up the tissue and knotting it about her waist, without noticing Lulu's averted head, "I always think of that charming poem of 'Hero and Leander,' so admirably put into verse by Arnold. Do you remember the bridal scene? You know the line—'With that soft leave he loosed her virgin zone!'" (64)

The poem is of an unwed couple having sexual intercourse. It is hard to escape the insinuation here. It is ironic that this passage was not selected for *Dark Angels: Lesbian Vampire Stories*.

The rest is compatible with a romantic friendship. "Let us prove to ourselves if to none others, that there can exist between two women a love, holy, pure, exalted, which no change of circumstance can alter, no selfishness or jealousy can make less true." But again the friendship is a violation of norms. Sybil deliberately leads Lulu away from her relationship with Guy so it is in competition with marriage. It is one thing to deny an offer of marriage because one finds friendship far more satisfying, it is another for it to arise in the midst of an engagement and work for its ruin. We have seen that before with *Princess Daphne*. But there it is inadvertent. This relationship also commences with the intention to destroy the integrity of one of its members, again the naïve one. However one cannot doubt the sincerity of Sybil's feelings for Lulu.

I have to say that Brian Stableford's thesis on "The Glass of Blood" is difficult to follow. Everything points to a deeply devoted relationship of a stepmother with her stepdaughter. Rosario already worshiped La Barnarina long before they met. When they did, her affection turned out to be contagious. The decadent part of the story is not their kisses but that they are mediated through the blood from an abattoir. Deep feelings of connection and their physical display between young girls and adult women were much more common at that time than they are today.

Finally there is *The Blood of a Vampire*. There is simply no way that her staying up all night with Olga could be coded language for lesbianism; her friend is so sick that she is near death. With regard to Margaret, her attention is fixed on her one evening and the next morning. And she interprets it herself—she spent ten years in a convent where friendships were forbidden. She so desperately wants a friend after her liberation but she has no sense of propriety. So she moves in much too quickly and with far too much enthusiasm. It is hardly lesbianism; it is an attempt to force a romantic friendship.

When that does not work out immediately she turns her overwhelming attention to Margaret's baby; she never wants it to be out of her arms. And after she learns that with her hungry eyes she can seduce any man, she focuses them on the fiancé of Margaret's close friend, Elinor. Only hours after they meet they are kissing and declaring their love to one another. When he leaves surreptitiously with Elinor she goes into wild fits of desperation and anger. It is only at the end that she has learned some sense of self-control and when her husband dies on their honeymoon, apparently due to his intimacy with her, she takes her own tragic life to end her blood-borne vampirism and her lineage as well.

The violations in woman-to-woman relationships, with one exception, do not appear to be sexual. They pertain to a rushed and false intimacy in friendships, except between Sardia and Lulu, which we will discuss shortly. There is another exception to that as well and that is between Rosario and La Barnarina, which is also clearly genuine. That story also lacks any homoeroticism, much less homosexuality. And this is something we must again address. These texts, for the most part, strike us as erotic, but there is no reason for classifying them as such. They seem to be ardently homosocial; they refer to romantic friendships. That they strike us as homoerotic, and we are accustomed to calling them "lesbian," says a lot about us as a culture; that they were not taken as such at the time, says a lot about them and their culture.

But there is the one scene with Sybil and Lulu that appears to be genuinely lesbian. Although the fall of her sheer clothing onto the floor is accidental, Sybil tries to arouse Lulu sexually and she seems to be ready to take it to another level, a physical one, if she responds. When Lulu does not and even rejects a kiss on the mouth, Sybil never tries that tactic again, but settles into all the indications of an intense friendship. If Sybil were not so universally cast as evil and manipulative, it may even have had elements of a genuine one in the text.

So from my perspective, we need to exercise considerable caution before we simply call these stories lesbian. It does not appear the nineteenth century was as open to lesbian relationships as we have believed.

Works cited

Alger, William Rounsville. *The Friendships of Women.* Boston: Roberts Brothers, 1868.
Anatol, Giselle Liza. *The Things That Fly in the Night: Female Vampires in Literature of the Circum-Caribbean and African Diaspora.* New Brunswick: Rutgers University Press, 2015.
Auerbach, Nina. *Our Vampires, Ourselves.* Chicago: University of Chicago Press, 1995.
Beer, John. 1986. "Coleridge, Hazlitt, and 'Christabel.'" *The Review of English Studies* 37: 145 (1986), 40-54.
Case, Sue-Ellen. "Tracking the Vampire." *Differences* 3 (1991), 1-20.
Coffman, Christine E. *Insane Passions: Lesbianism and Psychosis in Literature and Film.* Middletown: Wesleyan University Press, 1986.
Coleridge, Samuel. *Christabel; Kubla Khan; The Pains of Sleep.* 3. London: John Murray, 1816.
Coleridge, Samuel. *The Poetical Works of S.T. Coleridge: Including the Dramas of Wallenstein, Remorse, and Zapolya.* Lonon: William Pickering, 1829.
Daniels, Cora Lynn. *Sardia: A Story of Love.* Boston: Lee & Shepard Publishers, 1891.
Davis, Octavia. "Morbid Mothers: Gothic Heredity in Florence Marryat's The Blood of the Vampire." *Horrifying Sex: Essays on Sexual Difference in Gothic Literature.* Ed. Ruth Bienstock Anolik. Jefferson, NC: McFarland, 2007. 40-54.
Depledge, Greta. "Introduction." *The Blood of the Vampire.* By Florence Marryat. Ed. Greta Depledge. Brighton: Victorian Secrets, 2010. iii-xxxiv.
Dyer, Richard. "Children of the Night: Vampirism as Homosexuality, Homosexuality as Vampirism." *Sweet Dreams: Sexuality, Gender, and Popular Fiction.* Ed. Susannah Radstone. London: Lawrence & Wishart. 47-72.
Elfenbein, Andrew. *Romantic Genius: The Prehistory of a Homosexual Role.* New York: Columbia University Press, 1999.

Faderman, Lillian. *Odd Girls and Twilight Lovers: A History of Lesbian Life in Twentieth Century America.* New York: Columbia University Press, 1991.

Faderman, Lillian. *Surpassing the Love of Men: Romantic Friendship and Love Between Women from the Renaissance to the Present.* New York: William Morrow, 1981.

Fanu, Le, Sheridan. *Carmilla: A Critical Edition.* Ed. Kathleen Costello-Sullivan. New York: Syracuse University Press, 2013.

Fox, Renée. "Carmilla and the Politics of Indistinguishability." *Carmilla: A Critical Edition.* By Sheridan Le Fanu. Ed. Kathleen Costello-Sullivan. New York: Syracuse University Press, 2013. 110-121.

Frayling, Christopher. *Vampyres: Lord Byron to Count Dracula.* London: Faber & Faber, 1991.

Furneaux, Holly. "Female Romantic Friendship and the Anguish of Marriage." *Journal of Victorian Studies* 14: 2 (2009), 25-37.

Garber, Eric, and Lyn Paleo. *Uranian Worlds: A guide to alternative sexuality in sceince fiction and horror.* 2nd. Boston: G. K. Hall & Co., 1990.

Geddis, Catherine. "Ghost and Horror Fiction." *Gay and Lesbian Literary Heritage: A Reader's Companion to the Writers and Their Works, from Antiquity to the Present.* Ed. Claude J. Summers. New York: Routledge, 2002. 324-326.

Gelder, Ken. *Reading the Vampire.* London: Routledge, 1994.

Gordon, Joan. "Sharper than a Serpent's Tooth: The Vampire in Search of Its Mother." *Blood Read.* Eds. Joan Gordon and Verone Hollinger. Philadelphia: University of Philadelphia Press, 1997. 45-55.

Graham, Chelsea. "Defanged and Desirable: An Examination of Violence and the Lesbian Vampire Narrative." M.A. Thesis, Bowling Green State University, 2016.

Grenfell, Laura. "*Carmilla*: The 'Red Flag' of Late Nineteenth Century Vampire Narratives?" *Tessera* 33/34 (2000), 152-167.

Grajko, Dalin Thomas. *'Christabel' and the Politics of Fragmentation.* MA Thesis: Rutgers, State University of New Jersey, 2013. https://rucore.libraries.rutgers.edu/rutgers-lib/40276/.

Grossberg, Benjamin Scott. "Making Christabel: Sexual Trangression and its Implications in Coleridge's 'Christabel.'" *Journal of Homosexuality* 41: 2 (2001), 145-165.

Haefle-Thomas, Ardel. *Queer Others in Victorian Gothic: Transgressing Monstrosity.* Cardiff: University of Wales Press, 2012.

Haley, William. *The Young Widow Or, The History of Cornelia Sedley.* Vol. 1. London: G. G. J. & J. Robinson, 1789.

Hazlitt, William. "Review of *Christabel: Kubla Khan, a Vision. The Pains of Sleep.* The *Edinburgh Review.* September 1816, 58-67.

Heron-Allen, Edward, and Selina Delaro. *Princess Daphne.* Chicago: Belford, Clarke & Co, 1888.

Hobson, Amanda. "Dark Seductress: The Hypersexualization of the Female Vampire." *Gender in the Vampire Narrative.* Ed. Amanda Hobson; U. Melissa Aniwo. Rotterdam: Sense Publishers, 2016. 9-27.

Holmes, Richard. *Coleridge: Darker Reflections.* London: HarperCollins, 1998.

Holmes, Trevor. "Coming Out of the Coffin: Gay Males and Queer Goths in Contgemporary Vampire Fiction." *Blood Read: the Vampire as Metaphor in Contemporary Culture.* Eds. Joan Gordon and Veronica Hollinger. Philadelphia: University of Philadelphia Press, 1997. 169-188.

"Human Vampires." *Westport Times* 10 (1876), 4.

Hypocrasy Unveiled, and Calumny Detected: In a Review of Blackwood's Magazine. Edinburgh: Francis Pillans, 1818.

Keesey, Pam. *Dark Angels: Lesbian Vampire Stories.* Pittsburgh: Cleis Press, 1995.

Killeen, Jarlath. "An Irish Carmilla?" *Carmilla: A Critical Edition.* By Sheridan Le Fanu. Ed. Kathleen Costello-Sullivan. Syracuse: Syracuse University Press, 2013. 99-109.

Le Fanu, J. T. Sheridan. "Carmilla." *The Dark Blue.* February 1872.

Lorrain, Jean. *Buveurs d'âmes*. Paris: Bibliotèque-Charpentier, 1893.

Lorrain, Jean. *Nightmares of an Ether Drinker*. Trans. Brian Stableford. Leyburn: Tartarus Press, 2002.

Lowczanin, Agnieszka. "Damsels and Demons: Transgressive Females from Clarissa to Carmilla." *Reading Subversion and Transgression*. Ed. Paulina Mirowska and Joanna Kazik: Lódź: Lódź University Press, 2013. 189-199.

Macfie, Sian. "'They Suck Us Dry': A Sudy of Late Nineteenth-Century Projections of Vampiric Women." *Subjectivity and Literature from the Romantics to the Present Day*. Eds. Philip Shaw and Peter Stockwell. London: Pinter Publishers, 1991. 58-67.

Major, Adrienne Antrim. "Other Love: Le Fanu's Carmilla as Lesbian Gothic." *Horrifying Sex: Essays in Sexual Difference in Gothic Literature*. Ed. Ruth Bienstock Anolik. Jefferson, NC: McFarland, 2007. 151-166.

Marcus, Sharon. *Between Women: Friendship, Desire, and Marriage in Victorian England*. Princeton: Princeton University Press, 2007.

Marryat, Florence. *The Blood of the Vampire*. Leipzig: Bernard Tauchnitz, 1897.

Melton, J. Gordon. *The Vampire Book: The Encyclopedia of the Undead*. London: Visible Ink, 2011.

Moore, Lisa. "'Something More Tender Still than Friendship': Romantic Friendship in Early-Nineteenth-Century England." *Feminist Studies* 18: 3 (1992), 499-520.

Musaeus, Grammaticus. *Hero and Leander: From the Greek of Musaeus*. Trans Edwin Arnold. London: Cassell, Petter & Galpin, 1873.

Nethercot, Arthur. "Coleridge's 'Christabel' and Lefanu's 'Carmilla.'" *Modern Philology* 47: 1 (1949), 32-38.

Paglia, Camille. "'Christabel.'" *Samuel Taylor Coleridge*. Ed. Harold Blood. New York: Chelsea House, 1986. 217-229.

Paglia, Camille. *Sexual Personae: Art and Decadence from Nefertiti to Emily Dickenson*. New York: Vintage Books, 1991.

Patrick, Michael D. "Christabel: A Brief Critical History and Reconsideration." *Salzburg Studies in English Literature under the Direction of Professor Erwin Stürzl*, Vol. 11. Ed. James Hogg. Salzburg: Universität Salzburg, 1973. 1-35.

Ridenhour, Jamieson. "'If I Wasn't a Girl, Would You Like Me Anyway?' Le Fanu's *Carmilla* and Alfredson's *Let the Right One In*." *Universal Vampire: Origins and Evolution of a Legend*. Eds. Barbara Brodman and James E. Doan. Blue Ridge Summit, PA: Fairleigh Dickinson, 2013. 165-176.

Rossetti, Christina. *The Goblin Market and Other Poems*. 2nd ed. London: Macmillan, 1865.

Rusking, John. *Sesame and Lilies, Two Lectures Delivered at Manchester in 1864*. London: Smith, Elder & Co, 1865.

Sabriye, Sezer. 2012. "Sheridan Le Fanu's 'Carmilla': A Different Vampire Story." *Mediterranean Journal Of Humanities* 2: 2 (2012), 143-49.

Signorotti, Elizabeth. 1996. "'Repossessing the Body': Transgressive Desire in 'Carmilla' and Dracula." *Criticism* 38: 4 (1996), 607-32.

Skal, David J. *V is for Vampire: The A-Z Guide to Everything Undead*. New York: Plum, 1996.

Smith, J. Percy. "Critic and Christabel." *University of Toronto Quarterly* 21: 1 (1951), 14-26.

Smith-Rosenberg, Carroll. "The Female World of Love and Ritual: Relations between Women in Nineteenth-Century America." *Signs* 1: 1 (1975), 1-29.

Spielmann, Marion Harry. "The Paris Salons." *The Magazine of Art* 22 (1898), 489-497.

Stableford, Brian. "The Glass of Blood." *Blood and Roses: the vampire in 19th century literature*. Ed. Adele Oivia Gladwell. London: Creation Books, 1999.

Stableford, Brian. "Sang for Supper: Notes on the Metaphorical Use of Vampires in The Empire of Fear and Young Blood." *Blood Read: The Vampire as Metaphor in Contemporary Culture*. Eds. Loan Gordon and Veronica Hollinger. University of Pennsylvania Press, Philadelphia, 1997. 69-84.

Swann, Karen. "Literary Gentlemen and Lovely Ladies: The Debate on the Character of Christabel." *EHL* 52: 2 (1985), 397-418.

Taylor, Anya. *Erotic Coleridge: Women, Love and the Law Against Divorce*. New York: Palgrave Macmillan, 2005.

Tracy, Robert. "Loving You All Ways: Vamps Vampires Necrophiles and Necrofilles in Nineteenth-Century Fiction." *Sex and Death in Victorian Literature*. Ed. Regina Barreca. Bloomington: Indiana University Press, 1990. 32-59.

Tracy, Robert. "Sheridan Le Fanu and the Unmentionable." *The Unappeasable Host: Studies in Irish Identity*. Ed. Robert Tracy. Dublin: University College of Dublin Press, 1998. 57-72.

Twitchell, James B. *The Living Dead: A Study of the Vampire in Romantic Literature*. Durham, NC: Duke University Press, 1981.

"The Vampire versus the Phaenix." *The Pharmaceutical Journal and Transactions* 5. 1874. 20.

Willburn, Sarah. "The Savage Magnet: Racialization of the Occult in Late Victorian Fiction." *Women's Writing* 15: 3 (2008), 436-453.

IV.

The Sympathetic and Merciful Vampire

Carmilla: Illustrated by D. H. Friston. In *The Dark Blue*, March 1872, 70-71.

10.
"My Greatest Torture is Life Itself:" The Tragic or Sympathetic Vampire in the Nineteenth Century

Introduction

From the partial vampire Ruth (*I Am Legend*) to Eli (*Let the Right One In*); from Barnabas (*Dark Shadows*) to Spike (*Buffy the Vampire Slayer*); from Louis (*Interview with a Vampire*) to Tara (*True Blood*); from Gilda (*The Gilda Stories*) to Cassidy (*The Preacher*), books, television, and the movies are full of tragic and sympathetic vampires. Did they just spring on the scene *ex nihilo*, responding simply to contemporary conditions and attitudes, or did they have antecedents, even as far back as the nineteenth century? If the latter what is the current state of research on the subject?

There have been two opposing ways to deal with the questions in works examining the issue. The first is to hold that the nineteenth century was completely void of them; there were no precursors to the twentieth and twenty-first ones. This take on the living-impaired is largely due to the fact that investigators are preoccupied with Dracula. There may be a passing phrase about other options, but there generally will be little attempt to describe them. As Jules Zanger in "Metaphor into Metonymy" (1997) wrote "Although the vampire myth had appeared in literature in a variety of forms from the beginning of the nineteenth century, it was Stoker's vampire that caught and dominated the public imagination" (Zanger 17).

So in this context, the nineteenth-century vampire is mostly treated as Dracula writ small and therefore as lacking anything that might elicit sympathy. It is a creature of darkness; an Antichrist; a devil devoid of humanity;[141] an immoral and inhuman monster existing solely to ruin lives;[142] a Gothic,[143] evil,[144] power-hungry villain.[145]

There have been a few attempts to note alternatives to Dracula, yet they arrive at the same conclusion. Victoria Nelson, *Gothicka* (2021) adds Polidori's Lord Ruthven to Dracula which for her also precludes the possibility of a tragic vampire in the era, since Ruthven is not one either (Nelson 121). Samantha George and Bill Hughes point to the diversity of the nineteenth-century vampire detailed in Christopher Frayling's celebrated book, *Vampyres: Lord Byron to Count Dracula*, and with him deny there could be a sympathetic vampire at the time (George and Hughes 1-2) They are, of course, limited by Frayling's four categories: the Satanic

---

[141] See Fenicchia 1, 2, 17, 24.
[142] See Orlomoski 1, 46.
[143] See Melton 120-21.
[144] Guðmundsdóttir 6.
[145] Hudders 15.

Lord; the Fatal Woman; the Unseen Force; the Folkloric Vampire, so the closure to such an alternative is already there.[146] The new strand that they locate with Frayling—the vampire with a conscience—does not belong in the nineteenth century; because it is "new," it pertains only to what was recent in 1991.

Polidori's vampire, Lord Ruthven, was clearly Byronic, as will be shown. In her "The deformed transformed" (2013), Conrad Aquilina writes "'Aristocratically aloof, unfailingly elegant, and invariably merciless' is how Anne Rice's Lestat describes Byron's descendants" (33; cf. Rice 436), that is, the nineteenth-century vampire.[147]

The other course holds that there were such vampires. The first and primary one is, surprisingly, Polidori's Lord Ruthven. Beyond simply asserting it as does Lima 266, one can declare him sympathetic by superimposing the Byronic hero on him, as, for example, Recht 87-88 does. Another is to note that Ruthven uses different methods than Dracula to entrap his prey and takes alternative measures with men and with women. With men this includes friendship and intimacy.[148]

René Carat (*Une Forme du Mal du Siècle*, 1904) described the Byronic hero thus: he is cold and keeps to himself; he tends to isolate himself and to detest human company; he is doleful, fierce, and proudly silent (Carat 50). Lord Macaulay famously said in his 1903 "Moore's Life of Lord Byron" that he is "a man proud, moody, cynical, with defiance on his brow, and misery in his heart, a scorner of his kind, implacable in revenge, yet capable of deep and strong affection" (335). It is the doleful and miserable side, the capacity for affection that is missing not only from Lord Ruthven but from Darvell, the antihero of a story fragment by Lord Byron that Polidori depended upon. Leonard Wolf, in *British writers. Supplement III* (1996), has typified him as "aloof, brilliant, chilling, fascinating to women, and coolly evil" (385).[149] Nothing of sorrow here. Darvell is too undeveloped to draw any conclusions. He could go either way, but goes neither as things stand.

Moreover Ruthven's friendship appears to be inauthentic from the beginning. He perceives and takes advantage of Aubrey's naiveté. He openly acts in ways that will provoke Aubrey's disdain. When Aubrey reacts, Ruthven punishes him by killing his beloved in Greece. Then he restores the friendship and gives his life for him, first exacting from him an oath. Finally, restored by moonlight, he uses the promise to silence Aubrey and drive him mad as he prepares to marry and kill his beloved sister.

---

[146] The same may be said about Perkowski's four categories: Psychotic, Psychic, Folkloric, Literary (*The Darkling* 54; *Vampire Lore* 611-12. The first two are real; the latter mythic and fictional. Cf. Cornwell 106.
[147] See also Svoboda 38.
[148] It is said to go back to Auerbach 14-18. Cf Abbott 145. 1995 may seem a late date to start analysis, but Tim Kane (*The Changing Vampire of Film and Television*, 2005) finds that the appearance of sympathetic vampires in visual media does not begin in earnest until 1987. Cf. Dudek 15. She traces the sympathetic vampire in print to Anne Rice's *Interview with a Vampire* (1976).
[149] Nodier's Lord Ruthwen (1820) might qualify depending on how one interprets his speech when he first meets Malvina: "Oh, my friend, my whole being is reassured by her sight. You know, blasted by misfortunes, isolated on earth, you see me ever ready to abandon, without regret, the nothingness which surrounds me to seek a nothingness as yet unknown. This angel, this dream alone can attach me to existence. It's with her that I am awaiting a new life" (Nodier, Jouffroy, Merle 110. I read it as manipulation; Stuart 48-49, considers it at face value. There are two renditions of the Lord Ruthven character that do qualify but they will be considered later.

Everything is calculated. He seems to develop friendships with men to exploit them, undercut them, and destroy them ruthlessly as a game. He uses their sense of personal honor in order to exploit them, even to make them work against the social good to their ultimate discredit. It is hard for me to see this as eliciting sympathy.

One might want to make a case for Dracula, as Kathryn McGinley in her "Development of the Byronic" (1996), does with her comments about him, as a development of the Byronic vampire. Dracula's statement, to which McGinley refers, that "I too can love" has no tragic overtones since there is no loss, separation, or even vulnerability. One can argue, also with McGinley, that he was tormented because of the change in his visage as he is crumbling to dust: "there was in the face a look of peace" (Stoker 1897, 352). But there is no sign of it in his undead existence. And from Lucy we know a vampire experiences no reluctance or sorrow when first risen from the dead.

I therefore must reject the claim. He is an example, in part, of the vampire who is described by the anonymous author of "Vampires" (1887), as "showing marked partiality in its choice of a victim, being attracted to some one person in especial, lavishing upon him or her unwholesome endearments, delaying with an epicure's instinct the gratification of its abominable propensity, and gloating over the unconscious doomed one with something of a lover's ecstasy" (144). That is about it.

This leaves us with only four genuine precursors: Lamia and Clarimonde receive a sentence apiece by Margaret Carter in "The Vampire" (2007): the former presents "a sympathetic perspective on the title character" (621) and the latter is an "early example of the sympathetic vampire" (623). These are hardly more than assertions. Varney glides by in but a couple of sentences by Milly Williamson in her article on the *The Lure of the Vampire*: "Varney's was not the threat of domination, but instead the lure of intimacy.... This vampire continues to depict the essence of the outsider, the tortured soul, a figure at odds with its ontological being" (71-72).[150] Likewise *Carmilla* is covered in only half a page in Stacey Abbott's *Undead Apocalypse* (2016): "Le Fanu's *Carmilla* is told from the human Laura's point of view and largely presents Carmilla as sympathetic, a much needed companion. ... [D]espite Laura's seeming reticence, the story remains one of intimacy and friendship" (145-146). We shall be dealing with these below.

There are other alternatives, but they are beyond the scope of this paper. Milly Williamson is primarily interested in themes from the nineteenth century that make for the sympathetic vampires of the twentieth and twenty-first centuries rather than individual vampires: rebelliousness, domestication, intimacy, melodrama (29-30). And there also has been an endeavor to find an antecedent outside the vampire—in H. Rider Haggard's *She* (Lauren Fleck-Steff, "H. Rider Haggard's She and the Birth of the Sympathetic Vampire," 2010).[151]

In any case, with either of the two ways described above, there is precious little to work with. The one zero; the other four. In actual fact, I want to argue, there are actually quite a few, around fifty, and they approach the idea of the tragic vampire that elicits our sympathy in, by my count, eleven different ways.

---

[150] Dudek (16) concurs. Recht (88) argues that Varney was the first sympathetic vampire of serial literature and had a large influence on Barnabas Collins, Louis de Pointe du Lac, Angel, and Spike.
[151] I had access only to the introduction before it seemingly was expunged from the internet.

Let me end with a *caveat lector*: the reader may want to take issue with some of the divisions and selections, for they include so-called human vampires, where one might expect sympathy to arise. But I consider such inclusion to be necessary. This metaphorical application of the term to living humans was the primary way the vampire was treated in the latter half of the century. To cut this off would create an obstacle to a full analysis on account of contemporary prejudices of what a vampire can be in this context. And like the vampire monster, living ones are mainly evil. The following examples of human vampires are tragic; they were called and understood as vampires at the time; they obviously precede current sympathetic vampires and so can be seen as opening space for their existence and development later.

The Tragic Vampire

Tragic due to Inadvertency

First are the ones who live under the burden of being vampires while alive and possibly living an ostracized life. They are designated such at birth, creating the risk that they will grow up conforming to society's expectations and become what it fears. In South Russia, according to Juljan Jaworskij, "Südrussishche Vampyre" (1898), it is said that if a pregnant woman looks at the "grand entrance" of the priest, her child will be a vampire. Vampires, it continues, are powerful and nefarious in life and even worse in death (331). In Prussia infants born with a thin membrane over their faces have to have rituals performed otherwise they will turn into vampires (Knoop 138-139). Living vampires were not just theoretical then. Dick Donovan, for example, tells in his book of short stories, "The Woman with the 'Oily Eyes" (1899), a tale he heard of a woman in India who was beaten to death as a vampire because she allegedly lured men to her by mesmerism and drank their blood (40).

Lokis is a story told by Prosper Mérimée (1869), of a count, thought to be and therefore treated by his mother from infancy onward as the product of her being raped by a bear. On his wedding night, he murders his bride by biting open her throat.

Annette, as told by Dick Donovan, in "Sequel to the Woman with the 'Oily Eyes'" (1899), did not open her eyes until she was one year old and they were reputed to be like those of a snake. She went through an exorcism ceremony. As a child, her strange, but harmless behavior provoked calls for her death so she had to be secreted away to a convent. She grows up to be a serial polyandrist, marrying strong and wealthy men only to cause them to weaken, leeched of their blood, before they die and she inherits their fortunes.

Then there are good people who, to their horror, face becoming vampires after death. John Stagg, "The Vampyre" (1810), tells the tale of Herman who is being attacked nightly by his dead friend and is dying. He tells his wife 'When dead I too shall seek your death" and so asks her that when he pass away she stake him.

A young lady, according to Prosper Mérimée, "Sur Le Vampirisme" (1827), is assaulted by a vampire and immediately begins to fade, although her parents try everything to save her. On her deathbed she calls her father and makes him promise that after she passes he will cut off her head and sever the tendons behind her knees "that she not become a vampyre."

Edmund Ollier, in "Vampyres" (1855) paints a personal picture of an encounter with a vampire. Each night it comes, he states, and sucks your blood at the heart and you grow paler and more languid. You die and then the worst begins. "You are then yourself forced to become a Vampyre and to create fresh victims, who, as they die, add to the phantom stock" (39).

Tragic because of Religion or Philosophy

Théophile Gautier in his *Arria Marcella* (1852), tells a story of how Octavian, on a tour of Pompeii, falls in love with the form of a woman molded in the fiery lava. By force of this love, he is transported over the centuries and she from deep within the realm of death to meet in the old city before the volcanic destruction and dally with each other.[152] In the midst of their delight and enjoyment, an austere Christian enters uninvited and against their wills sends her back into the void prepared for unrepentant pagans and him to his own era. Octavian grieves for her the rest of his life, although he lives a good one.

John Keats writes in 1820, that the eponymous goddess Lamia had become infatuated with a young Corinthian, so she changes her shape into a woman from that of a snake. When he meets her, he falls instantly in love. They spend time in bliss together, Lamia taking a big risk in making herself vulnerable to him. Finally, due to his persistent requests, Lamia consents to marry him as long as his philosophy teacher Apollonius is not invited. He turns up at the ceremony anyway and discovers her true identity as a lamia. She laments her loss as he destroys her. The groom dies that same night, so Apollonius has done him no favor.

Herinrich Heine in "Gods in Exile" (1853) imagines what if the Greek and Latin gods were real. Early Christianity treated them as demons, dethroning them and destroying their holy places. Many of them were forced to become day laborers drinking beer instead of nectar. Apollo, in his fantasy, was discovered, confessed under torture, and was executed. When suspicions arose that he was a vampire they moved to disinter and stake him but his grave was found empty. Bacchus became a Franciscan monk who once a year celebrated his ancient revelry in secret accompanied by vampires. All of them have been harassed by Christians into living clandestinely.

Tragic due to Inevitability or Necessity

The story of Julius Courtney may be placed here, but it is better suited for the final category: Tragic for not Wanting to Victimize. So we turn to Poe's 1839 "The house of Usher." The title refers to both lineage of the inhabitants and structure of the house: the two are in a feedback loop, feeding on each other like vampires.[153] In the lineage, the brother and sister, the last members of the family,

---

[152] She is called an "orientalized female vampire" by Pal-Lapinski (3).
[153] James Twitchell has argued "The Fall of the House of Usher" became, early in the twentieth century, a central means to discuss the use of the vampire in Poe (124-127).

are vampires to each other; the house is inextricably linked to them both. The brother buries his twin sister alive and she rises to confront him. This proves the death of both of them. With this final encounter the house falls in both senses. The dialectic at both levels leaves the destruction inescapable and the inhabitants know it.

Francis Faversham is the most miserable of men, according to T. F. Ridgwell's "Told in a First-Class Smoker" (1898) for he thinks he is causing his beloved fiancée's deathly illness by unwillingly sapping her life's energy to bolster his own. The doctor, after several dead ends with a diagnosis, remains dubious. However in Faversham's absence she does improve and with his return she weakens near death again. They break up, he tries to commit suicide, and in the end he dies on the battlefield in an act of conspicuous bravery.

Florence Marryat in her 1897 *The Blood of the Vampire* writes a tale where her heroine, Harriet Brandt, is one of the most, if not the most tragic vampire of the nineteenth century. After ten years in a convent where she was under strict surveillance and friendships were forbidden, she is released and tries desperately to be close to people with her limited social skills. They either pull away or become ill. Near the end of the story, she discovers that she has a hereditary vampirism so that whosoever she draws close to suffers and often dies. Finally, after a very brief period of marital bliss, after which her husband dies while still on the honeymoon, she decides to end her endangerment to others, her own misery, and her lineage by taking her life.

Tragic on account of Longevity

"The Pale Woman" by Arthur Symons (1898) is the portrait of a woman who has experienced so much death in her lifetime, has outlived so many of those she has loved, that she has entered a kind of living death void of all desire except the desiring of desire. The eponymous Vampire Countess exclaims four times in her story variations of "Kill me! My greatest torture is life itself" (Féval 1856). Rymer's Varney the Vampire (1845-1847) laments that it has been 180 years since he was happy. "How long is this hated life to last?" he mutter[s]. "When shall I cease to be the loathsome creature I am?" More than once he has tried unsuccessfully to kill himself. Eventually he climbs the volcano Mt. Vesuvius and "tired and disgusted with a life of horror, he flung himself in to prevent the possibility of a reanimation of his remains" (ch. 170).[154]

According to Sabine Baring-Gould the eponymous heroine of "Margery of Quether" (1884) prayed for everlasting life to her Christian God and like Greek mythic figures Glaucus and the Sibyl of Cumae with their non-Christian gods her prayer is answered but without eternal youth and with endless aging.[155] She

---

[154] This is obviously based on the fabled suicide of the pre-Socratic philosopher, Empedocles, by throwing himself into the volcanic Mt. Etna (which, according to Diogenes Laertius' *Lives of Eminent Philosophers* [5.69] was to prove he had become a god). He became the subject of sentimentalist treatments at the time, like those by the great German Romantic poet, Friedrich Hölderlin, who published three different versions of his play *Tod des Empedokles* (*Death of Empedocles*) between 1798 and 1826.

[155] Margery is counted as a vampire by Eighteen-Bisang and Dalby (2011). I have argued above that the vampire here is the bat.

is forced to be alone and live in concealment, except for a short time when she was shown love and was able to draw youth from a man. He does not mind the transfer and prepares for death but she finally is forced to give most of it back. He does not want her to go back to what she was so he stops at middle age and he worries about her wellbeing afterward as she must hide away (337-360; 466-485).

Winzy works for an alchemist and unwittingly drinks an elixir for everlasting life (Mary Wollstonecraft, "The Mortal Immortal," 1834).[156] He marries the love of his life and lives with her as she grows old and dies. He is now in his 323rd year and has never remarried. "[T]he more I live, the more I dread death, even while I abhor life." Thus unwilling to kill himself, he is setting off on an expedition no mortal can endure, hoping this will liberate his soul, which thirsts for freedom, from its tenacious bodily cage. In 1,600 BCE, according to Arthur Conan Doyle in his "Ring of Thoth" (1890), a young Egyptian man inoculates himself with a serum of immortality, but his beloved dies before he can do the same to her.[157] For some 3,500 years he has been faithful to her and has sought to find an antidote in order to rejoin her in the afterlife. He finally finds it and dies hugging to himself the mummy of his lover.

Tragic by Reason of an Assignment

The eponymous Spalatro, a wayward youth, meets an old man in Rome and through him his "daughter," whom the old man conjures up and who is the archetype of beauty to him, albeit "pale and bloodless as the dead (Sheridan Le Fanu, "Spalatro" 453)."[158] He encounters her several times alone and in company; her face always showing a sorrow and pity for him. She warns him not to pursue her or, especially, declare his love to her, but he does both. Upon doing the latter, she disappears back into her "quiet," her appeals unheeded, until the male powers have need of her again. He is now owned by these same forces and becomes an outlaw, his soul promised to hell.

As the above is an ambassador from hell, the *Virgin Vampire* is one from heaven, although she likewise is destined for hell—in Lamothe-Langon's 1825 story.[159] A colonel is severely wounded in Hungary, comes to love his benefactress, and takes a blood oath pledging himself to her in marriage. Upon recovery he goes his way and has a proper French family. She meanwhile commits suicide and is sent back to him as a vampire by God's providence to punish him with hell for his infidelity. The repeated descriptions of her suffering after he left her are deeply moving. At first she is emotionless and mechanical in her mission but as she slowly kills his son and wife she begins to regret it. She warns him not to want

---

[156] This is seen as a vampire story by Jo Zebedee (*The Secret Bookshelf* 2014). Gordon and Hollinger in their "Introduction: The Shape of Vampires" (1997), without citing this story, that it is the change of perspective or point of view, adapting Wollstonecraft/ Shelley's narrative strategy in *Frankenstein*, that made the "domestication" (hence the "sympathetication") of the vampire possible (2). The innovation here is particularly striking, since the vampire's story is told completely in the first-person.

[157] This seems a strange selection for a vampire tale, but it appears as such in Robert Eighteen-Bisang and Martin H. Greenberg, *Vampire Stories: Sir Arthur Conan Doyle* (2009), 66-85.

[158] The daughter is called a vampire, for example, by Andrew Boylan (59-62).

[159] Theodor Hildebrand, *Der Vampyr* basically duplicates this French story in German (1828).

to marry her after the death of his wife, but he becomes insistent. At the wedding, she does not touch him with her hidden, skeleton hand to kill him, so it appears she sacrifices herself to eternal perdition without taking him with her.

Tragic because of Unintentionality

We have already noted the stories about Faversham and Brandt. Penthesilea meets Achilles on the battlefield of the Trojan War as adversaries and in their competitions come to love and respect each other (Heinrich von Kleist *Penthesilea: A Tragic Drama*, 1808).[160] Achilles finally sets aside his armor to surrender himself to her, but she, in full battle fury, attacks him with her dogs and tears him apart with her teeth. When she regains her senses and learns what she has done, she takes her life. Charles Nodier, "De Quelques Phénomènes du Sommeil" (1831), relates the story of a young man who was on the run from the law and was joined by a woman who would not leave him. In a severely weakened state she seemed to say to him, "Eat me if you are hungry." She died shortly thereafter and he buried her. Now, nightly in a nightmare, he disinters and devours her. He thus describes himself, in his despair and under this curse, as a vampire.

Tragic due to Loss of Companionship

There are two types here: a vampire living without his companion; a vampire sacrificing herself for her companion.[161] We have already noted the stories of Winzy and the Egyptian, where men live faithful but lonely lives for centuries even millennia after their one true love has died. One somewhat like them is a folktale from Santorin told by James Emerson, *Letters from the Aegean* (1829). While Demetrio is abroad he loses his reputation and his beloved dies of sorrow. When he returns he is ostracized, but is unbothered by it in his grief for his lover. He disappears and weeks later begins to appear again without hurting anyone and avoiding all; he simply visits his fiancée's grave in the dead of the night. The villagers, now repentant, locate his exposed, deceased body, exorcize it so it may rest, and bury it next to his love. Interestingly he is not reunited with her with his first death. He is called a "Vampire of the Cyclades."

A story of Apollonius is related by Philostratus in the early third century CE of his disciple marrying a lamia (*Life of Apollonius of Tyana*, 402-409). He unmasks her and declares to his disciple that he has been cherishing a snake (ὄφιν θάλπεις καὶ σὲ ὄφις). She admits, with false tears, that she was seducing him to feed on him and he forces her to disappear, thereby saving him. In 1621, Robert Burton retells it in a section of his book, *The Anatomy of Melancholy* dealing with "love-melancholy" (434). This time there is no reference to deception—she appears really to love him and her weeping seems sincere. This allows space for early female vampires to regret what they do and to miss their lovers legitimately as they vanish, as we saw in Keats' poem.

---

[160] Susanne Kord calls Penthesilea a "domesticated" or "virtuous vampire," one conforming to gender and sexual stereotypes at the time (Kord 72), whereas Christopher Frayling, *Vampyres: From Lord Byron to Count Dracula*, says she defies a single vampire categorization (42-43).

[161] It is gendered this way. It would take us too far afield to analyze why.

Then there is the most tragic in this category and it is a development of Lamia and the virgin vampire. According to Alexandre Dumas in his *The Vampire: Drama in 5 Acts* (1851), a female vampire falls in love with a young man and saves him from an attack by a male vampire but cannot save his sister. Later she attaches herself to his fiancée and when the two mortals are assaulted by the same male vampire she offers to save him again if he will only declare his love to her. When he pleads for the life of his beloved in addition to his own she explains she cannot without dying herself, for revealing how to kill another vampire is a capital offence. When he and his fiancée make a suicide pact rather than die by the vampire, she sacrifices herself and tells him the secret so he shall live and be happy, even without her. She dies in his arms.

Tragic on account of Separation by Death

Here dead women become vampires to maintain their relationship with their living beloved. The partner of a deceased woman awakens with yellow bruises on his body and remembers stories of the dead returning, lying down next to their love, and leaving behind such marks by their kisses (Théophile Gautier, "The Yellow Marks," 1845). Did she return during the night "to pay the debt of kisses" she owes him? Heinrich Heine aks in his *Book of Songs* (1827). A young monk conjures up his dead lover. She approaches him mournfully and sits down beside him. "They gaze at each other and are silent." Heine also writes in number 46 of his "Lyrical Interlude" in the *Book of Songs*, about the daughter of a king with a pallid and tear-stained face who sits next to her love as he explains that he cares not for the throne and wants only her. She responds by reminding him she is dead "And only by night can I be by your side, To your loving caresses replying" (79).

A Countess dies (in Villiers de l'Isle-Adam's *Sardonic Tales*, 1874). The Count, rather innocently, creates the conditions for her return, by living as if she did not die, by treating her as present in everything he does. The decision, then, to include her in everything "as if" she were still physically there, draws her back by an irresistible attraction. She struggles and fights to make herself tangible to him again. But when she finally succeeds, when she has left the confines of her coffin, taken up the key, exited the crypt, and entered the room, the spell is momentarily broken for him and his mental control falters by the sudden recognition of her as dead. With that, the natural irreversible separation between the dead and the living resumes and she disappears.

Emily Brontë in *Wuthering Heights* (1847) relates a story how a boyhood of cruelty against Heathcliff results in a cruel, vengeful man, who adores the only one who ever loved him when he was young. And she loves him preeminently although she married another. Both see themselves as two bodies with a single soul. There are a number of studies noting the vampiric features of this man, Heathcliff, and there are worries expressed in the book itself about him being one. Catherine is another sympathetic vampire according to Carol A. Senf (83-84). She haunts him after her death, because she wished never to be parted from him and so promised she would be restless in her grave for him and because he demanded that she do so. This becomes magnified and more tangible when he opens up her casket shortly before his death of lovesickness, for she appears undecayed and then is seen abroad by others as well and heard trying to return to her old room. Neither had ever responded to the Christian notion of heaven. To her it was the Heights where she grew up and for him simply to be with her. When he dies, twenty years after her, both are reported to be observed walking together on the moors. They attack no one; they simply stroll together and look out at her paradise, as they did as children.

Tragic by Reason of Misidentification

Richard Dowling's "A Gruesome Tale" (1895) describes a couple that neighbors are betting will divorce, but they have a son, making it less likely they will. They take in a renter who does not go out, is, as seen from the window, very friendly with the wife during the day, and does not stand when she enters the room, so rumors start again. A fire breaks out when the husband is away and the wife is running errands. A window breaks and a creature emerges. A dog? No. A bear? No. Now it appears to be a vampire bat. Finally the bat turns into a legless man carrying the son in a sheet. He lowers the child to safety and then declares to the neighbors that he himself is going to re-enter the fire to keep from "the laughter of your eyes and the jeering of your tongues." He vanishes in the smoke and flames.

A young man, two years married, is on holiday in the city where his mother and sister live (in Stanislaw Przybyszewski's "De Profundis," 1895). Recently he has been suffering sudden fevers which bring on delirium and hallucinations. He, in a fit of madness, reads a letter from his wife which convinces him that his sister, Agaj, is in love with him. In this state of mind she comes to him and they make violent, passionate love together. He sees her as his savior and terror—his Mother Mary and his vampire. Soon he actually does meet Agaj and he declares to her his love and adoration; she is horrified with, dumbstruck by, and disappointed in him. It goes back and forth from real encounters where she keeps her distance to wild visions where his fantasies are played out. In one of them she refers to herself as his vampire. But she is in actuality neither his vampire nor his Virgin Mary. Rather she is being assaulted by her brother as he plays out the wish for an incestuous affair brought on by fits of insanity.

Jan Neruda's "Vampire" (1871) tells of a local artist who joins a group on an excursion to Vienna which includes a Polish girl, who is seriously ailing, her lover, and her family. He sketches while everyone else enjoys the view. When her lover later asks a hotel-keeper about the artist, he answers venomously that he is called "The Vampire" because unerringly whoever he paints dies when he is done. The young man then attacks the artist, the girl appears to faint, and the portrait is exposed to everyone: it is of the girl. This does not appear to be deliberate or done with malicious intent.

Angelo is thought to be a vampire because he was subject to a *Scheintod*,[162] an apparent death, two years before the action in the novel, which left him with a permanently pale complexion (in Carl Spindler's "Der Vampyr und seine Braut," 1826). He keeps it a secret but one of the guests of a party he attends witnessed a death and burial at that time, and is certain this is the man. Using this revelation as leverage, his enemies play upon the vampire superstitions of his fiancée and her brother to destroy his chances of happiness. Then a duel is provoked in which he is mortally wounded. Right before his death his fiancée learns the truth—of his rescue by a grave robber and of his saving of her son's life by sucking a wound he had received to get the blood flowing and not to drink it, as he was accused—so he is able to die in peace.

Arsène Arnaud Clarétie tells the story (in *The Man with the Waxen Hands*, 1866) of a Marquis who knows what the distinguishing characteristic of a vampire is—pale, waxen, delicate hands—and his fiancée's family is acquainted with such a man. That man, in turn, believes a mark of distinction is the same and so sleeps with his hands suspended above him. When the Marquis' beloved complains of being sick, he is certain what he must do. He gains access to the man's bedchamber and executes him.

Adèle is sure she knows what is causing the general illness of the village and specifically of her son, and it is not living next to an undrained swamp (Eliza Lynn Linton, "The Fate of Madame Cabanel," 1872). It is her master's new, gentle, healthy wife, an outsider. Certain she has been proved a vampire when her son dies, Adèle whips up some men of the village who abduct her and take her to the pit outside the village to throw her in. Due to their rough handling, she dies on the way.

The worst of these tales, related by Balzac, "The Succubus" (1837), is of a young woman standing before the inquisition in the thirteenth century on charges of being a succubus, or a "vampire who feeds on souls, [a] tigrish nature that drinks blood." (42). Over thirty witnesses testify and all but two, one a Jew, damn her as a seductress and blasphemer. She is condemned to be burned alive. A rescue attempt is thwarted and then she escapes, leading the guards on a prolonged chase, but she is apprehended and committed to the flames. It is later demonstrated that she was innocent and the charges the result of various jealousies.

Tragic by Virtue of Needing to be Loved

Carmilla by Sheridan Le Fanu (1871-72) has two types of victims: peasants who are beneath her and whose lives she takes quickly; those who are of her own station whom she loves and whose affection she seeks in return. She takes their lives slowly and seductively and seems to want to savor their blood. She may be sly, cunning, well practiced at subterfuge, and operating with a treacherous motive, but she also sincerely wants a romantic friendship and bonds of care with her prey.

---

[162] Apparent deaths were, of course, a topic of discussion in the nineteenth century. Perhaps the most celebrated early example was Anne Greene, *Newes from the dead. Or A true and exact narration of the miraculous deliverance of Anne Greene* (1651). Part of this book was republished in John Ashton, "Sus. per Coll." (1887), 51-54.

Further she did not want the vampirism that was inflicted upon her; she herself was a victim. Laura asks her about her first ball. "'I remember everything

"Carmilla" illustrated by M. Fitzgerald (705).

about it—with an effort. I see it all, as divers see what is going on above them ... There occurred that night what has confused the picture, and made its colours faint. I was all but assassinated in my bed, wounded here,' she touched her breast, 'and never was the same since'" (604). A modern reader can hardly but feel regret when the patriarchal authorities step in, pursue Carmilla, mutilate her body, and usurp the narrative from Laura to give Carmilla the most crass of intentions.

Tragic for not Wanting to Victimize

There are essentially three types: initial hesitation with the current victim; anguish over killing one's family; self-loathing at what one is.

Of the lamia or vampire Geraldine, before climbing into bed with Christabel, it is said: "Ah! what a stricken look was hers!/ Deep from within she seems half-way/ To lift some weight with sick assay,/ And eyes the maid and seeks delay" (Coleridge 54). "The Cold Beloved" by Joseph Freiherr von Eichendorff ("Das kalte Liebschen," 1816) tries to talk her lover out of wanting to join her in the tomb, but when he touches her their exchange ends "He: Chills and shivers run through my skin. She: The kiss of death brings insanity.—He: Alas! this breaks my young life within! She: You'll join me in the grave endlessly."[163] The victim of "La Belle Dame" is developed by John Keats (1820) and he declares, after being left dying by the woman, "She took me to her elfin grot,/ And there she wept and sighed full sore."[164]

---

[163] Heide Crawford, *The Origins of the Literary Vampire* (2016), includes an analysis of this poem albeit without a full translation (59-65). I am no poet, so I apologize for my translation.
[164] Twitchell sees this as about a lamia (100-101). It is hard to disagree.

According to Augustus Harris, *Ruthven: A Drama in Four Acts* (1859), Lord Ruthven, before the wedding, after which he must kill his wife, reflects "How beautiful she looks! I would spare her!" before he overcomes the feeling. In James Robinson Planché's 1820 play, *The Vampire: or, The Bride of the Isles*, Lord Ruthven has to feed on his virgin bride at a particular time each year to continue his existence. He reflects on his situation: "Demon as I am, that walks the earth to slaughter and devour! The little that remains of heart within this wizard frame, sustained alone by human blood, shrinks from the appalling act of planting misery in the bosom of this veteran chieftain. Still must the fearful sacrifice be made" (7).

Then there is the second type. Lord Byron in his *Giaour, A Fragment of a Turkish Tale* (1813), describes how a curse is laid on an infidel by the family of one he has killed that he will become a vampire: ". . . from thy daughter, sister, wife,/ At midnight drain the stream of life;/ Yet loathe the banquet which perforce/ Must feed thy livid living corse." His family will recognize the infidel and die hating him. Worst of all he shall take the life of his beloved little daughter last. This malediction will be picked up by German renditions of the Lord Ruthven saga, the most recognizable vampire story of the nineteenth century, but as a confession of torment by the vampire of his first act after being turned; for example Marschner's 1828 opera, *Der Vampyr*. After that, however, he murders remorselessly.

A vampyre laments, in Feilix Dahn's "The Vampire" (1875), "Gladly would I like the other/ Dead my grave in quiet keep;/ Yet a ban eternal, cursèd,/ Makes me wander when all sleep" (22-23). He must visit his beloved and take her life. Finally we are directed to a story by William H. G. Kingston, "The Vampire; or, Pedro Pacheco and the Bruxa" (1863), of witch mothers, bruxas, who after an orgy and flying around as vampire bats, "Though feeling a human loathing for this terrific task, their horrible propensities overcome their maternal love, and seizing on their babes, their black wings fanning them to repose, they suck the life-blood from their veins—dreadful fate!" (74).

We have already noted Varney, Francis Faversham, and Harriet Brandt for the third kind. Goethe has a quick reference in his "*vampyrisches Gedicht*," as he called it[165] in "The Bride of Corinth" (1797). The vampire bride is promised to her living beloved and he will soon die to join her. She asks her Christian mother to incinerate their bodies according to the pagan customs and not to bury them. Otherwise "When his race is run, I must hasten on,/ And the young must 'neath my vengeance sink." She wants only to take him with her; she has no desire for others, although she would be driven by her nature to take their lives. This story also belongs among those who are separated due to religion and those who have lost a companion.

Count Vardalek is invited to stay with a family and he is drawn to the youngest child to supply him with life force (Eric Stanislaus Stenbock, "The Sad Story of a Vampire," 1894). He pines while psychically depleting him, "My darling, I fain would spare thee; but thy life is my life, and I must live, I who would rather die. Will God not have any mercy on me? Oh! oh! life; oh the torture of life! . . . O Gabriel, my beloved! my life, yes life—oh, why life?"

G. J. Whyte-Melville, "Bones and I" (1868) reveals Bones telling of his encounter with a beautiful vampire. As innocent, kindly men "sacrifice fortune

---

[165] For this turn of phrase see Goethe, *Tagebücher* 1, 381-82, the 4th and 6th of June 1797.

and profession" for her, even their lives, she exudes a sorrow and sadness at being trapped in such a life. She accepts it as inevitable, however, as something she cannot change—*c'est plus fort que moi*, she declares ("it is stronger than I," 144). She wishes she could age and die. Yet given a life in which she can mesmerize her prey as a snake and that renews itself from the vitality of its victims, she lives it as it is given to her. "Mine has been an unhappy life, and there seems to be no end, no resting-place," she laments.

Julius Courtney in Cobban's "Master of His Fate" (1889), is a man of uncommon charm and learning among his peers, but he also has a particularly close relationship to nature—its interchange of power and its indifference; he can draw life force from all around him but cannot feel sympathy or compassion.[166] That is until he falls in love with Nora and then he is horrified by his effect on her. He had been able to renew his youth, first by drawing from nature alone, then by limited contact with people, now only by prolonged contact pushing his victims into comatose states of sheer exhaustion. He needs to replenish more often, as well, or slip quickly into old age. He has never taken a life, but he is terrified, in this advanced state, he will kill the love of his life by their intimate touching. In light of this he goes out to sea, slips into the water, and disappears.

Thus far we have the options of continuing one's life as it is given or taking it. There is one other alternative however. Australie, "The Vampire Race" (1873) describes how Leonardo has learned that he is part of a vampire race where the males in the family have fed on the "strong warm life" of those closest to them, especially their wives who would only last a year after marriage. Although he is already involved with a woman he foreswears any hope of marriage and leaves her, ensuring the end of his race. Abroad he is informed that since he has left, his lover has weakened and is close to death, so he returns, tells her he loves her and that when she is strong enough he will explain to her his family secret so she can make an informed decision about her future with him. When she recovers and discovers the mystery she gladly marries him and one year later, as she lay dying, she rejoices in her decision. "Not for one hour have I repented of the choice I made."

Conclusion

It would be anachronistic to argue that the nineteenth-century tragic vampire exactly parallels the twentieth- and twenty-first-century ones. It does not. But it offers a far richer palette of options than it has previously been asserted to have. And many of the later strategies to garner reader sympathy are already being experimented with in the nineteenth century. In the story of Julius Courtney we have a vampire that is able to extract its nutrition without killing its victims. He even makes sure they will have treatment to recover. There are a number in which the vampire is at odds with its own nature, regretting it and wishing it were otherwise. The topic of longevity is broached—outliving one's mortal beloved.

Others include a fit of irrationality leading one accidently to kill one's lover; the intervention of religion destroying a mixed relationship; a vampire putting

---

[166] Courtney, in 1890, is called a spiritual vampire ("Reviews" 1890, 297) and a moral one (William Wallace, "Review of 'Master of his Fate'" 1890, 114).

itself at risk for intimacy with a human or sacrificing oneself for the life of a mortal lover; the mortal sacrificing oneself for a relationship with a vampire. All of these and more open the portals for later development. One need not look outside vampire literature for something similar to the current preoccupation with the sympathetic vampire. It is right there in its earliest manifestations. *Dracula* may have had a chilling effect on them, as the first approach delineated in the introduction avers,[167] but they were there all the time waiting to be rediscovered.

Works cited

Abbott, Stacey. *Undead Apocalypse: Vampires and Zombies in the Twenty-First Century.* Edinburgh: Edinburgh University Press, 2016.

Aquilina, Conrad. "The deformed transformed; of, from bloodsucker to Byronic hero—Polidori and the literary vampire." *Open graves, open minds: Representations of vampires and Undead from the Enlightenment to the present day.* Ed. Sam George and Bill Hughes. Manchester: Manchester University Press, 2013. 36-78.

Ashton, John. "Sus. per Coll." *Gentleman's Magazine.* January 1887. 48-57.

Auerbach, Nina. *Our Vampires, Ourselves.* Chicago: University of Chicago Press, 1995.

"Australie". "The Vampire Race: A Dramatic Poem." *The Sydney Mail and New South Wales Advertiser,* October 18, 1873. 515; 547.

Balzac, Honoré de. "The Succubus." *Droll Stories Collected from the Abbeys of Touraine.* London: John Camden Horen, 1874. 20-88 [1837].

Barring-Gould, Sabine. "Margery of Quether." *Cornhill Magazine,* April & May 1884. 337-60; 466-85.

Brontë, Emily (Ellis Bell). *Wuthering Heights: A Novel.* 2 vols. London: Thomas Cautley Newby, 1847

Boylan, Andrew M. *The Media Vampire: A Study of Vampires in Fictional Media.* Lulu.com, 2012.

Burdet, W. *A wonder of wonders. Being a faithful narrative and true relation of one Anne Green.* London: John Clowes, 1651.

Burmeister, Ludewig Peter August. *Der Vampyr.* Vols. 2-3, in *1838 Abendländische tausend und eine nacht, oder Die schönsten mährchen und sagen aller europäischen völke* Meissen: F. W. Goedsche, 1838. 235-254; 1-21.

Burton, Robert. *The Anatomy of Melancholy.* London: Henry Cripps, 1621.

Byron, George Gordon, Lord. *Giaour, A Fragment of a Turkish Tale.* London: Thomas Davison, 1813.

Canat, René. *Une Forme du Mal du Siècle, du Sentiment de la Solitude Morale au XIXe Siècle .* Paris: Libraire Hachette et Compagnie, 1904.

Carter, Margaret. "The Vampire." *Icons of Horror and the Supernatural: An Encyclopedia of Our Worst Nightmares.* 2nd ed. Ed. S. T. Joshi. Westport, CT: Greenwood Press, 2007. 619-52.

Clarétie, Arsène Arnaud. *The Man with the Waxen Hands.* Vol. 11, in *Sensation Novels: Pretty Babiole.* Ed. Du Boisgobey. London: Vizetelly, 1886. 184-192 [1866].

---

[167] Tim Kane, *The Changing Vampire of Film and Television* (2005) names the first cycle of vampire cinema as malignant (1931-48) followed by the erotic (1957-85), and only then by the sympathetic (1987-present). Sam George in her October 13, 2015, posting for *Open Graves, Open Minds* entitled ""The Emergence of the Sympathetic or Reluctant Vampire in Twentieth-Century Culture" places the first sympathetic vampire as Barnabas Collins in *Dark Shadows.* Many others have as well.

Cobban, James Maclaren. "Jules Courtney, Or, Master of his Fate." *Blackwood's Edinburgh Magazine* October-December 1889. 439-466; 581-591; 770-789.

Coleridge, Samuel Taylor. "Christabel." *Christabel; Kubla Khan, a vision; The pains of sleep.* London: William Bulmer, 1816. 3-48 [1800].

Conan Doyle, Arthur. "The Ring of Thoth." *Vampire Stories: Sir Arthur Conan Doyle.* Eds. Robert Eighteen-Bisang and Martin H. Greenberg. New York: Skyhorse Publishing, 2009. 66-85 [1890].

Cornwell, Neil. "European Gothic and nineteenth-century Russian literature." *European Gothic: A spirited exchange 1760-1960.* Ed. Avril Horner. Manchester: Manchester University Press, 2002. 104-127.

Crawford, Heide. *The Origins of the Literary Vampire.* Lanham: Rowman & Littlefield, 2016.

Dahn, Felix. "The Vampire." *German Lyrics.* Trans. Henry Phillips, Jr. Philadelphia: Printed for Private Circulation, 1892. 22-23 [1875].

Donovan, Dick. "Sequel to the Woman with the 'Oily Eyes:' The Story of Annette." *Tales of Terror.* London: Chatto & Windus, 1899. 41-50.

Donovan, Dick. "The Woman with the 'Oily Eyes.'" *Tales of Terror.* London: Chatto & Windus, 1899. 1-40.

Dowling, Richard. "A Gruesome Tale." *The Aukland Star.* 11 December 1895. 6 Christmas Supplement.

Dudek, Debra. *The Beloved Does Not Bite: Moral Vampires and the Humans Who Love Them.* New York: Rutledge, 2018.

Dumas, Alexandre. *The Vampire: Drama in 5 Acts. Lord Ruthven Returns.* Trans. Frank J. Morlock. Encino: Black Coat Press, 2004 [1851].

Eichendorff, Joseph Freiherr von. "Das kalte Liebschen." *Frauentaschenbuch für das Jahr*, 1816. 230-31.

Eighteen-Bisang, Robert, and Richard Dalby. *Vintage Vampire Stories.* New York: Skyhorse Publishing, 2011.

Emerson, James. *Letters from the Aegean.* Vol. 2. London: Henry Colburn, 1829.

Fenicchia, Lindsey M. "The Modern Vampire as Romantic Hero: Acceptance, Love and Self-Control." English Master's Thesis. State University of New York College at Brookport, 2012.

Féval, Paul. *The Vampire Countess.* Trans. Brian Stableford. Encino, CA: Black Coat Press, 2003 [1856].

Fleck-Steff, Lauren. "H. Rider Haggard's She and the Birth of the Sympathetic Vampire." Senior Thesis. Endicott College, 2010.

Frayling, Christopher. *Vampyres: Lord Byron to Count Dracula.* London: Faber & Faber, 1991.

Gautier, Théophile. *Arria Marcella.* in *The Works of Théophile Gautier.* 11. Trans. F. C. de Sumichrast. Cambridge: University Press, 1906. 315-67 [1852].

Gautier, Théophile. "The Yellow Marks." *One of Cleopatra's Nights and Other Fantastic Stories,* Trans. Lafcadio Hearn. New York: Worthington Co., 1882. 318-19 [1845].

George, Sam, and Bill Hughes. "Introduction: Undead Reflections: The Sympathetic Vampire and its Monstrous Other." *Gothic Studies* 15 :1 (May 2013), 1-7.

Goethe, Johann Wolfgang Goethe. *Tagebücher 1770-1810.* 1. *Gesammtausgabe.* 11 Ed. Gerhart Baumann. Stuttgart: J. G. Cotta'scher, 1806.

Goethe, Johann Wolfgang von. "The Bride of Corinth." *The Poems of Goethe.* Trans. Edgar Alfred Bowring. London: John W. Parker & Son, 1853. 182-88 [1797].

Goethe, Johann Wolfgang von. "Die Braut von Korinth." *Musen-Almanach für das Jahr 1798.* 1897. 88-99.

Gordon, Joan, and Veronica Hollinger. "Introduction: The Shape of Vampires." *Blood Read: The Vampire as Metaphor in Contemporary Culture.* Eds. Joan Hollinger & Veronica Gordon. Philadelphia: University of Pennsylvania Press, 1997. 1-7.

Guðmundsdóttir, Berglind. "The Vampire's Evolution in Literature: The Influence Bram Stoker's Dracula Has Had on the Works of Writers of Modern Young Adult Vampire Fiction." B.A. Essay. University of Iceland, 2015.

Harris, Augustus. *Ruthven: A Drama in Four Acts*. London: Thomas Hailes Lacy, 1859.

Heine, Heinrich. "Gods in Exile." *The Prose Writings of Heinrich Heine*. Ed. Havelock Ellis, London: Walter Scott, 1887. 268-89 [1853].

Heine, Heinrich. "Lyrical Interlude." *The Poems of Heine: Complete*. Trans. Edgar Alfred Bowring. London: William Clowes & Sons, Limited, 1887. 65-191 [1827].

Hildebrand, Theodor. *Der Vampyr, Oder: Die Todtenbraut: Ein Roman nach Neugriechischen Volkssagen*. Leipzig: Christian Ernst Kollmann, 1828.

Hudders, Anthony. "The Southern Vampire in American Popular Fiction." Master in de Vergelijkende Moderne Letterkunde. Universiteit Gent, 2010.

Jaworskij, Juljan. "Südrussishche Vampyre." *Zeitschrift des Vereins für Volkskunde* 8: 3 (1898), 331-336.

Joshi, S. T. *Icons of Horror and the Supernatural: An Encyclopedia of Our Worst Nightmares*. 2. Westport, CT: Greenwood Press, 2007.

Kane, Tim. *The Changing Vampire of Film and Television: A Critical Study of the Growth of a Genre*. Jefferson, NC: MacFarland, 2005.

Keats, John. *La Belle Dame*. Vol. 1. *The Indicator: a Miscellany for the Fields and the Fireside*. By Leigh Hunt. New York: Wiley & Putnam, 1845. 211-13 [1819].

Keats, John. *Lamia, Isabella, the Eve of Saint Agnes, and Other Poems*. London: Thomas Davison, 1820 (rpt. 1927).

Kingston, William H. G. "The Vampire; or, Pedro Pacheco and the Bruxa." *Tales for All Ages*. London: Bickers & Bush, 1863. 72-80.

Kleist, Heinrich von. *Penthesilea: A Tragic Drama*. Trans. Joel Agee. New York: HarperCollins, 1998 [1808].

Knoop, Otto, ed. *Sagen und Erzählungen aus der Provinz Posen Posen: Eigenthum der Gesellschaft, 1893*. Posen: Eigenthum der Gesellschaft, 1893.

Kord, Susanne. *Murderesses in German Writing, 1720-1860: Heroines of Horror*. Cambridge: Cambridge University Press, 2009.

Lamothe-Langon, Etienne-Leon de. *The Virgin Vampire*. Trans. Brian Stableford. Encino: Black Coat Press, 2011 [1825].

Le Fanu, J. T. Sheridan. "Spalatro: From the Notes of Fra Giacomo." *The Dublin University Magazine: A Literary and Political Journal* 21 (March & April 1843), 338-51; 446-58.

Le Fanu, Joseph Sheridan. *Carmilla: A Critical Edition*. Ed. Kathleen Costello-Sullivan. Syracuse: Syracuse University Press, 2013 [1871-1872].

Le Fanu, Joseph Sheridan. "Carmilla." *The Dark Blue*. 2. January 1872.

Lima, Maria Antónia. "Forever Young, Though Forever Changing: Evolution of the Vampire." *Dracula and the Gothic in Literature, Pop Culture and the Arts*. Ed. Isabel Ermida. Leiden: Brill Rodopi, 2016. 256-70.

Linton, Eliza Lynn. "The Fate of Madame Cabanel." *All the Year Round*. 16 December 1872. 6-12.

Lohrli, Anne. *Household Words: A Weekly Journal 1850-1859. Conducted by Charles Dickens*. Toronto: University of Toronto Press, 1973.

Macaulay, Thomas Babington Baron. "Moore's Life of Lord Byron." *Critical and Historical Essays Contributed to the Edinburgh Review*. Ed. F. C. Montague. London: Methuen & Co, 1903. 303-42.

Marryat, Florence. *The Blood of the Vampire*. Leipzig: Bernard Tauchnitz, 1897.

Marschner, Heinrich. "The Vampyr." *Opera Glass*. 1997 [1828]. (accessed January 4, 2017).

McGinley, Kathryn. "Development of the Byronic Vampire: Byron, Stoker, Rice." *The Gothic World of Anne Rice*. Eds. Gary Hoppenstand & Ray B. Browne. Bowling Green, OH: Bowling Green State University Popular Press, 1996. 71-90.

Melton, J. Gordon. *The Vampire Book: The Encyclopedia of the Undead*. Canton, MI: Visible Ink Press, 2011.

Mérimée, Prosper. "Sur le Vampirisme." *La Guzla, ou choix de poésies illyriques, recueillies dans la Dalmatie, la Bosnie, la Croatie et l'Herzegowine*. Paris: F. G. Levrault, 1827. 145-157.

Mérimée, Prosper. *Works of Prosper Mérimée*. Ed. George Saintsbury. Vol. 4. New York: Bigelow, Brown & Co., Inc., 1905 [1869].

Montaclair, Florent. *Le vampire dans la littérature romantique française 1820-1868 : Textes et documents*. Besançon: Presses universitaires de Franche-Comté, 2010.

Nelson, Victoria. *Gothicka: Vampire Heroes, Human Gods, and the New Supernatural*. Cambridge: Harvard University Press, 2012.

Neruda, Jan. "Vampire." *Czechoslovak Stories*. Trans. Sarka B. Hrbkova. New York: Duffield & Company, 1920. 75-80 [1871].

Newes from the dead. Or A true and exact narration of the miraculous deliverance of Anne Greene. Oxford: Leonard Lichfield, 1651.

Nodier, Charles. "De Quelques Phénomènes du Sommeil." *Revue de Paris* 23 (1831), 27-44.

Nodier, Charles, Achille de Jouffroy, and Jean-Toussaint Merle. *Lord Ruthven: The Vampire*. Trans. Frank J. Morlock. Encino: Black Coat Press, 2004 [1820].

Ollier, Edmund. "Vampyres." *Household words*. 30 (February 1855), 247-256.

Orlomoski, Caitlyn. "From Monsters to Victims: Vampires and Their Cultural Evolution from the Nineteenth to the Twenty-First Century." Honors Scholar Theses. University of Connecticut, 2011.

Pal-Lapinski, Piya. *The Exotic Woman in Nineteenth-century British Fiction and Culture: A Reconsideration*. Durham: University of New Hampsire Press, 2005.

Perkowski, Jan L. *The Darkling: A Treatise on Slavic Vampirism*. Columbus: Slavica Publishing, Inc., 1989.

Perkowski, Jan Louis. *Vampire Lore: From the Writings of Jan Louis Perkowski*. Bloomington: Slavica Publishers, 2006.

Philostratus. *Life of Apollonius of Tyana*. Trans. R. C. Conybeare. Vol. 1. London: William Heinemann, 1912.

Planché, James Robinson. *The Vampire: or, The Bride of the Isles*. London: John Dicks, 1820.

Poe, Edgar A. "The Fall of the House of Usher." *Burton's Gentleman's Magazine* 5 (September 1839), 145-52.

Przybyszewski, Stanislaw. "De Profundis." *Lasst die Toten ruhen: Deutsche Vampirgeschichten aus dem 19. Jahrhundert*. Stolberg: Atlantis, 2012. 253-301 [1895].

Recht, Marcus. *Der Sympathische Vampir: Visualisierungen Männlichkeiten in der TV-Serie Buffy*. Frankfurt: Campus Verlag, 2011.

"Reviews." *The American: Journal of Literature, Science, the Arts, and Public Affairs*, January 1890. 297.

Rice, Ann. *The Vampire Chronicles: Interview with the Vampire*. New York: Ballantine Books, 2002.

Ridgwell, T. F. "Told in a First-Class Smoker: A Modern Vampire." *The Raiway Magazine* 2 (April 1898), 334-343.

Roxana, Stuart. *Stage Blood: Vampires of the 19th-Century Stage*. Bowling Green: Bowling Green State University Popular Press, 1998.

Rymer, James Malcolm. *Varney the Vampyre*. Ed. Devendra P. Varma. New York: Arno Press, 1970 [1845-1847].

Senf, Carol A. *The Vampire in Nineteenth-Century English Literature*. Madison: University of Wisconsin Press, 1988.

Spindler, Carl. "Der Vampyr und seine Braut: Ein Nachtstück aus der neuesten Zeit." *Zwillinge. Zwei Erzählungen. Nebst einem Anhange von Originalbriefen*. Hanau: C J. Edler'schen Buchhandlung, 1826. 1-106.

Stagg, John. "The Vampyre." *The minstrel of the North; or, Cumbrian legends; being a poetical miscellany of legendary, Gothic and romantic, tales.* London: Hamblin & Seyfang, 1810. 261-68.

Stenbock, Eric Stanislaus. "The True Story of a Vampire." *The Shadow of Death; Studies of Death.* New York: Garland Publishing, Inc., 1984. 120-147 [1884].

Stuart, Roxana. *Stage Blood: Vampires of the 19th-Century Stage.* Bowling Green: Bowling Green State University Popular Press, 1998.

Svoboda, Jan. "Toward the Sympathetic Vampire: From Bram Stoker's *Dracula* to Stephanie Meyer's *The Twilight Saga.*" Bachelor's Thesis. Masaryk University, 2012.

Symons, Arthur. "The Pale Woman." *Images of Good and Evil.* London: Heinemann, William, 1899. 90.

Tille, Rebecca. *Der Vampir als Element der Literaturgeschichte : literaturwissenschaftliche Untersuchung zur schwarzromantischen Vampirmotivik.* Hamburg: Diplomica, 2013.

Villiers de l'Isle-Adam, August Compte de. *Sardonic Tales.* Trans. Hamish Miles. A. A. Knopf, 1927 [1874].

Wallace, William. "Review of 'Master of his Fate'." *The Academy: A Weekly Review of Literature, Science, and Art* 37 (February 1890), 114.

Whyte-Melville, G. J. "Bones and I; or, The Skeleton at Home." *London Society* 13 (January-June 1868): 3-12; 137-49; 269-78; 369-74; 442-47; 541-49; *London Society* 14 (July 1868), 160-170.

Williamson, Milly. "Let Them All In: The Evolution of the 'Sympathetic' Vampire." *Screening the Undead: Vampires and Zombies in Film and Television.* Eds. Leon Hunt, Sharon Lockyer, & Milly Williamson. London: I. B. Tauris & Co Ltd, 2014. 71-92.

Williamson, Milly. *The Lure of the Vampire: Gender, Fiction and Fandom from Bram Stoker to Buffy.* London: Wallflower Press, 2005.

Wolf, Leonard. "Abraham Stoker." *British writers. Supplement III, James M. Barrie to Mary Wollstonecraft.* Eds. George Stade and Carol Howard. New York: Charles Scribner's Sons, 1996.

Wollstonecraft, Mary. "The Mortal Immortal: A Tale," *The Keepsake for 1834.* Ed. Frederic Mansel Reynolds. London: Longman, Rees, Orme, Brown, Green, and Longman, 1833. 71-87.

Zanger, Jules. "Metaphor into Metonymy: The Vampire Next Door." *Blood Read: The Vampire as Metaphor in Contemporary Culture.* Philadelphia: University of Pennsylvania Press, 1997. 17-26.

Zebedee, Jo [The Secret Bookshelf], ed. *Selected Vampire Stories (Annotated).* CreateSpace Independent Publishing Platform, 2014.

11.
"I Am Not as These: I Have Mercy:" The Benign or Benevolent Vampire of the Nineteenth Century

Introduction

> Take, for example, the NBC *Dracula* (2013-2014), whose central character of Dracula . . . , our customary archetype of evil, is decidedly "good," a quality that, arguably, was unachievable in the previous century.
> John Edgar Browning, "Listening to our Vampires: Dracula from the Grave to the Page to Stage and Cinema" (2017), 134.

Mutatis mutandis, much the same can have been said of the vampire in the twentieth century. It has been so inconceivable, considered so unachievable, that I know of no study of the nineteenth-century vampire as benevolent.

I shall, therefore, work from Browning's salient observation of the twenty-first- and twentieth-century Draculas. Jules Zanger, in "Metaphor into Metonymy" (1997), uses Dracula as the paradigm of the "old vampire," that is, the one of the nineteenth century, which is "wholly evil and morally unredeemable . . . the earthly embodiment of supernal Evil . . . the Anti-Christ. (17). Lindsey Fenicchia ("The Modern Vampire as Romantic Hero," 2012) has argued that nineteenth-century vampires "were seen as antichrist figures which epitomize a life of sin" and that Dracula "epitomizes the century: vampire as a damned figure" (see 1, 2, 17, 24). Anthony Hudders in his "The Southern Vampire in American Popular Fiction" (2010) makes the case that the "vampire emerged as a power-hungry villain in the nineteenth century" (15).

The essay "From Monsters to Victims" by Caitlyn Orlomoski (2011), states unequivocally that during the 1800s, "the bloodsuckers were monsters that existed solely to ruin the lives of the innocent humans around them; they [were] purely evil, delighting in the misfortunes of others and causing tragedy whenever possible" (46). Victoria Nelson in *Gothicka: Vampire Heroes, Human Gods, and the New Supernatural* (2012), adds Polidori's vampire, Lord Ruthven (1819) to Dracula, for it "remained the Gothick vampire standard in England and America until the publication of Bram Stoker's *Dracula* (1897)" (121). Ruthven is typified as "Satanic," a "vile seducer and murderer of maidens."

This paper is meant to see if such assertions are warranted. My conclusion is that they are, except for a handful of examples. It is this select group of tales on which I wish to focus. I will divide the subject matter into nineteenth-century vampires who act beneficently, those who are benign or harmless, and those who are benevolent. The focus is on action—doing good deeds—with the first; with the second and third it is on character.

Proto-Vampires

Being helpful is not unknown before vampires; that is, among proto- or urvampires. In Norse mythology, the mound dweller was a particular type of proto-vampire or "again walker" (*aptrgangr*). It was usually violent and protective of its buried wealth, but not always. In the thirteenth century there arose a story of King Hreggvid who dies in battle and is placed in an impregnable barrow along with a great many treasures (*Göngu-Hrólfs Saga* 3, 16, 32). Hreggvid himself, as a revenant ("returner"), places further spells on the mound, so only one man, Hrolf, can penetrate, the man he wants to marry his daughter.

Hrolf, by sheer force of will and strength, makes it to the king's mound, fully prepared to have to fight for what he requires. But Heggvid meets him outside and provides him unbegrudgingly with what he needs from his wealth. Later, in battle, Hrolf once more must seek help from King Hreggvid, who, again without reservation, gives him the wherewithal to prevail. After his success, Hrolf marries Hreggvid's daughter, the princess, and Hreggvid is heard from no longer.

Norse myths were remote influences upon the West's construction of the vampire, showing up in vampire reports by 1689, but the Continental European and British revenant is proximate. And I mean "influence" literally, for it flowed directly into the vampire. This, however, does not mean the Western revenant was somehow insulated; the introduction of the idea of purgatory in the Roman Church changed some of its manifestations from the twelfth century on. And then from Eastern European states, through imperialist expansions and contractions, new features were introduced from their revenants starting in earnest in the fifteenth century.

An interesting example of the helpful revenant in this tradition is that of a baker (c. 1425). He died, but a few days later, he rejoined his family in the early morning hours, kneading the bread and encouraging them to work skillfully and vigorously (see Martin 631-33). The neighbors, in fear, ran him off, so he started pelting them with rocks. They therefore dug him up and broke his legs. Another one is a story from 1465 included in Joseph Klapper's "Die Schlesischen Geschichten von den Schädingenden Toten" (1909), where a dead man returns to his grieving wife and they comfort each other. She feels much better now that he is back. But the mother-in-law spies them together and calls a Dominican friar who brings the host with him and exorcises the demon leaving behind a rotting corpse.

What made the Western vampire differ from an ordinary revenant like the ones above was having a credible and skeptical Westerner report it and list his source(s). To show the continuity between the revenant and the early vampire, let me turn to a similar account from 1657, related by François Richard. The revenants above are from Bohemia; the following vampire is from Greece, another new influence on the development of the vampire. After the death of a shoemaker, he reappeared and returned to his occupation: "he repaired the shoes of his children, he drew water at the cistern, and often he was seen in the valleys to cut wood for the sustenance of his family (212)."[168] The neighbors eventually became alarmed at this, exhumed the body, and set it aflame.

Vampires Acting Beneficently

The eponymous Varney the Vampire, depicted by James Malcolm Rymer, (1845-1847) is, at the end of his 180 years of being a vampire, guilty of many dastardly deeds including some murders done to those who were trying to aid him as one human being to another. But he is also able to act charitably. Varney is challenged to a duel; his adversary fires but Varney does not. Instead moments later he raises his pistol to the sky and shoots (ch. 39). Thereafter he hands his opponent back his bullet. Varney joins with a co-conspirator to abduct a man for strategic purposes. When their plans fail, his companion wants to kill the hostage but Varney secretly releases him (chs. 65; 68). When he is caught by some men emerging from a house he appears to have robbed and told he was going to be searched he draws a gun, shoots one of them in the face, and escapes. It turns out the man is unharmed, for Varney used a blank (ch. 81). A plot is being carried out to disinherit a young woman; Varney discovers this and alerts her lover so the young man can save her wealth (ch. 175).

Antonia, according to Ludwig von Baczko, *The Sorcerers* (c. 1815), is a spoiled girl who is being tutored by Marie.[169] Marie includes lessons on mocking God and being vain, so Antonia soon loses her friends, including steadfast Agnes. When she "comes out" as a debutante she loses her favored suitor, Ignatius, to Countess Constance, who is as virtuous as Antonia is sinful. With the help of Marie, she finds a sorcerer who gives her powers for thirty years in exchange for selling her soul to the devil. Her first act is to curse Ignatius with blindness, but Constance's reputation only climbs with her faithful service to her husband. Antonia then reduces them to poverty, but again the two acclimate themselves to it with dignity.

Having given herself to cursing and debauchery for many years, she becomes disenchanted and turns from her vampirism to God. Marie tries everything to keep her under the power of Satan, but Antonia remains faithful. At her first opportunity, she divides all her property, gives it to Agnes and Constance, and joins a convent, giving herself to acts of penance the remainder of her life. After a life of vice, then, she performs the good deed of giving her wealth to those whom she hurt the most.

---

[168] There is a more colorful variation of this tale in Earl of Carnarvon, *Reminiscences of Athens and the Morea* (1869), 162-64.

[169] This is primarily a Faust story but is considered to be about vampires by Andrew Barger (195). Both Antonia and Marie are treated as vampires; the latter has no redeeming characteristics, whereas the former repents of her misdeeds. Barger attributes the story to Ludwig Tieck, but this is an error; rather it was originally part of a collection of stories gathered and reworked by Ludwig von Baczko. It appeared in book form around 1800 under the title of *Legenden, Volkssagen, Gespenster- und Zaubergeschichten* — at least that is the date given it by Indiana University, a copy of which is digitalized by Hathi Trust. The original has no date, but another impression, when it is noted to be the first of three volumes, is dated 1815. To err on the safe side (and stay with the best evidence), then, I am adopting the later date.

Lucy Mary Jane Garnett and John Stuart Glennie in their *Greek Folk-songs* (1885) tell of a widow who allows her daughter, Areté, to marry a distant suiter as long as her son, Constantine, keeps his word and brings her home every summer and winter.[170] But Constantine is murdered and his mother, in her destitution, prays to God for her son to arise and bring Areté home. God allows him do so and upon his arrival at his sister's home, Areté tells him if he has come in joy to permit her to dress up but if for evil she will remain as is. He responds with the latter. When Constantine drops her off to see her mother he returns to his grave; the two reunite and die of grief. All of this was arranged according to God's providence, so Constantine becomes a vampire to carry out his promise and to be an answer to his mother's prayer. What happens subsequently is not his doing (126-128).[171]

Dr. Prestwitch, a man of very modest means, secretly receives the corpse of a hanged man, a forger, for experimentation when he realizes the man is still alive, so he works to revive him (Mary Elizabeth Braddon, "The Dreaded Guest," 1871).[172] Once done the criminal has leverage on the physician because helping a felon can be a capital offense so he begins to come weekly to extort money. But he also starts referring people to him, many of whom are criminals, but they pay their bills. So this begins to offset the costs of the blackmail.

F. W. Lawson, illustrator, 112-13.

---

[170] The original Greek can be found in Passow 396-97. There are several versions; this is 518. A translation from another version (517) is located in Tozer 95-97. There is still the same beneficent action, but there is no reunion. The title is Ο Βουρκόλακας which is translated as "vampire." Number 519 is merely partial consisting of the story up to Constantine's departure.
[171] There are a number of parallels between this poem and the eighteenth-century "vampire" Lenore." One appears to be that if one calls upon the dead, they inevitably bring death with them. The difference here is the function of religion. One is in the context of rebellion against God; the other in that of piety.
[172] As far as being a vampire, it is a necrophiliac who is called a "perfect vampire" in the story. More to the point, however, it is not unusual for someone recovered from an apparent death (*Scheintod*) to be called a vampire. See Spindler, "Der Vampyr und seine Braut" (1826) and Catherine Grace Frances Gore, *The Elizabethines* (1829), as early examples. Finally anyone involved in extorting another was subject to the name.

For three years he does this until he disappears. Years pass and the doctor hears nothing, except once he receives a package of forged money, which he burns. Then at Christmas eleven years after he goes missing, he shows up and turns out to be a most respectable and pleasant fellow. The last three years of his life, the ex-convict is generous to the family and at his death he bequeaths his fortune—in real money—to the doctor.

As told by Frank R. Stockton in his "A Borrowed Month" (1886), Clinton travels to Switzerland to paint for a month, for that is all he can afford.[173] The second day of his stay, he is struck down with rheumatism in his left leg and this severely limits his ability to find and sketch landscapes. At the suggestion of a rather strange man, Clinton decides that by the sheer force of his will, he can transfer his ailment to his many friends back home and borrow their health for a day. He knows they would not begrudge this given his circumstances. It works like a charm and upon returning home he hears about how the shifting of his illness around opened up the possibility for him to wed the woman he loves. His actions are beneficent because the exchange is only for a day and focuses on caring friends.

A king's son rescues a corpse that was being beaten for a debt of money, which the son pays, as reported by Lucy M. J. Garnett, *The Women of Turkey and their Folk-Lore* (1890).[174] The dead man joins him and leads him to a maiden who weds husbands only to find them dead in the morning. The corpse arranges for the two to marry and then sleeps in the same room as they their first night. During the night a three-headed dragon emerges from the maiden's mouth and the dead body chops off its heads. So the young man is alive in the morning. The corpse then demands that they cut the maiden in half to distribute her evenly between them just as they had already split the wealth from the dowry. When she screams the dragon's body falls from her mouth. The dead man then says that he needs neither her nor the riches; they are his for the kindness he showed in rescuing him. He is named "The Grateful Vampire."

The reader knows from the last chapter that according to Dumas *The Vampire: Drama in 5 Acts* (1851), the female vampire, Ziska, continues to feed on the innocent as she acts beneficently toward her human love interest, Gilbert. Gilbert is on his way to his sister's wedding, when she, in disguise, pulls him down on his horse right as a rifle is fired, saving his life. The shooter is a male vampire, Lord Ruthwen, who is going to marry his sister. She forewarns him of the danger his sister is in, but he is unable to save her from Ruthwen and she dies.

Later when Ruthwen attacks to kill Gilbert's and his fiancée, she wants to save him once more, but this time only if he will declare his love for her. This would mean, however, his beloved must die alone at Ruthwen's hands. Instead, Gilbert and his lover prepare to poison themselves to avoid Ruthwen killing them. Ziska stops them and betrays Ruthwen by telling Gilbert how to kill him. Because vampires cannot do this without sacrificing their immortal lives, she dies in his arms and he is able to eliminate Ruthwen. This act of self-sacrifice for the life of the man she loves makes her beneficence the highest of this category.

---

[173] Brian J. Frost, *The Monster with a Thousand Faces* (1889) lists this as a psychic vampire story (49). One could subtitle it: "How I Made Vampirism Work for Me."
[174] The original is in Aléandros Paspátis, *Études sur les Tchinghianés* (1870), 601-605.

Benign or Harmless Vampires

Paul Miflitt died in his fifties and is remembered by a friend: "He was a lover of children, and as a consequence young people were drawn to him. He used to say he stole a little of child's life by associating with them, but though it benefitted him, they were none the losers by the operation as the magnet imparts of its life a portion to the negative iron, imbuing it with its own life, yet losing none. So Paul Miflitt felt he was no thief by partaking of their youthful vitality" (Ford 295).

Dracula, as told by Bram Stoker 1897, chs 10-12, has been feeding on Lucy for some time with the intention of making her a vampire. She has reached the point where she is near death from blood loss. Dr. Van Helsing realizes he must perform a transfusion. Arthur, her fiancé, steps up to be the donor. Upon completion her breathing is stronger and her cheeks have regained some of their color. After two nights of supervision during the night, she seems to be recovering nicely. The third night she is left alone and she is found in the morning to be near death again. Another transfusion is required. Another setback, another transfusion; one more and a fourth.[175] With the last one Lucy rallies a little but then dies. Kathryn McGinley in her "Development of the Byronic Vampire" (1996), calls her a "passive vampire" (76), drawing the blood from her four benefactors.[176]

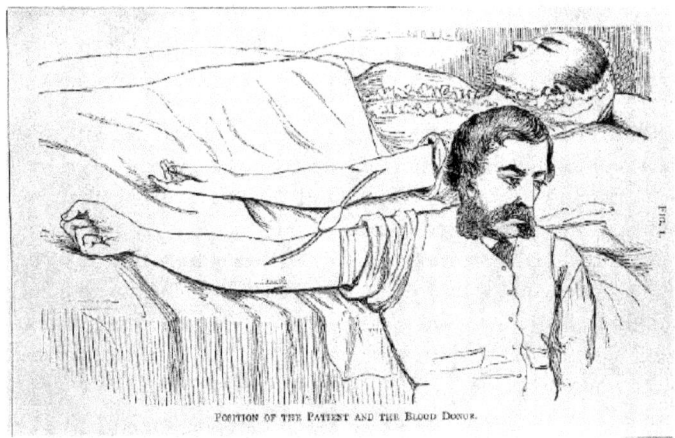

"Immediate transfusion in England: Position of the Patient and the Blood Donor." In J. H. Aveling, "Immediate transfusion in England" 1873, 303.

Mahmouré di Zulueta has lived as a Bohemian, resolved to preserve her uncompromised independence in Edward Heron-Allen and Selina Delaro's

---

[175] That this, in Christopher Craft's mind, parallels a gang rape is absurd and merits no response (see Craft 128).
[176] Robert Tracy, in "Loving You All Ways: Vamps Vampires Necrophiles and Necrofilles in Nineteenth-Century Fiction" (1990), says much the same thing although he sexualizes it: Lucy "mimics the vampire by receiving constant blood transfusions which are specifically described as sexual acts" (42). In actual fact, Van Helsing thinks it grimly comical when Arthur says, after his transfusion to her, that this makes her his wife; he does not take it seriously — for him or for the others who transfuse her afterwards.

Princess Daphne (1888).[177] After she divorced the husband of her youth "[s]he had no lover and wanted none—later on she had lovers and still wanted none" (42). But her lifestyle ended up destroying her health and she has fallen ill, hovering near death for the past five months. A young, bright, and strong young man comes into her life and works to seduce her. She lets herself be seduced. He promises "you shall live again and your veins shall throb with the pulses of my love" (50). He begins to mesmerize her and transfer his health to her. When she protests because his vitality is waning, he chides her for "posing as a charming little vampire" (84). Caught up in the power of mesmerism he eventually drives himself to an early grave and she lives on by the force of his life.

Dr. Lefevre has developed a technique known as psycho-dynamics that works through a machine whereby "the electricity stored with the human body can be driven out by the human will . . . into another human body" in James Maclaren Cobban's "Jules Courtney" (1889).[178] This is important because the city has been experiencing a rash of episodes of life-force depletion due to a psychic vampire (452). Lady Mary Fane is attacked and the technique does not work. He jury rigs the device so as to draw his own nervous force, the volatile and at the same time very searching fluid of life, and transfer it into her, like blood. She recovers. When he recuperates from the process he proposes to her. She replies "You made me well by putting your own life into me; so what could I do but give you the life that was already your own" (772). She is a vampire enabled by her physician.

Benevolent Vampires

The first two here can be read, with equal validity, as descents-into-madness or as ascents-into-enlightenment. I choose the latter. Being taken by a friend to hear the eponymous Clara Mílitch sing and recite, Yakoff is less than impressed, but is puzzled that she seemed to have been looking directly at him during her performance (Turgenev).[179] A few days later she communicates to him that she would like a rendezvous. He is formal, distant, and impatient with her, causing her to upbraid herself; she says she should have understood that he comprehended nothing of her. She pushes past him and disappears. A few weeks later he reads she had committed suicide.

Thus begins his pilgrimage. He meets Clara's sister and learns that she had an almost mystical approach to finding the one she was destined to marry. Should she be wrong she covenanted that she would kill herself. He finds evidence he was the one, which causes him to declare his love for her. He feels haunted and begins to feel an ecstasy when he perceives she is near. When she finally appears to him, he kisses her in bliss and faints near death. He dies joyfully declaring that love is stronger than death.

The second one is related by Théophile Gautier, "Spirite" (1865). Told by a Swedenborgian that a spirit is trying to contact him, Guy de Malivert prepares

---

[177] This is called vampiric by Brian Frost (49).
[178] This was quickly named a vampire tale, but the passage here has been unnoticed, e.g., Baron de Book-Worm & Co., "Our Booking Office" (1890), 10 and *Edinburgh Medical Journal* (1890), 759.
[179] Militch is called a vampire by Dorothy Scarborough (162).

himself for the encounter.[180] The spirit, a woman of surpassing beauty, tells him her story. She was, when alive, around seven years younger than he and fell hopelessly in love with him. Forced by convention not to express it, she languished in the cloud of his ignorance. At seventeen, certain Guy would never learn of her existence, she joined a convent and prayed to God that she would be able, in the next life, to reveal her love to him. Being frail, mixed with a life of self-sacrifice, she soon died.

Having himself fallen in love with her heavenly self, he begins to live a double life: a real one and a spiritual one. Opting to adopt the latter more and more he thus finds her increasingly visible and the world recedes from his view. When he dies he does so with total joy on his face and a companion sees a lovely celestial woman collect his soul and take it up into the heavens with her.

Manwed enters an old, rundown castle and finds himself with a choice according to Leopold Ritter von Sacher-Masoch's "Die Toten sind unersättlich" (1875). He either can mount marble steps to a statue of Jesus representing self-sacrifice, or another which will take him to a statue of Venus. He takes the latter, placing his engagement ring on her finger, around which she closes her hand so he cannot remove it. He kisses her and feels like she is acting like a vampire, sucking his life's blood from him, but with his consent and enjoyment.

He kisses her until she has a human body and takes on the role of his dominatrix. He lies at her knees, kisses her feet, allows her to tread on his head, lets her tie his hands with her hair, and performs menial tasks for her pleasure. He revels in his "wonderous exhaustion" as she continues to gain strength from him. She asks what he would do if she strangled him and he replies he would die a "sweet death." She is offering him an alternative to a religiously sanctioned patriarchal marriage, which he obviously does not want, and thus is acting for him as a benefactor, a benevolent vampire.[181]

J. T. Sheridan Le Fanu, "Spalatro: From the Notes of Fra Giacomo" (1843), tells how Spalatro helps an old man home and therein the man conjures up his daughter, who is the embodiment of beauty itself. "Henceforward life had lost for me all interest. I had beheld loveliness which was not of this earth" (454). She, on the other hand, is always sad and warning him that she is "the unwilling thrall of agencies hated and feared, but from which never—never in time or eternity [can she] escape" (456). She wants him to leave her alone, but he continues to pursue her.

One evening he follows her to her home. She motions him away and when he will not desert her, she explains to him, "Speak to me no more of love, as you would save your soul alive. In sin and sorrow my lot is fixed for ever. Beware how you court me here. I strive to save you. We are not all alike. I am not as these: I have mercy: I would deliver you" (457). Yet he does speak of love and she disappears; his soul becomes the devil's until the end of his days and is eternally damned thereafter.

---

[180] Melton 283 names the story vampiric.
[181] This is a wonderful inversion of a story long used to show the superiority of Christianity to paganism. It goes back to about 1140 with William Malmesbury, *William of Malmesbury's Chronicle of the Kings of England* 1847, 232-34. Its most famous rendition in the nineteenth century for English speakers was Henry Thomas Liddell "The Vampire Bride" 1833, 31-56.

Bettina is the victim of the vampire Lord Ruthwen; her lover, Léonti, swears to pursue and kill him (Cyprien Bérard, *The Vampire Lord Ruthwen*, 1820). Strangely enough, Léonti, in his travels, encounters her and she tells him that the vampire is there, known as Lord Seymour, high in the royal court. She then explains why she is there. She has been resurrected by God as a "vampire woman" to be the "terror of the guilty and the safeguard of virtuous lives" (129-131). Thus she is there to expose her murderer, who right now has his eye on the duke's only daughter Eleonora to marry and to kill.

Ruthwen arranges things so he can wed her; Bettina, on the other hand, arranges matters to get Léonti into the court. Ruthwen succeeds in his plans, but Bettina then appears before the court, reveals who she is, and tells the company to avenge Eleonora and herself on their murderer. She then falls and dies in horrible convulsions. Taking advantage of the chaos, Léonti runs forward and plunges his sword through the vampire's heart. Because a deadly illness begins to spread in the royal household, Ruthwen's corpse is exhumed and a red hot iron is thrust in his eyes and through his heart.

Conclusion

In the preceding chapter, I have argued that the image of a sympathetic vampire was experimented with in the nineteenth century much more than current scholarship recognizes. Here I have gone one step further. I believe I have located sixteen examples of vampires that were harmless or willfully helpful and, in this case, academics and committed amateurs do not appear to have considered them as possible. The general consensus on the evil vampire in the nineteenth century seems to have blinded such experts from the richness of actual depictions.

There are several ways to act beneficently. Most are positive. They can be religious in nature. A dead man is raised by God to keep his vow to his mother; a vampire woman messianically sacrifices her eternal life for the good of the mortal man whom she loves; a young woman repents of her evil life and, in keeping with her contrition, she makes restitution to those she hurt most. One other is simply secular gratitude. A physician saves the life of a felon who uses his skills as a forger to become a productive member of society and bequeaths his fortune to the doctor, thankful for his second chance of life. And two are negative. Varney decides three times to exercise mercy and not kill men that he easily could have; Clinton limits his vampirism to enjoying the health of his many friends for but one day in a single month.

The volitionally benign are generally those (i.e. women) acted upon by others (men), who mean to help them—whom we may want to call enablers. Mahmouré is made to receive her beau's health; Lady Fane her physician's; Lucy that of four males who love her and want to help her regain her health. There is one exception to this passivity and it is a man. Mifflitt actively draws energy from children with no ill effects on them.

The benevolent vampire (i.e., a woman) usually is one providing an alternative to the beloved (a man) that is vastly preferred by him and acts in a religiously charged environment. Yakoff and Guy are both given heavenly love and Manwed a pagan one of masochism. Yet there are the cases of Spalatro disobeying the directives of his compassionate vampire love interest to the detriment of his eternal soul and a dead woman becoming an adventurous Virgin-Mary vampire carrying out God's providential will to end the unlife of a Satanic one, helping at the same time her lover avenge her death.

It is true that the vast majority of references to the vampire, in news stories and literature, whether literal or metaphorical, were negative in the nineteenth century. The vampire was a "customary archetype of evil." But more emphasis must be placed on "customary" than it hitherto has, for it was not universal.

Works cited

Aveling, J. H. "Immediate transfusion in England." *Obstetrics Journal* 1 (1873), 303.
Baczko, Ludwig von. *The Sorcerers*. Vol. 1. *Popular Tales and Romances of the Northern Nations*. London: W. Simpkin & R. Marshall, 1823. 123-189 [1815].
Barger, Andrew, ed. *The Best Vampire Stories 1800-1849*. Bottletree Books LLC, 2011.
Bérard, Cyprien. *The Vampire Lord Ruthwen*. Trans. Brian Stableford. Encino, CA: Black Coat Press, 2011 [1820].
Book-Worm. Baron de. "Our Booking Office." *Punch, Or the London Charivari* January 1890, 10.
Braddon, Mary Elizabeth. "The Dreaded Guest." *Belgravia: A London Magazine* December 1871, 112-28.
Carnarvon, Earl. *Reminiscences of Athens and the Morea, extr. from a journal of travels in Greece in 1839*. Ed. Henry Howard M. Herbert. London: John Murray, 1869.
Cobban, James Maclaren. "Jules Courtney, Or, Master of his Fate." *Blackwood's Edinburgh Magazine* October-December 1889, 439-466; 581-591; 770-789.
Craft, Christopher. "'Kiss Me with Those Red Lips': Gender and Inversion in Bram Stoker's *Dracula*." *Representations* 8 (1984), 107-33.
Dumas, Alexandre. *The Vampire: Drama in 5 Acts. Lord Ruthven Returns*. Trans. Frank J. Morlock. Encino: Black Coat Press, 2004 [1851].
Edinburgh Medical Journal, February 1890, 759.
Fenicchia, Lindsey M. "The Modern Vampire as Romantic Hero: Acceptance, Love and Self-Control." English Master's Thesis. State University of New York College at Brookport, 2012.
Ford, D. N. *Born Again: Or, The Romance of a Duel Life*. Falmouth: Chas. Francis Adams, 1893.
Frost, Brian J. *The Monster with a Thousand Faces: Guises of the Vampire in Myth and Literature*. Bowling Green: Bowling Green State University Popular Press, 1989.
Garnett, Lucy Mary Jane, and John Stuart Glennie. *Greek Folk-songs from the Turkish Provinces of Northern Hellas*. London: Elliot Stock, 1885.
Garnett, Lucy M. J. *The Women of Turkey and their Folk-Lore*. London: David Nutt, 1890.
Gautier, Théophile. "Spirite…." *The Works of Théophile Gautier*. Trans. F. C. Sumichast. Vol. 6. Boston: C. T. Brainard, 1901 [1865].
Göngu-Hrólfs Saga. Trans. Hermann Pálsson & Paul Edwards. Toronto: University of Toronto Press, 1980 [14th Century].
Gore, Catherine Grace Frances. *The Elizabethines*. Vol. 2. *Hungarian Tales*. London: Saunders & Outley, 1829.
Heron-Allen, Edward, and Selina Delaro. *Princess Daphne*. Chicago: Belford, Clarke & Co., 1888.

Hudders, Anthony. "The Southern Vampire in American Popular Fiction." Master in de Vergelijkende Moderne Letterkunde. Universiteit Gent, 2010.

Klapper, Joseph. "Die Schlesischen Geschichten von den Schädingenden Toten." *Mitteilungen der Schlesischen Gesellschaft für Volkskunde* 11 (1909), 58-93.

Le Fanu, J. T. Sheridan. "Spalatro: From the Notes of Fra Giacomo." *The Dublin University Magazine: A Literary and Political Journal* 21 (March-April 1843), 338-51; 446-58.

Liddell, Henry Thomas. "The Vampire Bride." *The Wizard of the North; The Vampire Bride; and Other Poems*. Edinburgh: William Blackwood, 1833. 29-58.

Malmesbury, William. *William of Malmesbury's Chronicle of the Kings of England*. Trans. J. A. Giles. London: Henry G Bohn, 1847 [c. 1140].

Martin, Hervé. "A la recherche de la culture populaire bretonne à travers les manuscrits du bas Moyen Age." *Annales de Bretagne et des Pays de l'Ouest* 86: 4 (December 1979), 631-33.

McGinley, Kathryn. "Development of the Byronic Vampire: Byron, Stoker, Rice." *The Gothic World of Anne Rice*. Eds. Gary Hoppenstand & Ray B. Browne. Bowling Green, OH: Bowling Green State University Popular Press, 1996. 71-90.

Melton, J. Gordon. *The Vampire Book: The Encyclopedia of the Undead*. Canton, MI: Visible Ink Press, 2011.

Nelson, Victoria. *Gothicka: Vampire Heroes, Human Gods, and the New Supernatural*. Cambridge: Harvard University Press, 2012.

Orlomoski, Caitlyn. "From Monsters to Victims: Vampires and Their Cultural Evolution from the Nineteenth to the Twenty-First Century." Honors Scholar Theses. University of Connecticut, 2011.

Paspátis, Aléandros. *Études sur les Tchinghianés, ou Bohémiens de l'empire Ottoman*. Constaninople: Antoine Koroméla, 1870.

Passow, Arnoldus. *Popularia Carmina: Graeciae Recentioris*. Leipzig: B. G. Tevrneri, 1860.

Richard, François. *Relation de ce qui s'est passé de plus remarquable a Saint-Erini isle de l'Archipel depuis l'établissement des Peres de la Compagnie de Jesus en icelle*. Paris: Sebastien Cramoisy, 1657.

Sacher-Masoch, Leopold Ritter von. "Die Toten sind unersättlich." *Lasst die Toten ruhen: Deutsche Vampirgeschichten aus dem 19. Jahrhundert*. Ed. Oliver Kotowski, Atlantis, 2012. 143-176. [1875].

Scarborough, Dorothy. *The Supernatural in Modern English Literature*. New York: G. P. Putnam's Sons, 1917.

Spindler, Carl. "Der Vampyr und seine Braut: Ein Nachtstück aus der neuesten Zeit." *Zwillinge. Zwei Erzählungen. Nebst einem Anhange von Originalbriefen*, 1-106. Hanau: C J. Edler'schen Buchhandlung, 1826.

Stockton, Frank R. "A Borrowed Month." *The Century Illustrated Monthly Magazine* February-March 1886, 537-44; 730-736.

Tozer, Henry Farshawe. *Researches in the Highlands of Turkey: Including Visits to Mounts Ida, Athos, Olympus, and Pelion, to the Mirdite Albanians, and other remote Tribes*. Vol. 2. London: John Murray, 1869.

Tracy, Robert. "Loving You All Ways: Vamps Vampires Necrophiles and Necrofilles in Nineteenth-Century Fiction." *Sex and Death in Victorian Literature*. Ed. Regina Barreca. Bloomington: Indiana University Press, 1990. 32-59.

Turgenev, Ivan. *Clara Mílitch. The Novels and Stories of Iván Turgénieff*. Trans. Isabel F. Hapgood. Vol. 16. New York: Charles Scribner's Sons, 1922 [1883].

"Vampires." *The Eclectic Magazine of Foreign Literature, Science, and Art*. July 1887, 143-144.

Zanger, Jules. "Metaphor into Metonymy: The Vampire Next Door." *Blood Read: The Vampire as Metaphor in Contemporary Culture*. Philadelphia: University of Pennsylvania Press, 1997. 17-26.

www.ingramcontent.com/pod-product-compliance
Lightning Source LLC
Chambersburg PA
CBHW072022240426
43667CB00044B/2211